RPC for NT

Guy Eddon

R&D Publications
Lawrence, Kansas 66046

R&D Publications, Inc.
1601 West 23rd Street, Suite 200
Lawrence, Kansas 66046-2700
USA

Distributed by Prentice Hall
ISBN 0-13-100223-6

Cover Design: T. Watson Bogaard

To my grandfather
Samuel Weingarten (1914-1990)

Remote Procedure Calls and You

The Remote Procedure Call (RPC) paradigm is simple, its implementation complex, and its power enormous. A *remote procedure call* is what occurs when your application calls a procedure located on another computer. This makes your application the client. The remote procedure then executes on a remote computer called the server. RPC is built upon the model of client/server architecture. While this paradigm has been around for quite some time, RPC lends it a new meaning and a bright future. In this book I hope to shed light upon a topic that will shape the future of distributed computing.

Why This Book Is For You

This book was written for software engineers who want to learn about Microsoft Remote Procedure Calls (RPC) version 1.0. Whether you are developing a new application or enhancing an existing one, RPC is something you should know about. Microsoft RPC provides a standardized method for developing distributed applications. This allows your software to break free of one computer and spread across a network, utilizing all available CPU horsepower. Utilizing RPC, you can increase the power and efficiency of your software exponentially. Most of the text in this book is targeted for the software engineer who needs to add RPC features into his software and wants to get up to speed quickly.

But I Don't Know Windows NT

You do not need to be a Windows NT programmer to use Microsoft RPC version 1.0. Currently, RPC-aware applications can be developed in MS-DOS, Windows for Workgroups, and Windows NT. In addition, Chapter 1 and Appendix 4 describe new features of Windows NT, and how they relate to RPC. If you are an MS-DOS or Windows 3.1 developer you will probably find that Windows NT is much easier to program than you expected. This is due mainly to the fact that Windows NT supports 32- bit flat model programming. As we go along I will explain any new feature in Windows NT that an MS-DOS or Windows 3.1 programmer might not be familiar with. All of the examples in this book are written in C, and the text assumes a moderate level of proficiency with the C language. While you do not have to be a Windows programmer to understand the material contained in this book, it may be useful to read up on some subjects related to general Windows programming. This book is for anyone who wants to get a feel for the power of RPC, but it will be most useful to those who want to harness that power.

The Examples

I have tried to make the examples in this book as clear as possible, always focusing on the current topic of discussion and leaving out as many unnecessary details as possible. The goal of the examples in this book is twofold. First, to provide a framework for developing RPC applications. Second, to show distributed computing paradigms that are made possible by RPC.

To run the examples in this book, you must have at least one computer capable of running Windows NT. To try these programs across a network you will need two computers, both with supported network cards. One must be capable of running Windows NT, and the other MS-DOS, Windows for Workgroups, or Windows NT. If you intend to use MS-

DOS or Windows 3.1 you will also need to have Microsoft LAN Manager 2.1 client software with NetBEUI, Named Pipes, or TCP/IP for the secondary computer. If you are using only one Windows NT computer you do not need a network card. To build the examples you will need the Windows NT SDK. For the Windows for Workgroups applications you will need the Windows 3.1 SDK in addition to the Microsoft C/C++ 7.0 compiler required for the MS-DOS programs.

Acknowledgments

This book will make me the pride and joy of two women: My great aunt Julia Pirotte-Sokolska, who enjoys splendid health in Poland, and my grandmother Bluma Weingarten in Israel who in the manner of all grandmothers will make good use of the copy I send her.

I would like to thank my father for patiently helping me with the RPC examples; my mother and Sherri Berman for their invaluable editing assistance; my sister Maya for saying that I will never finish it (I did!)

At R&D Publications I would like to thank Robert Ward and Berney Williams for making this project possible.

Rohan Phillips and Bruce Ramsey of Microsoft Developers Support Services patiently answered my questions and provided me with up-to-the-minute information on RPC.

This is an exciting time to be part of the software development world. Computers are everywhere, and the future belongs to those who can use these resources effectively.

Guy Eddon
July 1994
CompuServe: 71172,1014

Table of Contents

Preface . . . . *v*

Chapter 1 — The RPC Model *1*

RPC and Distributed Computing; The Client/Server Model; The RPC
Charade; Interface Definition Language; How IDL Works; RPC and
LPC; Windows NT and the OSF DCE.

Chapter 2 — Hello, RPC! *15*

Hello, World in RPC; The Hello Client; Exception Handling Macros.

Chapter 3 — The HELLO *Server* *23*

Binding; UUID; The Protocol Sequence; The Network Address; The
End Point; The Options; The HELLO Server; Memory Allocator; The

HELLO Procedure; The *HELLO* Interface Definition; *HELLO* makefile; Building RPC Applications; Debugging; The *HELLO* files.

Chapter 4 — Passing Data: Pointers, Arrays, and Strings 43

RPC and References; Reference Pointers; Unique Pointers; Full Pointers; Arrays; Strings.

Chapter 5 — Building the PRIME Applications 53

Console Management; The Prime Number Algorithm; The I/O Library; Running *PRIME1*; Building *PRIME1*.

Chapter 6 — Multithreading: Developing PRIME2 75

Multithreading; Adding Critical Sections; Distributing the Work; The User Interface.

Chapter 7 — The PRIME3 Client — RPCs at Last 91

Binding to the Server; Creating Binding Handles; Automatic Binding; Types of Binding Handles; Manual Binding; Implicit Binding Handles; Explicit Binding Handles; The String Binding; The *PRIME3* Client; Structured Exception Handling; Binding to the *PRIME3* Server; The *PRIME3* Client Stub; Terminating the *PRIME3* client; The *PRIME3* Interface.

Chapter 8 — The PRIME3 Server 123

Starting the *PRIME3* Server; Registering the Server Interface; The *PRIME3* Server Stub; Terminating the *PRIME3* Server.

Chapter 9 — PRIME4 — Fault-Tolerant Servers *147*

Context Handles; Context Rundown Routines; Stateless Servers; The *PRIME4* Context Handle; Supporting DOS and WFW.

Chapter 10 — PRIME5 — RPC Name Service *227*

The *PRIME5* client; Running *PRIME5*; The *PRIME5* Server.

Chapter 11 — PRIME6 — Overview *265*

Multiple Clients, Multiple Servers; The *PRIME6* Client; The *PRIME6* Interface; Debugging *PRIME6*.

Chapter 12 — A Distributed Mandelbrot Application *303*

Lossless vs. Lossy Compression; The Mandelbrot Set; Design Issues; Using a Local Server; Running *Mandelbrot*; The *Mandelbrot* Server.

Appendix 1 — Evolution of PC Operating Systems *365*

MS-DOS; Comaptibility; OS/2 and the 286; DOS Extenders; The Surrogate OS/2; Enhanced Mode in Three Flavors; Windows 3.0; Windows 3.1; Windows for Workgroups; The Future.

Appendix 2 — What is Win32? *373*

How Win32s Differs from Win32; Developing Win32s Applications.

Appendix 3 — OSF DCE *377*

OSF DCE Distributed Computing Models; Integration of the DCE Technology Components; DCE Threads; DCE Remote Procedure Call (RPC); DCE Directory; DCE Time; DCE Security; DCE Distributed File Service; Management; Cells.

Appendix 4 — What's New in Windows NT? *383*

Compatibility and Portability; Subsystems and Compatibility; File Systems and Compatibility; Portability; Hardware Abstraction Layer; Segmented Memory Models; Thunking; Separate Address Spaces; Preemptive Multitasking; Windows 3.1 and the Virtual Machine; Threads; Multithreading; Symmetric Multiprocessing; GUIs; Improved Graphics Device Interface (GDI); Console; Other Features.

Glossary *397*

Annotated Bibliography *413*

Index *417*

Chapter 1

The RPC Model

The Remote Procedure Call (RPC) is an exciting development in operating system and network technology. The RPC model, defined in the Open Software Foundation's Distributed Computing Environment (DCE) standard (see Appendix 3), allows a computer to act as a compute server, sharing its CPU cycles with other computers on the network, even with those of completely different computer architectures.

Microsoft Remote Procedure Call version 1.0 is an implementation of the RPC standard. An application that you write using Microsoft RPC can call a function located on another computer. The application making the call — the client — can run under MS-DOS, Windows 3.1, Windows for Workgroups, or Windows NT. The server machine, however, must run Windows NT.

This book shows you how to use Microsoft RPC to incorporate remote procedure calls into your applications. We'll develop working examples of RPC-enabled applications and we'll go behind the scenes to explore the mechanisms that make distributed computing through RPC possible.

RPC: The Foundation of Distributed Computing

For the application developer, RPC hides the complexity of the network by making a remote procedure call look just like a local procedure call. Most modern programming languages, including C, offer the procedure as the basic programming construct. Procedures allow the programmer to organize code into discrete groups, with each group performing a specific function. For example, the following procedure accepts two parameters and returns their sum:

```
int sum(int x, int y)
    {
    return x + y;
    }
```

In these Procedure Oriented Programming (POP) languages, procedures relate to one another as "black boxes." *Procedure_A* can call *Procedure_B* without knowing how *Procedure_B* is implemented. Procedures thus offer a level of abstraction. It is possible to replace *Procedure_B* with a *Procedure_C*, whose interface is identical, without modifying *Procedure_A*. This abstraction has led to the proliferation of libraries in which related procedures are grouped together.

In modern POP languages, it has become unnatural, and at times difficult, to incorporate the network. Whereas a programming language facilitates the writing of code, a network simply transmits data. Little work had been done on integrating program code and the network until Birrell and Nelson published a paper in 1984 introducing a new concept: the RPC. Birrell and Nelson proposed extending the POP model to encompass the network. This simple and elegant solution allows programmers

In the remainder of the book, unless noted otherwise, the term "local procedure call" refers to the standard C function call. Don't confuse this term with Windows NT's Local Procedure Call (LPC), which is an optimized message-passing facility used (among other things) to communicate with the operating system.

to add a procedure-oriented layer to the communication-oriented network, thereby permitting access to the network in a familiar manner.

RPCs are designed to alleviate the difficulty commonly associated with building distributed applications. As anyone who has ever done low-level network programming knows, the number of potential network errors one must anticipate is mind-boggling. Someone may trip over the network cable, the server might crash, or a computer may fail. In other words, if something can go wrong with the network, it usually will. By creating a high-level, procedural interface to the network, the RPC model hides most of these network programming details from the application programmer.

Since RPC was designed to work in a computing environment with heterogeneous computer architectures, RPC also insulates the programmer from details such as different endian schemes, network protocols, and the default sign of a character. The RPC facility handles these for you, allowing you to concentrate on building your application.

The Client/Server Model

Applications that use remote procedure calls are intrinsically distributed. Such applications are usually divided into two parts: a client and a server. The client always makes requests of the server, whose sole purpose is to provide the client with the information it requests.

Servers are usually classified by the type of resource they offer. On today's networks, it is common to find file servers, print servers, and communication servers. In Windows NT, it is possible for a server to share not only its peripherals, such as hard disk space, printers, and modems, but also its computational horsepower — i.e., it can become a "compute server."

Normally, in the RPC model the party which makes the call to the remote procedure is called the client, while the party that services the remote procedure call is the server. It is possible for a server to service multiple requests from multiple clients simultaneously. The distinction

"A distributed system is one that runs on a collection of machines that do not have shared memory, yet looks to its users like a single computer." Andrew Tanenbaum's (Modern Operating Systems, *1992)*

between client and server blurs, however, when a server becomes a client to yet another server. In fact, it is possible for the two parties to be both a client and server for each other at the same time.

The RPC Charade

On the client side of a distributed application, a remote procedure call usually looks exactly the same as a local procedure call. However, the events triggered by a remote procedure call differ radically from those caused by a call to a local procedure. When a remote procedure call is executed, the computer jumps to a *client stub*. This stub is generated automatically by one of the RPC development tools (the IDL compiler, discussed more below) and has the same name as the remote procedure, so the jump will be transparent to the programmer.

The client stub packages the function parameters into a complex data structure in the Network Data Representation (NDR) format. This structure is then transmitted over the network to the server, where it is unpacked by the server stub (also generated by the IDL compiler), and delivered to the remote procedure as regular function parameters, thereby invoking the remote procedure on behalf of the client. The result is then translated into network messages and transmitted back to the client as a return value.

Figure 1.1 shows the RPC mechanism in action. The remote procedure call originates at the client application. From there, it travels through the client stub and into the clutches of the RPC client runtime. The runtime translates it into a network message understood by the transport, so that the call can be transmitted across the network to the server. The server transport decodes the network messages and passes them through the RPC server runtime and to the server stub. The server stub then calls the remote procedure using the local procedure call method. The remote procedure executes and returns the result back to the client application through the same mechanism.

As you can see, a lot of work goes on behind the scenes to make a remote procedure call look and feel like a local procedure call. The goal of RPC is to be as unobtrusive as possible by adhering closely to the local procedure call model. The RPC model accomplishes this so well, in fact, that a programmer need not even know whether a function will execute remotely or locally. This seamlessness is made possible by a special RPC language called the Interface Definition Language (IDL).

Interface Definition Language

The Interface Definition Language (IDL) was originally set forth by the Open Software Foundation's Distributed Computing Environment as part of an attempt to establish standards for RPC. (See Appendix 3.) The language was originally known as the Network Interface Definition Language (NIDL), a more accurate name since IDL is a network contract. Microsoft chose to name their implementation the Microsoft Interface Definition Language (MIDL).

IDL defines the interface between the client and the server. All the communication between a client and the server passes through the IDL interface. Programmers who have worked on an application that must communicate with another application — written by a different team — can appreciate the importance of defining an interface to which both sides will adhere. When the interface is not well-defined, each side usually ends up

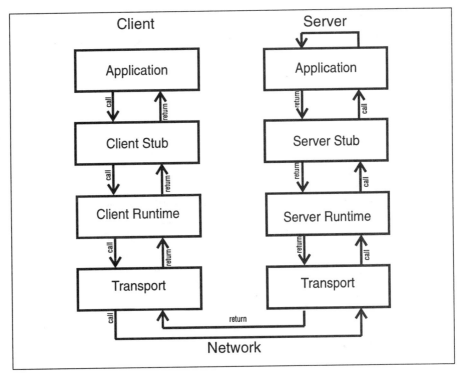

Figure 1.1   *RPC mechanism in action. Logically, the client application calls the server application directly. Actually, the call passes through several support layers on both hosts.*

blaming the other for not following the specifications. With IDL, however, this process is automated. Once you've defined the interface in IDL, both sides (server and client) must adhere to it, else their programs will not even compile.

Strictly speaking, MIDL is a translator and not a compiler. It does not produce machine code, but instead translates IDL code into C. The C code generated by MIDL forms the remote procedure stubs in both the client and the server. Thus the master IDL file produces code that is compiled and linked in by both sides of the distributed application. Microsoft's RPC manual says that IDL is not a flavor of C. While true, this assertion leads some people to believe that IDL is a new programming language. In fact, however, IDL is not a *programming* language. One does not actually direct the computer to execute specific instructions in the IDL file. Rather, the IDL file defines the interface between the client and server parts of a distributed application.

MIDL is a strongly typed language compared to C. C is considered weakly typed because it allows implicit casts between variables of different types. MIDL, on the other hand, does not permit the programmer to cast variables into different types because MIDL must arbitrate between different applications on potentially different computer architectures. Therefore, it cannot allow any ambiguities of syntax. Table 1.1 lists the MIDL base types and their properties.

Base type	Description
boolean	A data item that can have the values TRUE or FALSE.
byte	An 8-bit data item guaranteed to be transmitted without modification.
char	An 8-bit unsigned character data item.
double	A 64-bit floating point number.
float	A 32-bit floating point number.
handle_t	A primitive handle that can be used for RPC binding.
hyper	A 64-bit integer that may be declared as either signed or unsigned. The hyper specifier is not supported in Microsoft RPC version 1.0.
long	A 32-bit integer that may be declared as either signed or unsigned.
short	A 16-bit integer that may be declared as either signed or unsigned.
small	An 8-bit integer that may be declared as either signed or unsigned, with the same default sign as the *char* type.
wchar_t	Wide character type that is supported as Microsoft extension to IDL. To use *wchar_t*, you must specify the *-ms_ext* switch when compiling the IDL file.

Table 1.1   *MIDL base types and their properties. Note that these types are more precisely specified than their C counterparts.*

How IDL Works

The programmer uses IDL to create the *interface definition file*, which specifies the name, version, and the Universally Unique IDentifier (UUID) of the interface. The UUID, as its name suggests, is a unique identifier that ensures that a client's remote procedure calls are made to the correct server. The interface definition file also includes special prototypes for all the exported functions (functions which the client may call) on the server. Interface definition files end with a *.IDL* extension. In the following chapters, I'll show you several .IDL files and explain the important features in each.

While IDL defines the interface between the client and the server, the actual logical connection is accomplished by a process called binding. The concept of binding is somewhat similar to that of linking, whereby the caller links with the remote procedure. However, in a distributed application no correct address can ever be determined by the caller, because the remote procedure resides in the server's address space. Thus, the client never truly calls the remote procedure, but rather requests that the server do so on its behalf. We'll cover binding in more detail in Chapter 3 and then again in Chapter 7.

RPC and LPC

Although the remote procedure call mechanism strives for transparency to the application programmer, total transparency is not possible. Address space differences, binding requirements, exception handling, and operating system differences force the programmer to take into account the application's distribution across the network. While RPC adheres very closely to the local procedure call model, there are some subtle issues a programmer must be aware of.

Global variables present one particularly notable problem. Since the client and the server are two different programs, they cannot share global variables. If a remote procedure attempts to access one of the client's global variables, the linker will report an unresolved external. The solution to this problem is to pass the global variable as a function parameter to the remote procedure. We'll cover other issues relating to shared data in Chapter 4 and again in Chapter 8.

Windows NT and the OSF DCE

Microsoft's RPC implementation conforms to the RPC specification included in the Open Software Foundation (OSF) Distributed Computing Environment (DCE) standard. Thus, a server developed to run on Windows NT should be able to work correctly with an OSF compatible client,

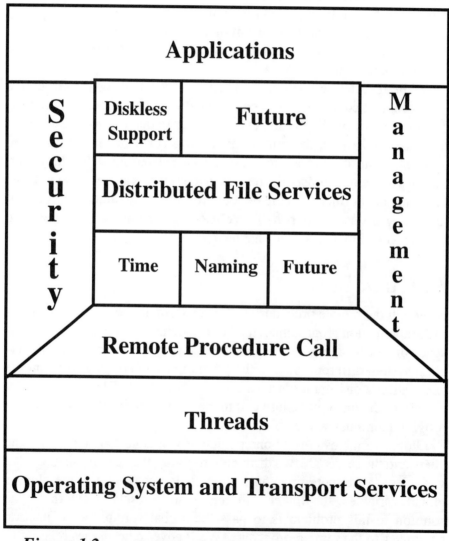

Figure 1.2   *The entire set of DCE services proposed by the OSF. Note that the RPC facility is a crucial foundation for higher-level services.*

regardless of the client platform. Moreover, if an RPC application is written to use only POSIX compliant operating services, it should port (with minor changes in some function names) easily from Windows NT to other POSIX compliant RPC environments. (See Appendix 4 for more information about Windows NT's compatibility features.)

The OSF is a consortium of companies formed to define the components of an environment that supports distributed computing. Many corporations and universities from around the world are members of the OSF, including IBM and Microsoft. Thus, the OSF standard has strongly influenced the design of distributed environments.

Originally an outgrowth of the Network Computing System (NCS) on the Apollo computer, the OSF DCE standards define a complete set of services to support the development, use, and maintenance of applications in an environment in which all systems and their resources are widely available. Figure 1.2 depicts the entire set of DCE services proposed by the OSF. Note that the RPC facility serves as the crucial foundation of distributed computing. Many of the other services proposed in the OSF DCE — including security, distributed file services, threads, and transport services — are implemented using RPC. Microsoft RPC is an implementation of the RPC portion of the OSF DCE standards. Since Windows NT is the host environment, it must supply most of the other DCE services.

DCE assumes that the underlying operating system provides these services:

- Multitasking
- Timers
- Local interprocess communications
- Basic file system operations (VFS layer)
- Memory management
- Local security mechanisms (if appropriate)
- Threads (or the ability to use DCE Threads)
- General system utility functions

From among MS-DOS, Windows for Workgroups, and Windows NT, only Windows NT provides all of the services listed and thus is the only environment that can support RPC server applications. While Windows for Workgroups comes close, it is missing threads. True multithreading cannot be implemented in Windows for Workgroups (or Windows 3.1), because it is non-reentrant. MS-DOS is lacking in most respects. While only Windows NT can function as a server, all three environments can be clients, because a client application need only be able to access the network — a minimum for any RPC application.

In particular, Windows NT's built-in networking, multithreading, and RPC Structured Exception Handling (SEH) are crucial to the success of RPC.

Networking

Windows NT incorporates the same peer-to-peer networking available in Windows for Workgroups. Windows NT allows a computer to share its resources with another computer. You can share most peripherals between Windows NT and Windows for Workgroups. For instance, even if you do not yet have a Windows NT driver for your CD-ROM, you may still access it from a Windows NT workstation via a shared volume from Windows for Workgroups. In both Windows NT and Windows for Workgroups, the enhanced File Manager lets users share and connect drives.

Programmers may also take advantage of these features with the special networking functions available in the Win32 API. (See Appendix 2 for more information about the Win32 API and its relationship to other operating systems.) In addition to drives, users can share printers, modems, or even data. For instance, Windows for Workgroups allows a user at one computer to paste data into another computer's clipboard or initiate a DDE conversation with another computer on the network. Windows NT also includes the low-level network protocol support required for RPC, including network protocols such as named pipes and TCP/IP.

Multithreading

Among all the Windows platforms, Windows NT is the only one that can support multithreading. An application can create multiple threads of execution within one process by invoking the *CreateThread()* function.

Multithreading combined with RPC is a potent combination. Multithreading gives RPC servers the ability to support multiple clients while simultaneously doing other computations locally. In addition, RPC clients running on Windows NT can make multiple remote procedure calls to multiple servers.

Threads are crucial to enhancing an RPC application's performance. Without threads, a call to a remote procedure will block the client program until the remote procedure completes execution and returns.

Since RPC was designed to look and feel like a local procedure call, which requires the calling function to wait for its completion, RPC behaves in the same manner. However, since a remote procedure call executes remotely, the client CPU is simply waiting for its return.

Multithreading allows this "wait" time on the local host to be used for computation. In a multithreaded Windows NT application, the thread that makes the remote procedure call is blocked. By this I mean that the thread is suspended; it does not receive execution focus until the remote procedure call returns. The blocked thread therefore does not waste valuable CPU time. Instead, other local threads continue processing. Thus, distributing a task across two multithreaded machines will increase the peak performance available at either machine by tapping the power of both CPUs.

Object Oriented Programming

Object Oriented Programming (OOP) is a useful paradigm for developing a distributed application with RPC (whether you are programming in C or C++). Within the OOP construct, the RPC server should be an encapsulated object that appears as a black box to the client. In this way, future application programmers never need know that RPCs play a crucial role in the implementation of their application program. Within OOP, RPCs should be used very thoughtfully.

When programming in an object-oriented style, you should very clearly define the objectives of each remote procedure, as kludges work very poorly in RPC. You cannot simply decide that a remote procedure should allocate memory so that the client will be able to receive some extra data you did not think of before. You should clearly define each remote procedure as if you were designing an API (which, in effect, you are). Be sure to explore the relationships among the different remote procedures and how the client will operate within them.

The ability to suspend a thread makes Windows NT the most productive platform for using RPC. A multithreaded application can have a thread executing while waiting for the return of the remote procedure call. Since a multithreading mechanism is not available in MS-DOS or Windows for Workgroups, applications in those environments must wait until the remote procedure call returns before continuing local processing.

In MS-DOS, the local CPU's power is wasted until the remote procedure call returns. In Windows, an application can (through careful

Application Development

Development Methods

Bjarne Stroustrup in The C++ Programming Language, has this to say about development methodology:

"A program needs to be produced and maintained by an organization that can do this [development] despite changes of personnel, direction, and management structure. A popular approach to coping with this problem has been to try to reduce system development into a few relatively low-level tasks slotted into a rigid framework; that is, create a class of easy-to-train (cheap) and interchangeable low-level programmers ("coders "), and a class of somewhat less cheap but equally interchangeable (and therefore equally dispensable) designers. The coders are not supposed to make design decisions, and the designers are not supposed to concern themselves with the grubby details of coding. This approach often fails, and where it does work it produces overly large systems with poor performance."

American corporations that develop software have a tendency to cover problems with money. If a project is delayed or has bugs, they add more people to the project team. This almost never helps, as the new people are usually just a burden to the existing team. The root of this problem lies with the fact that no one on the development team fully understands the entire project. This is because projects are usually broken into small pieces by the managers, so that they can retain full control. As long as the managers don't know what's going on, they want to be sure that no one else does either.

programming) allow other Windows applications to run while it is waiting for the remote procedure call's return. Though Windows is not a multithreaded operating system, it is a multitasking environment, where multiple tasks can execute while an application is involved in a remote procedure call. Due to these limitations, RPC for MS-DOS and Windows applications will most likely come as an optional extension, when an application requires a particular service from a server that it cannot provide itself. (See Appendix 2 for an overview of how DOS has evolved.)

The Contributing Manager

There is a solution to this problem. In order for project development to succeed, there must be at least one person on the team, be it the project manager or the secretary, who completely understands every single aspect of the project. This person must usually write a large portion of system himself. The other people on the team can write and test many other parts of the application. One person, however, must always be in control and take full responsibility for the success of the entire project. This is the concept of the contributing manager, which is being implemented by most successful software firms. Contributing managers must have management skills, but must also be technically knowledgeable. In fact, a contributing manager is sometimes the most technical person on the team.

Testing is the most frequently overlooked part of application development. Successful software development does not occur when programmers work weekends two weeks before due project is due, but when the project is finished two months in advance and then tested the last two months (refer to Greg Pope, Software Testophobia 1992). Part of this problem is due to the fact that companies have a peculiar tendency to hire software development managers from many unrelated fields. For instance, one prominent package shipping company has hired former cake testers, and department store sales managers to work as system managers in their Information Services (IS) department. In any other field this would be unthinkable. Imagine an advertising agency hiring a restaurant manager to manage a group of graphic artists. Somehow in the software development industry this has become acceptable. Hopefully these tendencies will change as the industry matures.

Multithreading, despite its advantages, can be a double-edged sword. Multithreading can cause subtle problems relating to reentrancy. Every thread in your application must be fully reentrant. Since the operating system can interrupt your thread at any time, access to global variables must also be synchronized. If your thread depends on a global variable that another thread may modify, your code can become corrupted. Local variables, on the other hand, are completely safe in a multithreading environment. Each time a thread loses execution focus, its stack and variables are saved and later restored when the thread is resumed. Since all local variables are saved in a function's stack, they cannot be modified by another thread.

RPC Exception Handling

Windows NT's Structured Exception Handling (SEH) is a powerful, new error handling mechanism that allows an application to catch system calls that fail and react appropriately. With RPC, exception handling is not an option. It is a must. Exception handling simplifies the enormous task of handling the errors that can occur in an RPC application under this complex operating system. RPC structured exception handling is also available under MS-DOS and Windows, an important point to developers who must write portable code. I'll explain more about structured error handling in the next chapter.

Summary

One of the major incentives for companies to switch to Windows NT may be its RPC facility. (For an overview of other important NT features, see Appendix 4.) Initially, those applications that take advantage of RPC will probably offer distributed features as an optional service. If a server is unavailable, the application will attempt to perform the service locally, albeit more slowly. This scheme makes sense so long as RPC is considered optional. At some point, however, RPC will become a required feature, in much the same way that a network is a required business tool today. In the near future, corporate software will be advertised as RPC-compliant and will quickly be integrated into workgroup software where the advantages of RPC will be immediately seen. RPC will have the greatest impact upon corporate information services where it will connect worlds of data from diverse sources. At the very least, it will become the hotbed for a whole generation of new acronyms.

## Chapter 2

Hello, RPC!

This chapter will present a trivial RPC-based client application, modeled after the classic "Hello, world" program from Kernighan and Ritchie's *The C Programming Language*:

```
#include <stdio.h>

main()
    {
    printf("Hello, world\n");
    }
```

The first line of the non-distributed *HELLO* program *#includes* the definitions in *STDIO.H*, including the definition of the *printf()* function. As in most C programs, the application begins execution at the *main()* function. Inside the *main()* function body is a call to *printf()*, which displays the string passed to it — "*Hello, world.*"

The code for the *printf()* function is not contained in the source file, but rather in the standard C library. When the *HELLO* program is compiled, the resulting object file indicates to the linker that the call to *printf()* must be resolved before the program can be executed. The linker must locate *printf()* in the library and combine it with the *HELLO* program.

In this non-distributed *HELLO* program, the call to *printf()* is eventually resolved to a jump to the *printf()* function's actual address in the final executable. The code that implements the *printf()* function is located in the same executable file as the calling code. Since both the code that calls the *printf()* function and the code that implements it are in the same address space, the calling code can simply jump to the correct address, trusting that the *printf()* function will execute.

On the other hand, what if the *printf()* function were a remote procedure? Since a remote procedure executes in a different address space than its caller, the calling program cannot simply jump to the *printf()* function's address. There would be no correct address to jump to. Herein lies the problem that RPC must overcome.

Your First RPC Program

A distributed version of the *HELLO* program will demonstrate how RPC addresses these problems. RPC applications are usually split into two pieces: the client and the server. Generally, the client makes the remote procedure calls to the server, which stores the code for the remote procedures. It is not particularly difficult to find a clear division of work in the *HELLO* program, since the only function call in the entire program is made to *printf()*. Therefore, the *printf()* function will become the remote procedure that the client will call. The server will then display the string passed and return to the client.

Source File	Listing	Description
HELLOC.C	2.1	The client source code file
RPC.H	2.2	A client header file
HELLOS.C	3.1	The server source code file
HELLOP.C	3.2	The procedure source code file
HELLO.IDL	3.3	The interface definition file
HELLO.ACF	3.4	The attribute configuration file
HELLO.MAK	3.5	The make file

Table 2.1   HELLO *client project source files.*

Table 2.1 lists the application source files for the RPC *HELLO* program. The *HELLO* client source file, *HELLOC. C,* (Listing 2.1) does not look very different from the classic "Hello, world" program. The source file adds two header files. The first, *RPC. H,* defines the RPC exception handlers used in the application:

```
#include <RPC.H>
```

The *HELLO* client also includes the *HELLO. H* header file

```
#include "hello.h"
```

HELLO. H is generated by the MIDL compiler at build time.

Other than the header files, *HELLOC* 's major oddity is several statements related to the RPC exception handler:

```
RpcTryExcept
    HelloRPC("Hello, RPC!\n");
RpcExcept(1)
    printf("The RPC runtime module reported an exception.\n");
RpcEndExcept
```

HelloRPC( ) is the remote procedure call. When execution reaches this point, the remote procedure *HelloRPC( )* is called on the server. The client then waits for the *HelloRPC( )* function call to return before resuming execution. The remote procedure call is made within the context of the exception handler. Thus the exception handler takes on special importance in this example.

The exception handler has the form:

```
RpcTryExcept
    /* Make remote procedure call */
    /* Other code... */
RpcExcept(1)
    /* Exception occurred, respond gracefully */
RpcEndExcept
```

If the remote procedure call executes smoothly, then the exception code is not executed. However, if the remote procedure call causes an exception, any code following it does not execute — execution immediately jumps to the exception handling code.

Microsoft RPC v1.0 defines the following exception handling macros and API functions:

- □ *RpcAbnormalTermination*
- □ *RpcEndExcept*
- □ *RpcEndFinally*
- □ *RpcExcept*
- □ *RpcExceptionCode*
- □ *RpcFinally*
- □ *RpcTryExcept*
- □ *RpcTryFinally*

The header file *RPC.H* (Listing 2.2) shows how these macros and functions are implemented.

When an exception occurs, the exception handling code should take appropriate action. In the *HELLO* example, this means notifying the user:

```
RpcExcept(1)
    /* Exception occurred, respond gracefully */
    printf("The RPC runtime module reported an exception.\n");
RpcEndExcept
```

The *HELLO* client appears to remain simple, in part, for the same reasons that the *hello, world* program appeared simple — both trivial applications rely heavily upon defaults and hidden mechanisms. The *#include <stdio.h>* directive hides the complex data structures required for buffered I/O. By quietly invoking the startup code, *main()* hides the difficulties involved in opening an output stream and initializing a runtime environment. By implictly directing output to *stdout*, *printf()* avoids the need for file pointers.

The "trivial" *HELLO* client also relies upon implicit behavior and hidden code. For one thing, Listing 2.1 is only one of several source files required to construct the *HELLO* client. (The *HELLO.H* header, as I mentioned before, is actually *generated* by the MIDL compiler.) The *HELLO* client also uses *automatic binding* and *implicit binding handles*. In later chapters, I'll expose what's really happening by detailing applications that use manual binding and explicit binding handles.

Summary

The *HELLO* client illustrates how the RPC model succeeds in hiding the network complexity from the application designer. The most significant change between the non-distributed and distributed client application is the use of structured exception handling (SEH) and the need to create some auxiliary files.

Chapter 3 presents the *HELLOC* server and the IDL and ACF files necessary to compile both *HELLO* components. As you will see, implementing the server side is not nearly as trivial.

Listing 2.1 — HELLOC.C

```
/*********************************************************************\
* HELLOC.C - Client side of automatic binding HELLO program        *
*            (c) Guy Eddon, 1993                                    *
*                                                                   *
* To build:  NMAKE HELLO                                            *
*                                                                   *
* Usage:     HELLOC                                                 *
*                                                                   *
* Comments:  This distributed application prints a string such as   *
*            "Hello, RPC!\n" on the server. The client uses         *
*            automatic binding to bind to the server.               *
\*********************************************************************/

#include <STDIO.H>
#include <RPC.H>
#include "hello.h"

void _CRTAPI1 main(void)
   {
   RpcTryExcept
      HelloRPC("Hello, RPC!\n");
   RpcExcept(1)
      printf("The RPC runtime module reported an exception.\n");
   RpcEndExcept
   }

/* End of File */
```

Listing 2.2 — RPC.H

```
/****************************************************************\
* RPC.H                                                        *
\****************************************************************/

/*++

Copyright (c) 1991-1993 Microsoft Corporation

Module Name:

    rpc.h

Abstract:

    Master include file for RPC applications.

--*/

#ifndef __RPC_H__
#define __RPC_H__

#ifndef RC_INVOKED
#pragma pack(4)
#endif /* RC_INVOKED */

#ifdef __cplusplus
extern "C" {
#endif

#define __RPC_WIN32__

#ifndef __MIDL_USER_DEFINED
#define midl_user_allocate MIDL_user_allocate
#define midl_user_free     MIDL_user_free
#define __MIDL_USER_DEFINED
#endif

typedef void * I_RPC_HANDLE;
typedef long RPC_STATUS;
```

Listing 2.2 — *(continued)*

```
#define RPC_UNICODE_SUPPORTED
#if   (_MSC_VER >= 800)
#define __RPC_FAR
#define __RPC_API  __stdcall
#define __RPC_USER __stdcall
#define __RPC_STUB __stdcall
#define RPC_ENTRY  __stdcall
#else
#define __RPC_FAR
#define __RPC_API
#define __RPC_USER
#define __RPC_STUB
#define RPC_ENTRY
#endif

#ifdef IN
#undef IN
#undef OUT
#undef OPTIONAL
#endif /* IN */

#include "rpcdce.h"
#include "rpcnsi.h"
#include "rpcnterr.h"

#ifndef RPC_NO_WINDOWS_H
#include <windows.h>
#endif // RPC_NO_WINDOWS_H

#include <excpt.h>
#include <winerror.h>

#define RpcTryExcept \
    try \
        {

// trystmts

#define RpcExcept(expr) \
        } \
    except (expr) \
        {
```

Listing 2.2 — (continued)

```
// exceptstmts

#define RpcEndExcept \
        }

#define RpcTryFinally \
    try \
        {

// trystmts

#define RpcFinally \
        } \
    finally \
        {

// finallystmts

#define RpcEndFinally \
        }

#define RpcExceptionCode() GetExceptionCode()
#define RpcAbnormalTermination() AbnormalTermination()

RPC_STATUS RPC_ENTRY
RpcImpersonateClient (
    IN RPC_BINDING_HANDLE BindingHandle OPTIONAL
    );

RPC_STATUS RPC_ENTRY
RpcRevertToSelf (
    );

unsigned long RPC_ENTRY
I_RpcMapWin32Status (
    IN RPC_STATUS Status
    );

#ifdef __cplusplus
}
#endif

#ifndef RC_INVOKED
#pragma pack()
#endif /* RC_INVOKED */

#endif // __RPC_H__
/* End of File */
```

## Chapter 3

The HELLO *Server*

The *HELLO* client in Chapter 2 resembled the classic C "Hello, world" program. The *HELLO* server, however, will probably be unrecognizable to you. The server side application is much more complex because it must deal with issues such as multiple clients, networks, and protocol sequences, to name a few. These are the attributes upon which the client and server must agree when establishing a binding.

Binding

A binding is a logical connection between the client and the server. Of the two standard types of linking, static and dynamic, binding is most similar to the latter.

With static linking (the type of linking used by most MS-DOS applications) all the application's code is linked together at compile-time to produce one large executable. This type of linking is ideal in a single process operating system such as MS-DOS. Since every MS-DOS application assumes it is the only program running, it may freely use all available memory.

Windows programs, on the other hand, can use static linking or dynamic linking. Dynamic linking is a much more advanced form of linking because applications are not linked with their libraries until runtime. When compiled for dynamic linking, an application's object module is not fully linked; it still contains unresolved references to externals. These externals are then resolved at runtime by the operating system's dynamic linking mechanism. Microsoft Windows provides this functionality to Windows applications. This type of linking has resulted in the Dynamic Link Library (DLL) in which an entire library can be linked to, at runtime. Table 3.1 shows the runtime libraries implementing RPC on each Microsoft platform. (See Figure 3.1, "Dynamic Linking versus Static Linking," for a comparison of dynamic and static linking.)

In the *RPC* model, applications link to their remote procedures at runtime, which could be called a type of dynamic linking. Nevertheless, *RPC* never actually *links* to a function call in the conventional manner. With conventional linking methods, the address of the called procedure must eventually be computed, be it at compile time or at runtime. In the *RPC* model, an application can never get the address of a remote procedure, because the called procedure is

Microsoft DOS DLLs	
Pseudo-DLL	**Description**
RPCLTC1.RPC	Client named pipe transport
RPCLTC3.RPC	Client TCP/IP transport
RPCLTC5.RPC	Client NetBIOS transport
RPCNS.RPC	Name Service

Microsoft Windows DLLs	
DLL	**Description**
RPCRT1.DLL	Core RPC API function
RPCNS1.DLL	Name service API functions

Microsoft Windows NT DLLs	
DLL	**Description**
RPCLTC1.DLL	Client named pipe transport
RPCLTS1.DLL	Server names pipe transport
RPCLTC3.DLL	Client TCP/IP transport
RPCLTS3.DLL	Server TCP/IP transport
RPCNS4.DLL	Name service
RPCRT4.DLL	Windows runtime
RPCLTC5.DLL	Client NetBIOS transport
RPCLTS5.DLL	Server NetBIOS transport

Table 3.1   *Runtime libraries implementing RPC on each Microsoft platform.*

not located in the same address space as the caller. Thus, instead of actually linking to the target address, the application creates a *dynamic binding* to a remote procedure and uses this binding to call the function.

All bindings are created with calls to *RPC* runtime functions.

The Binding Components

Each unique binding is identified by a sequence of components, consisting of the Universally Unique Identifier, the protocol sequence, the network address, the end point, and some network-specific options.

The UUID

A Universally Unique IDenitifier (UUID) is a special number used to pair RPC servers with clients. Each UUID string contains five groups of hexadecimal digits separated by hyphens:

```
651AB8D0-C73B-BDC7-B34A-0183BD0342DA
```

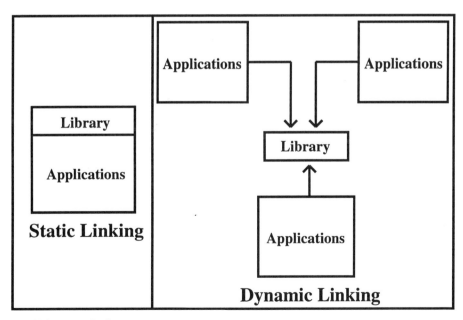

Figure 3.1   *Dynamic linking vs. static linking*

To generate UUIDs, you use the *UUIDGEN* program that comes with Microsoft RPC. UUIDs are compatible with the Windows NT GUID (Globally Unique IDentifier). These numbers must be unique if the applications are going to function properly. *UUIDGEN* uses the sytstem date, the system time, the network card number, and a random factor to create a unique UUID. In the string binding, the UUID specifies an optional number used for identification purposes. It allows clients and servers to distinguish different objects from one another. RPC servers can expose several interfaces, each with a different UUID. This ensures that some clients have access only to specific interfaces.

The Protocol Sequence

The protocol sequence specifies the network protocol used on your network. Microsoft RPC v1.0 supports several protocols; others are planned for the future. The most common is the named pipes (*ncacn_np*) protocol, native to Windows NT. Table 3.2 lists the currently supported network protocols and the strings you use to identify them.

The Network Address

The network address is the address of the server to which the client wishes to bind. In this example, the named pipes protocol sequence uses the form

```
\\servername
```

where *servername* is the name of the server computer. The type of valid network address depends on the protocol sequence used. Different protocol sequences have very different methods of defining network addresses.

Protocol	String
Named Pipes	ncacn_np
Internet Address	ncacn_ip_tcp
DECNet Phase IV	ncacn_dnet_nsp
DECNet Phase V	ncacn_osi_dna
Internet Address	ncadg_ip_udp
NetBIOS	ncacn_nb
Local RPC	ncalrpc
To be specified	ncadg_dds

Table 3.2   *Network protocols currently supported by Microsoft RPC.*

The End Point

The end point specifies the network end point at which the server application is listening. The actual mechanism will depend on the underlying network protocol. With named pipes, the valid end point specifies the pipe to which the server is listening. A valid end point for the named pipes protocol sequence is

    \pipe\pipename

where *pipename* is an application-defined name for the *pipe* used for the low-level network communication between the client and the server.

The Options

The options parameter is a miscellaneous string for special settings appropriate for a particular protocol sequence. For the named pipes protocol sequence, the only option currently available is *security=true*. This statement turns on security mechanisms for the remote procedure call. For other network protocols, valid options will vary.

The HELLO *Server*

Like the *HELLO* client, the *HELLO* server (Listing 3.1) includes the *RPC.H* and *HELLO.H* header files, but there the similarity ends. The server makes much more extensive use of the RPC functions and types than does the client. The first RPC function the *HELLO* server calls is *RpcServerUseProtseqEp( )*:

```
RPC_STATUS status;

unsigned char *pszEndpoint = "\\pipe\\auto";
unsigned char *pszProtocolSequence = "ncacn_np";
unsigned char *pszSecurity = NULL;
unsigned int  cMaxCalls = 20;

status = RpcServerUseProtseqEp(pszProtocolSequence,
    cMaxCalls,   /* max concurrent calls */
    pszEndpoint,
    pszSecurity);/* Security descriptor */
```

RpcServerUseProtseqEp() notifies the RPC runtime module that the server will be listening for client calls using the specified protocol sequence and endpoint. Next, the server registers its interface with the RPC runtime:

```
RPC_STATUS status;

status = RpcServerRegisterIf(
    hello_ServerIfHandle, /* interface to register   */
    NULL,                 /* MgrTypeUuid             */
    NULL);                /* MgrEpv; NULL - use default */
```

The *RpcServerRegisterIf()* function registers the server interface, as defined in the *HELLO.IDL* file (Listing 3.3), making the server's interface available to all compatible clients (i.e., clients with matching UUIDs).

The server then calls the *RpcServerInqBindings()* function:

```
RPC_STATUS status;
RPC_BINDING_VECTOR *pBindingVector;

status = RpcServerInqBindings(&pBindingVector);
```

This function retrieves all available binding handles for communication and returns a pointer to a binding vector. The binding vector, *pBindingVector*, is used in the next RPC function call:

```
RPC_STATUS status;

unsigned int fNameSyntaxType = RPC_C_NS_SYNTAX_DEFAULT;
unsigned char *pszAutoEntryName = "/.:/Autohandle_sample";
RPC_BINDING_VECTOR *pBindingVector;

status = RpcNsBindingExport(
    fNameSyntaxType,      /* name syntax type        */
    pszAutoEntryName,     /* nsi entry name          */
    hello_ServerIfHandle,
    pBindingVector,       /* set in previous call    */
    NULL);                /* UUID vector             */
```

RpcNsBindingExport() exports the server's interface and binding handles so that clients can import them and connect to the server, thus permitting the execution of remote procedure calls. The final RPC call the server makes during its initialization phase is to the *RpcServerListen()* function:

```
RPC_STATUS status;

status = RpcServerListen(cMinCalls, cMaxCalls, fDontWait);
```

The *RpcServerListen()* function turns execution over to the RPC runtime module. This function notifies the RPC runtime module that the server is now ready and waiting to receive client requests.

Memory Allocator

Two other functions worthy of attention are user-defined memory allocation and deallocation functions.

RPC's design allows the programmer to install custom memory handling functions which are called whenever the server stubs need to allocate or free memory for incoming data. The *HELLO* example uses only very simple memory handling functions (at the end of Listing 3.1), but one could replace them with something much more sophisticated. This flexibility is one way in which RPC defines itself as an open standard. Nearly all its features are either user-defined or can be overridden by the programmer. Such flexibility can often get in the way, but in the long run, is a major advantage.

The HELLO *Procedure*

The actual remote procedure the client calls, *HelloRPC()*, is contained in a separate source file: *HELLOP.C* (Listing 3.2). This source file is linked in with the server side of the *HELLO* application:

```
#include <RPC.H>
#include "hello.h"
void HelloRPC(unsigned char *string)
    {
    printf(string);
    }
```

HelloRPC()'s implementation makes it easy to see why the "Hello, RPC!" string is displayed on the server. When the client makes the remote procedure call, it passes a string to the *HelloRPC()* function. *HelloRPC()* uses the standard *printf()* function to display the string. Since the server is executing the *HELLO* application at this point, the string appears in the *server's* display space.

The HELLO *Interface Definition*

The *HELLO* application's interface definition is contained in *HELLO. IDL* (Listing 3.3). This special file contains the application's UUID, version, pointer type, interface name, and function prototypes:

```
[ uuid (6B29FC40-CA47-1067-B31D-0183BD0342DA),
  version(1.0),
  pointer_default(unique)]
interface hello
{
void HelloRPC([in, string] unsigned char *string);
}
```

The Universally Unique IDentifier (UUID) is the special number used for matching prospective clients and servers. The version number ensures that only compatible versions of the client and server are connected. So long as the major version numbers are the same, a client and server are considered compatible. For instance, if the version numbers of a prospective client and server pair were 1.3 and 1.7 respectively, they would be considered compatible. If they were 1.7 and 2.0, they would not be permitted to connect.

The default pointer signifies the type of pointer to be used in remote procedure calls. Chapter 4 and the PRIME program examples later in the book will explore the options for pointers.

The interface name defined in the Interface Definition Language (IDL) must be the same used previously in the server code. Within the body of the interface definition are prototypes for all the remote procedures. In this case there is only one: the *HelloRPC( )* function. The prototypes used in the IDL file are slightly different from those in standard C header files, as each function parameter must have a special tag specifying the direction (relative to the server) the parameter will be transmitted over the network. In this case, since the string is going from the client to the server, the parameter used is: *[in, string]*.

The *HELLO. IDL* file is compiled by the MIDL (Microsoft Interface Definition Language) compiler along with an optional Attribute Configuration File, *HELLO.ACF*. Whereas the IDL file includes all the information regarding the transmission of function parameters, the Attribute Control File contains general purpose attributes not pertaining to the network.

makefile

Even simple RPC applications generally consist of two executables, built from several source files. Therefore the building of such programs is obviously complex. The makefile provided with the *HELLO* application (Listing 3.5) is designed to automate this process for you. It handles the execution of the MIDL and C compilers, and the linker in the proper order.

The *HELLO* makefile first executes the MIDL compiler to generate the procedure stubs:

```
# Stubs, auxiliary and header file from the IDL file
hello.h hello_c.c hello_x.c hello_s.c hello_y.c : hello.idl hello.acf
    midl -cpp_cmd $(cc) -cpp_opt "-E"  hello.idl
```

The source files are then compiled with the C compiler.

```
.c.obj:
    $(cc) $(cflags) $(cvars)$<
    $(cvtomf)
```

The MIDL C files are also compiled, but with special switches.

```
# hellos auxiliary file
hello_y.obj : hello_y.c hello.h
    $(cc) $(cflags) $(cvars) $(WARN) hello_y.c
    $(cvtomf)
```

Lastly, all the object files are linked to produce two executables.

```
# The Client
helloc : helloc.exe
helloc.exe : helloc.obj hello_c.obj hello_x.obj
    $(link) $(conflags) -out:helloc.exe \
    helloc.obj hello_c.obj hello_x.obj \
    rpcrt4.lib rpcns4.lib $(conlibs)

# The Server
hellos : hellos.exe
hellos.exe : hellos.obj hellop.obj hello_s.obj hello_y.obj
    $(link) $(conflags) -out:hellos.exe \
    hellos.obj hello_s.obj hellop.obj hello_y.obj \
    rpcrt4.lib rpcndr.lib rpcns4.lib $(conlibs)
```

```
[auto_handle]
interface hello
{
}
```

In this case, the only information given is the *[auto_handle]* attribute.

In this context, a handle is an object through which a program can identify a specific binding. The *[auto_handle]* attribute directs the MIDL compiler to generate stubs that "hide" the binding handle from the programmer. We'll return to handles again in Chapter 8 when we discuss manual binding.

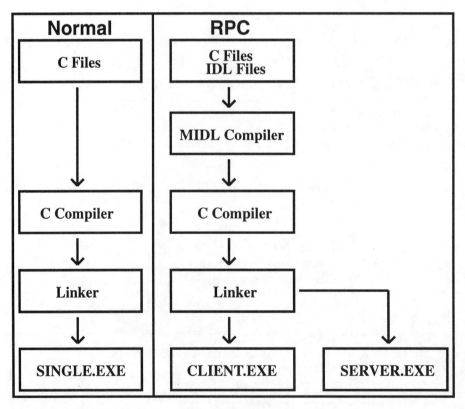

Figure 3.2   *RPC Development Cycle.*

Building RPC Applications

An RPC program consists of the following kinds of files:

1. C source and header files
2. IDL (Interface Definition Language) file
3. ACF (Attribute Configuration File)
4. makefile

Figure 3.2, The RPC Development Cycle, compares the build process of a normal, non-distributed application to that of a distributed RPC

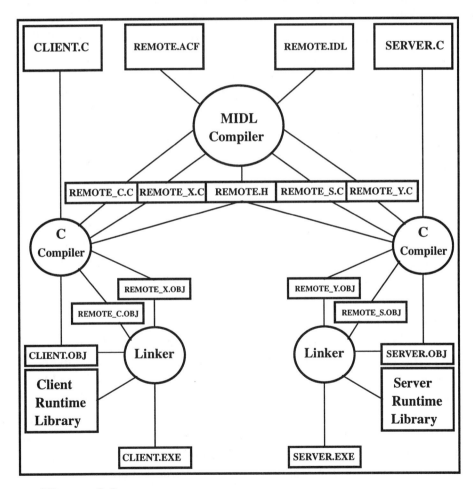

Figure 3.3   *Relationships among source files in an RPC application.*

application. The main difference between the two is the MIDL compiler. The MIDL compiler translates the IDL and ACF files into C source files. These five source files, along with the client and server source files, are compiled by the C compiler to produce six object files, three for the client and three for the server. The linker then links these object files with the correct RPC runtime library to produce the client and server executables. This entire build process is managed by the makefile. Figure 3.3 shows the relationships among source files for both client and server in an RPC application.

Nearly all RPC applications use some sort of script file to handle the build process. The Windows NT SDK provides a simple build program called *NMAKE*, which I will use in all the examples in this book. While more robust, third-party build tools are being ported to Windows NT, *NMAKE* is satisfactory for the examples provided here.

Windows NT makefiles are structured in a manner that will probably be new to most programmers. They include a special system makefile, *NTWIN32.MAK* (see Appendix 2), which contains numerous macros for building standard applications.

The *NTWIN32.MAK* file provides a level of abstraction between your makefile and the tools and libraries actually used to build your application. For instance, if your application is a text-mode, multithreaded application, you can specify *conlibsmt* macro for multithreaded console libraries. If a future library release should change the names of the functions that implement these services, only the *NTWIN32.MAK* file will need to be updated. Your makefile, however, can continue to use the *conlibsmt* macro without modification. This technique is used in the makefiles of most Windows NT applications.

Debugging

In distributed applications, the remote procedures should always reside in a different source file than the rest of the code. With this arrangement, during development and debugging, the application may be linked to the client and server portions, producing a regular (i.e., not distributed) version of the application. Debugging this version of the application is no different than debugging any other non-distributed application. Only after you have debugged the code as a normal executable (or executable and DLLs) should you separate it into a client/server application.

The HELLO *Files*

The *HELLO* application consists of seven source files (listed in Table 3.3).
To build the *HELLO* application, type

```
NMAKE HELLO.MAK
```

The *NMAKE* makefile for this project is specially designed to build both the client and server executables for this application. To run the program on one computer, open two command shells. In the first, type:

```
HELLOS
```

In the second type:

```
HELLOC
```

If you plan to run the *HELLO* program on two computers, you must first modify your client computer's registry information. On the computer where you intend to execute the *HELLO* client, run the *C:\WINNT\SYSTEM32\REGEDT32.EXE* program. Select the *HKEY_LOCAL_MACHINE* window and choose *SOFTWARE – Microsoft – Rpc – NameService*. Then double click on *ServerNetworkAddress* and enter "*\\servercomputername*," where *servercomputername* is the name of the computer on which the *HELLO* server program will be running.

When you run the client program *HELLOC*, it executes a remote procedure call to the server instructing it to display the string. The "Hello, RPC!" string immediately appears in the server's display space.

To see the exception handler in action, start the *HELLO* client without first executing the *HELLO* server. The client will immediately report an exception. The ability to quickly determine the status of a server will become important

Source File	Listing	Description
HELLOC.C	2.1	The client source code file
RPC.H	2.2	A client header file
HELLOS.C	3.1	The server source code file
HELLOP.C	3.2	The procedure source code file
HELLO.IDL	3.3	The interface definition file
HELLO.ACF	3.4	The attribute configuration file
HELLO.MAK	3.5	The makefile

Table 3.3   Hello *project source files.*

Running this program the first time might take a while. Before your program can start, Windows NT must first start the RPC Service and the RPC Locator. To avoid this initial delay, you can configure Windows NT to automatically start these services each time you load Windows NT.

shortly. Even more important, and more difficult, is the ability of a server to determine a client's status. We'll explore both topics in the *PRIME* program examples later in the book.

Summary

Even though it is "trivial," the distributed *HELLO* application illustrates many important features of RPC programming. To build a working *HELLO* client and server, you must come to terms with at least the fundamentals of binding, IDL files, ACF files, and the entire RPC development cycle.

Unlike a real application, though, the *HELLO* program really doesn't move very much data between the client and the server. As I've hinted earlier, applying the RPC model to non-trivial data transfers and pointers raises some interesting problems. I'll explain how the RPC model addresses these problems in the next chapter.

Listing 3.1 — HELLOS.C

```
\*******************************************************************/
*                                                                  *
* HELLOS.C - Server side of automatic binding HELLO program        *
*           (c) Guy Eddon, 1993                                     *
*                                                                  *
* To build:  NMAKE HELLO                                            *
*                                                                  *
* Usage:     HELLOS                                                 *
*                                                                  *
* Comments:  This distributed application prints a string such as   *
*            "Hello, RPC!\n" on the server. The client uses        *
*            automatic binding to bind to the server.              *
*                                                                  *
\*******************************************************************/

#include <STDLIB.H>
#include <STRING.H>
#include <STDIO.H>
#include <RPC.H>
#include "hello.h"

void _CRTAPI1 main(int argc, char *argv[])
   {
   RPC_STATUS status;
   RPC_BINDING_VECTOR *pBindingVector;

   unsigned char *pszAutoEntryName   = "/.:/Autohandle_sample";
   unsigned char *pszEndpoint        = "\\pipe\\auto";
   unsigned char *pszProtocolSequence = "ncacn_np";
   unsigned char *pszSecurity        = NULL;
   unsigned int   cMinCalls          = 1;
   unsigned int   cMaxCalls          = 20;
   unsigned int   fDontWait          = FALSE;
   unsigned int   fNameSyntaxType    = RPC_C_NS_SYNTAX_DEFAULT;

   status = RpcServerUseProtseqEp(pszProtocolSequence,
                         cMaxCalls,      /* max concurrent calls */
                         pszEndpoint,
                         pszSecurity);   /* Security descriptor  */

   printf("RpcServerUseProtseqEp returned 0x%x\n", status);

   if(status)
      exit(status);
```

Listing 3.1 — (continued)

```
status = RpcServerRegisterIf(
    hello_ServerIfHandle, /* interface to register      */
    NULL,                 /* MgrTypeUuid                 */
    NULL);                /* MgrEpv; null means use default */

printf("RpcServerRegisterIf returned 0x%x\n", status);

if(status)
    exit(status);

status = RpcServerInqBindings(&pBindingVector);

printf("RpcServerInqBindings returned 0x%x\n", status);

if(status)
    exit(status);

status = RpcNsBindingExport(
    fNameSyntaxType,  /* name syntax type    */
    pszAutoEntryName, /* nsi entry name      */
    hello_ServerIfHandle,
    pBindingVector,   /* set in previous call */
    NULL);            /* UUID vector         */

printf("RpcNsBindingExport returned 0x%x\n", status);

if(status)
    exit(status);

printf("Calling RpcServerListen\n");

status = RpcServerListen(cMinCalls, cMaxCalls, fDontWait); /* wait */
                                                          /* flag */

printf("RpcServerListen returned: 0x%x\n", status);

if(status)
    exit(status);

if(fDontWait)
    {
    printf("Calling RpcMgmtWaitServerListen\n");

    status = RpcMgmtWaitServerListen(); /* wait operation */

    printf("RpcMgmtWaitServerListen returned: 0x%x\n", status);
```

Listing 3.1 — (continued)

```
    if(status)
        exit(status);
    }
}

/* MIDL allocate and free */
void *MIDL_user_allocate(size_t len)
    {
    return(malloc(len));
    }

void MIDL_user_free(void *ptr)
    {
    free(ptr);
    }
/* End of File */
```

Listing 3.2 — HELLOP.C

```
/*********************************************************************\
*                                                                   *
* HELLOP.C - Remote procedures linked with the server              *
*            (c) Guy Eddon, 1993                                    *
*                                                                   *
* To build:  NMAKE HELLO                                            *
*                                                                   *
* Comments:  This version of the distributed application that prints *
*            "hello, world" (or other string) on the server features *
*            a client that uses automatic binding.                  *
*                                                                   *
\*********************************************************************/

#include <STDLIB.H>
#include <STDIO.H>
#include <TIME.H>
#include <RPC.H>
#include "hello.h"

void HelloRPC(unsigned char *string)
    {
    printf(string);
    }

/* End of File */
```

Listing 3.3 — HELLO.IDL

```
/*********************************************************************\
* HELLO.IDL- Interface Definition                                   *
*           (c) Guy Eddon, 1993                                     *
\*********************************************************************/

[ uuid (7A32DE30-CDA7-1457-BE1D-0DFD0573452A),
  version(1.0),
  pointer_default(unique)]
interface hello
{
void HelloRPC([in, string] unsigned char *string);
}
```

Listing 3.4 — HELLO.ACF

```
/*********************************************************************\
* HELLO.ACF- Attribute Configuration File                           *
*           (c) Guy Eddon, 1993                                     *
\*********************************************************************/

[auto_handle]
interface hello
{
}
```

Listing 3.5 — HELLO.MAK

```
################################################################
# HELLO.MAK - makefile
################################################################

!include <ntwin32.mak>

!if "$(CPU)" == "i386"
cvtomf =
cflags = $(cflags:G3=Gz)
!endif
!if "$(CPU)" == "MIPS"
cvtomf = mip2coff $@
!endif

.c.obj:
   $(cc) $(cflags) $(cvars) $<
   $(cvtomf)

.obj.exe:
    $(link) $(conflags) -out:$(@R).exe $(@R).obj $(conlibs)

all : helloc hellos

helloc : helloc.exe
helloc.exe : helloc.obj hello_c.obj hello_x.obj
    $(link) $(conflags) -out:helloc.exe \
      helloc.obj hello_c.obj hello_x.obj \
      rpcrt4.lib rpcns4.lib $(conlibs)

# helloc main program
helloc.obj : helloc.c hello.h

# helloc stub
hello_c.obj : hello_c.c hello.h
   $(cc) $(cflags) $(cvars) hello_c.c
   $(cvtomf)

# helloc auxiliary file
hello_x.obj : hello_x.c hello.h
   $(cc) $(cflags) $(cvars) hello_x.c
   $(cvtomf)
```

Listing 3.5 — (continued)

```
# Make the hellos
hellos : hellos.exe
hellos.exe : hellos.obj hellop.obj hello_s.obj hello_y.obj
    $(link) $(conflags) -out:hellos.exe \
     hellos.obj hello_s.obj hellop.obj hello_y.obj \
     rpcrt4.lib rpcndr.lib rpcns4.lib $(conlibs)

# hellos main loop
hellos.obj : hellos.c hello.h

# remote procedures
hellop.obj  : hellop.c hello.h

# hellos stub file
hello_s.obj : hello_s.c hello.h
   $(cc) $(cflags) $(cvars) hello_s.c
   $(cvtomf)

# hellos auxiliary file
hello_y.obj : hello_y.c hello.h
   $(cc) $(cflags) $(cvars) hello_y.c
   $(cvtomf)

# Stubs, auxiliary and header file from the IDL file
hello.h hello_c.c hello_x.c hello_s.c hello_y.c : hello.idl hello.acf
    midl -cpp_cmd $(cc) -cpp_opt "-E"  hello.idl
```

## Chapter 4

Passing Data: Pointers, Arrays, and Strings

By mirroring the familiar local procedure call (LPC) model, RPC camouflages the network, thereby creating a more managable environment for the programmer. As the *HELLO* example demonstrates, accessing network resources involves little more than a simple function call (at least from the client side).

Conceptually, at least, the sequence is very straightforward:

1. The client stub packages the function parameters and sends them across the network to the server stub.

2. The server stub gets control and unpackages the function parameters.

3. The server stub calls the remote procedure with the correct function parameters using the local procedure call mechanism.

4. The same process is repeated in reverse order to transmit the return value back to the client.

What happens, though, when the client and server both need to refer to the same large data structure? RPC's method of packaging and transmitting function parameters strongly resembles the local procedure call (LPC) model's call-by-value, in which the called function receives a copy of the variable, not the variable itself. For large data structures, call-by-value is inherently expensive.

LPC programs can avoid the copying overhead of call-by-value by passing only a *reference* to the data structure, i.e., a pointer. For convenience and consistency, the RPC model should also support pointers. But, if the client and server tasks are executing in different address spaces, a reference constructed in one space will have no meaning in the other.

This chapter explains how the RPC model deals with pointers, and what the programmer needs to know in order to make informed decisions about passing large data structures between client and server.

RPC and References

Remote procedures execute in an address space different from that of their caller. If you were to pass a pointer to a remote procedure in the same manner in which you pass a variable, the pointer's value would still be the variable's address on the client. If the remote procedure were to access the data object, the user would immediately see an error message regarding a memory exception error, such as the one in Figure 4.1. The exception occurs because the pointer attempted to access memory that the server application does not own. Although the pointer was valid on the client, it is not valid on the server.

To correct this problem, RPC treats pointers in a manner that completely contradicts a C programmer's normal expectations. When a client passes a pointer to a remote procedure, the client stub transmits both the pointer and the data object to which it points. Thus, using a pointer invokes at least as much data copying as passing the referenced object. This feature is often referred to as *pointer emulation*. Emulating pointers consists of the following steps:

1. The client stub is called to package the function parameters and send them across the network to the server stub. The data object to which the pointer points is also packaged and sent.

2. The server stub unpackages the function parameters. In addition, it calls the user-defined memory allocation function to allocate memory on the server. It then copies the data object into the memory buffer and modifies the value of the pointer parameter to point to its address on the server.

3. The server stub calls the remote procedure with the correct function parameters using the local procedure call mechanism. The remote procedure can then access and modify the data object via the pointer, with no harmful side effects.

4. The same process is repeated in reverse order to transmit the return value back to the client. This may also include returning the modified data object as well.

The RPC method above avoids the necessity of transmitting the client's entire address space to the server. Such a move would be extremely inefficient and might require several seconds to complete.

It should be clear now why pointers passed to remote procedures must be treated differently than pointers passed to local procedures. When using the local procedure model, pointers are one of the most efficient methods of passing data to functions. When using RPC, pointers are a very inefficient method. Thus, you should design your distributed applications to minimize the amount of network traffic generated.

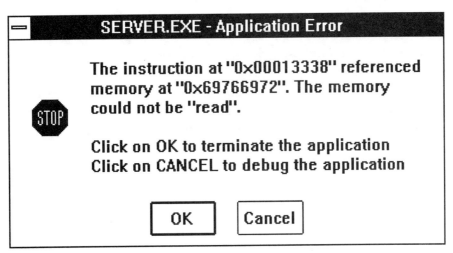

Figure 4.1   *Using a pointer incorrectly will produce a memory fault.*

Pointers

Call-by-value is usually contrasted with the call-by-reference model in which the function called receives the address of the variable. In other words, it receives a pointer. Any change made to the data object within the scope of the called function affects the value of the object to which the original pointer points. Pointers under RPC require special attention because the LPC and RPC models must diverge in how they handle them. When you pass a pointer in the LPC model, the callee receives a copy of that pointer. The function is then free to access the memory to which it points . If the function modifies the data object pointed to, then any other function that accesses the data will find it modified as well.

In C, most function calls use the *cdecl* calling convention. This convention involves pushing the last parameter on the stack first and allows a function to accept a variable number of parameters. For example, the standard C function *printf()* accepts a variable number of parameters. In Windows, however, many functions use the *PASCAL* calling convention, in which the first function parameter is pushed on the stack first. This convention allows a function to accept only a predefined number of parameters. By default, Windows NT uses a *stdcall* convention that is similar to the *cdecl* calling convention, but does not allow a function to accept a variable number of function parameters.

No matter which calling convention you use, C is very efficient compared to most other high-level languages. In C, passing a pointer to a function is one of the most efficient ways to provide the function access to data. Instead of pushing all the data on the stack — a very unrealistic idea when the data is a large buffer or a number of large data structures — only the pointer to the data is pushed. By placing only a few bytes on the stack, a function can conceivably access several megabytes of memory. Unfortunately, this elegant method is impossible in RPC.

The rest of this chapter focuses on RPC mechanisms that attempt to reduce the overhead inherent in passing data objects across the network. In this vein, RPC provides three distinct types of pointers: Reference, Unique, and Full. Table 4.1 compares these pointer types.

Reference Pointers

Reference pointers are the most efficient type of pointers available to RPC applications but also the most restricted. Reference pointers must always obesrve these limitations:

1. A reference pointer must always point to a valid memory address and may never contain the value *NULL*.

2. The value of a reference pointer must never change during a remote procedure call. In other words, it must point to the same data object before, during, and after the remote procedure call.

3. A data object returned from a remote procedure is copied over the existing data object.

4. The data object pointed to by a reference pointer may not be accessed by any other pointer (no aliasing).

If any of these requirements is not met, the application's behavior is undefined. Though restrictive, the reference pointer requirements allow the MIDL compiler to generate efficient stubs.

Pointer Type	Description
Reference	The most restricted pointer type. Reference pointers are usually used to implement pass-by-value semantics and to allow for *out* parameters.
Unique	The default pointer type used for most pointer operations. The unique pointer imposes fewer restrictions than reference pointers.
Full	The most sophisticated pointer type, with no restrictions. Full pointers are less efficient because the generated stubs cannot make any assumptions. Not supported in Microsoft RPC v1.0.

Table 4.1   *RPC pointer types.*

Unique Pointers

Unique pointers are less efficient than reference pointers because they impose fewer restrictions. Unlike reference pointers, the value of a unique pointer may change. Like reference pointers, unique pointers do not allow aliasing of data, meaning that you may not access the data object through any other pointer. The unique pointer is the default pointer type used when another type is not explicitly indicated. The following rules must be followed when using unique pointers:

1. Unique pointers may have the value *NULL*.

2. The value of a unique pointer may change during a remote procedure call.

3. A data object returned from a remote procedure is copied over the existing data object unless the pointer's value was *NULL*. In such cases, new memory is allocated for the data object on return.

4. The data object pointed to by a unique pointer may not be accessed (aliased) by any other pointer.

Full Pointers

Full pointers provide all the flexibility available to regular pointers in C. The remote procedure stubs generated by the MIDL compiler do all the fancy footwork required to make RPC transparent to the pointer operations. This mode may be useful for distributing existing applications quickly. You can get your application working and worry later about efficiency. Unfortunately, though full pointers are part of the OSF DCE specifications, Microsoft RPC v1.0 does not support them. In the future, should full pointers be supported, they will probably be the least efficient of the three pointer types.

Arrays, Strings, and Other Special Memory Structures

I have described how a data object referenced by a pointer is transmitted across the network to the server. I have not mentioned, however, the methods the RPC runtime uses to determine the amount of data to transmit. If the RPC runtime had no way of ascertaining a data object's size, it would be obliged to transmit the client's entire address space. To avoid this unbearable overhead, programmers can employ several methods to specify the amount of data the RPC runtime should send.

Arrays

The size of an array and the range of its elements transmitted to the remote procedure can be either constant or variable. When the size of an array to be transmitted is variable, the IDL file must contain special attributes to indicate the variables that will arbitrate the amount of data transmitted. Table 4.2 lists the MIDL attributes that support array bounds. Unfortunately Microsoft chose not to implement the *min_is* attribute in its RPC v1.0. The lowest valid array element therefore is always assumed to be *0*. Following are several examples of how these attributes may be used in the IDL file:

```
size_is

interface RPC_Array
    {
    extern short Size;

    void CalcArray([in, out, size_is(Size)] char Array[*]);
    }
```

Attribute	Description
first_is	Index of the first array element to be transmitted.
last_is	Index of the last array element to be transmitted.
length_is	Total number of array elements to be transmitted.
min_is	Lowest valid array element.
max_is	Highest valid array element.
size_is	Total number of elements allocated for the array.

Table 4.2   **MIDL attributes that support array bounds.**

length_is

```
interface RPC_Array
    {
    extern short Size;
    extern short Length;

    void CalcArray([in, out,
        size_is(Size),
        length_is(Length)] char Array[*]);
    }
```

first_is and last_is

```
interface RPC_Array
    {
    extern short Size;
    extern short First;
    extern short Last;

    void CalcArray([in,
        size_is(Size),
        first_is(First)
        last_is(Last)] char Array[*]);
    }
```

max_is

```
interface RPC_Array
    {
    extern short Max;

    void CalcArray([in, max_is(Max)] char Array[*]);
    }
```

In the following example, the array operator and the pointer operator can be used interchangeably:

```
interface RPC_Array
    {
    extern short Size;

    void CalcArray1([in, size_is(Size)] char *Array);
    void CalcArray2([in, size_is(Size)] char Array[*]);
    }
```

In these examples, the variables declared as *extern*, such as *Size* and *Length*, must be defined in the client application. The RPC runtime uses the values contained in these variables to determine what portion of the array it must transmit to the server. The runtime knows which variables to use because the MIDL compiler generates code that defines them as *extern*. The asterisks in these examples are simply optional place holders for the variable array's dimension.

In some instances, the RPC compiler can reduce network traffic by transmitting the array as a *variant array*. Only a certain range of a variant array's elements are transmitted to the remote procedure.

Strings

Before passing a null-terminated string to a remote procedure, you must indicate the *string* attribute in the procedure's IDL function prototype. The *string* attribute notifies the MIDL compiler that the data will be a null-terminated string. The code that the MIDL compiler generates then uses either the *strlen()* or *_wstrlen()* function to dynamically determine the string's actual length and transmits only the data up to and including the terminating *NULL*. Since the runtime determines the data's length dynamically by the position of the terminating *NULL*, passing a string is one of the easiest and most efficient ways to send a variable-length array to a remote procedure:

```
RPC_Array
    {
    void CalcArray([in, out, string] char Array[*]);
    }
```

Summary

It is important to remember that although the RPC facility was designed to resemble the standard C local procedure call, the two are very different underneath. Therefore, to develop the most efficient RPC applications, you must comprehend how the mechanism works internally. Parameters, especially pointers, arrays, and strings, are implemented differently and thus require the programmer to use slightly different conventions.

## Chapter 5

Building the PRIME *Applications*

The next several chapters introduce six programs, the last four of which are full-fledged RPC applications. Each program computes and displays prime numbers. I admit it is hard to envision a corporation developing a full-blown RPC application simply to produce a mountain of prime numbers. However, given that the process of finding prime numbers is computationally intensive, I find it ideal for demonstrating the usefulness of RPC.

In developing the six *PRIME* example applications, I will focus on the most important issues a programmer will face in his or her first time plunge into RPC application development. These issues include console management, multithreading, client/server architecture, Microsoft RPC, and a host of general Windows NT programming issues. Each *PRIME* program includes a feature lacking in the previous one (see Table 5.1). Thus, each succeeding example is increasingly complex. The final product, *PRIME6*, is a multithreaded, RPC-based application in which multiple servers respond to multiple clients.

Console Management

Windows NT provides two distinct user interfaces: the graphical user interface (GUI) and the console. Current Windows 3.1 applications use the GUI exclusively. Until recently, only the GUI interface was available to Windows developers. The GUI model, as shown in Figure 5.1, consists of re-sizable, overlapping windows in which the applications' user interface is displayed. Such programs usually utilize standard Windows features such as pull-down menus, push buttons, list boxes, and edit controls. The console interface, on the other hand, is a special category of Windows NT applications written for character mode. The *PRIME* examples use the console application interface.

An application written to the console interface can take advantage of all the Windows NT features except the graphic functions. Since console applications can run either windowed or full screen, they resemble MS-DOS applications running in Windows 3.1 enhanced mode. (In Windows 3.1 enhanced mode, an MS-DOS application can run either in full-screen mode or as a windowed application.) Their appearance notwithstanding, console Windows NT applications are full-fledged Windows NT applications and have much more control over their display than MS-DOS programs running in a window. The console application's major limitation (or feature, depending upon what your application does) is its inability to display graphics. This limitation results from the need to run the program in full-screen character mode.

I chose to write the *PRIME* program examples using the console interface because the same RPC example written as a graphical Windows

Features	1	2	3	4	5	6
Computes Prime Numbers	x	x	x	x	x	x
Multithreaded		x	x	x	x	x
Remote Procedure Calls			x	x	x	x
Multiple Clients — Single Server			x	x	x	x
Multiple Clients — Multiple Servers						x
Name Service					x	

Table 5.1   *Features of the six* PRIME *Examples.*

application would be at least twice as long, and all its interesting features would be hidden in massive switch-case constructs.

PRIME1

PRIME1 is a simple Windows NT application that computes and displays prime numbers. The *PRIME1* application does not make use of RPC or the multithreading capabilities of Windows NT. Later versions of *PRIME* will include these features. *PRIME1* just gets the basics down.

The Prime Number Algorithm

The algorithm I'll use to compute prime numbers is straight-forward, though not especially efficient. All the *PRIME* examples will use this *IsPrime()* function to compute prime numbers:

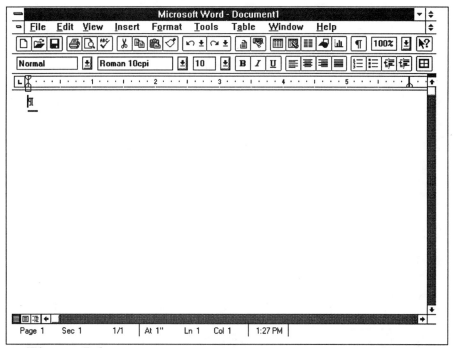

Figure 5.1   *The Standard Windows Interface.*

The I/O Library

To facilitate creating the console display, I ported my *DIRECTIO* library from MS-DOS to Windows NT. As an MS-DOS library, *DIRECTIO* provides high-speed direct memory access for real-mode MS-DOS applications. The Windows NT version provides an interface to the Win32 API console management functions. Table 5.2 lists the library functions used in the *PRIME* examples. Each of the *PRIME* applications calls functions in the *DIRECTIO* library, which in turn call Win32 console functions (listed in Table 5.3) to perform the actual display. The source for the NT *DIRECTIO* library appears as Listings 5.3 and 5.4. The original MS-DOS version appears in Listings 9.7 and 9.8.

Function	Description
set_vid_mem	Initializes the console display space. Must be called before any of the other *DIRECTIO* functions.
box	Creates a box with the specified dimensions using the extended ASCII character set. Can create a box with a single- or double-border.
clear	Clears the specified area with the desired attribute.
clearscreen	Clears the entire console space with the desired attribute.
get_character_no_wait	Determines if a character is waiting in the keyboard buffer, and if so, retrieves it. If no character is waiting, returns immediately.
get_character_wait	Waits for the user to input a character.
moutchar	Displays a character a specified number of times with the desired attribute starting from a specified location.
mxyputc	Displays a character at the specified location with the desired attribute.
mxyputs	Displays a string at the specified location with the desired attribute.
read_field	Creates an input field and returns a string.

Table 5.2   *Library Functions Used in the* PRIME *Examples.*

```
unsigned char IsPrime(unsigned long TestNumber)
{
unsigned long count;
unsigned long HalfNumber = TestNumber / 2 + 1;

for(count = 2; count < HalfNumber; count++)
        if(TestNumber % count == 0)
                return NOT_PRIME;
return PRIME;
}
```

Running PRIME1

Once you've compiled and linked *PRIME1*, you can execute it by opening a single command shell (the Windows NT command line) and typing

PRIME1

Function	Description
FillConsoleOutputAttribute	Write a character attribute to a specified number of consecutive character cells in a screen buffer.
FillConsoleOutputCharacter	Write a character to a specified number of consecutive character cells in a screen buffer.
FlushConsoleInputBuffer	Empty an input buffer.
GetConsoleMode	Get a mask indicating the current mode of a console input buffer or an output screen buffer.
GetConsoleScreenBufferInfo	Returns information about a screen buffer, including its size in character rows and columns, cursor position, the location of its window, its default text display attribute.
PeekConsoleInput	Read data from the input buffer without removing it.
SetConsoleCtrl Handler	Add or remove a Ctrl-C and Ctrl-Break handler for the calling process.
SetConsoleMode	Sets the mode for either an input or an output console handle.
WriteConsoleOutputAttribute	Write a string of consecutive character attributes to a specified location in a screen buffer.
WriteConsoleOutputCharacter	Write a string of consecutive characters to a specified location in a screen buffer.

Table 5.3　　*Win32 Console Functions.*

PRIME1 clears the screen, sets up its user interface, and begins to compute prime numbers. For information about the available command line parameters, run:

```
C:\PRIME1>PRIME1 /?
```

which produces the message:

```
Usage: PRIME1
       -f first number
```

PRIME1 computes prime numbers from numeral one (1) unless you specify a different starting number with the *-f* option.

When you start *PRIME1*, it first displays its console window (Figure 5.2). Within the console window, *PRIME1* creates two display boxes using the *DIRECTIO box()* function. Immediately, the boxes are filled with numbers that zoom by. The box on the left displays the numbers that the *PRIME* algorithm is testing. The box on the right displays the numbers that the algorithm has determined to be prime. Once a number has been

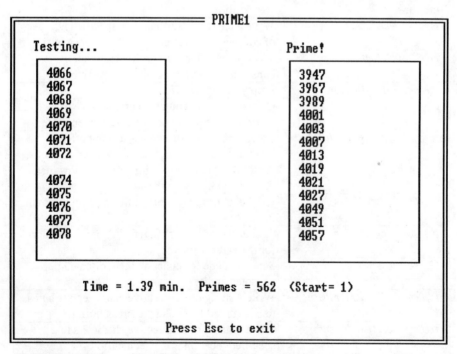

Figure 5.2   The PRIME1 *Display.*

displayed, the box scrolls up one row, overwrites the number at the top of the box, and creates an empty space for the next entry, thus providing the user with the illusion of scrolling. You can create this effect easily using the Win32 *ScrollConsoleScreenBuffer()* function.

PRIME1 computes prime numbers in a loop:

```
while(NextNumber <= ULONG_MAX)
    {
    IsPrime(NextNumber++);
    }
```

The program will run until *NextNumber* hits the 4,294,967,296 limit or until the user presses the *Esc* key. Before terminating, the application executes some cleanup code and returns to the single command shell from which it started.

Building PRIME1

The *PRIME1* program consists of the following source files:

File	Listing	Description
PRIME1.C	5.1	The *PRIME1* source code
PRIME1.MAK	5.2	The *PRIME1* makefile
DIRECTIO.C	5.3	The *DIRECTIO* source code
DIRECTIO.H	5.4	The *DIRECTIO* header file

To build *PRIME1*, type

```
NMAKE PRIME1.MAK
```

PRIME1.MAK in Listing 5.2 is a standard Windows NT makefile and, as such, includes the *NTWIN32.MAK* file. As described in Chapter 1, *NTWIN32.MAK* sets up many standard macros for developing Windows NT applications.

The target executable is *PRIME1.EXE*, and its dependencies are *PRIME1.OBJ* and *DIRECTIO.OBJ*. On the link line, *PRIME1.MAK* specifies the use of the *$(conflags)* and *$(conlibs)*, which are set up in the *NTWIN32.MAK* file. Since *PRIME1* is a console application, these flags trigger the use of standard flags and libraries required for console applications.

The compile line specifies the use of *$(cflags)* and *$(cvars)*, which in turn indicate the standard Windows NT compiler flags and variables:

```
.c.obj:
    $(cc) $(cflags) $(cvars) $<
    $(cvtomf)
```

Lastly, all the object files are linked to produce the executable:

```
PRIME1 : PRIME1.exe
PRIME1.exe : PRIME1.obj directio.obj
    $(link) $(conflags) -out:PRIME1.exe \
    PRIME1.obj directio.obj $(conlibs)
```

In future chapters the details of command syntax and compilation will be presented in manual page form (see page 61).

Summary

PRIME1 is a simple, nondistributed Windows NT program that computes prime numbers. The following chapters will build on this basic foundation, adding features specific to a distributed application built with remote procedures calls. The first of these features, multithreading, is required for an RPC server. The *PRIME2* program in Chapter 6 incorporates multithreading.

PRIME1   PRIME1

Command Syntax

```
PRIME1 [options]
```

Options

All options may be given in UNIX style (a leading hyphen) or DOS style (a leading slash).

```
-f n Start search at n instead of 1 (1 is the default).
-?
-h   Print usage summary and stop.
```

Termination

Program terminates when *NextNumber* reaches 4,294,967,296 or when the user presses the *Esc* key, whichever comes first.

Limitations

The program cannot search beyond 4,294,967,296 (2^32).

Files

Makefile

```
PRIME1.MAK
```

File	Listing	Description
PRIME1.C	5.1	The *PRIME1* source code
PRIME1.MAK	5.2	The *PRIME1* makefile
DIRECTIO.C	5.3	The *DIRECTIO* source code
DIRECTIO.H	5.4	The *DIRECTIO* header file

Table 5.4   *Source files for* PRIME1.

Listing 5.1 — PRIME1.C

```c
/*********************************************************************\
*                                                                   *
* PRIME1.C - Prime number example                                   *
*           (c) Guy Eddon, 1993                                     *
*                                                                   *
* To build:  NMAKE PRIME1.MAK                                       *
*                                                                   *
* Usage:     PRIME1                                                 *
*                                                                   *
* Comments:  This example computes prime numbers.                   *
\*********************************************************************/

#include <STDIO.H>
#include <STRING.H>
#include <STDLIB.H>
#include <STDARG.H>
#include <LIMITS.H>
#include <WINDOWS.H>
#include "directio.h"


/* Coordinates for displaying numbers to be tested */

#define TESTING_X1    10
#define TESTING_Y1     3
#define TESTING_X2    30
#define TESTING_Y2    18

/* Coordinates for displaying prime numbers */

#define PRIME_X1      50
#define PRIME_Y1       3
#define PRIME_X2      70
#define PRIME_Y2      18


#define PRIME          1
#define NOT_PRIME      0
#define ERROR_EXIT     2
#define SUCCESS_EXIT   0
#define STRING_LENGTH 256

#define WHITE_ON_BLUE FOREGROUND_WHITE|FOREGROUND_INTENSITY|BACKGROUND_BLUE
#define WHITE_ON_CYAN FOREGROUND_WHITE|FOREGROUND_INTENSITY|BACKGROUND_CYAN
#define RED_ON_BLUE   FOREGROUND_RED  |FOREGROUND_INTENSITY|BACKGROUND_BLUE

unsigned char IsPrime(unsigned long TestNumber);
void InitializeApplication(void);
void Usage(void);
```

Listing 5.1 — (continued)

```c
unsigned long NextNumber = 1, StartTime, CurrTime,
  NoPrime, StartNumber = 1;

void main(int argc, char **argv)
    {
    int count;
    char Buffer[STRING_LENGTH];
    SMALL_RECT psrctScrollRectTesting, psrctScrollRectPrime;
    COORD coordDestOriginTesting, coordDestOriginPrime;
    CHAR_INFO pchiFill;
    WORD Color[TESTING_X2-TESTING_X1-3], Normal[TESTING_X2-TESTING_X1-3];
    DWORD dummy;
    COORD PrimeCoord;

    psrctScrollRectTesting.Left   = TESTING_X1+1;
    psrctScrollRectTesting.Top    = TESTING_Y1+2;
    psrctScrollRectTesting.Right  = TESTING_X2-1;
    psrctScrollRectTesting.Bottom = TESTING_Y2-1;

    coordDestOriginTesting.X = TESTING_X1+1;
    coordDestOriginTesting.Y = TESTING_Y1+1;

    psrctScrollRectPrime.Left   = PRIME_X1+1;
    psrctScrollRectPrime.Top    = PRIME_Y1+2;
    psrctScrollRectPrime.Right  = PRIME_X2-1;
    psrctScrollRectPrime.Bottom = PRIME_Y2-1;

    coordDestOriginPrime.X = PRIME_X1+1;
    coordDestOriginPrime.Y = PRIME_Y1+1;

    /* Allow the user to override settings with command line switches */

    for(count = 1; count < argc; count++)
        {
        if((*argv[count] == '-') || (*argv[count] == '/'))
            {
            switch(tolower(*(argv[count]+1)))
                {
                case 'f': /* first number */
                    NextNumber = StartNumber = atol(argv[++count]);
                    break;

                case 'h':
                case '?':
                default:
                    Usage();
                }
```

Listing 5.1 — (continued)

```
      }
   else
      Usage();
   }

InitializeApplication();

pchiFill.Char.AsciiChar = (char)32;
pchiFill.Attributes =  RED_ON_BLUE;

for(count = 0; count < TESTING_X2-TESTING_X1-3; count++)
    Color[count] = RED_ON_BLUE;

for(count = 0; count < TESTING_X2-TESTING_X1-3; count++)
    Normal[count] = WHITE_ON_BLUE;

while(NextNumber <= ULONG_MAX)
   {
   if(VK_ESCAPE == get_character_no_wait())
      break;

   NextNumber++;

   ScrollConsoleScreenBuffer(hStdOut, &psrctScrollRectTesting, NULL,
                        coordDestOriginTesting, &pchiFill);
   sprintf(Buffer, " %-18d", NextNumber - 1);
   mxyputs((unsigned char)TESTING_X1+1, (unsigned char)TESTING_Y2-1, Buffer, WHITE_ON_BLUE);

   if(IsPrime(NextNumber - 1) != 0)
      {
      PrimeCoord.X = TESTING_X1 + 2;
      PrimeCoord.Y = TESTING_Y2 - 1;

      WriteConsoleOutputAttribute(hStdOut, Color, TESTING_X2-TESTING_X1-3, PrimeCoord, &dummy);
      mxyputs((unsigned char)TESTING_X2-2, (unsigned char)(TESTING_Y2-1), "*", RED_ON_BLUE);

      PrimeCoord.X = PRIME_X1 + 2;
      PrimeCoord.Y = PRIME_Y2 - 1;

      WriteConsoleOutputAttribute(hStdOut, Normal, PRIME_X2-PRIME_X1-3, PrimeCoord, &dummy);
      ScrollConsoleScreenBuffer(hStdOut, &psrctScrollRectPrime, NULL,
                        coordDestOriginPrime, &pchiFill);
      WriteConsoleOutputAttribute(hStdOut, Color, PRIME_X2-PRIME_X1-3, PrimeCoord, &dummy);

      sprintf(Buffer, " %-18d", NextNumber - 1);
      mxyputs((unsigned char)(PRIME_X1+1), (unsigned char)PRIME_Y2-1, Buffer, RED_ON_BLUE);
      NoPrime++;
      }
```

Listing 5.1 — (continued)

```c
        CurrTime = (GetTickCount() - StartTime)/1000;
        sprintf(Buffer,"Time = %d.%02d min.  Primes = %d   (Start= %d)",
                CurrTime/60, CurrTime%60, NoPrime, StartNumber);
        mxyputs(27, 20, Buffer, WHITE_ON_CYAN);
        }

    clearscreen(0);
    }

/* Tests for prime numbers */

unsigned char IsPrime(unsigned long TestNumber)
    {
    unsigned long count;
    unsigned long HalfNumber = TestNumber / 2 + 1;

    for(count = 2; count < HalfNumber; count++)
        if(TestNumber % count == 0)
            return NOT_PRIME;

    return PRIME;
    }

/* Displays command line options */

void Usage(void)
    {
    printf("\nSimple prime number example.\n\n");
    printf("Usage: PRIME1\n");
    printf(" -f first number\n");
    exit(SUCCESS_EXIT);
    }

/* Screen initialization and colors and title lines */

void InitializeApplication(void)

    {
    set_vid_mem();

    clearscreen(BACKGROUND_CYAN);
    StartTime = GetTickCount();
    box(0, 0, 79, 24,DOUBLE);
    mxyputs(37, 0, " PRIME1 ", WHITE_ON_CYAN);
```

Listing 5.1 — (continued)

```
    mxyputs(10, 2, "Testing...", WHITE_ON_CYAN);
    box(TESTING_X1, TESTING_Y1, TESTING_X2, TESTING_Y2,SINGLE);

    mxyputs(50, 2, "Prime!", WHITE_ON_CYAN);
    box(PRIME_X1, PRIME_Y1, PRIME_X2, PRIME_Y2,SINGLE);

    mxyputs(32, 23, "Press Esc to exit", WHITE_ON_CYAN);
    }

/* End of File */
```

Listing 5.2 — PRIME1.MAK

```
#################################################################
#                                                               #
# PRIME1.MAK - makefile                                         #
#                                                               #
#################################################################

!include <ntwin32.mak>

!if "$(CPU)" == "MIPS"
cdebug =
cvtdebug =
linkdebug =
!endif

all: prime1.exe

prime1.exe: prime1.obj directio.obj
  $(link) $(conflags) -out:$*.exe $** $(conlibs)

.c.obj:
  $(cc) $(cflags) $(cvars) $*.c
```

Listing 5.3 — DIRECTIO.C

```
/*********************************************************************\
*                                                                   *
* DIRECTIO.C -  Uses the console API to do video I/O                *
*               (c) Guy Eddon, 1993                                 *
*                                                                   *
*                                                                   *
* Comments:     Port of MS-DOS direct screen access to NT.          *
*                                                                   *
\*********************************************************************/

#include <STDIO.H>
#include <STRING.H>
#include <STDLIB.H>
#include <STDARG.H>
#include <LIMITS.H>
#include <WINDOWS.H>
#include "directio.h"

#define WHITE_ON_CYAN FOREGROUND_WHITE|FOREGROUND_INTENSITY|BACKGROUND_CYAN

/* Declaration for Ctrl-C and Ctrl-Break handler */

extern BOOL WINAPI CtrlHandler(DWORD CtrlType);

HANDLE hStdOut;
CONSOLE_SCREEN_BUFFER_INFO csbi;

/* Initialize Screen Access and set Ctrl-C and Ctrl-Break handlesr */

void set_vid_mem(void)
   {
   hStdOut = GetStdHandle(STD_OUTPUT_HANDLE);
   GetConsoleScreenBufferInfo(hStdOut, &csbi);
   SetConsoleCtrlHandler(CtrlHandler, TRUE);
   }

/* Display string pointed by str at location (x,y) with attribute attr */

void mxyputs(unsigned char x, unsigned char y, char *str, unsigned  attr)
   {
   COORD BufferCoord;
   DWORD dummy;
   WORD Color[MAX_STR];
   unsigned count;

   BufferCoord.X = x;
   BufferCoord.Y = y;
```

Listing 5.3 — (continued)

```c
    WriteConsoleOutputCharacter(hStdOut, str, strlen(str), BufferCoord, &dummy);

    for(count = 0; count < strlen(str); count++)
       Color[count] = attr;

    WriteConsoleOutputAttribute(hStdOut, Color, strlen(str), BufferCoord, &dummy);
    }

/* Display character ch num times starting at (x,y) with attribute atr */

void mxyputc(unsigned char x, unsigned char y, char ch, unsigned char num, unsigned char attr)
    {
    COORD BufferCoord;
    DWORD dummy;

    BufferCoord.X = x;
    BufferCoord.Y = y;

    FillConsoleOutputCharacter(hStdOut, ch, num, BufferCoord, &dummy);
    FillConsoleOutputAttribute(hStdOut, attr, num, BufferCoord, &dummy);
    }

/* Display character ch at location (x,y) with attribute attr    */

void moutchar(unsigned char x, unsigned char y, char ch, unsigned char attr)
    {
    COORD BufferCoord;
    DWORD dummy;

    BufferCoord.X = x;
    BufferCoord.Y = y;

    FillConsoleOutputCharacter(hStdOut, ch, 1, BufferCoord, &dummy);
    }

/*
    Display Box from (x1,y1) to (x2,y2), S_D flag for single or double border
*/

void box(unsigned char x1, unsigned char y1, unsigned char x2, nsigned char y2, char S_D)
    {
    COORD BufferCoord;
    DWORD dummy;
    unsigned char count;
    char chr;
```

Listing 5.3 — (continued)

```
for(count = y1 + 1; count < y2; count++)
    {
    BufferCoord.X = x1;
    BufferCoord.Y = count;

    chr = S_D ? 186 : 179;

    FillConsoleOutputCharacter(hStdOut, chr, 1, BufferCoord, &dummy);
    FillConsoleOutputAttribute(hStdOut, WHITE_ON_CYAN, 1, BufferCoord, &dummy);

    BufferCoord.X = x2;

    FillConsoleOutputCharacter(hStdOut, chr, 1, BufferCoord, &dummy);
    FillConsoleOutputAttribute(hStdOut, WHITE_ON_CYAN, 1, BufferCoord, &dummy);
    }
BufferCoord.X = x1 + 1;
BufferCoord.Y = y1;

count = x2 - x1 - 1;
chr =   S_D ? 205 : 196;

FillConsoleOutputCharacter(hStdOut, chr, count, BufferCoord, &dummy);
FillConsoleOutputAttribute(hStdOut, WHITE_ON_CYAN, count+1, BufferCoord, &dummy);

BufferCoord.Y = y2;

chr = S_D ? 205 : 196;

FillConsoleOutputCharacter(hStdOut, chr, count, BufferCoord, &dummy);
FillConsoleOutputAttribute(hStdOut, WHITE_ON_CYAN, count+1, BufferCoord, &dummy);

BufferCoord.X = x1;
BufferCoord.Y = y1;

chr = S_D ? 201 : 218;

FillConsoleOutputCharacter(hStdOut, chr, 1, BufferCoord, &dummy);
FillConsoleOutputAttribute(hStdOut, WHITE_ON_CYAN, 1, BufferCoord, &dummy);

BufferCoord.Y = y2;

chr = S_D ? 200 : 192;

FillConsoleOutputCharacter(hStdOut, chr, 1, BufferCoord, &dummy);
FillConsoleOutputAttribute(hStdOut, WHITE_ON_CYAN, 1, BufferCoord, &dummy);
```

Listing 5.3 — (continued)

```
    BufferCoord.X = x2;
    BufferCoord.Y = y1;

    chr = S_D ? 187 : 191;

    FillConsoleOutputCharacter(hStdOut, chr, 1, BufferCoord, &dummy);
    FillConsoleOutputAttribute(hStdOut, WHITE_ON_CYAN, 1, BufferCoord, &dummy);

    BufferCoord.Y = y2;

    chr = S_D ? 188 : 217;

    FillConsoleOutputCharacter(hStdOut, chr, 1, BufferCoord, &dummy);
    FillConsoleOutputAttribute(hStdOut, WHITE_ON_CYAN, 1, BufferCoord, &dummy);
    }

/*
    Reads field from (x1,y) to (x2,y), saves value in a variable pointed by buffer
*/
void read_field(unsigned char x1, unsigned char x2, unsigned char y, char *buffer)
    {
    unsigned char col = x1;
    unsigned char count;

    for(count = x1; count <= x2; count++)
       moutchar(count, y, (char)32, 0);
    for(count = x1; ; count++)
       {
       buffer[count - x1] = toupper(get_character_wait());
       if(buffer[count - x1] == '\r')
          break;
       if(buffer[count - x1] == '\b')
          {
          count--;
          if(col != x1)
             {
             moutchar(--col, y, (char)32, 0);
             count--;
             }
          }
       else
          moutchar(col++, y, buffer[count - x1], 0);
       if(col < x1)
          col = x1;
```

Listing 5.3 — (continued)

```c
        else
            if(col > ((unsigned char)(x2 + 1)))
                {
                count--;
                col = x2 + 1;
                moutchar(col, y, (char)32, 0);
                }
        }
    buffer[count - x1] = 0;
    }

/* Clears screen from (x1,y1) to (x2,y2) */

void clear(unsigned char x1, unsigned char y1, unsigned char x2,
            unsigned char y2, unsigned char attr)
    {
    unsigned char row;

    for(row = y1; row <= y2; row++)
        mxyputc(x1, row, (char)32, (unsigned char)((x2-x1)+1), attr);
    }

/* Clears the entire screen    */

void clearscreen(WORD attr)
    {
    COORD BufferCoord;
    DWORD dummy;

    BufferCoord.X = 0;
    BufferCoord.Y = 0;

    FillConsoleOutputCharacter(hStdOut, (char)32, 80*25, BufferCoord, &dummy);
    FillConsoleOutputAttribute(hStdOut, attr, 80*25, BufferCoord, &dummy);

    if(!attr)
        SetConsoleCtrlHandler(CtrlHandler, FALSE);
    }

/* Waits for a character and returns it */

char get_character_wait(void)
    {
    HANDLE hStdIn;      /* standard input         */
    DWORD dwInputMode; /* to save the input mode */
    DWORD dwRead;
    char chBuf;         /* buffer to read into    */
```

Listing 5.3 — (continued)

```
    hStdIn = GetStdHandle(STD_INPUT_HANDLE);
    GetConsoleMode(hStdIn, &dwInputMode);
    SetConsoleMode(hStdIn, dwInputMode & ~ENABLE_LINE_INPUT & ~ENABLE_ECHO_INPUT);
    ReadFile(hStdIn, &chBuf, sizeof(chBuf), &dwRead, NULL);
    SetConsoleMode(hStdIn, dwInputMode);
    return chBuf;
    }

/* If there is a character, returns it. Otherwise, returns */

char get_character_no_wait(void)
    {
    HANDLE hStdIn;      /* standard input        */
    INPUT_RECORD aInputBuffer;
    DWORD dummy;
    DWORD dwInputMode; /* to save the input mode */

    hStdIn = GetStdHandle(STD_INPUT_HANDLE);
    GetConsoleMode(hStdIn, &dwInputMode);
    SetConsoleMode(hStdIn, dwInputMode & ~ENABLE_LINE_INPUT & ~ENABLE_ECHO_INPUT);
    PeekConsoleInput(hStdIn, &aInputBuffer, 1, &dummy);
    SetConsoleMode(hStdIn, dwInputMode);
    FlushConsoleInputBuffer(hStdIn);

    if(aInputBuffer.EventType == KEY_EVENT)
       return (char)(aInputBuffer.Event.KeyEvent.wVirtualKeyCode);
    }

BOOL WINAPI CtrlHandler(DWORD CtrlType)
    {
    switch (CtrlType)
       {
       case CTRL_BREAK_EVENT:
       case CTRL_C_EVENT:
          return TRUE;
          break;
       }
    return TRUE;
    }

/* End of File */
```

Listing 5.4 — DIRECTIO.H

```
/*********************************************************************\
*                                                                   *
* DIRECTIO.H -  Defines for DIRECTIO.C                              *
*               (c) Guy Eddon, 1993                                 *
*                                                                   *
* Comments:     Port of MS-DOS direct screen access to NT.          *
\*********************************************************************/

#define FOREGROUND_YELLOW (WORD)0x0006
#define FOREGROUND_CYAN   (WORD)0x0003
#define BACKGROUND_CYAN   (WORD)0x0030
#define FOREGROUND_WHITE  (WORD)0x0007
#define FOREGROUND_BLUE        0x0001
#define FOREGROUND_GREEN       0x0002
#define FOREGROUND_RED         0x0004
#define FOREGROUND_INTENSITY   0x0008
#define BACKGROUND_BLUE        0x0010
#define BACKGROUND_GREEN       0x0020
#define BACKGROUND_RED         0x0040
#define BACKGROUND_INTENSITY   0x0080


#define SINGLE   0
#define DOUBLE   1
#define MAX_STR 100

extern HANDLE hStdOut;
extern CONSOLE_SCREEN_BUFFER_INFO csbi; /*used to get current attribute*/

extern void clearscreen(WORD);
extern void clear(unsigned char x1, unsigned char y1, unsigned char x2,
                  unsigned char y2, unsigned char attribute);
extern void read_field(unsigned char x1, unsigned char x2, unsigned char y, char *buffer);
extern void mxyputs(unsigned char x, unsigned char y, char *buffer, unsigned attribute);
extern void set_vid_mem(void);
extern void mxyputc(unsigned char x, unsigned char y, char ch,
                  unsigned char num, unsigned char attr);
extern void moutchar(unsigned char x, unsigned char y, char character,
                  unsigned char attribute);
extern void box(unsigned char x1, unsigned char y1, unsigned char x2,
                unsigned char y2, char S_D);
extern char get_character_wait(void);
extern char get_character_no_wait(void);


/* End of File */
```

## Chapter 6

Multithreading: Developing PRIME2

Like the *PRIME1* program, this chapter's *PRIME2* computes and displays prime numbers. Unlike *PRIME1*, however, *PRIME2* uses Windows NT's preemptive multithreading capabilities to engage multiple threads in its computations. The multithreading features presented in *PRIME2* will become critical in the *PRIME3* example in which they will form the basis of RPC.

Multithreading

PRIME2 can create up to 10 threads, each of which uses the algorithm from Chapter 5 to test whether or not a number is prime. The program creates these threads via a call to the Win32 *CreateThread()* function:

```
for(count = 1; count <= NumThreads; count++)
    hthread[count-1] = CreateThread(
                NULL,    /*No security descriptor   */
                0,       /*use previous stack size   */
                (LPTHREAD_START_ROUTINE)thread,
```

```
count,          /*input to the prime routine*/
0,              /*no special creation flags */
&lpIDThread[count-1]);
```

Though not yet an RPC application, *PRIME2* is a multithreaded application; through `CreateThread()`, `Prime2` can create multiple instances of its `Thread()` function, each of which calls the `IsPrime()` function to compute prime numbers:

```
unsigned long NextNumber = 0;

void Thread(int count)
    {
    while(NextNumber <= ULONG_MAX)
            {
            IsPrime(NextNumber++);
            }
    }
```

Windows NT's multithreading facility is a very powerful feature, but is subject to the pitfalls inherent in concurrent programming. The *PRIME2* example gives us an opportunity to observe how these problems may arise.

Adding Critical Sections

PRIME2's `Thread()` function incorporates the `while` loop from the body of *PRIME1*. The most serious problem in just blindly adding the code to the `Thread()` function lies in the use of the global variable `NextNumber`.

Windows NT is built in a very structured, orthogonal manner. There is a logical and organized method by which different parts of the operating system interact and interface. In Windows NT, WinExec actually calls the `CreateProcess()` *function. The* `CreateProcess()` *function eventually calls the* `CreateThread()` *function. In this way the new application becomes another child thread of the operating system itself. Different parts of the operating system are really just threads, each with a different purpose and access rights.*

Thread() uses the value in *NextNumber* to determine the next number to test.

NextNumber is incremented after each call to *IsPrime()* so that individual threads don't repeat each others' work. In other words, *NextNumber* is used to ensure that no two threads test the same number. The variable must therefore be global so that multiple instances of the *Thread()* function can determine the next number to test.

Unfortunately, since the operating system may interrupt a thread at any moment, it is possible for two threads to attempt to increment *NextNumber* simultaneously. In such cases the *NextNumber* variable can become corrupted. While this scenario might not occur during a project's testing phase, it will more than likely occur once the product is released to end-users. These kinds of concurrency problems are very difficult to track down because threads may interrupt one another at different times. While the application appears to work well most of time, a seemingly unexplained bug occasionally appears.

To prevent the problems that can arise when concurrent threads access a single resource, *PRIME2* embeds the access to those resources within a critical section. A critical section permits safe, serialized access to resources shared among threads, such as global variables. Although Windows NT offers other synchronization objects, critical sections constitute one of the more efficient mechanisms available to serialize access to shared resources.

Before using a critical section, you must initialize it via a call to the Win32 *InitializeCriticalSection()* function:

```
InitializeCriticalSection(&GlobalCriticalSection);
```

For more information about Win32 synchronization objects — including Semaphores, Mutex objects, and event objects — see the chapter on Synchronization objects in The WIN32 API manual. *If you are unfamiliar with the problems created by concurrent access to shared resources, we suggest you find a textbook on operating system theory, such as* Operating System Principles *by Brinch Hansen.*

where *GlobalCriticalSection* is an instance of a critical section type synchronization object. *PRIME2* is then free to enter and leave a critical section by calling the *EnterCriticalSection()* and *LeaveCriticalSection()* functions, respectively. Proper placement of these function calls is critical, since improper placement can have undesired side effects. For example consider the *Thread()* function below, complete with a critical section:

```
unsigned long NextNumber = 0;

void Thread(int count)
    {
    EnterCriticalSection(&GlobalCriticalSection);
    while(NextNumber <= ULONG_MAX)
            {
            IsPrime(NextNumber++);
            }
    ExitCriticalSection(&GlobalCriticalSection);
    }
```

In this example, prime numbers can no longer be computed concurrently because the first thread that gains control of *IsPrime()* will never release it. To prevent this lockup, *PRIME2* copies the value of the *NextNumber* variable to a safe, local variable and then increments *NextNumber* within the critical section. It next calls *IsPrime()* outside the critical section:

```
unsigned long NextNumber = 0;

void Thread(int count)
    {
    unsigned long safe_temp;

    while(NextNumber <= ULONG_MAX)
            {
            EnterCriticalSection(&GlobalCriticalSection);
            safe_temp = NextNumber++;
            ExitCriticalSection(&GlobalCriticalSection);
            IsPrime(safe_temp);
            }
    }
```

PRIME2 modifies the global *NextNumber* only from within the context of a critical section. The *IsPrime()* function is called with a safe, local copy of *NextNumber*. The *safe_temp* variable is "safe" because it is local to the thread and, as such, is not subject to modification by any other thread. *PRIME2* can now call *IsPrime()*, which performs its lengthy computation outside of the critical section, thus allowing other threads to proceed concurrently.

The *PRIME2* application terminates when the user presses the *ESC* key. *PRIME2* then calls the Win32 *DeleteCriticalSection()* function to delete the critical section object created when the program was initially executed.

```
DeleteCriticalSection(&GlobalCriticalSection);
```

The program then calls the standard C *exit()* function to terminate the application. When a multithreaded application is terminated, the operating system terminates all its threads simultaneously, thereby avoiding the "chicken without a head" effect.

Distributing the Work

In deciding how *PRIME2* should distribute work to its multiple threads, you can choose one of two approaches:

- ☐ Dole out work as threads become available.
- ☐ Engage in "social engineering," preventing a thread from getting ahead of others just because its task is simpler.

I wrote *PRIME2* to take advantage of the first approach. In a multiprocessor or distributed environment, the first method is more efficient than the second because a slow thread will not degrade the performance of the other threads. For example, *PRIME2* can send work to, say, thread number seven, even if thread number two has not yet completed its task.

The second method of distributing work is significantly easier to implement, but is less efficient. Using this approach, *PRIME2* would farm out a number to each thread sequentially and wait for the first thread to become available before passing out new numbers. This method can

The PVIEW utility, provided with the Windows NT 3.1 SDK, lets you monitor the threads you create.

Distributing work efficiently is important when there is spare CPU time to go around. On a uniprocessor machine, one CPU executes all threads; it is not important which thread is executing. As long as one thread is executing, the CPU will be busy performing necessary work. The point is not which thread is executing, but that you exploit every CPU cycle available. In a distributed environment, however, where RPCs engage multiple CPUs in executing the threads, it is important to distribute work efficiently. If you let a CPU sit idle when it could be executing a thread, efficiency is lost.

easily waste CPU time if, for instance, thread number eight becomes available before thread number one does. Such a scenario is quite likely to occur, considering that thread number one might receive a prime number and therefore must test all the possibilities up to that number divided by two, whereas thread number eight may receive an even number and toss it out immediately.

If thread number eight finishes before thread number one, *PRIME2* will display thread eight's results first. The prime numbers will therefore occasionally appear out of sequence on the screen. If the situation required that the data processed appear in a sequential format, then *PRIME2* might engage the threads in the less efficient, sequential manner.

The User Interface

The *PRIME2* display (Figure 6.1) is very similar to that of *PRIME1*. I have added a thread column next to the column of numbers being tested and next to those determined to be prime. I've also added a box to the right which lists the threads and the number each is testing.

Depending on the options you specify, *PRIME2* will seem to behave differently. For example, if you execute *PRIME2* with the maximum number of threads and a large starting number (e.g., *PRIME2 -t 9 -f 500000*), you will notice that a few numbers will scroll by quickly. The primes in the sequence are not acknowledged until later, when the thread which received the number has had time to process it. In the meantime, the other nine threads continue searching for a prime number. Since half of all numbers are even and therefore thrown out quickly, most threads keep searching for a prime until they find a reasonable candidate. This behavior is simply a byproduct of the threading mechanism and the prime number search algorithm. If you watch closely, you will notice that once the numbers stop zooming by, all threads become busy. The first one to find a prime displays it on the "prime side," and then searches for the next prime. Figure 6.1 presents a snapshot of the PRIME2 display.

Summary

By including support for multiple threads, the *PRIME2* program is a step closer to our primary goal — a multithreaded, distributed application. The program also introduces critical sections, which protect data against the corruption multiple threads may introduce.

Yet *PRIME2* does not employ RPCs to distribute work to other machines across the network. In the next chapter, *PRIME3* tackles this formidable task head on.

```
============================= PRIME2 =============================

  Testing...  Thread(5)   Prime!    Thread(5)    Thread/Prime

      213        0          151         2          0-      7
      214        5          149         1          1-     11
      215        3          157         4          2-     10
      217        1          163         5          3-      8
      216        4          167         4          4-      7
      219        5          173         5          5-      5
      218        0          179         1
      220        3          181         4        Primes = 48
      221        4          193         1        Time  = 0.11 min.
      222        2          191         5        First = 1
                            197         2
      225        0          199         0
      226        3          211         2
      224        5


                         Press Esc to exit
```

Figure 6.1   The PRIME2 *display.*

PRIME2 PRIME2

Command Syntax

```
PRIME2 [options]
```

Options

All options may be given in UNIX style (a leading hyphen) or DOS style (a leading slash).

```
-f n  Start search at n instead of one (one is the default).
-t n  Start n (0 - 9) threads. By default no threads are started
      (i.e., only the main process calculates primes).
-?
-h    Print usage summary and stop.
```

Termination

NextNumber reaches 4,294,967,296.
The user presses the *ESC* key.

Files

Makefile

```
PRIME2.MAK
```

Listing	Figure	Description
DIRECTIO.C	5.3	The *DIRECTIO* source code
DIRECTIO.H	5.4	The *DIRECTIO* header file
PRIME2.C	6.1	The *PRIME2* source code
PRIME2.MAK	6.2	The *PRIME2* makefile

Table 6.1   *Source files for* PRIME2.

Listing 6.1 — PRIME2.C

```
/***********************************************************************\
*                                                                      *
* PRIME2.C - Multithreaded prime number example                        *
*           (c) Guy Eddon, 1993                                        *
*                                                                      *
* To build:  NMAKE PRIME2.MAK                                          *
*                                                                      *
* Usage:     PRIME2                                                    *
*                                                                      *
* Comments: This example uses multiple threads to compute prime numbers. *
\***********************************************************************/

#include <STDIO.H>
#include <STRING.H>
#include <STDLIB.H>
#include <STDARG.H>
#include <LIMITS.H>
#include <WINDOWS.H>
#include "directio.h"

#define PRIME       1
#define NOT_PRIME   0
#define MAX_THREADS 9

/* Coordinates for displaying numbers to be tested */

#define TESTING_X1   3
#define TESTING_Y1   3
#define TESTING_X2  23
#define TESTING_Y2  18

/* Coordinates for displaying prime numbers */

#define PRIME_X1    30
#define PRIME_Y1     3
#define PRIME_X2    50
#define PRIME_Y2    18

#define ERROR_EXIT    2
#define SUCCESS_EXIT  0
#define STRING_LENGTH 256
#define WAIT         350

#define WHITE_ON_BLUE FOREGROUND_WHITE|FOREGROUND_INTENSITY|BACKGROUND_BLUE
#define WHITE_ON_CYAN FOREGROUND_WHITE|FOREGROUND_INTENSITY|BACKGROUND_CYAN
#define RED_ON_BLUE   FOREGROUND_RED  |FOREGROUND_INTENSITY|BACKGROUND_BLUE
```

Listing 6.1 — (continued)

```c
unsigned char IsPrime(unsigned long TestNumber);
void thread(int count);
void Usage(void);
void InitializeApplication(void);

/* Number of threads available to the application */

int NumThreads;

CRITICAL_SECTION GlobalCriticalSection;
char HighLight[MAX_THREADS+1];
unsigned long NextNumber = 1, StartTime, CurrTime, NoPrime[MAX_THREADS+1], StartNumber = 1;

void main(int argc, char **argv)
  {
  DWORD  lpIDThread[MAX_THREADS];
  HANDLE hthread[MAX_THREADS];
  int count;

  /* Allow the user to override settings with command line switches */

  for(count = 1; count < argc; count++)
    {
    if((*argv[count] == '-') || (*argv[count] == '/'))
      {
      switch(tolower(*(argv[count]+1)))
        {
        case 'f': /* first number */
          NextNumber = StartNumber = atol(argv[++count]);
          break;

        case 't': /* number of threads */
          NumThreads = atoi(argv[++count]);
          if(NumThreads > MAX_THREADS)
            NumThreads = MAX_THREADS;
          break;

        case 'h':
        case '?':
        default:
          Usage();
        }
      }
    else
      Usage();
    }
```

Listing 6.1 — *(continued)*

```
    InitializeApplication();

    InitializeCriticalSection(&GlobalCriticalSection);

    for(count = 1; count <= NumThreads; count++)
        hthread[count-1] = CreateThread(NULL, 0, (LPTHREAD_START_ROUTINE)thread, count, 0,
                                &lpIDThread[count-1]);

    thread(0);

    DeleteCriticalSection(&GlobalCriticalSection);

    clearscreen(BACKGROUND_CYAN);
    }

void thread(int count)
    {
    char Buffer[STRING_LENGTH];
    unsigned long temp;
    int loop;

    SMALL_RECT psrctScrollRectTesting, psrctScrollRectPrime;
    COORD coordDestOriginTesting, coordDestOriginPrime;
    CHAR_INFO pchiFill;
    WORD Color[TESTING_X2-TESTING_X1-3], Normal[TESTING_X2-TESTING_X1-3];
    DWORD dummy;
    COORD PrimeCoord;

    psrctScrollRectTesting.Left   = TESTING_X1+1;
    psrctScrollRectTesting.Top    = TESTING_Y1+2;
    psrctScrollRectTesting.Right  = TESTING_X2-1;
    psrctScrollRectTesting.Bottom = TESTING_Y2-1;

    coordDestOriginTesting.X = TESTING_X1+1;
    coordDestOriginTesting.Y = TESTING_Y1+1;

    psrctScrollRectPrime.Left   = PRIME_X1+1;
    psrctScrollRectPrime.Top    = PRIME_Y1+2;
    psrctScrollRectPrime.Right  = PRIME_X2-1;
    psrctScrollRectPrime.Bottom = PRIME_Y2-1;

    coordDestOriginPrime.X = PRIME_X1+1;
    coordDestOriginPrime.Y = PRIME_Y1+1;

    pchiFill.Char.AsciiChar = ' ';
    pchiFill.Attributes = WHITE_ON_BLUE;
```

Listing 6.1 — (continued)

```
for(loop = 0; loop < TESTING_X2 - TESTING_X1 - 3; loop++)
    Color[loop] = RED_ON_BLUE;

for(loop = 0; loop < TESTING_X2 - TESTING_X1 - 3; loop++)
    Normal[loop] = WHITE_ON_BLUE;

while(1)
    {
    if(VK_ESCAPE == get_character_no_wait())
        {
        EnterCriticalSection(&GlobalCriticalSection);
        Sleep(WAIT);
        clearscreen(0);
        exit(SUCCESS_EXIT);
        LeaveCriticalSection(&GlobalCriticalSection);
        }

    EnterCriticalSection(&GlobalCriticalSection);
    if((temp = ++NextNumber) >= ULONG_MAX)
        break;
    LeaveCriticalSection(&GlobalCriticalSection);

    EnterCriticalSection(&GlobalCriticalSection);
    ScrollConsoleScreenBuffer(hStdOut, &psrctScrollRectTesting, NULL,
                         coordDestOriginTesting, &pchiFill);
    sprintf(Buffer, " %-17d", temp - 1);
    mxyputs((unsigned char)TESTING_X1+2, (unsigned char)(TESTING_Y2-1),
            Buffer, WHITE_ON_BLUE);
    sprintf(Buffer, "%d",  count);
    mxyputs((unsigned char)TESTING_X2-4, (unsigned char)(TESTING_Y2-1), Buffer, WHITE_ON_BLUE);
    for(loop = 0; loop <= NumThreads; loop++)
        HighLight[loop]++;
    HighLight[count] = 0;

    LeaveCriticalSection(&GlobalCriticalSection);

    if(IsPrime(temp - 1) != 0)
        {
        EnterCriticalSection(&GlobalCriticalSection);
        PrimeCoord.X = TESTING_X1 + 2;
        PrimeCoord.Y = TESTING_Y2 - 1 - HighLight[count];
        if(PrimeCoord.Y > TESTING_Y1)
            {
            WriteConsoleOutputAttribute(hStdOut, Color,
            TESTING_X2-TESTING_X1-3, PrimeCoord, &dummy);
            mxyputs((unsigned char)TESTING_X2-2, (unsigned char)(PrimeCoord.Y), "*", RED_ON_BLUE);
            }
        LeaveCriticalSection(&GlobalCriticalSection);
```

Listing 6.1 — *(continued)*

```
    PrimeCoord.X = PRIME_X1 + 2;
    PrimeCoord.Y = PRIME_Y2 - 1;

    EnterCriticalSection(&GlobalCriticalSection);
    WriteConsoleOutputAttribute(hStdOut, Normal, PRIME_X2-PRIME_X1-3, PrimeCoord, &dummy);
    ScrollConsoleScreenBuffer(hStdOut, &psrctScrollRectPrime, NULL,
                              coordDestOriginPrime, &pchiFill);
    WriteConsoleOutputAttribute(hStdOut, Color, PRIME_X2-PRIME_X1-3, PrimeCoord, &dummy);
    sprintf(Buffer, "%-18d", temp - 1);
    mxyputs((unsigned char)(PRIME_X1+2), (unsigned char)PRIME_Y2-1, Buffer, RED_ON_BLUE);
    sprintf(Buffer, "%d", count);
    mxyputs((unsigned char)(PRIME_X2-4), (unsigned char)PRIME_Y2-1, Buffer, RED_ON_BLUE);
    LeaveCriticalSection(&GlobalCriticalSection);
    NoPrime[count]++;
    }
  CurrTime = (GetTickCount() - StartTime)/1000;

    {
    long unsigned TotalNoPrime;

    TotalNoPrime = 0;

    for(loop = 0; loop <= NumThreads; loop++)
       TotalNoPrime += NoPrime[loop];

    sprintf(Buffer, "Primes = %d", TotalNoPrime);
    mxyputs(60, (unsigned char)(NumThreads+5+1), Buffer, WHITE_ON_CYAN);

    sprintf(Buffer, "Time = %d.%02d min.", CurrTime/60, CurrTime%60);

    mxyputs(60, (unsigned char)(NumThreads+5+2), Buffer, WHITE_ON_CYAN);

    if(NumThreads)
       for(loop = 0;loop <= NumThreads; loop++)
          {
          sprintf(Buffer,"%d-%5d", loop,NoPrime[loop]);
          mxyputs((unsigned char)(62), (unsigned char)(loop+4), Buffer, WHITE_ON_CYAN);
          }
    }
  }
}
```

Listing 6.1 — (continued)

```c
/* Tests for prime numbers. */

unsigned char IsPrime(unsigned long TestNumber)
    {
    unsigned long count;
    unsigned long HalfNumber = TestNumber / 2 + 1;

    for(count = 2; count < HalfNumber; count++)
        if(TestNumber % count == 0)
            return NOT_PRIME;

    return PRIME;
    }

/* Displays command line options    */

void Usage(void)
    {
    printf("\nMultithreaded prime number example.\n\n");
    printf("Usage: PRIME2\n");
    printf(" -f first number\n");
    printf(" -t number of threads (0 - 9)\n");
    exit(SUCCESS_EXIT);
    }

/* Screen initialization and colors and title lines */

void InitializeApplication(void)
    {
    char Buffer[20];

    set_vid_mem();

    clearscreen(BACKGROUND_CYAN);
    StartTime = GetTickCount();

    box(0, 0, 79, 24, DOUBLE);
    mxyputs(37, 0, " PRIME2 ", WHITE_ON_CYAN);
    sprintf(Buffer, "%d", NumThreads);

    mxyputs(3, 2, "Testing...  Thread( )", WHITE_ON_CYAN);
    mxyputs(22, 2, Buffer, WHITE_ON_CYAN);
    box(TESTING_X1, TESTING_Y1, TESTING_X2, TESTING_Y2, SINGLE);

    mxyputs(30, 2, "Prime!     Thread( )", WHITE_ON_CYAN);
    mxyputs(49, 2, Buffer, WHITE_ON_CYAN);
    box(PRIME_X1, PRIME_Y1, PRIME_X2, PRIME_Y2, SINGLE);
```

Listing 6.1 — (continued)

```
  if(NumThreads)
    {
    mxyputs(60, 2, "Thread/Prime", WHITE_ON_CYAN);
    box(60, 3, 70, (unsigned char)(NumThreads+5), SINGLE);
    }

  sprintf(Buffer, "First = %d", StartNumber);
  mxyputs(60, (unsigned char)(NumThreads+5+3), Buffer, WHITE_ON_CYAN);

  mxyputs(32, 23, "Press Esc to exit", WHITE_ON_CYAN);
  }

/* End of File */
```

Listing 6.2 — PRIME2.MAK

```
#########################################################################
#                                                                       #
# PRIME2.MAK - makefile                                                 #
#                                                                       #
#########################################################################

!include <ntwin32.mak>

!if "$(CPU)" == "MIPS"
cdebug =
cvtdebug =
linkdebug =
!endif

all: prime2.exe

prime2.exe: prime2.obj directio.obj
  $(link) $(conflags) -out:$*.exe $** $(conlibsmt)

.c.obj:
  $(cc) $(cflags) $(cvarsmt) $*.c
```

Chapter 7

The PRIME3 *Client —*
RPCs At Last

PRIME3 is the first *PRIME* application that makes remote procedure calls using Microsoft RPC v1.0. In addition to computing prime numbers locally, the client uses RPCs to take advantage of the server computer's processing power. By default, this server resides on the same computer as the client. To use a server on another computer, you must supply the server's name as a command line option. The *HELLO* client in Chapter 2 did not require you to specify the server's name because it used automatic binding to connect to the server. *PRIME3*, on the other hand, uses manual binding, so you must specify the computer to which the client will connect. This chapter explains both manual and automatic binding and why you would choose one over the other. *PRIME5* will show how manual binding can locate the server automatically.

Binding to the Server

RPC client programs maintain a logical connection to a server through a binding handle. Just as the *CreateWindow()* function creates a window and returns a window handle, the RPC function *RpcBindingFromStringBinding()*

takes a *struct* of type *handle_t* that describes the network connection and returns a binding handle that references the server. The client side then uses this binding handle each time it calls a remote procedure on a particular server. Whether your application or the client stub manages the binding handle depends on the type of handle you define in the *. IDL and *.ACF files.

Creating Binding Handles

As mentioned earlier, binding handles can be created automatically or manually. This distinction is based upon whether the application or the stubs manage the binding handle by calling the RPC runtime functions. With automatic binding, the stubs — not your application code — create and maintain the binding handles. The *HELLO* client program in Chapter 2 used automatic binding and therefore made no direct calls to the RPC runtime. Manual binding, on the other hand, requires the client application to call the RPC runtime to manage the binding handle. Table 7.1, RPC Handles, lists the different binding handles and gives a description of each.

Automatic Binding

A client application that uses automatic binding, such as the *HELLO* program, does not call the RPC runtime itself. Instead, the remote procedure stubs generated by the MIDL compiler make all the necessary

Handle Type	Description
Automatic	A binding handle created and maintained by the client stubs as generated by the MIDL compiler.
Context	A handle the maintains information about the state of a server. Also used for rundown routines.
Primitive	A binding handle of the *RPC_HANDLE* (*handle_t*) type.
Explicit	A binding handle passed by the programmer as the first parameter to every remote procedure call.
Implicit	A binding handle passed as the first parameter to every remote procedure call by the client stubs as generated by the MIDL compiler.
User-defined	A binding handle of a user-defined type.

Table 7.1   *RPC Handles.*

Types of Binding Handles

Primitive Binding Handles

Primitive binding handles are of the type *handle_t*. Except for the *HELLO* program, all the RPC examples in this book use primitive binding handles. Ultimately, all binding handles are mapped to primitive binding handles by the RPC runtime. Primitive binding handles are the norm, whereas user-defined binding handles are considered special cases only. Primitive binding handles are either implicit or explicit.

User-defined Binding Handles

Just as you can associate data with a window handle, you can associate data with a binding handle. A user-defined binding handle is simply a structure that you define as a binding handle. To create a user-defined binding handle, you must specify the handle attribute on a type definition in the program's interface definition file.

```
typedef [handle] struct
    {
    char *pszUuid;
    char *pszProtocolSequence;
    char *pszNetworkAddress;
    char *pszEndpoint;
    char *pszOptions;
    } DATA_HANDLE_TYPE;
```

You must also provide the marshalling and unmarshalling routines that the client stub calls before and after each remote procedure call. These functions convert your user-defined binding handle to and from a primitive binding handle that the RPC runtime requires. These functions must be defined as follows:

```
handle_t type_bind()
Binding routine

void type_handle(type, handle_t)
Unbinding routine
```

These routines are necessary because the RPC runtime cannot know the structure of your user-defined binding handle. This translation is in keeping with the statement that all binding handles are eventually mapped to primitive binding handles of type *handle_t*.

RPC runtime calls to import the server's interface and bind to it. When an application will use automatic binding, the ACF (Attribute Configuration File) should include the [*auto_handle*] attribute.

```
[auto_handle]
interface autoh
{
}
```

The MIDL compiler reads the IDL and ACF files and creates the appropriate client and server stubs. Automatic binding simplifies the application programmer's job at the expense of relinquishing direct control over the binding process. The automatic binding facility causes the client to bind to the first available compatible server. In addition, if a binding is lost, the client immediately rebinds to the next available

		CREATION METHOD	
		AUTOMATIC	**MANUAL**
PASSING METHOD	**IMPLICIT**	**PRIMITIVE ONLY**	**PRIMITIVE OR USER-DEFINED**
	EXPLICIT	**NA**	**PRIMITIVE OR USER-DEFINED**

Figure 7.1   *This matrix shows how the choices for handle type are influenced by usage decisions.*

compatible server. This mechanism is useful for clients that do not require a specific server. Automatic binding uses the Name Service to locate prospective servers.

Manual Binding

Manual binding requires that the client application create and maintain a binding to each server to which it will make remote procedure calls. Under manual binding, the remote procedure stubs generated by the MIDL compiler perform less work than those generated with automatic binding. Stubs using the manual binding facility have only to package the function parameters and transmit them to the server.

As you'd expect, manual binding is more complex than automatic binding, but it affords the programmer much better control of the binding process. Since the client application makes all the RPC runtime function calls, it does not necessarily have to use the Name Service facility, though it may do so (see Chapter 10). Once a binding handle has been created, it may be passed between client and server *implicity* or *explicitly*. The actual handle object may be a primitive or a user-defined type (see sidebar on page 93). Additionally, a special form of handle (a context handle) supports client-specific data storage on the host (see Chapter 11). Figure 7.1 shows how the object types relate to handle usage. The next sections explain the differences between passing the handle implicitly and passing it explicitly.

Implicit Binding Handles

All the calls to the RPC runtime include a binding handle as the first parameter, though the programmer need not always be aware of this fact. With implicit handles, the programmer creates a binding via the RPC runtime functions and stores the binding handle in a global variable. The stubs then access the binding handle and package it as the first parameter to the remote procedure calls.

The MIDL compiler determines the kind of binding handle from the information in the ACF file. *PRIME3* uses implicit binding handles:

```
[implicit_handle(handle_t prime_IfHandle)]
interface prime
{
}
```

The programmer creates the binding but lets the stubs handle packaging it as the first parameter to the runtime. This approach has one restriction: Since the client does not control the binding handle in each remote procedure call, it can make calls to only one server at a time.

Explicit Binding Handles

Explicit binding handles require the client application to supply the binding handle as the first parameter to every remote procedure call. Explicit handles require more work on the part of the programmer and add to total program complexity. They provide, however, a means to specify the binding handle used in each remote procedure call. Armed with this power, a programmer can manage bindings to multiple servers concurrently, directing each remote procedure call to the desired server. The *PRIME6* program in Chapter 11 uses explicit binding handles to manage connections to multiple *PRIME6* servers simultaneously.

When using explicit binding handles, you do not need to create an ACF file for the MIDL compiler. In this case, the MIDL compiler generates the default stubs, which do very little compared with the implicit binding handle stubs.

The String Binding

The RPC string binding functions simplify the binding process. Using these functions, the programmer can specify the parameters for a particular binding as a single string. These parameters include the UUID, the protocol sequence (the network protocol), the server's network address, the endpoint at which the server is listening, and other "options." For example, a complete string binding for the named pipes protocol sequence might be

```
12345678-1234-1234-1234-123456789ABC@ncacn_np:\\servername
[\pipe\pipename]
```

This string breaks down into the following components:

UUID	12345678-1234-1234-1234-123456789ABC
Protocol Sequence	ncacn_np
Network Address	\\servername
Endpoint	\pipe\pipename
Options	none

The *PRIME3* client assembles the string binding via a call to the *RpcStringBindingCompose()* function.

```
status = RpcStringBindingCompose(NULL, "ncacn_np",
        "\\servername", "\pipe\prime3", NULL,
        &pszStringBinding);
```

RpcStringBindingCompose() significantly reduces the complexity of building a string binding. The string binding must include specific punctuation to separate its elements. In addition, certain protocol sequences require the components to be ordered differently. The RPC function insulates the programmer from these network-specific issues by handling them automatically. It even allocates the memory necessary to store the returned string binding. (You must later free this memory with a call to the *RpcStringFree()* function.)

Another convenience function, *RpcStringBindingParse()*, operates in the reverse direction. It accepts a complete string binding and separates it into its component parts. Table 7.2 lists these and the other RPC string binding functions.

The client application then calls the *RpcBindingFromStringBinding()* function to transform the string binding into the actual binary binding.

```
status = RpcBindingFromStringBinding(pszStringBinding,
        &prime_IfHandle);
```

The binding handle, *prime_IfHandle*, is actually a pointer to the binding structure itself. As mentioned earlier, the application uses the binding handle in every subsequent remote procedure call.

Function	Description
RpcBindingFromStringBinding	Returns a binding handle from a string representation
RpcBindingToStringBinding	Returns a string representation of a binding handle
RpcStringBindingCompose	Combines the components of a string binding into a string binding
RpcStringBindingParse	Returns, as separate strings, the components of a string binding
RpcStringFree	Frees the memory used for the string binding

Table 7.2   **RPC String Binding Functions.**

The elements that make up the string binding (the UUID, protocol sequence, network address, end point, and options) were also discussed in Chapter 3.

The PRIME3 *Client*

The *PRIME3* client display (Figure 7.2) is quite similar to that of *PRIME2*. The numbers that *PRIME3* is testing are displayed in a box on the left. Those numbers discovered to be prime are displayed in a box on the right. Instead of listing a thread number next to each prime number, the *PRIME3* client displays the word *CLIENT* if the client determined the number to be prime, or *SERVER*, if the server performed the computations.

The server does not perform any computations without a request from the client. Therefore, the server display simply blinks a message to notify the *PRIME3* server administrator that it is waiting for client requests. When a client request arrives, the server performs the necessary computations and returns the result to the client. In addition, the results of the computations are also displayed on the *PRIME3* server screen (Figure 7.3).

PRIME2 allowed the user to create a variable number of threads to compute prime numbers. The *PRIME3* program, however, creates only two threads.

```
══════════════════ PRIMEC3 ══════════════════

 Testing...              Prime!              Number of Primes
 ┌─────────────────┐   ┌─────────────────┐  ┌──────────────────┐
 │                 │   │  167    LOCAL   │  │ LOCAL :    46    │
 │  230    LOCAL   │   │  173    LOCAL   │  └──────────────────┘
 │                 │   │  179    LOCAL   │
 │  232    LOCAL   │   │  181    LOCAL   │   Primes = 53
 │  233    LOCAL   │   │  191    LOCAL   │   Time  = 0.17 min.
 │                 │   │  193    LOCAL   │   First = 1
 │  235    LOCAL   │   │  197    LOCAL   │
 │  236    LOCAL   │   │  199    LOCAL   │
 │  237    LOCAL   │   │                 │
 │  238    LOCAL   │   │  223    LOCAL   │
 │                 │   │                 │
 │  240    LOCAL   │   │                 │
 │  241    LOCAL   │   │  233    LOCAL   │
 │  242    LOCAL   │   │  241    LOCAL   │
 └─────────────────┘   └─────────────────┘

                  Press Esc to exit
```

Figure 7.2   *The* PRIME3 *client display.*

```
hthread_local = CreateThread(NULL, 0,
                    (LPTHREAD_START_ROUTINE)thread_local,
                    NULL, 0, &lpIDThreadLocal);

hthread_remote = CreateThread(NULL, 0,
                    (LPTHREAD_START_ROUTINE)thread_remote,
                    NULL, 0, &lpIDThreadRemote);
```

The first thread computes prime numbers by calling a local *IsPrime()* function; this thread is nearly identical to the *Thread()* function in *PRIME2*. The second thread, while appearing the same as the first thread, calls a remote version of *IsPrime()*, called *RemoteIsPrime()*.

RemoteIsPrime() is a remote procedure that computes prime numbers on a *PRIME3* server. It uses the same algorithm as the local *IsPrime()* function. When the client calls *RemoteIsPrime()*, execution focus is transferred to the client's remote procedure stub. The stub packages and transfers the request to the RPC runtime. Once the RPC runtime has issued the request for the remote procedure to execute, it suspends the current thread. Thus the application does not waste any CPU cycles waiting for the remote procedure to return. This process is the heart of the RPC mechanism that we'll examine in this chapter.

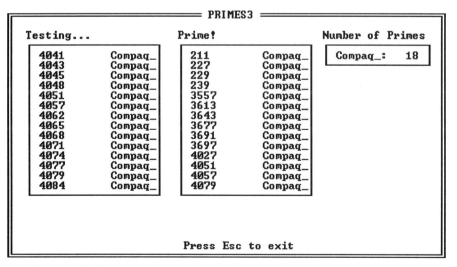

Figure 7.3   *The PRIME3 server display.*

Structured Exception Handling

PRIME3 calls *RemoteIsPrime()* from within an RPC exception handler, just as the *HELLO* client called *HelloRPC()* in Chapter 2. Should the call fail for any reason, program execution is immediately transferred to the *RpcExcept* block; the code following the remote procedure call in the *RpcTryExcept* block is not executed.

```
RpcTryExcept
    {
    if(RemoteIsPrime(PrimeServerHandle, temp - 1) != 0)
            {
            /* Do stuff */
            /* Not executed if exception occurred */
            }
    }
RpcExcept(1)
    {
    while(ServerStatus())
            {
            /* If exceptions occur */
            /* Wait for server to come on-line */
            }
    }
RpcEndExcept
```

A common exception is one where the server is off-line. Once inside the *RpcExcept* block, the client enters a *while(TRUE)* loop that it does not exit until the server comes on-line. While in the loop, the client calls the *ServerStatus()* function, which attempts to call the server.

```
char ServerStatus(void)
    {
    char value = FALSE;

    RpcTryExcept
        {
        PrimeServerHandle = InitializePrimeServer(computer_
                                                  name_buffer);
        }
```

```
RpcExcept(1)
  {
  value = TRUE;
  }
RpcEndExcept

return value;
}
```

If the call to *InitializePrimeServer()* does not raise an exception, then the client assumes that the server is on-line. If the opposite is true, the client displays a message to alert the user to the server's condition. The *thread_remote()* function then calls the *sleep()* function twice with a value *WAIT* of 350 milliseconds to avoid wasting processor cycles. While the *thread_remote()* function spends most of its time blocked in the *sleep()* function, the *thread_local()* function continues to execute.

A Caveat

In real-world applications, client RPC programs should attempt to determine when a remote procedure call is most efficient. If the local computer cannot service the request under any circumstance, then a remote procedure call must be made. However, if the task can be serviced either locally or remotely, the client application should then decide whether to employ RPC.

In most cases the client may assume that the server is the more powerful computer and will therefore offload work to the server. Nevertheless, it is smart programming practice to determine the type of computer on which the server application is running. This is possible by making one remote procedure call to the server and asking it to provide system information about itself.

Binding to the PRIME3 *Server*

Since *PRIME3* uses manual binding, the client code must establish binding with a compatible server before calling a remote procedure. This process involves calls to several RPC run-time functions. The client first calls *RpcStringBindingCompose()* to combine all the pieces of a string binding together. The combined string is returned in a character array allocated by the *RpcStringBindingCompose()* function. This memory is later freed by a call to the *RpcStringFree()* function. The following code fragment illustrates how the *RpcStringBindingCompose()* function is used:

```
status = RpcStringBindingCompose(NULL, "ncacn_np",
        "\\servername", "\pipe\prime3", NULL,
        &pszStringBinding);
```

The *PRIME3* client then calls *RpcBindingFromStringBinding()* to convert the resulting string binding into an actual "binary binding" used to communicate with the server.

To assist the server administrator, the *PRIME3* client passes its computer name to the server during the *InitializePrimeServer()* remote procedure call. To do so, it uses a new Win32 function, *GetComputerName()*:

```
GetComputerName(computer_name_buffer,
    &Max_ComputerName_Length);
```

As a result of this, the *PRIME3* server screen, will display the name of the client computer adjacent to all the prime numbers computed by the server on behalf of this client.

The PRIME3 *Client Stub*

When the *PRIME3* client calls the *RemoteIsPrime()* remote procedure, program control passes to the stub generated by the MIDL compiler. As you can see in Listing 7.1, the stub packs all the function parameters into a variable *_message* of type *RPC_MESSAGE*:

```
typedef struct _RPC_MESSAGE
    {
    RPC_BINDING_HANDLE Handle;
    unsigned long DataRepresentation;
    void PAPI *Buffer;
    unsigned int BufferLength;
    unsigned int ProcNum;
    PRPC_SYNTAX_IDENTIFIER TransferSyntax;
    void PAPI *RpcInterfaceInformation;
    void PAPI *ReservedForRuntime;
    RPC_MGR_EPV PAPI *ManagerEpv;
    void PAPI *ImportContext;
    unsigned long RpcFlags;
    } RPC_MESSAGE, PAPI * PRPC_MESSAGE;
```

Because *PRIME3* uses implicit binding handles, the stub also packs the binding handle into the first field of *RPC_MESSAGE* structure.

```
_message.Handle = prime_IfHandle;
```

The client stub demonstrates how the RPC exception handling mechanism works. The exception handling is not simply an interrupt that notifies you when things have gone awry. Instead, the stub tests the return value *_status* of each function it calls. If *_status* is any value but zero, the stub raises an exception with the *RpcRaiseException()* function:

```
_status = I_RpcGetBuffer(&_message);
if(_status)
    RpcRaiseException(_status);
```

RpcRaiseException() automatically triggers the exception handler. Structured exception handling is actually the only way to trap errors when utilizing RPC. If errors were returned as function return codes, there would be no way to distinguish them from a real value returned by the remote procedure itself. Therefore, an alternate method of error handling is required, and structured exception handling works superbly.

When the client stub has finished filling the fields of the *RPC_MESSAGE* structure, it makes the actual remote procedure call with the *char_from_ndr()* function.

```
char_from_ndr(_prpcmsg, (unsigned char *)&_ret_value);
```

Function	Return Value
char_from_ndr()	unsigned *char*
char_array_from_ndr()	pointer to unsigned *char*
short_from_ndr()	unsigned *short*
short_array_from_ndr()	pointer to unsigned *short*
long_array_from_ndr()	pointer to *long*
float_from_ndr()	*float*
float_array_from_ndr()	pointer to *float*
double_from_ndr()	*double*
double_array_from_ndr()	pointer to *double*

Table 7.3   *Functions that make calls to the RPC runtime and their return values.*

This function accepts two parameters, the address of the *_message* variable and the address of the remote procedure's return value. *char_from_ndr()* is just one of several functions that make calls into the RPC runtime. Table 7.3 contains a list of the functions, which are classified by the type of their return value. Recall that the abbreviation *ndr* stands for Network Data Representation. The RPC runtime converts all data values to this format so that data from various platforms can be exchanged, regardless of their size or endian scheme.

At this point, control passes to the RPC runtime module, which sends the required messages over the network to the server stub. Once the remote procedure *RemoteIsPrime()* finishes its calculations, the server stub packages the return value in the *ret_value* parameter, which the client receives in the *char_from_ndr()* function call that initiated the remote procedure call in the first place:

```
/* receive data into &_ret_value */
char_from_ndr(_prpcmsg, (unsigned char *)&_ret_value);
```

The client stub returns this value to the remote procedure call:

```
return (_ret_value);
```

The client application then receives execution focus to continue processing. It obtains the return value in the same manner it would from a local procedure call.

```
IsItPrime = RemoteIsPrime(PrimeServerHandle, NumberToTest);
```

Terminating the PRIME3 Client

The discussion up to now has focused on how an RPC-enabled client establishes a connection with a server. Equally important is how an RPC application goes about terminating it.

When the user terminates the client, the program calls the *TerminatePrimeServer()* function. This function uses RPC services to notify the server that the client is exiting. While this function does not actually shut-down the server (the server may still have other clients), it alerts the server of its plans. The server must recognize which client is terminating so that it can then take appropriate action, such as freeing whatever memory the client may be using, and recycling the client's handle.

The actual RPC runtime clean-up functions are called by the client after placing the *TerminatePrimeServer()* RPC. The first function, *RpcStringFree()*, frees the string allocated by the call to *RpcStringBindingCompose()*:

```
status = RpcStringFree(&pszStringBinding);
```

The *RpcStringBindingCompose()* function initially allocates the memory necessary to contain the string binding. Therefore this memory must be freed by the RPC runtime with the *RpcStringFree()* function. The last RPC runtime function called by the *PRIME3* client, *RpcBindingFree()*, frees the binding created by the *RpcBindingFromStringBinding()* function:

```
status = RpcBindingFree(&prime_IfHandle);
```

This function frees and terminates the binding that represented the logical connection between the client and the server. At this point the client is no longer bound to the server and is free to exit.

The PRIME3 *Interface*

The *PRIME3* interface definition file, *PRIME3.IDL* (Listing 8.4), specifies the interface between the client and server.

```
[ uuid (906B0CE0-C70B-1067-B317-00DD010662DA),
  version(1.0),
  pointer_default(unique) ]
interface prime
    {
    char RemoteIsPrime(
            [in] unsigned long PrimeServerHandle,
            [in] unsigned long TestNumber);
    }
```

File	Description
PRIME3.H	The remote procedure function declarations
PRIME3_C.C	Client side remote procedure stubs
PRIME3_S.C	Server side remote procedure stubs
PRIME3_X.C	Client side auxiliary file
PRIME3_Y.C	Server side auxiliary file

Table 7.4   *Files produced from the PRIME3.IDL and PRIME3.ACF files.*

It includes the UUID, version number, pointer type, and function prototype of the remote procedure *RemoteIsPrime()*. The function prototype includes a special tag to indicate the direction that the parameter will be transmitted, relative to the remote procedure.

From the *PRIME3.IDL* and *PRIME3.ACF* files, the MIDL compiler produces the files listed in Table 7.4. You compile and link these files with your other source files to produce the client- and server-side executables.

As in the previous *PRIME* programs, both the *PRIME3* client and its server call functions in the *DIRECTIO* library for screen I/O.

Summary

The main advantage of manual binding is the power it gives the developer. Manual binding forces the programmer to take full responsibility for the binding process. With manual binding, the client application can choose to bind with any available server. In Chapter 11, we will use manual binding to allow our client applications to connect with multiple servers simultaneously. Clients using automatic binding can only connect to one server at a time. Automatic binding makes the client application much easier to develop by handling the binding process. While this may be acceptable under some circumstances, it does not afford the programmer the full control of manual binding. It can also be advantageous when it doesn't matter which server provides the necessary information. A global time service is a good example of such a case. In the next chapter, we will explore the *PRIME3* server, which provides a distributed prime number service for our client.

PRIME3   (CLIENT)   PRIME3

Command Syntax (Client)

```
PRIME3 [options]
```

Options

All options may be given in UNIX style (a leading hyphen) or
DOS style (a leading slash).

-f n   Start search at n instead of one (one is the default).
-p   protocol_sequence
-n   network_address
-e   endpoint
-o   options

The *-p -n -e* and *-o* options correspond to the elements that determine the binding between the client and server.

-?
-h   Print usage summary and stop.

Examples

```
PRIME3 -n \\ServerMachineName -f 1000
```

This connects the *PRIME3* client to the *PRIME3* server running on a
machine named *ServerMachineName* and searches for prime numbers greater than 1,000.

Termination

NextNumber reaches 4,294,967,296.
The user presses the *ESC* key.

Files

Makefile (builds both server and client)

```
PRIME3.MAK
```

File	Listing	Description
DIRECTIO.C	5.3	*DIRECTIO* source code
DIRECTIO.H	5.4	*DIRECTIO* header file
PRIMEC3.C	7.2	*PRIME3* client source code
PRIMEP3.C	8.2	*PRIME3* remote procedures source code
PRIME3.MAK	8.3	*PRIME3* makefile
PRIME3.IDL	8.4	*PRIME3* interface definition language file
PRIME3.ACF	8.5	*PRIME3* attribute configuration file

Table 7.5   **Source files for the PRIME3 client.**

Listing 7.1 — STUBC3.C

```
/* **************************************
 *
 * Client Stub, as generated from the
 * MIDL compiler
 * **************************************/

unsigned char RemoteIsPrime(
        unsigned long PrimeServerHandle,
        unsigned long TestNumber)
        {
        unsigned char _ret_value;
        unsigned char *_packet;
        unsigned char *_tempbuf;
        RPC_STATUS _status;
        RPC_MESSAGE _message;
        PRPC_MESSAGE _prpcmsg = &_message;

#ifdef TIMERPC
        I_RpcTimeReset();
#endif

        _message.Handle = prime_IfHandle;
        _message.RpcInterfaceInformation = &___RpcClientInterface;
        _message.BufferLength = 8;
        _message.ProcNum = 0;
        _status = I_RpcGetBuffer(&_message);
        if(_status)
                RpcRaiseException(_status);
        _packet = _message.Buffer;

        /* send data from PrimeServerHandle */

        *(*(long **)&_prpcmsg->Buffer)++ = (long)PrimeServerHandle;
```

Listing 7.1 — (continued)

```
        /* send data from TestNumber */

        *(*(long **)&_prpcmsg->Buffer)++ = (long)TestNumber;
        _message.Buffer = _packet;
        _status = I_RpcSendReceive(&_message);
        if(_status)
                RpcRaiseException(_status);
        _packet = _message.Buffer;
RpcTryFinally
        {
        /* receive data into &_ret_value */
        char_from_ndr(_prpcmsg, (unsigned char *)&_ret_value);
        }
RpcFinally
        {
        _message.Buffer = _packet;
        _status = I_RpcFreeBuffer(&_message);
        if(_status)
                RpcRaiseException(_status);
        }
RpcEndFinally

#ifdef TIMERPC
        I_RpcTimeCharge(TIME_STUB);
        I_RpcTimeGet("RemoteIsPrime");
#endif
        return (_ret_value);
        }

/* End of File */
```

Listing 7.2 — PRIMEC3.C

```c
/********************************************************************\
*                                                                  *
*                                                                  *
*                                                                  *
* PRIMEC3.C - Distributed prime number example                     *
*             (c) Guy Eddon, 1993                                  *
*                                                                  *
* To build:    NMAKE PRIME3.MAK                                    *
*                                                                  *
* Usage:       PRIMEC3                                             *
*                                                                  *
* Comments:    This is the client side prime number program.      *
*                                                                  *
\********************************************************************/

#include <STDIO.H>
#include <STRING.H>
#include <STDLIB.H>
#include <STDARG.H>
#include <LIMITS.H>
#include <CTYPE.H>
#include <WINDOWS.H>
#include <RPC.H>
#include "prime3.h"
#include "directio.h"

/* Coordinates for displaying numbers to be tested */

#define TESTING_X1      3
#define TESTING_Y1      3
#define TESTING_X2      23
#define TESTING_Y2      18

/* Coordinates for displaying prime numbers */

#define PRIME_X1        30
#define PRIME_Y1        3
#define PRIME_X2        50
#define PRIME_Y2        18

/* If we found a prime then return PRIME, otherwise return NOT_PRIME */

#define PRIME           1
#define NOT_PRIME       0
```

Listing 7.2 — (continued)

```
/* Number of threads available to the application */

#define MAX_THREADS    10
#define ERROR_EXIT      2
#define SUCCESS_EXIT    0
#define STRING_LENGTH 256

/* Delay time in microseconds */

#define WAIT          350

/* Colors used in this application */

#define WHITE_ON_BLUE FOREGROUND_WHITE|FOREGROUND_INTENSITY|BACKGROUND_BLUE
#define WHITE_ON_CYAN FOREGROUND_WHITE|FOREGROUND_INTENSITY|BACKGROUND_CYAN
#define RED_ON_BLUE   FOREGROUND_RED|FOREGROUND_INTENSITY|BACKGROUND_BLUE

/* Prototypes of functions used in this application */

extern unsigned char IsPrime(unsigned long TestNumber);
extern char ServerStatus(void);
extern void thread_local(void);
extern void thread_remote(void);
extern void Usage(void);
extern void InitializeApplication(void);
extern void statistics(void);
extern void NotifyServer(void);

/* Critical Section for choosing next available number for testing */

CRITICAL_SECTION GlobalCriticalSection;

/* Storage for Computer Name */

char computer_name_buffer[MAX_COMPUTERNAME_LENGTH];

/* Unique number returned by the server */

unsigned long PrimeServerHandle;

/*
NextNumber    - Next available number to test
StartTime     - Time that we start to compute primes
CurrTime      - Current Computer time
NoPrimeLocal  - Number of primes computed locally
NoPrimeRemote - Number of primes computed on the remote computer
StartNumber   - The starting number for testing primes
*/
```

Listing 7.2 — (continued)

```c
unsigned long NextNumber = 1, StartTime, CurrTime, NoPrimeLocal, NoPrimeRemote, StartNumber = 1;

void _CRTAPI1 main(int argc, char **argv)
    {
    RPC_STATUS status;

    unsigned char *pszUuid            = NULL;
    unsigned char *pszProtocolSequence = "ncacn_np";
    unsigned char *pszNetworkAddress   = NULL;
    unsigned char *pszEndpoint         = "\\pipe\\prime";
    unsigned char *pszOptions          = NULL;
    unsigned char *pszStringBinding    = NULL;

    DWORD  Max_ComputerName_Length = MAX_COMPUTERNAME_LENGTH;
    DWORD  lpIDThread;
    HANDLE hthread_remote;

    int count;

/* Allow the user to override settings with command line switches */

    for(count = 1; count < argc; count++)
        {
        if((*argv[count] == '-') || (*argv[count] == '/'))
            {
            switch(tolower(*(argv[count]+1)))
                {
                case 'p': /* protocol sequence */
                    pszProtocolSequence = argv[++count];
                    break;

                case 'n': /* network address */
                    pszNetworkAddress = argv[++count];
                    break;

                case 'e':
                    pszEndpoint = argv[++count];
                    break;

                case 'o':
                    pszOptions = argv[++count];
                    break;

                case 'f': /* first number */
                    NextNumber = StartNumber = atol(argv[++count]);
                    break;
```

Listing 7.2 — (continued)

```
            case 'h':
            case '?':
            default:
                Usage();
            }
        }
    else
        Usage();
    }

/*
  Use a convenience function to concatenate the elements of
  the string binding into the proper sequence
*/

    status = RpcStringBindingCompose(
        pszUuid,
        pszProtocolSequence,
        pszNetworkAddress,
        pszEndpoint,
        pszOptions,
        &pszStringBinding);

    if(status)
        exit(ERROR_EXIT);

/* Set the binding handle that will be used to bind to the server */

    status = RpcBindingFromStringBinding(pszStringBinding,
        &prime_IfHandle);

    if(status)
        exit(ERROR_EXIT);

    GetComputerName(computer_name_buffer, &Max_ComputerName_Length);
    ServerStatus();
    InitializeApplication();

    InitializeCriticalSection(&GlobalCriticalSection);

/*  Create thread with normal priority, the name of the thread routine is thread_remote
*/

    hthread_remote = CreateThread(NULL, 0,
        (LPTHREAD_START_ROUTINE)thread_remote, NULL, 0, &lpIDThread);
```

Listing 7.2 — (continued)

```
/* function to compute primes */

    thread_local();

    DeleteCriticalSection(&GlobalCriticalSection);

/*
    The calls to the remote procedures are complete. Free the string and the binding handle
*/

    /* remote calls done - unbind */

    status = RpcStringFree(&pszStringBinding);

    if(status)
        exit(ERROR_EXIT);

    /* remote calls done - unbind */

    status = RpcBindingFree(&prime_IfHandle);

    printf("Unbinding from the prime number server.\n", status);

    if(status)
        exit(ERROR_EXIT);

    exit(SUCCESS_EXIT);
    }

void thread_local(void)
    {
    unsigned long temp;
    char Buffer[STRING_LENGTH];
    int loop;

    SMALL_RECT psrctScrollRectTesting, psrctScrollRectPrime;
    COORD coordDestOriginTesting, coordDestOriginPrime;
    CHAR_INFO pchiFill;
    WORD Color[TESTING_X2-TESTING_X1-3], Normal[TESTING_X2-TESTING_X1-3];

    COORD ComputTestCoord;
    COORD ComputPrimeCoord;

    DWORD dummy;
    COORD PrimeCoord;
```

Listing 7.2 — (continued)

```
psrctScrollRectTesting.Left    = TESTING_X1+1;
psrctScrollRectTesting.Top     = TESTING_Y1+2;
psrctScrollRectTesting.Right   = TESTING_X2-1;
psrctScrollRectTesting.Bottom  = TESTING_Y2-1;

coordDestOriginTesting.X = TESTING_X1+1;
coordDestOriginTesting.Y = TESTING_Y1+1;

psrctScrollRectPrime.Left    = PRIME_X1+1;
psrctScrollRectPrime.Top     = PRIME_Y1+2;
psrctScrollRectPrime.Right   = PRIME_X2-1;
psrctScrollRectPrime.Bottom  = PRIME_Y2-1;

coordDestOriginPrime.X = PRIME_X1+1;
coordDestOriginPrime.Y = PRIME_Y1+1;

pchiFill.Char.AsciiChar = (char)32;
pchiFill.Attributes = WHITE_ON_BLUE;

ComputTestCoord.X  = TESTING_X2-7;
ComputTestCoord.Y  = TESTING_Y2-1;
ComputPrimeCoord.X = PRIME_X2-7;
ComputPrimeCoord.Y = PRIME_Y2-1;

for(loop = 0; loop < TESTING_X2-TESTING_X1-3; loop++)
    {
    Color[loop]  = RED_ON_BLUE;
    Normal[loop] = WHITE_ON_BLUE;
    }

while(1)
    {

    /* If the user pressed ESC then notify the server and the exit */

    if(VK_ESCAPE == get_character_no_wait())
        {
        EnterCriticalSection(&GlobalCriticalSection);
        Sleep(WAIT);
        NotifyServer();
        clearscreen(0);
        exit(0);
        LeaveCriticalSection(&GlobalCriticalSection);
        }
```

Listing 7.2 — (continued)

```
      /* To make sure that we won't test the same number twice */

      EnterCriticalSection(&GlobalCriticalSection);
      if((temp = ++NextNumber) >= ULONG_MAX)
         break;
      LeaveCriticalSection(&GlobalCriticalSection);

      EnterCriticalSection(&GlobalCriticalSection);
      ScrollConsoleScreenBuffer(hStdOut, &psrctScrollRectTesting, NULL,
                              coordDestOriginTesting, &pchiFill);
      sprintf(Buffer, "%d", temp - 1);
      mxyputs((unsigned char)TESTING_X1+2, (unsigned char)(TESTING_Y2-1),
            Buffer, WHITE_ON_BLUE);
      WriteConsoleOutputAttribute(hStdOut, Normal, 7, ComputTestCoord, &dummy);
      mxyputs((unsigned char)(TESTING_X2-7), (unsigned char)TESTING_Y2-1,
            "LOCAL ", WHITE_ON_BLUE);
      LeaveCriticalSection(&GlobalCriticalSection);

      if(IsPrime(temp - 1) != 0)
         {
         PrimeCoord.X = PRIME_X1 + 2;
         PrimeCoord.Y = PRIME_Y2 - 1;

         EnterCriticalSection(&GlobalCriticalSection);
         ScrollConsoleScreenBuffer(hStdOut, &psrctScrollRectPrime, NULL,
                                 coordDestOriginPrime, &pchiFill);
         sprintf(Buffer, "%-17d", temp - 1);
         mxyputs((unsigned char)(PRIME_X1+2), (unsigned char)PRIME_Y2-1,
                 Buffer, WHITE_ON_BLUE);
         WriteConsoleOutputAttribute(hStdOut, Normal, 7, ComputPrimeCoord,&dummy);
         mxyputs((unsigned char)(PRIME_X2-7), (unsigned char)PRIME_Y2-1,
                 "LOCAL ", WHITE_ON_BLUE);
         LeaveCriticalSection(&GlobalCriticalSection);
         NoPrimeLocal++;
         }

      statistics();
      }
   }

void thread_remote(void)
   {
   unsigned long temp;
   char Buffer[STRING_LENGTH];
   int loop;
```

Listing 7.2 — (continued)

```
SMALL_RECT psrctScrollRectTesting, psrctScrollRectPrime;
COORD coordDestOriginTesting, coordDestOriginPrime;
CHAR_INFO pchiFill;
WORD Color[TESTING_X2-TESTING_X1-3], Normal[TESTING_X2-TESTING_X1-3];

COORD ComputTestCoord;
COORD ComputPrimeCoord;

DWORD dummy;
COORD PrimeCoord;

psrctScrollRectTesting.Left   = TESTING_X1+1;
psrctScrollRectTesting.Top    = TESTING_Y1+2;
psrctScrollRectTesting.Right  = TESTING_X2-1;
psrctScrollRectTesting.Bottom = TESTING_Y2-1;

coordDestOriginTesting.X = TESTING_X1+1;
coordDestOriginTesting.Y = TESTING_Y1+1;

psrctScrollRectPrime.Left   = PRIME_X1+1;
psrctScrollRectPrime.Top    = PRIME_Y1+2;
psrctScrollRectPrime.Right  = PRIME_X2-1;
psrctScrollRectPrime.Bottom = PRIME_Y2-1;

coordDestOriginPrime.X = PRIME_X1+1;
coordDestOriginPrime.Y = PRIME_Y1+1;

pchiFill.Char.AsciiChar = (char)32;
pchiFill.Attributes = WHITE_ON_BLUE;

ComputTestCoord.X  = TESTING_X2-7;
ComputTestCoord.Y  = TESTING_Y2-1;
ComputPrimeCoord.X = PRIME_X2-7;
ComputPrimeCoord.Y = PRIME_Y2-1;

for(loop = 0; loop < TESTING_X2-TESTING_X1-3; loop++)
   {
   Color[loop]  = RED_ON_BLUE;
   Normal[loop] = WHITE_ON_BLUE;
   }

while(1)
   {
```

Listing 7.2 — (continued)

```
    /* If the user pressed ESC then notify the server and the exit */

    if(VK_ESCAPE == get_character_no_wait())
        {
        EnterCriticalSection(&GlobalCriticalSection);
        Sleep(WAIT);
        NotifyServer();
        clearscreen(0);
        exit(0);
        LeaveCriticalSection(&GlobalCriticalSection);
        }

    /* To make sure that we won't test the same number twice */

    EnterCriticalSection(&GlobalCriticalSection);
    if((temp = ++NextNumber) >= ULONG_MAX)
        break;
    LeaveCriticalSection(&GlobalCriticalSection);

    EnterCriticalSection(&GlobalCriticalSection);
    ScrollConsoleScreenBuffer(hStdOut, &psrctScrollRectTesting, NULL,
                              coordDestOriginTesting, &pchiFill);
    sprintf(Buffer, " %-17d", temp - 1);
    mxyputs((unsigned char)TESTING_X1+1, (unsigned char)(TESTING_Y2-1), Buffer, RED_ON_BLUE);
    WriteConsoleOutputAttribute(hStdOut, Color, 7, ComputTestCoord, &dummy);
    mxyputs((unsigned char)(TESTING_X2-7), (unsigned char)TESTING_Y2-1, "REMOTE ", RED_ON_BLUE);
    LeaveCriticalSection(&GlobalCriticalSection);

TryAgain:
    RpcTryExcept
        {
        if(RemoteIsPrime(PrimeServerHandle, temp - 1) != 0)
            {
            EnterCriticalSection(&GlobalCriticalSection);
            PrimeCoord.X = TESTING_X1 + 2;
            LeaveCriticalSection(&GlobalCriticalSection);

            PrimeCoord.X = PRIME_X1 + 2;
            PrimeCoord.Y = PRIME_Y2 - 1;

            EnterCriticalSection(&GlobalCriticalSection);
            ScrollConsoleScreenBuffer(hStdOut, &psrctScrollRectPrime, NULL,
                coordDestOriginPrime, &pchiFill);
            sprintf(Buffer, " %-17d", temp - 1);
            mxyputs((unsigned char)(PRIME_X1+1), (unsigned char)PRIME_Y2-1, Buffer, RED_ON_BLUE);
            WriteConsoleOutputAttribute(hStdOut, Color, 7, ComputPrimeCoord, &dummy);
            mxyputs((unsigned char)(PRIME_X2-7), (unsigned char)PRIME_Y2-1, "REMOTE ", RED_ON_BLUE);
            LeaveCriticalSection(&GlobalCriticalSection);
```

Listing 7.2 — (continued)

```
            NoPrimeRemote++;
            }

        statistics();
        }

    RpcExcept(1)
        {

/* if exceptions occur */

        while(ServerStatus())
            {
            for(loop = 0; loop < 5; loop++)
                {
                mxyputs((unsigned char)15, (unsigned char)21, "Prime number server is off-line.
                        Please restart it.", WHITE_ON_CYAN);
                Sleep(WAIT);
                mxyputc((unsigned char)15, (unsigned char)21, (char)32, 52,
                        FOREGROUND_CYAN|FOREGROUND_INTENSITY|BACKGROUND_CYAN);
                Sleep(WAIT);
                }
            }

        goto TryAgain;
        }
    RpcEndExcept
    }
}

/* Tests for prime number on the local computer */

unsigned char IsPrime(unsigned long TestNumber)
    {
    unsigned long count;
    unsigned long HalfNumber = TestNumber / 2 + 1;

    for(count = 2; count < HalfNumber; count++)
        if(TestNumber % count == 0)
            return NOT_PRIME;

    return PRIME;
    }
```

Listing 7.2 — (continued)

```
/* Displays command line options */

void Usage(void)
    {
    printf("\nDistributed client/server prime number example.\n\n");
    printf("Usage: PRIMEC3\n");
    printf(" -p protocol_sequence\n");
    printf(" -n network_address\n");
    printf(" -e endpoint\n");
    printf(" -o options\n");
    printf(" -s string\n");
    printf(" -f first number\n");
    exit(1);
    }

/* Screen Initialization and colors and title lines */

void InitializeApplication(void)
    {
    char Buffer[STRING_LENGTH];
    set_vid_mem();

    clearscreen(BACKGROUND_CYAN);
    StartTime = GetTickCount();

    box(0, 0, 79, 24,DOUBLE);
    mxyputs(37, 0, " PRIMEC3 ", WHITE_ON_CYAN);

    mxyputs(TESTING_X1, 2, "Testing...", WHITE_ON_CYAN);
    box(TESTING_X1, TESTING_Y1, TESTING_X2, TESTING_Y2, SINGLE);

    mxyputs(PRIME_X1, 2, "Prime!",WHITE_ON_CYAN);
    box(PRIME_X1, PRIME_Y1, PRIME_X2, PRIME_Y2, SINGLE);

    mxyputs(58, 2, "Number of Primes", WHITE_ON_CYAN);
    box(58, 3, 73, (unsigned char)(1+5), SINGLE);

    sprintf(Buffer,"First = %d", StartNumber);
    mxyputs(58,(unsigned char)(1+5+3), Buffer, WHITE_ON_CYAN);

    mxyputs(32, 23, "Press Esc to exit", WHITE_ON_CYAN);
    }
```

Listing 7.2 — (continued)

```c
/* Check the Server status if it is of line, then try to connect, return server status */

char ServerStatus(void)
   {
   char value = FALSE;

   RpcTryExcept
      {
      PrimeServerHandle = InitializePrimeServer(computer_name_buffer);
      }
   RpcExcept(1)
      {
      value = TRUE;
      }
   RpcEndExcept

   return value;
   }

/* Dislay information about the progress of computing prime numbers */

void statistics(void)
   {
   char Buffer[STRING_LENGTH];

   CurrTime = (GetTickCount() - StartTime)/1000;
   sprintf(Buffer, "Primes = %d", NoPrimeLocal+NoPrimeRemote);
   mxyputs(58, (unsigned char)(7), Buffer, WHITE_ON_CYAN);
   sprintf(Buffer, "Time = %d.%02d min.", CurrTime/60, CurrTime%60);
   mxyputs(58, (unsigned char)(8), Buffer, WHITE_ON_CYAN);
   sprintf(Buffer, "%s:%5d", "LOCAL ", NoPrimeLocal);
   mxyputs((unsigned char)(60), (unsigned char)(4), Buffer, WHITE_ON_BLUE);
   sprintf(Buffer, "%s:%5d", "REMOTE", NoPrimeRemote);
   mxyputs((unsigned char)(60), (unsigned char)(5), Buffer, RED_ON_BLUE);
   }

/* Let the Server know that we are about to exit */

void NotifyServer(void)
   {
   RpcTryExcept
      {
      TerminatePrimeServer(PrimeServerHandle);
      }
```

Listing 7.2 — (continued)

```
RpcExcept(1)
    {
    return;
    }
RpcEndExcept
}

/* End of File */
```

Chapter 8

The PRIME3 *Server*

In Chapter 7, I introduced the client side of the *PRIME3* client application and explained how it and the client stubs use manual binding to bind to a *PRIME3* server. This chapter explains the other half of the story: the *PRIME3* server.

The *PRIME3* server consists of two source files. The first contains the startup code that prepares the server to receive client requests, *PRIMES3.C* in Listing 8.1. The other part, *PRIMEP3.C* in Listing 8.2, is the remote procedure code called by the client. Although you link the startup and procedure files to produce the server application, the startup code in *PRIMES3.C* never calls the procedure code in *PRIMEP3.C*. Instead, the server stubs call the remote procedures (local to the server) on behalf of the client.

I separated the server code into two source files for the purpose of testing the application as a non-RPC program. Before attempting to incorporate RPC into your application, you should verify that it works as a conventional program. Separating the procedures from the RPC initialization code lets you link the procedure code directly with the client, thus producing a non-distributed application that you can test using conventional methods.

Starting the PRIME3 *Server*

When you start the *PRIME3* server, it registers its interface, displays its console window, and listens for client calls. The *PRIME3* server allows you to specify several command-line parameters. Before the *PRIME3* client begins to compute prime numbers, it calls the *InitializePrimeServer()* function, a remote procedure that notifies the server to prepare itself for a client. *InitializePrimeServer()* is not an RPC API function, but is coded in the *PRIMEP3.C* file. The function accepts a character array containing the name of the computer on which the client is executing, *computer_name_buffer* (see the manual page for usage details):

```
RpcTryExcept
    {
        PrimeServerHandle = InitializePrimeServer
                            (comuter_name_buffer);
    }
```

The *PRIMEP3* server code stores this name in the *GlobalComputerNameBuffer* buffer for future use and returns a handle to the client. The client will use this handle in all subsequent remote procedure calls so that the server can identify the client. Ignoring some status reporting, *InitializePrimeServer()* is defined thus:

```
unsigned long InitializePrimeServer(unsigned char *ComputerName)
    {
    char Buffer[STRING_LENGTH];
    unsigned long unique_handle;
    EnterCriticalSection(&GlobalCriticalSection);
    unique_handle = handles + 10 * handle_mod++;
    strcpy(GlobalComputerNameBuffer[handles], ComputerName);
    GlobalComputerHandleBuffer[handles] = unique_handle;
    NoPrimes[handles] = 0;
    handles++;
    LeaveCriticalSection(&GlobalCriticalSection);
    return unique_handle;
    }
```

InitializePrimeServer() creates the unique handle within a critical section to prevent two clients from corrupting the *GlobalComputerNameBuffer* buffer by calling the function concurrently. While it is unlikely that two clients would call this function at nearly the same time, they might, especially if an off-line server were to come on-line while clients are already executing. At that moment, several clients may discover the server's existence and simultaneously call the *InitializePrimeServer()* function.

The server uses the handle returned by the *InitializePrimeServer()* function whenever a client calls the server to compute a prime number. The server is able to retrieve the computer name from the *GlobalComputerNameBuffer* buffer, based upon the handle passed by the client. The server displays the number being tested and the name of the computer for which it is testing the number.

Registering the Server Interface

For the *PRIME3* server program to accept remote procedure calls from clients, it must register its interface with the RPC runtime. In addition, it must register the protocol sequences and end points it wishes to support with a call to the *RpcServerUseProtseqEp()* function:

```
status = RpcServerUseProtseqEp(pszProtocolSequence,
        cMaxCalls, pszEndpoint, pszSecurity);
```

The RPC runtime library contains several variations on this function. However, all share the goal of registering the protocol sequences and end points with the RPC runtime.

The first parameter *to RpcServerUseProtseqEp()* is the protocol sequence, which must match the one the client registers with the *RpcStringBindingCompose()* function. This call tells the RPC runtime which network protocols it should listen to for client requests. A server can register one, several, or all available protocol sequences so that it can honor requests from clients using any of the registered protocols.

RpcServerUseProtseqEp()'s second parameter is the maximum number of calls the particular protocol sequence can handle simultaneously. Any client that attempts to bind to your server application after the specified maximum has been reached will receive the *RPC_NT_SERVER_TOO_BUSY* exception error code. That client should wait some random grace period and then attempt to call the remote procedure again.

The end point specified in the *RpcServerUseProtseqEp()* function must be a legal end point for the protocol sequence specified. The combination of the protocol sequence and end point determines the channel on which the server is listening for remote procedure calls. All clients with the correct authentication may access this server, provided they use the same protocol sequence and end point.

The security attribute accepted by *RpcServerUseProtseqEp()* is optional and is applicable only to named pipes (*ncacn_np*). The string *security=true* is the only security attribute currently available for the named pipes protocol. Microsoft has stated an interest in including Kerberos security in a future version of Microsoft RPC.

Once the protocol and endpoint are registered, the server registers its interface with a call to the *RpcServerRegisterIf()* function. You must call *RpcServerRegisterIf()* for each interface you wish to register.

```
status = RpcServerRegisterIf(prime3_ServerIfHandle, NULL, NULL);
```

The first parameter is the interface name provided in the interface definition file, *prime3*. The MIDL compiler adds the text *_ServerIfHandle* to the interface name to produce the *prime3_ServerIfHandle* interface handle. This interface handle and the resulting C code is contained in the *PRIME3_S.C* source file.

The other two parameters specify the UUID and the entry point vector. Both of these parameters are optional, and, in this case both are *NULL*. Since a server can register an unlimited number of interfaces, each providing a different service, the last two optional parameters allow the clients to distinguish between the different interfaces by using an object UUID. Since the *PRIME3* server offers one interface only, these options are unimportant.

The *PRIME3* server application then initializes its console window, displays its user interface, and calls the *CreateThread()* function to create a maintenance thread. The server calls *CreateThread()* with the *CREATE_SUSPENDED* attribute so that the thread is initially suspended. The thread's priority can be set with the *SetThreadPriority()* function before it begins to execute. Since the thread does not perform mission-critical work — merely maintenance and clean-up work — *PRIME3* sets the *server_thread()* function to a low priority with the *THREAD_PRIORITY_LOWEST* attribute.

In the *PRIME3* server program, *thread_server()* checks only to see if the user has pressed the ESC key. If so, it shuts down the server, notifies clients, and exits. The *thread_server()* function also computes some statistics, both on the prime numbers computed and on the client for whom the work was done.

The last function *PRIMES3* calls is the *RpcServerListen()* function:

```
status = RpcServerListen(cMinCalls, cMaxCalls, fDontWait);
```

The *cMinCalls* parameter specifies the minimum number of clients that must be connected at one time; this value is usually one. *cMaxCalls* specifies the maximum number of clients the server can service concurrently. If this value is greater than one (as it is in *PRIME3*) the server is responsible for concurrent programming issues. The *fDontWait* parameter indicates whether or not the function should wait for remote procedure calls requests, or if it should return immediately.

The PRIME3 *Server Stub*

The server stub, *PRIME3_RemoteIsPrime()*, does not have the same name as the actual remote procedure, *RemoteIsPrime()*. The MIDL compiler prepends the interface definition name to the function so that the linker does not encounter multiply-defined symbols: the remote procedure stub and the remote procedure itself.

The server stub receives the *RPC_MESSAGE* that the client prepared and sent across the network. From the information in the *PRIME3.IDL* file, the MIDL compiler determined that the stub must call the *long_from_ndr()* function twice to extract the parameters necessary for the actual call to *RemoteIsPrime()*:

```
/* receive data into &PrimeServerHandle */
long_from_ndr(_prpcmsg,(unsigned long *)&PrimeServerHandle);
/* receive data into &TestNumber */
long_from_ndr(_prpcmsg, (unsigned long *)&TestNumber);
```

The stub then calls *RemoteIsPrime()* using the standard local procedure call mechanism.

```
ret_value = RemoteIsPrime(PrimeServerHandle, TestNumber);
```

After the actual remote procedure executes, its return value is saved in the *ret_value* variable, which is then packed back into the *RPC_MESSAGE* structure for transmission back to the client:

```
/* send data from _ret_value */
*(*(char **)&_prpcmsg->Buffer)++ = (char)_ret_value;
```

The server stub then returns control back to the RPC runtime module. The runtime sends the network messages back to the client stub.

Terminating the PRIME3 *Server*

The *PRIME3* server terminates only when the user presses the ESC key. The server performs the necessary clean-up and exits. In this implementation, when the server terminates, all currently connected clients are "blown out of the water." In a commercial application the server should give clients an opportunity to complete their current task before exiting.

PRIME3   (SERVER)   PRIME3

Command Syntax (Server)

```
PRIMES3 [options]
```

Options

All options may be given in UNIX style (a leading hyphen) or DOS style (a leading slash).

```
-p protocol_sequence
-e endpoint
```

The -p and -e correspond to the elements that determine the binding between the client and server.

```
-m maxcalls
-n mincalls
-f flag_wait_op
-s security_descriptor
-?
-h  Print usage summary and stop.
```

Termination

NextNumber reaches 4,294,967,296.
The user presses the *ESC* key.

Files

Makefile (builds both server and client)

```
PRIME3.MAK
```

File	Listing	Description
DIRECTIO.C	5.3	*DIRECTIO* source code
DIRECTIO.H	5.4	*DIRECTIO* header file
PRIMES3.C	8.1	*PRIME3* server source code
PRIMEP3.C	8.2	*PRIME3* remote procedures source code
PRIME3.MAK	8.3	*PRIME3* makefile
PRIME3.IDL	8.4	*PRIME3* interface definition language file
PRIME3.ACF	8.5	*PRIME3* attribute configuration file

Table 8.1   *Source files for the* PRIME3 *server.*

Listing 8.1 — PRIMES3.C

```
/*********************************************************************\
*                                                                    *
* PRIMES3.C - Distributed prime number example                       *
*             (c) Guy Eddon, 1993                                    *
*                                                                    *
* To build:    NMAKE PRIME3.MAK                                      *
*                                                                    *
* Usage:       PRIMES3                                               *
*                                                                    *
* Comments:    This is the server side prime number example.         *
*                                                                    *
\*********************************************************************/

#include <STDIO.H>
#include <STRING.H>
#include <STDLIB.H>
#include <STDARG.H>
#include <LIMITS.H>
#include <CTYPE.H>
#include <WINDOWS.H>
#include <RPC.H>
#include "prime3.h"
#include "directio.h"

/* If we found a prime then return PRIME, otherwise return NOT_PRIME */

#define PRIME        1
#define NOT_PRIME    0

/* Maximum Number of Clients to respond to */

#define MAX_CALLS    10

/* Coordinates for displaying numbers to be tested */

#define TESTING_X1   3
#define TESTING_Y1   3
#define TESTING_X2   23
#define TESTING_Y2   18
```

Listing 8.1 — (continued)

```
/* Coordinates for displaying prime numbers */

#define PRIME_X1      30
#define PRIME_Y1       3
#define PRIME_X2      50
#define PRIME_Y2      18

#define ERROR_EXIT     2
#define SUCCESS_EXIT   0
#define STRING_LENGTH 256

/* Delay time in microseconds */

#define WAIT          350
#define WAIT_DISPLAY 2000

/* Colors used in this application */

#define WHITE_ON_BLUE FOREGROUND_WHITE|FOREGROUND_INTENSITY|BACKGROUND_BLUE
#define WHITE_ON_CYAN FOREGROUND_WHITE|FOREGROUND_INTENSITY|BACKGROUND_CYAN
#define RED_ON_BLUE   FOREGROUND_RED|FOREGROUND_INTENSITY|BACKGROUND_BLUE
#define RED_ON_CYAN   FOREGROUND_RED|FOREGROUND_INTENSITY|BACKGROUND_CYAN
#define CYAN_ON_CYAN  FOREGROUND_CYAN|BACKGROUND_CYAN

/* Number of characters in computer name to display on the screen */

#define COMP_NAME_LENGTH 7

extern char IsPrime(unsigned long TestNumber);
extern void Usage(void);
extern void InitializeApplication(void);

/* Number of primes for each client */

extern unsigned long NoPrimes[MAX_CALLS];

/* Number of clients that we are connected to */

extern unsigned long handles;

extern void thread_server(void);
```

Listing 8.1 — (continued)

```
/* Names of clients that we are connected to */

extern char GlobalComputerNameBuffer[MAX_CALLS][MAX_COMPUTERNAME_LENGTH];

DWORD   lpIDThread;
HANDLE hthread_server;
CRITICAL_SECTION GlobalCriticalSection;

/* main: register the interface, start listening for clients */

void _CRTAPI1 main(int argc, char *argv[])
   {
   RPC_STATUS status;

   unsigned char *pszProtocolSequence = "ncacn_np";
   unsigned char *pszSecurity         = NULL;
   unsigned char *pszEndpoint         = "\\pipe\\prime";
   unsigned int cMinCalls             = 1;
   unsigned int cMaxCalls             = MAX_CALLS;
   unsigned int fDontWait             = FALSE;

   int i;

/* allow the user to override settings with command line switches */

   for(i = 1; i < argc; i++)
      {
      if((*argv[i] == '-') || (*argv[i] == '/'))
         {
         switch(tolower(*(argv[i]+1)))
            {
            case 'p': /* protocol sequence */
               pszProtocolSequence = argv[++i];
               break;

            case 'e':
               pszEndpoint = argv[++i];
               break;

            case 'm':
               cMaxCalls = (unsigned int) atoi(argv[++i]);
               break;

            case 'n':
               cMinCalls = (unsigned int) atoi(argv[++i]);
               break;
```

Listing 8.1 — (continued)

```
            case 'f':
                fDontWait = (unsigned int) atoi(argv[++i]);
                break;

            case 's':
                pszSecurity = argv[++i];
                break;

            case 'h':
            case '?':
            default:
                Usage();
            }
        }
    else
        Usage();
    }

/* Tells the RPC runtime to use the specified protocol sequence combined
   with the specified endpoint for receiving remote procedure calls */

    status = RpcServerUseProtseqEp(
        pszProtocolSequence,
        cMaxCalls,        /* max concurrent calls */
        pszEndpoint,
        pszSecurity);  /* Security descriptor  */

    if(status)
        exit(status);

/* Registers an interface with RPC runtime */

    status = RpcServerRegisterIf(
        prime3_ServerIfHandle, /* interface to register       */
        NULL,                  /* MgrTypeUuid                 */
        NULL);                 /* MgrEpv; null means use default */

    if(status)
        exit(status);

    InitializeCriticalSection(&GlobalCriticalSection);

    InitializeApplication();

    mxyputs(23, 21, "Listening for prime number requests.", RED_ON_CYAN);
```

Listing 8.1 — (continued)

```
/* Tells the RPC runtime to listen for remote procedure calls */

    status = RpcServerListen(cMinCalls, cMaxCalls, fDontWait);

    if(status)
       exit(status);

    if(fDontWait)
       {
       status = RpcMgmtWaitServerListen(); /* wait operation */

       if(status)
          exit(status);
       }
    }

/* Displays command line options */

void Usage(void)
    {
    printf("\nDistributed client/server prime number example.\n\n");
    printf("Usage: PRIMES3\n");
    printf(" -p protocol_sequence\n");
    printf(" -e endpoint\n");
    printf(" -m maxcalls\n");
    printf(" -n mincalls\n");
    printf(" -f flag_wait_op\n");
    printf(" -s security_descriptor\n");
    exit(EXIT_SUCCESS);
    }

/* MIDL allocate and free */

void *MIDL_user_allocate(size_t len)
    {
    return(malloc(len));
    }

void MIDL_user_free(void * ptr)
    {
    free(ptr);
    }
```

Listing 8.1 — (continued)

```
void InitializeApplication(void)
   {
   set_vid_mem();

   clearscreen(BACKGROUND_CYAN);

   box(0, 0, 79, 24, DOUBLE);
   mxyputs(37, 0, " PRIMES3 ", WHITE_ON_CYAN);

   mxyputs(TESTING_X1, 2, "Testing...", WHITE_ON_CYAN);

   box(TESTING_X1, TESTING_Y1, TESTING_X2, TESTING_Y2,SINGLE);

   mxyputs(PRIME_X1, 2, "Prime!", WHITE_ON_CYAN);
   box(PRIME_X1, PRIME_Y1, PRIME_X2, PRIME_Y2, SINGLE);

   mxyputs(32, 23, "Press Esc to exit", WHITE_ON_CYAN);

/* Create thread with low priority to display server activity */

   hthread_server = CreateThread(NULL, 0, (LPTHREAD_START_ROUTINE)thread_server, NULL,
                        CREATE_SUSPENDED, &lpIDThread);

   SetThreadPriority(hthread_server, THREAD_PRIORITY_LOWEST);
   ResumeThread(hthread_server);
   }

/* Displays information about prime number production */

void thread_server()
   {
   while(1)
      {
      char Buffer[STRING_LENGTH], Buffert[STRING_LENGTH];
      unsigned char i;

      if(VK_ESCAPE == get_character_no_wait())
         {
         EnterCriticalSection(&GlobalCriticalSection);
         Sleep(WAIT);
         clearscreen(0);
         exit(EXIT_SUCCESS);
         LeaveCriticalSection(&GlobalCriticalSection);
         DeleteCriticalSection(&GlobalCriticalSection);
         }
```

Listing 8.1 — (continued)

```
    if(handles)
        {
        mxyputs(58, 2, "Number of Primes", WHITE_ON_CYAN);
        EnterCriticalSection(&GlobalCriticalSection);
        for(i = 0; i < handles; i++)
            {
            strncpy(Buffert, GlobalComputerNameBuffer[i], COMP_NAME_LENGTH);
            Buffert[COMP_NAME_LENGTH] = 0;
            sprintf(Buffer, " %7s:%5d ", Buffert, NoPrimes[i]);
            mxyputs(59, (unsigned char)(4+i), Buffer, WHITE_ON_CYAN);
            }
        box(58, 3, 74, (unsigned char)(3+1+handles), SINGLE);
        mxyputc(58, (unsigned char)(5+i), (char)32, 17, CYAN_ON_CYAN);
        LeaveCriticalSection(&GlobalCriticalSection);
        }
    else
        for(i = 0; i < 13; i++)
            mxyputc(58, (unsigned char)(2+i), (char)32, 17, CYAN_ON_CYAN);

    if(!handles)
        {
        mxyputs(23, 21, "Listening for prime number requests.",
            RED_ON_CYAN);
        Sleep(WAIT_DISPLAY);
        }
    mxyputc(23, 21, (char)32, 36, CYAN_ON_CYAN);
    }
}

/* End of File */
```

Listing 8.2 — PRIMEP3.C

```
/****************************************************************\
*                                                              *
* PRIMEP3.C - Distributed prime number example                 *
*            (c) Guy Eddon, 1993                               *
*                                                              *
* To build:   NMAKE PRIME3.MAK                                 *
*                                                              *
* Usage:      PRIMES3                                          *
*                                                              *
* Comments:   These are the remote procedures called by the clients. *
*                                                              *
\****************************************************************/

#include <STDIO.H>
#include <STRING.H>
#include <STDLIB.H>
#include <STDARG.H>
#include <LIMITS.H>
#include <CTYPE.H>
#include <WINDOWS.H>
#include <RPC.H>
#include "prime3.h"
#include "directio.h"

/* If we found a prime then return PRIME, otherwise return NOT_PRIME */

#define PRIME        1
#define NOT_PRIME    0

/* Maximum Number of Clients to respond to */

#define MAX_CALLS    10

/* Coordinates for displaying numbers to be tested */

#define TESTING_X1    3
#define TESTING_Y1    3
#define TESTING_X2    23
#define TESTING_Y2    18

/* Coordinates for displaying prime numbers */

#define PRIME_X1    30
#define PRIME_Y1     3
#define PRIME_X2    50
#define PRIME_Y2    18
```

Listing 8.2 — (continued)

```
#define ERROR_EXIT    2
#define SUCCESS_EXIT   0
#define STRING_LENGTH 256


/* Time delay in microseconds */


#define WAIT          350
#define WAIT_DISPLAY 2000


/* Colors used in this application */


#define WHITE_ON_BLUE FOREGROUND_WHITE|FOREGROUND_INTENSITY|BACKGROUND_BLUE
#define WHITE_ON_CYAN FOREGROUND_WHITE|FOREGROUND_INTENSITY|BACKGROUND_CYAN
#define RED_ON_BLUE   FOREGROUND_RED|FOREGROUND_INTENSITY|BACKGROUND_BLUE
#define RED_ON_CYAN   FOREGROUND_RED|FOREGROUND_INTENSITY|BACKGROUND_CYAN
#define CYAN_ON_CYAN  FOREGROUND_CYAN|BACKGROUND_CYAN


/* Number of characters in computer name to display on the screen */


#define COMP_NAME_LENGTH 7

/* Critical Section for choosing next available number for testing */

extern CRITICAL_SECTION GlobalCriticalSection;

/* Number of clients that we are connected to */

unsigned long handles = 0;

/* Names of clients that we are connected to */

char GlobalComputerNameBuffer[MAX_CALLS][MAX_COMPUTERNAME_LENGTH];

/* Number of primes for each client */

unsigned long NoPrimes[MAX_CALLS];

/* Unique identifier that we return to each client */

unsigned long GlobalComputerHandleBuffer[MAX_CALLS];

/* Global variable to help us to produce a unique number */

unsigned long handle_mod = 1;

/* This function is called by the client, we return a unique number,
   so in the future we can keep track who called us              */
```

Listing 8.2 — *(continued)*

```
unsigned long InitializePrimeServer(unsigned char *ComputerName)
   {
   char Buffer[STRING_LENGTH];
   unsigned long unique_handle;

   EnterCriticalSection(&GlobalCriticalSection);
   unique_handle = handles + 10 * handle_mod++;

   strcpy(GlobalComputerNameBuffer[handles], ComputerName);
   mxyputc(2, 21, (char)32, 75, CYAN_ON_CYAN);
   sprintf(Buffer, "Computer %s logged in.", ComputerName);
   mxyputs(27, 21, Buffer, RED_ON_CYAN);
   sprintf(Buffer,  "(%ld)",unique_handle);
   mxyputs(54, 21, Buffer, RED_ON_CYAN);
   Sleep(2*WAIT_DISPLAY);
   mxyputc(2, 21, (char)32, 75, CYAN_ON_CYAN);
   GlobalComputerHandleBuffer[handles] = unique_handle;

   NoPrimes[handles] = 0;

   handles++;

   LeaveCriticalSection(&GlobalCriticalSection);

   return unique_handle;
   }

/* This function was called by the client. The client supplied his
   identifier and the number to test if it is a prime            */

unsigned char RemoteIsPrime(unsigned long PrimeServerHandle,
   unsigned long TestNumber)
   {
   unsigned long count;
   unsigned long HalfNumber = TestNumber / 2 + 1;
   char Buffer[STRING_LENGTH];
   char LocalComputerName[MAX_COMPUTERNAME_LENGTH];
   int loop;

   SMALL_RECT psrctScrollRectTesting, psrctScrollRectPrime;
   COORD coordDestOriginTesting, coordDestOriginPrime;
   CHAR_INFO pchiFill;
   WORD Local[COMP_NAME_LENGTH];

   COORD ComputTestCoord;
   COORD ComputPrimeCoord;
   DWORD dummy;
```

Listing 8.2 — (continued)

```
/* Lets find out the name of client computer */

    EnterCriticalSection(&GlobalCriticalSection);
    for(loop = 0; loop < (int)handles; loop++)
        if(GlobalComputerHandleBuffer[loop] == PrimeServerHandle)
            {
            strcpy(LocalComputerName, GlobalComputerNameBuffer[loop]);
            PrimeServerHandle = loop;
            break;
            }

    LeaveCriticalSection(&GlobalCriticalSection);

    psrctScrollRectTesting.Left   = TESTING_X1+1;
    psrctScrollRectTesting.Top    = TESTING_Y1+2;
    psrctScrollRectTesting.Right  = TESTING_X2-1;
    psrctScrollRectTesting.Bottom = TESTING_Y2-1;

    coordDestOriginTesting.X = TESTING_X1+1;
    coordDestOriginTesting.Y = TESTING_Y1+1;

    psrctScrollRectPrime.Left   = PRIME_X1+1;
    psrctScrollRectPrime.Top    = PRIME_Y1+2;
    psrctScrollRectPrime.Right  = PRIME_X2-1;
    psrctScrollRectPrime.Bottom = PRIME_Y2-1;

    coordDestOriginPrime.X = PRIME_X1+1;
    coordDestOriginPrime.Y = PRIME_Y1+1;

    pchiFill.Char.AsciiChar = (char)32;
    pchiFill.Attributes = WHITE_ON_BLUE;

    ComputTestCoord.X  = TESTING_X2-7;
    ComputTestCoord.Y  = TESTING_Y2-1;
    ComputPrimeCoord.X = PRIME_X2-7;
    ComputPrimeCoord.Y = PRIME_Y2-1;

    for(loop = 0; loop < COMP_NAME_LENGTH; loop++)
        Local[loop] = WHITE_ON_BLUE;
```

Listing 8.2 — (continued)

```
/* If the user pressed ESC then exit */

   if(VK_ESCAPE == get_character_no_wait())
      {
      EnterCriticalSection(&GlobalCriticalSection);
      Sleep(WAIT);
      clearscreen(0);
      exit(SUCCESS_EXIT);
      LeaveCriticalSection(&GlobalCriticalSection);
      DeleteCriticalSection(&GlobalCriticalSection);
      }

   sprintf(Buffer, "%d", TestNumber);

   EnterCriticalSection(&GlobalCriticalSection);
   ScrollConsoleScreenBuffer(hStdOut, &psrctScrollRectTesting, NULL,
                             coordDestOriginTesting, &pchiFill);
   sprintf(Buffer, "%d", TestNumber);
   mxyputs((unsigned char)TESTING_X1+2, (unsigned char)(TESTING_Y2-1), Buffer, WHITE_ON_BLUE);
   WriteConsoleOutputAttribute(hStdOut, Local, COMP_NAME_LENGTH, ComputTestCoord, &dummy);
   LocalComputerName[COMP_NAME_LENGTH] = 0;
   mxyputs((unsigned char)(TESTING_X2-7), (unsigned char)TESTING_Y2-1,
           LocalComputerName, WHITE_ON_BLUE);
   LeaveCriticalSection(&GlobalCriticalSection);

   for(count = 2; count < HalfNumber; count++)
      if(TestNumber % count == 0)
         return NOT_PRIME;

   sprintf(Buffer, "%d", TestNumber);

   EnterCriticalSection(&GlobalCriticalSection);
   ScrollConsoleScreenBuffer(hStdOut, &psrctScrollRectPrime, NULL,
                             coordDestOriginPrime, &pchiFill);
   sprintf(Buffer, "%d", TestNumber);
   mxyputs((unsigned char)(PRIME_X1+2), (unsigned char)PRIME_Y2-1, Buffer, WHITE_ON_BLUE);
   WriteConsoleOutputAttribute(hStdOut, Local, COMP_NAME_LENGTH, ComputPrimeCoord, &dummy);
   mxyputs((unsigned char)(PRIME_X2-7), (unsigned char)PRIME_Y2-1,
           LocalComputerName, WHITE_ON_BLUE);
   NoPrimes[PrimeServerHandle]++;
   LeaveCriticalSection(&GlobalCriticalSection);

   return PRIME;
   }
```

Listing 8.2 — (continued)

```c
/* Notification from a client that he is done */

void TerminatePrimeServer(unsigned long PrimeServerHandle)
   {
   char Buffer[256+MAX_COMPUTERNAME_LENGTH];
   unsigned char loop, loopshift;

   EnterCriticalSection(&GlobalCriticalSection);

   for(loop = 0; loop < (unsigned char)handles; loop++)
      {
      if(GlobalComputerHandleBuffer[loop] == PrimeServerHandle)
         {

/* Let's put terminating message on the screen */

         mxyputc(2, 21, (char)32, 75, CYAN_ON_CYAN);
         sprintf(Buffer, "Computer %s Exited!", GlobalComputerNameBuffer[loop]);
         mxyputs(27, 21, Buffer, RED_ON_CYAN);
         mxyputc(59, (unsigned char)(4+loop), (char)32, 15, CYAN_ON_CYAN);
         Sleep(WAIT_DISPLAY);
         mxyputc(2, 21, (char)32, 75, CYAN_ON_CYAN);
         break;
         }
      }

/* Let's remove his name from our table */

   if(loop < handles-1)
      {
      loopshift = loop;
      for(loop = loopshift; loop < (unsigned char)(handles - 1); loop++)
         {
         strcpy(GlobalComputerNameBuffer[loop], GlobalComputerNameBuffer[loop+1]);
         GlobalComputerHandleBuffer[loop] = GlobalComputerHandleBuffer[loop+1];
         NoPrimes[loop] = NoPrimes[loop+1];
         }
      }

/* We have one client less */

   handles--;
   LeaveCriticalSection(&GlobalCriticalSection);
   }

/* End of File */
```

Listing 8.3 — PRIME3.MAK

```
###################################################################
#                                                                 #
# PRIME3.MAK - Makefile                                           #
#                                                                 #
###################################################################

!include <ntwin32.mak>

!if "$(CPU)" == "i386"
cvtomf =
cflags = $(cflags:G3=Gz)
!endif
!if "$(CPU)" == "MIPS"
cvtomf = mip2coff $@
!endif

.c.obj:
    $(cc) $(cflags) $(cvarsmt) $<
    $(cvtomf)

all : primec3 primes3

primec3 : primec3.exe
primec3.exe : primec3.obj prime3_c.obj prime3_x.obj directio.obj
    $(link) $(conflags) -out:primec3.exe \
    primec3.obj prime3_c.obj prime3_x.obj directio.obj rpcrt4.lib rpcndr.lib $(conlibsmt)

primec3.obj : primec3.c prime3.h

prime3_c.obj : prime3_c.c prime3.h
    $(cc) $(cflags) $(cvarsmt) prime3_c.c
    $(cvtomf)

prime3_x.obj : prime3_x.c prime3.h
    $(cc) $(cflags) $(cvarsmt) prime3_x.c
    $(cvtomf)

primes3 : primes3.exe
primes3.exe : primes3.obj primep3.obj prime3_s.obj prime3_y.obj
  directio.obj
    $(link) $(conflags) -out:primes3.exe \
    primes3.obj prime3_s.obj primep3.obj prime3_y.obj directio.obj \
    rpcrt4.lib rpcndr.lib $(conlibsmt)
```

Listing 8.3 — (continued)

```
primes3.obj : primes3.c prime3.h

primep3.obj : primep3.c prime3.h

prime3_s.obj : prime3_s.c prime3.h
   $(cc) $(cflags) $(cvarsmt) prime3_s.c
   $(cvtomf)

prime3_y.obj : prime3_y.c prime3.h
   $(cc) $(cflags) $(cvarsmt) prime3_y.c
   $(cvtomf)

prime3.h prime3_c.c prime3_x.c prime3_s.c
  prime3_y.c : prime3.idl prime3.acf
    midl -cpp_cmd $(cc) -cpp_opt "-E"  prime3.idl
```

Listing 8.4 — PRIME3.IDL

```
/*******************************************************************\
*                                                                   *
* PRIME3.IDL -  Interface Definition for PRIME3                     *
*              (c) Guy Eddon, 1993                                  *
*                                                                   *
\*******************************************************************/

[ uuid (651AB8D0-C73B-BDC7-B34A-0183BD0342DA),
  version(1.0),
  pointer_default(unique)]
interface prime3
{

char RemoteIsPrime([in] unsigned long PrimeServerHandle,[in] unsigned long TestNumber);
unsigned long InitializePrimeServer([in, string] unsigned char *ComputerName);

void TerminatePrimeServer([in] unsigned long PrimeServerHandle);
}
```

Listing 8.5 — PRIME3.ACF

```
/*******************************************************************\
*                                                                   *
* PRIME3.ACF -  Attribute Configuration File for PRIME3            *
*              (c) Guy Eddon, 1993                                  *
*                                                                   *
\*******************************************************************/

[implicit_handle(handle_t prime_IfHandle)]
interface prime3
{

}
```

## Chapter 9

PRIME4 — *Fault-Tolerant Servers*

The *PRIME4* application implements a fault-tolerant server by incorporating two important RPC features: *context handles* and *context rundown routines*. In their most general use, context handles are a special type of binding handle that cause the server to preserve context information specific to the binding. This example, however, uses context handles in a more limited role: to enable the server to detect when the client has terminated abnormally and invoke an appropriate context rundown routine.

In addition to providing a more robust server, the *PRIME4* application includes clients for MS-DOS and Windows for Workgroups. By traversing multiple operating environments, *PRIME4* demonstrates how RPC provides connectivity and interoperability among different platforms. It also involves a great deal more code!

Context Handles

From the client's perspective, context handles are a special type of pointer — a pointer to data (context) which resides solely on the server machine and whose state will be preserved between RPC calls. Since the handle (at least conceptually) is a pointer to data *not* in the client's address space, the client may never dereference the handle. The only meaningful operations a client may perform on a context handle are to test it for *NULL* and to pass it as a parameter in an RPC call. Anytime the server needs to preserve state information for individual clients, the client must create a context handle.

An arbitrary type is associated with the context handle and its reference by statements in the IDL file:

```
typedef [context_handle] void * PCONTEXT_HANDLE_TYPE;
typedef [ref] PCONTEXT_HANDLE_TYPE * PPCONTEXT_HANDLE_TYPE;
```

The client code creates local storage for the handle (not for the remote data) and makes a call to the server:

```
PCONTEXT_HANDLE_TYPE phContext = NULL;

PrimeServerHandle = InitializePrimeServer( &phContext,
                       computer_name_buffer);
```

In all subsequent RPCs the client will pass the context handle in place of the binding handle. The server uses the context handle to locate the data (state information) specific to the associated client.

For example, to create a remote procedure to open a file, one would first create the IDL interface (using the context handle type definitions from above):

```
short RemoteOpen([out] PPCONTEXT_HANDLE_TYPE Context_handle,
             [in, string] unsigned char *filename);
```

Then the server code would be called to initialize the local state information, in this case a file pointer:

```
typedef struct
{
    FILE * hFile;
}
FILE_CONTEXT_TYPE;
Short RemoteOpen(PPCONTEXT_HANDLE_TYPE Context_handle,
                 unsigned char *filename)
{
FILE * tempFile; FILE_CONTEXT_TYPE * localptr;
if ((tempFile = fopen(filename,"r")) == NULL)
    {
    *Context_handle = (PCONTEXT_HANDLE_TYPE) NULL;
    return (FAILURE);
    }
else
    {
    localptr = (FILE_CONTEXT_TYPE *)
                midl_user_allocate(sizeof(FILE_CONTEXT_TYPE));
    localptr-hFile = tempFile;
    *Context_handle = (PCONTEXT_HANDLE_TYPE) localptr;
    return (SUCCESS);
    }
}
```

Notice that when the call is successful, the server returns a (properly cast) pointer to a data object that was allocated from the server's user heap. This pointer *is* the context handle. Because the associated data is referenced through a context handle, it will be preserved until the associated server/client binding is terminated.

Context Rundown Routines

When the *PRIME3* client wanted to shut down gracefully, it called an RPC named *TerminatePrimeServer()* to notify the server of its plans. The server then had the opportunity to free resources associated with the client. This arrangement works well as long as the client never exits without calling *TerminatePrimeServer()*. Yet, a client program may crash or its computer fail. A robust server must be sufficiently fault-tolerant to prevent such events from impairing its performance for all the other clients still online. Otherwise, resources allocated by clients which terminated abnormally might never be freed. The context rundown routine — a form of exception handler invoked whenever the associated binding is broken — provides a mechanism for cleaning up after an abnormally terminated client.

The server's RPC runtime automatically (i.e., without any special application code) calls a context rundown routine whenever an active client binding unexpectedly breaks. This call happens without any special programming on the part of the application programmer. In an active binding, the server runtime is (through keep-alive packets) in continuous communication with the client runtime. Thus, the server can easily detect a loss of the client. You might think of a context rundown routine as a call-back function that the server executes whenever a client unexpectedly terminates.

To declare the context rundown routine, use the syntax

```
void type_rundown(type)
```

where *type* matches that of context handle. Since the MIDL compiler expects the context handle's type name to be imbedded in the rundown routine's name, you must declare a context handle to use a rundown routine.

The context rundown routine usually performs maintenance on the server, such as releasing memory or executing other clean-up tasks. The *PRIME4* rundown routine's only parameter is the context handle for the client that terminated unexpectedly. The routine passes the handle, cast as an *unsigned long*, to *TerminatePrimeServer()*:

```
void PCONTEXT_HANDLE_TYPE_rundown(PCONTEXT_HANDLE_TYPE phContext)
    {
    if(handlesp == handles)
            {
            mxyputs(27, 2, "Rundown Executed", RED_ON_CYAN);
            TerminatePrimeServer((unsigned long) phContext);
            Sleep(2000);
            mxyputs(27, 2, "                    ", CYAN_ON_CYAN);
            }

    handlesp = handles;
    }
```

When the *PRIME4* client terminates normally, it calls the *TerminatePrimeServer()* remote procedure, just as *PRIME3* did. However, if the client terminates abnormally or for some reason is unable to call *TerminatePrimeServer()*, the server's context rundown routine will automatically run and execute the *TerminatePrimeServer()* function.

To test the context rundown routine, terminate the *PRIME4* client by choosing *Settings... - Terminate* from the system menu box. Windows NT will ask whether you are sure you want to terminate the command shell. Click *OK*, then *Yes*. The *PRIME4* client will then terminate abnormally. On the *PRIME4* server side, you should see the client computer's name disappear from the list of active clients.

Stateless Servers

An RPC server can be either *stateless* or *stateful*. A stateless server does not maintain any information about the state of its clients. Stateful servers, on the other hand, keep information about clients between remote procedure calls. Whether or not a server maintains state is very important, since it greatly affects the way clients and servers are constructed.

When a client/stateless-server relationship requires state, the client must maintain the state. If the stateless server crashes and is restarted, the client knows the information it has already asked for and can resubmit the stateful requests. On the other hand, if the server is stateful, then the server becomes responsible for reconstructing all the client requests. Crash recovery on a server can be complicated, if not impossible. Stateful servers, usually keep a log of all requests. All the examples in this book use stateless servers, and the clients maintain all state information.

The PRIME4 *Context Handle*

The *PRIME4* client initiates the construction of the context handle when it issues a remote procedure call to the *InitializePrimeServer()* routine:

```
PCONTEXT_HANDLE_TYPE phContext = NULL;

PrimeServerHandle = InitializePrimeServer(&phContext,
                                 computer_name_buffer);
```

InitializePrimeServer() in *PRIMEP4.C* (Listing 9.3) computes a unique identifier for the server in question and returns that as the binding handle. The value is cast to type *PCONTEXT_HANDLE_TYPE* and assigned to the context handle *pphContext*. Note that in this instance there is *no* data on the server associated with the context handle. The context handle actually is the data. If the client only needed the unique identifier, I could easily return it as normal data, but in this example I wanted to show how to create a rundown routine — for that, I must have a context handle:

```
unsigned long InitializePrimeServer(PPCONTEXT_HANDLE_TYPE
                pphContext, unsigned char *ComputerName)
{
unsigned long unique_handle;

EnterCriticalSection(&GlobalCriticalSection);
unique_handle = handles + 10 * handle_mod++;

strcpy(GlobalComputerNameBuffer[handles], ComputerName);

GlobalComputerHandleBuffer[handles] = unique_handle;

*pphContext = (PCONTEXT_HANDLE_TYPE)unique_handle;

NoPrimes[handles] = 0;

handles++;
handlesp = handles;
LeaveCriticalSection(&GlobalCriticalSection);

return unique_handle;
}
```

From the server's perspective, the context handle's sole purpose is to identify the client and its resources on the server. The server's runtime automatically passes the context handle to the function you define as the context rundown routine. The context rundown routine thus knows automatically which client to "rundown."

Supporting DOS and WFW

The Windows NT *PRIME4* client is very similar to the *PRIME3* client. I have only added code to manipulate the context handles. This modification, along with corresponding changes on the server, allows the *PRIME4* client to terminate abnormally without creating any unpleasant side effects on the server.

Though you must run the *PRIME4* server under Windows NT, you can run the *PRIME4* client under MS-DOS, Windows for Workgroups, or

```
┌─────────────────────────────────────────────────────────────────┐
│ ▬            PRIMEC4 Windows Client                          ▼ │
├─────────────────────────────────────────────────────────────────┤
│ Remote Call   Help                                              │
├─────────────────────────────────────────────────────────────────┤
│ Prime...                 Testing...                             │
│  249    LOCAL      193    LOCAL      LOCAL : 29                  │
│  251    REMOTE     197    LOCAL      REMOTE: 32                  │
│  253    LOCAL      199    REMOTE                                │
│  255    REMOTE     211    REMOTE     Primes = 61                │
│  257    LOCAL      223    REMOTE     Time = 0.22 min.           │
│  259    REMOTE     227    REMOTE     First= 1                   │
│  261    LOCAL      229    LOCAL      WIN31                       │
│  263    REMOTE     233    LOCAL                                 │
│  265    LOCAL      239    REMOTE                                │
│  267    REMOTE     241    LOCAL                                 │
│  269    LOCAL      251    REMOTE                                │
│  271    REMOTE     257    LOCAL                                 │
│  273    LOCAL      263    REMOTE                                │
│  275    REMOTE     269    LOCAL                                 │
│  277    LOCAL      271    REMOTE                                │
│  279    REMOTE     277    LOCAL                                 │
│  281    LOCAL      281    LOCAL                                 │
│  283    REMOTE     283    REMOTE                                │
├─────────────────────────────────────────────────────────────────┤
│          Prime number server sti–486      [30]                  │
└─────────────────────────────────────────────────────────────────┘
```

Figure 9.1   *Windows for Workgroups* PRIME4 *client display.*

You must install the MS-DOS and Windows for Workgroups RPC runtime support before running RPC applications in these environments. To set up RPC support, launch Windows for Workgroups and choose File-Run from the Program Manager. Then type

`X:\MSTOOLS\RPC_DOS\DISK1\SETUP.EXE`

and proceed with the installation directions. (Drive X is the drive on which you installed the Windows NT CD-ROM.)

Windows NT. Both the Windows NT client and server use the displays from *PRIME3.* However, the Windows for Workgroups *PRIME4* client cannot use the NT console interface because Windows for Workgroups does not offer it. Figure 9.1 illustrates the Windows for Workgroups *PRIME4* client display, while Figure 9.2 shows the MS-DOS version. Note that the *PRIME4* MS-DOS client display resembles the Windows NT client display.

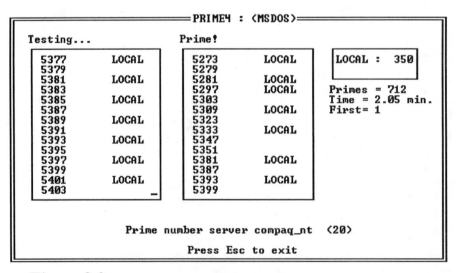

Figure 9.2   MS-DOS PRIME4 *client display.*

The MS-DOS and Windows for Workgroups versions of the *PRIME4* client are quite different from earlier examples since these environments do not support multiple threads of execution within a single process. Therefore, the *PRIME4* client in these environments is more limited than the Windows NT version. While the Windows NT *PRIME4* client makes RPCs, another thread in the same module continues to compute prime numbers locally, thereby taking advantage of two computers. When a MS-DOS or Windows for Workgroups *PRIME4* client makes remote procedure calls, it is blocked until the remote procedure returns.

PRIME4   (CLIENT)   PRIME4

Command Syntax (Client)

```
PRIMEC4 [options]
```

Options

All options may be given in UNIX style (a leading hyphen) or DOS style (a leading slash).

-f n   Start search at n instead of one (one is the default).
-p   protocol_sequence
-n   network_address
-e   endpoint
-o   options

The -p -n -e and -o options correspond to the elements that determine the binding between the client and server. If you with to run PRIME4 with a local server (on the same computer), do not specify a computer name (the -n option) on the command line.

-?
-h   Print usage summary and stop.

Examples

```
PRIMEC4 -n \\accounting
```

This connects the *primeC3* client to the PRIMES3 server running on a machine named accounting.

Termination

NextNumber reaches 4,294,967,296.
The user presses the *ESC* key.

Files

Makefile (builds both server and client)

```
PRIME4.MAK
```

File	Listing	Description
DIRECTIO.C	5.3	The *DIRECTIO* source code
DIRECTIO.H	5.4	The *DIRECTIO* header file
PRIMEC4.C	9.1	The *PRIME4* client C code
PRIMEP4.C	9.3	The *PRIME4* remote procedures C code
PRIME4.MAK	9.4	The *PRIME4* makefile
PRIME4.IDL	9.5	The *PRIME4* interface definition language file
PRIME4.ACF	9.6	The *PRIME4* attribute configuration file

Table 9.1   *Source files for NT version of* PRIME4 *client.*

PRIME4   (CLIENT)   PRIME4

File	Listing	Description
DIRECTIO.C	9.7	The *DIRECTIO* source code for MS-DOS
DIRECTIO.H	9.8	The *DIRECTIO* header file for MS-DOS
PRIME4.C	9.9	The *PRIME4* client C code for MS-DOS
PRIME4.DOS	9.10	The *PRIME4* makefile for MS-DOS
PRIME4.IDL	9.11	The *PRIME4* interface definition language file
PRIME4.ACF	9.12	The *PRIME4* attribute configuration file

Table 9.2   *Source files for MS-DOS version of* PRIME4 *client.*

File	Listing	Description
PRIMEC4.C	9.13	The *PRIME4* client C code for Windows for Workgroups
PRIMEC4.H	9.14	The *PRIME4* header file
PRIME4.WIN	9.15	The *PRIME4* makefile for Windows for Workgroups
PRIME4.IDL	9.16	The *PRIME4* interface definition language file
PRIME4.ACF	9.17	The *PRIME4* attribute configuration file
PRIME4.DEF	9.18	The *PRIME4* module definition file
PRIME4.RC	9.19	The *PRIME4* resource file
PRIME4.DLG	9.20	The *PRIME4* dialog box file
PRIME4.ICO	9.21	The *PRIME4* icon file

Table 9.3   *Source files for WFW version of* PRIME4 *client.*

Notes

Before running the MS-DOS client, you must start the network support provided in Windows for Workgroups. If you plan to run the MS-DOS client from straight DOS, type

```
net start workstation
```

before running the client. Alternatively, you can start the DOS client from a Windows for Workgroups DOS shell.

To run the Windows for Workgroups *PRIME4* client, you must decide whether you will use the real-mode redirector. If so, type

```
net stop workstation /y
```

before starting Windows for Workgroups. After you launch *PRIMEC4.EXE* from the Program Manager, the application will prompt you to enter the name of the server you wish to use.

PRIME4 (SERVER) PRIME4

Command Syntax (Server)

```
PRIMES4 [options]
```

Options

All options may be given in UNIX style (a leading hyphen) or DOS style (a leading slash).

```
-p    protocol_sequence
-e    endpoint
```

The -p and -e correspond to the elements that determine the binding between the client and server.

```
-m    maxcalls
-n    mincalls
-f    flag_wait_op
-s    security_descriptor
-?
-h    Print usage summary and stop.
```

Termination

NextNumber reaches 4,294,967,296.

The user presses the *ESC* key.

Files

Makefile (builds both server and client)

```
PRIME3.MAK
```

File	Listing	Description
DIRECTIO.C	5.3	The *DIRECTIO* source code
DIRECTIO.H	5.4	The *DIRECTIO* header file
PRIMES4.C	9.2	The *PRIME4* server C code
PRIMEP4.C	9.3	The *PRIME4* remote procedures C code
PRIME4.MAK	9.4	The *PRIME4* makefile
PRIME4.IDL	9.5	The *PRIME4* interface definition language file
PRIME4.ACF	9.6	The *PRIME4* attribute configuration file

Table 9.4   *Source files for NT version of* PRIME4 *server.*

Listing 9.1 — PRIMEC4.C (NT)

```
/*********************************************************************\
*                                                                   *
* PRIMEC4.C - Distributed prime number example                      *
*            (c) Guy Eddon, 1993                                     *
*                                                                   *
* To build:   NMAKE PRIME4.MAK                                      *
*                                                                   *
* Usage:      PRIMEC4                                               *
*                                                                   *
* Comments:   This is the client side prime number program.        *
*                                                                   *
\*********************************************************************/

#include <STDIO.H>
#include <STRING.H>
#include <STDLIB.H>
#include <STDARG.H>
#include <LIMITS.H>
#include <CTYPE.H>
#include <WINDOWS.H>
#include <RPC.H>
#include "prime4.h"
#include "directio.h"

/* Coordinates for displaying numbers to be tested */

#define TESTING_X1    3
#define TESTING_Y1    3
#define TESTING_X2    23
#define TESTING_Y2    18

/* Coordinates for displaying prime numbers */

#define PRIME_X1      30
#define PRIME_Y1       3
#define PRIME_X2      50
#define PRIME_Y2      18

/* If we found a prime then return PRIME, otherwise return NOT_PRIME */

#define PRIME         1
#define NOT_PRIME     0

/* Max number of threads for this application */

#define MAX_THREADS   10

#define ERROR_EXIT    2
#define SUCCESS_EXIT  0

/* Delay time in microseconds */

#define STRING_LENGTH 256
#define WAIT          350
```

Listing 9.1 — (continued)

```c
/* Colors used in this application */

#define WHITE_ON_BLUE FOREGROUND_WHITE|FOREGROUND_INTENSITY|BACKGROUND_BLUE
#define WHITE_ON_CYAN FOREGROUND_WHITE|FOREGROUND_INTENSITY|BACKGROUND_CYAN
#define RED_ON_BLUE   FOREGROUND_RED|FOREGROUND_INTENSITY|BACKGROUND_BLUE

/* Prototypes of functions used in this application */

unsigned char IsPrime(unsigned long TestNumber);
extern char ServerStatus(void);
extern void thread_local(void);
extern void thread_remote(void);
extern void Usage(void);
extern void InitializeApplication(void);
extern void statistics(void);
extern void NotifyServer(void);

/* Critical Section for choosing next available number for testing */

CRITICAL_SECTION GlobalCriticalSection;

/* Storage for Computer Name */

char computer_name_buffer[MAX_COMPUTERNAME_LENGTH];

/* Unique number returned by the server */

unsigned long PrimeServerHandle;

/*
NextNumber    - Next available number to test
StartTime     - Time that we start to compute primes
CurrTime      - Current Computer time
NoPrimeLocal  - Number of primes computed locally
NoPrimeRemote - Number of primes computed on the remote computer
StartNumber   - The starting number for testing primes
*/

unsigned long NextNumber = 1, StartTime, CurrTime, NoPrimeLocal,
   NoPrimeRemote, StartNumber = 1;

/*
   Context Handle - Contains binding information and information about
   the state of the processing task on the server. State information is not
   available to the client, it can be only accesses by the server
*/

PCONTEXT_HANDLE_TYPE phContext = NULL;

void _CRTAPI1 main(int argc, char **argv)
   {
   RPC_STATUS status; /* returned by RPC API function */
```

Listing 9.1 — (continued)

```
    unsigned char *pszUuid           = NULL;
    unsigned char *pszProtocolSequence = "ncacn_np";
    unsigned char *pszNetworkAddress  = NULL;
    unsigned char *pszEndpoint        = "\\pipe\\prime";
    unsigned char *pszOptions         = NULL;
    unsigned char *pszStringBinding   = NULL;

    DWORD  Max_ComputerName_Length = MAX_COMPUTERNAME_LENGTH;
    DWORD  lpIDThread;
    HANDLE hthread_remote;

    int count;

/* Allow the user to override settings with command line switches */

    for(count = 1; count < argc; count++)
        {
        if((*argv[count] == '-') || (*argv[count] == '/'))
            {
            switch(tolower(*(argv[count]+1)))
                {
                case 'p': /* protocol sequence */
                    pszProtocolSequence = argv[++count];
                    break;

                case 'n': /* network address   */
                    pszNetworkAddress = argv[++count];
                    break;

                case 'e':
                    pszEndpoint = argv[++count];
                    break;

                case 'o':
                    pszOptions = argv[++count];
                    break;

                case 'f': /* first number */
                    NextNumber = StartNumber = atol(argv[++count]);
                    break;

                case 'h':
                case '?':
                default:
                    Usage();
                }
            }
        else
            Usage();
        }
```

Listing 9.1 — (continued)

```
/* Use a convenience function to concatenate the elements of the string binding into the proper sequence */

    status = RpcStringBindingCompose(
        pszUuid,
        pszProtocolSequence,
        pszNetworkAddress,
        pszEndpoint,
        pszOptions,
        &pszStringBinding);

    if(status)
        exit(ERROR_EXIT);

/* Set the binding handle that will be used to bind to the server */

    status = RpcBindingFromStringBinding(pszStringBinding, &prime_IfHandle);

    if(status)
        exit(ERROR_EXIT);

    GetComputerName(computer_name_buffer, &Max_ComputerName_Length);
    ServerStatus();
    InitializeApplication();

    InitializeCriticalSection(&GlobalCriticalSection);

/* Create thread with normal priority, the name of the thread routine is thread_remote */

    hthread_remote = CreateThread(NULL, 0, (LPTHREAD_START_ROUTINE)thread_remote, NULL, 0, &lpIDThread);

/* function to compute primes */

    thread_local();

    DeleteCriticalSection(&GlobalCriticalSection);

/* The calls to the remote procedures are complete. Free the string and the binding handle */

    /* remote calls done - unbind */

    status = RpcStringFree(&pszStringBinding);

    if(status)
        exit(ERROR_EXIT);

    /* remote calls done - unbind */

    status = RpcBindingFree(&prime_IfHandle);

    printf("Unbinding from the prime number server.\n", status);

    if(status)
        exit(ERROR_EXIT);
```

Listing 9.1 — (continued)

```
    exit(SUCCESS_EXIT);
    }

void thread_local(void)
    {
    unsigned long temp;
    char Buffer[STRING_LENGTH];
    int loop;

    SMALL_RECT psrctScrollRectTesting, psrctScrollRectPrime;
    COORD coordDestOriginTesting, coordDestOriginPrime;
    CHAR_INFO pchiFill;
    WORD Color[TESTING_X2-TESTING_X1-3], Normal[TESTING_X2-TESTING_X1-3];

    COORD ComputTestCoord;
    COORD ComputPrimeCoord;

    DWORD dummy;
    COORD PrimeCoord;

    psrctScrollRectTesting.Left   = TESTING_X1+1;
    psrctScrollRectTesting.Top    = TESTING_Y1+2;
    psrctScrollRectTesting.Right  = TESTING_X2-1;
    psrctScrollRectTesting.Bottom = TESTING_Y2-1;

    coordDestOriginTesting.X = TESTING_X1+1;
    coordDestOriginTesting.Y = TESTING_Y1+1;

    psrctScrollRectPrime.Left   = PRIME_X1+1;
    psrctScrollRectPrime.Top    = PRIME_Y1+2;
    psrctScrollRectPrime.Right  = PRIME_X2-1;
    psrctScrollRectPrime.Bottom = PRIME_Y2-1;

    coordDestOriginPrime.X = PRIME_X1+1;
    coordDestOriginPrime.Y = PRIME_Y1+1;

    pchiFill.Char.AsciiChar = (char)32;
    pchiFill.Attributes = WHITE_ON_BLUE;

    ComputTestCoord.X  = TESTING_X2-7;
    ComputTestCoord.Y  = TESTING_Y2-1;
    ComputPrimeCoord.X = PRIME_X2-7;
    ComputPrimeCoord.Y = PRIME_Y2-1;

    for(loop = 0; loop < TESTING_X2-TESTING_X1-3; loop++)
        {
        Color[loop]  = RED_ON_BLUE;
        Normal[loop] = WHITE_ON_BLUE;
        }
```

Listing 9.1 — (continued)

```
while(1)
    {

    /* If the user pressed ESC then notify the server and the exit */

    if(VK_ESCAPE == get_character_no_wait())
        {
        EnterCriticalSection(&GlobalCriticalSection);
        Sleep(WAIT);
        NotifyServer();
        clearscreen(0);
        exit(0);
        LeaveCriticalSection(&GlobalCriticalSection);
        }

    /* To make sure that we won't test the same number twice */

    EnterCriticalSection(&GlobalCriticalSection);
    if((temp = ++NextNumber) >= ULONG_MAX)
        break;
    LeaveCriticalSection(&GlobalCriticalSection);

    EnterCriticalSection(&GlobalCriticalSection);
    ScrollConsoleScreenBuffer(hStdOut, &psrctScrollRectTesting, NULL, coordDestOriginTesting, &pchiFill);
    sprintf(Buffer, "%d", temp - 1);
    mxyputs((unsigned char)TESTING_X1+2, (unsigned char)(TESTING_Y2-1), Buffer, WHITE_ON_BLUE);
    WriteConsoleOutputAttribute(hStdOut, Normal, 7, ComputTestCoord, &dummy);
    mxyputs((unsigned char)(TESTING_X2-7), (unsigned char)TESTING_Y2-1, "LOCAL ", WHITE_ON_BLUE);
    LeaveCriticalSection(&GlobalCriticalSection);

    if(IsPrime(temp - 1) != 0)
        {
        PrimeCoord.X = PRIME_X1 + 2;
        PrimeCoord.Y = PRIME_Y2 - 1;

        EnterCriticalSection(&GlobalCriticalSection);
        ScrollConsoleScreenBuffer(hStdOut, &psrctScrollRectPrime, NULL, coordDestOriginPrime, &pchiFill);
        sprintf(Buffer, "%-17d", temp - 1);
        mxyputs((unsigned char)(PRIME_X1+2), (unsigned char)PRIME_Y2-1, Buffer, WHITE_ON_BLUE);
        WriteConsoleOutputAttribute(hStdOut, Normal, 7, ComputPrimeCoord, &dummy);
        mxyputs((unsigned char)(PRIME_X2-7), (unsigned char)PRIME_Y2-1, "LOCAL ", WHITE_ON_BLUE);
        LeaveCriticalSection(&GlobalCriticalSection);
        NoPrimeLocal++;
        }

    statistics();
    }
}
```

Listing 9.1 — *(continued)*

```c
void thread_remote(void)
   {
   unsigned long temp;
   char Buffer[STRING_LENGTH];
   int loop;

   SMALL_RECT psrctScrollRectTesting, psrctScrollRectPrime;
   COORD coordDestOriginTesting, coordDestOriginPrime;
   CHAR_INFO pchiFill;
   WORD Color[TESTING_X2-TESTING_X1-3], Normal[TESTING_X2-TESTING_X1-3];

   COORD ComputTestCoord;
   COORD ComputPrimeCoord;

   DWORD dummy;
   COORD PrimeCoord;

   psrctScrollRectTesting.Left   = TESTING_X1+1;
   psrctScrollRectTesting.Top    = TESTING_Y1+2;
   psrctScrollRectTesting.Right  = TESTING_X2-1;
   psrctScrollRectTesting.Bottom = TESTING_Y2-1;

   coordDestOriginTesting.X = TESTING_X1+1;
   coordDestOriginTesting.Y = TESTING_Y1+1;

   psrctScrollRectPrime.Left   = PRIME_X1+1;
   psrctScrollRectPrime.Top    = PRIME_Y1+2;
   psrctScrollRectPrime.Right  = PRIME_X2-1;
   psrctScrollRectPrime.Bottom = PRIME_Y2-1;

   coordDestOriginPrime.X = PRIME_X1+1;
   coordDestOriginPrime.Y = PRIME_Y1+1;

   pchiFill.Char.AsciiChar = (char)32;
   pchiFill.Attributes = WHITE_ON_BLUE;

   ComputTestCoord.X  = TESTING_X2-7;
   ComputTestCoord.Y  = TESTING_Y2-1;
   ComputPrimeCoord.X = PRIME_X2-7;
   ComputPrimeCoord.Y = PRIME_Y2-1;

   for(loop = 0; loop < TESTING_X2-TESTING_X1-3; loop++)
      {
      Color[loop]  = RED_ON_BLUE;
      Normal[loop] = WHITE_ON_BLUE;
      }

   while(1)
      {
```

Listing 9.1 — (continued)

```
/* If the user pressed ESC then notify the server and the exit */

     if(VK_ESCAPE == get_character_no_wait())
        {
        EnterCriticalSection(&GlobalCriticalSection);
        Sleep(WAIT);
        NotifyServer();
        clearscreen(0);
        exit(0);
        LeaveCriticalSection(&GlobalCriticalSection);
        }

     EnterCriticalSection(&GlobalCriticalSection);
     if((temp = ++NextNumber) >= ULONG_MAX)
        break;
     LeaveCriticalSection(&GlobalCriticalSection);


/* To make sure that we won't test the same number twice */

     EnterCriticalSection(&GlobalCriticalSection);
     ScrollConsoleScreenBuffer(hStdOut, &psrctScrollRectTesting, NULL, coordDestOriginTesting, &pchiFill);
     sprintf(Buffer, " %-17d", temp - 1);
     mxyputs((unsigned char)TESTING_X1+1, (unsigned char)(TESTING_Y2-1), Buffer, RED_ON_BLUE);
     WriteConsoleOutputAttribute(hStdOut, Color, 7, ComputTestCoord, &dummy);
     mxyputs((unsigned char)(TESTING_X2-7), (unsigned char)TESTING_Y2-1, "REMOTE ", RED_ON_BLUE);
     LeaveCriticalSection(&GlobalCriticalSection);

TryAgain:
     RpcTryExcept
        {
        if(RemoteIsPrime(PrimeServerHandle, temp - 1) != 0)
           {
           EnterCriticalSection(&GlobalCriticalSection);
           PrimeCoord.X = TESTING_X1 + 2;
           LeaveCriticalSection(&GlobalCriticalSection);

           PrimeCoord.X = PRIME_X1 + 2;
           PrimeCoord.Y = PRIME_Y2 - 1;

           EnterCriticalSection(&GlobalCriticalSection);
           ScrollConsoleScreenBuffer(hStdOut, &psrctScrollRectPrime, NULL, coordDestOriginPrime, &pchiFill);
           sprintf(Buffer, " %-17d", temp - 1);
           mxyputs((unsigned char)(PRIME_X1+1), (unsigned char)PRIME_Y2-1, Buffer, RED_ON_BLUE);
           WriteConsoleOutputAttribute(hStdOut, Color, 7, ComputPrimeCoord, &dummy);
           mxyputs((unsigned char)(PRIME_X2-7), (unsigned char)PRIME_Y2-1, "REMOTE ", RED_ON_BLUE);
           LeaveCriticalSection(&GlobalCriticalSection);

           NoPrimeRemote++;
           }

        statistics();
        }
```

Listing 9.1 — (continued)

```c
        RpcExcept(1)
            {

/* if exceptions occur */

            while(ServerStatus())
                {
                for(loop = 0; loop < 5; loop++)
                    {
                    mxyputs((unsigned char)15, (unsigned char)21,
                            "Prime number server is off-line.  Please restart it.",  WHITE_ON_CYAN);
                    Sleep(WAIT);
                    mxyputc((unsigned char)15, (unsigned char)21, (char)32, 52,
                            FOREGROUND_CYAN|FOREGROUND_INTENSITY|BACKGROUND_CYAN);
                    Sleep(WAIT);
                    }
                }

            goto TryAgain;
            }
        RpcEndExcept
        }
    }

/* Tests for prime number on the local computer */

unsigned char IsPrime(unsigned long TestNumber)
    {
    unsigned long count;
    unsigned long HalfNumber = TestNumber / 2 + 1;

    for(count = 2; count < HalfNumber; count++)
        if(TestNumber % count == 0)
            return NOT_PRIME;

    return PRIME;
    }

/* Displays command line options */

void Usage(void)
    {
    printf("\nContext Handle prime number example.\n\n");
    printf("Usage: PRIMEC4\n");
    printf(" -p protocol_sequence\n");
    printf(" -n network_address\n");
    printf(" -e endpoint\n");
    printf(" -o options\n");
    printf(" -f first number\n");
    exit(1);
    }
```

Listing 9.1 — (continued)

```c
/* Screen Initialization and colors and title lines */

void InitializeApplication(void)
    {
    char Buffer[STRING_LENGTH];
    set_vid_mem();

    clearscreen(BACKGROUND_CYAN);
    StartTime = GetTickCount();

    box(0, 0, 79, 24,DOUBLE);
    mxyputs(37, 0, " PRIMEC4 ", WHITE_ON_CYAN);

    mxyputs(TESTING_X1, 2, "Testing...", WHITE_ON_CYAN);
    box(TESTING_X1, TESTING_Y1, TESTING_X2, TESTING_Y2, SINGLE);

    mxyputs(PRIME_X1, 2, "Prime!",WHITE_ON_CYAN);
    box(PRIME_X1, PRIME_Y1, PRIME_X2, PRIME_Y2, SINGLE);

    mxyputs(58, 2, "Number of Primes", WHITE_ON_CYAN);
    box(58, 3, 73, (unsigned char)(1+5), SINGLE);

    sprintf(Buffer,"First = %d", StartNumber);
    mxyputs(58,(unsigned char)(1+5+3), Buffer, WHITE_ON_CYAN);

    mxyputs(32, 23, "Press Esc to exit", WHITE_ON_CYAN);
    }

/* Check the Server status if it is of line, then try to connect, return server status */

char ServerStatus(void)
    {
    char value = FALSE;

    RpcTryExcept
        {
        PrimeServerHandle = InitializePrimeServer(&phContext, computer_name_buffer);
        }
    RpcExcept(1)
        {
        value = TRUE;
        }
    RpcEndExcept

    return value;
    }
```

Listing 9.1 — (continued)

```c
/* Dislay information about the progress of computing prime numbers */

void statistics(void)
   {
   char Buffer[STRING_LENGTH];

   CurrTime = (GetTickCount() - StartTime)/1000;
   sprintf(Buffer, "Primes = %d", NoPrimeLocal+NoPrimeRemote);
   mxyputs(58, (unsigned char)(7), Buffer, WHITE_ON_CYAN);
   sprintf(Buffer, "Time = %d.%02d min.", CurrTime/60, CurrTime%60);
   mxyputs(58, (unsigned char)(8), Buffer, WHITE_ON_CYAN);
   sprintf(Buffer, "%s:%5d", "LOCAL ", NoPrimeLocal);
   mxyputs((unsigned char)(60), (unsigned char)(4), Buffer, WHITE_ON_BLUE);
   sprintf(Buffer, "%s:%5d", "REMOTE", NoPrimeRemote);
   mxyputs((unsigned char)(60), (unsigned char)(5), Buffer, RED_ON_BLUE);
   }

/* Let the Server know that we are about to exit */

void NotifyServer(void)
   {
   RpcTryExcept
      {
      TerminatePrimeServer(PrimeServerHandle);
      }
   RpcExcept(1)
      {
      return;
      }
   RpcEndExcept
   }

/* End of File */
```

Listing 9.2 — PRIMES4.C

```
/*************************************************************************\
*                                                                         *
* PRIMES4.C - Distributed prime number example                            *
*             (c) Guy Eddon, 1993                                         *
*                                                                         *
* To build:   NMAKE PRIME4.MAK                                            *
*                                                                         *
* Usage:      PRIMES4                                                     *
*                                                                         *
* Comments:   This is the server side prime number example.              *
*                                                                         *
\*************************************************************************/

#include <STDIO.H>
#include <STRING.H>
#include <STDLIB.H>
#include <STDARG.H>
#include <LIMITS.H>
#include <CTYPE.H>
#include <WINDOWS.H>
#include <RPC.H>
#include "prime4.h"
#include "directio.h"

/* If we found a prime then return PRIME, otherwise return NOT_PRIME */

#define PRIME       1
#define NOT_PRIME   0

/* Maximum Number of Clients to respond to */

#define MAX_CALLS   10

/* Coordinates for displaying numbers to be tested */

#define TESTING_X1    3
#define TESTING_Y1    3
#define TESTING_X2   23
#define TESTING_Y2   18

/* Coordinates for displaying prime numbers */

#define PRIME_X1   30
#define PRIME_Y1    3
#define PRIME_X2   50
#define PRIME_Y2   18

#define ERROR_EXIT      2
#define SUCCESS_EXIT    0
#define STRING_LENGTH 256
```

Listing 9.2 — (continued)

```
/* Delay time in microseconds */

#define WAIT         350
#define WAIT_DISPLAY 2000

/* Colors used in this application */

#define WHITE_ON_BLUE FOREGROUND_WHITE|FOREGROUND_INTENSITY|BACKGROUND_BLUE
#define WHITE_ON_CYAN FOREGROUND_WHITE|FOREGROUND_INTENSITY|BACKGROUND_CYAN
#define RED_ON_BLUE   FOREGROUND_RED|FOREGROUND_INTENSITY|BACKGROUND_BLUE
#define RED_ON_CYAN   FOREGROUND_RED|FOREGROUND_INTENSITY|BACKGROUND_CYAN
#define CYAN_ON_CYAN  FOREGROUND_CYAN|BACKGROUND_CYAN

/* Number of characters in computer name to display on the screen */

#define COMP_NAME_LENGTH 7

extern char IsPrime(unsigned long TestNumber);

extern void Usage(void);
extern void InitializeApplication(void);

/* Number of primes for each client */

extern unsigned long NoPrimes[MAX_CALLS];

/* Number of clients that we are connected to */

extern unsigned long handles;

extern void thread_server(void);

/* Names of clients that we are connected to */

extern char GlobalComputerNameBuffer[MAX_CALLS][MAX_COMPUTERNAME_LENGTH];

DWORD  lpIDThread;
HANDLE hthread_server;

/* Critical Section for choosing next available number for testing */

CRITICAL_SECTION GlobalCriticalSection;
```

Listing 9.2 — (continued)

```c
/* main: register the interface, start listening for clients */

void _CRTAPI1 main(int argc, char *argv[])
    {
    RPC_STATUS status;

    unsigned char *pszProtocolSequence = "ncacn_np";
    unsigned char *pszSecurity         = NULL;
    unsigned char *pszEndpoint         = "\\pipe\\prime";
    unsigned int cMinCalls             = 1;
    unsigned int cMaxCalls             = MAX_CALLS;
    unsigned int fDontWait             = FALSE;

    int i;

/* allow the user to override settings with command line switches */

    for(i = 1; i < argc; i++)
        {
        if((*argv[i] == '-') || (*argv[i] == '/'))
            {
            switch(tolower(*(argv[i]+1)))
                {
                case 'p': /* protocol sequence */
                    pszProtocolSequence = argv[++i];
                    break;

                case 'e':
                    pszEndpoint = argv[++i];
                    break;

                case 'm':
                    cMaxCalls = (unsigned int) atoi(argv[++i]);
                    break;

                case 'n':
                    cMinCalls = (unsigned int) atoi(argv[++i]);
                    break;

                case 'f':
                    fDontWait = (unsigned int) atoi(argv[++i]);
                    break;

                case 's':
                    pszSecurity = argv[++i];
                    break;
```

Listing 9.2 — (continued)

```
                case 'h':
                case '?':
                default:
                    Usage();
                }
            }
        else
            Usage();
        }

/* Tells the RPC runtime to use the specified protocol sequence combined
   with the specified endpoint for receiving remote procedure calls */

    status = RpcServerUseProtseqEp(
        pszProtocolSequence,
        cMaxCalls,      /* max concurrent calls */
        pszEndpoint,
        pszSecurity);   /* Security descriptor  */

    if(status)
        exit(status);

/* Registers an interface with RPC runtime */

    status = RpcServerRegisterIf(
        prime4_ServerIfHandle, /* interface to register      */
        NULL,                  /* MgrTypeUuid                */
        NULL);                 /* MgrEpv; null means use default */

    if(status)
        exit(status);

    InitializeCriticalSection(&GlobalCriticalSection);

    InitializeApplication();

    mxyputs(23, 21, "Listening for prime number requests.", RED_ON_CYAN);

/* Tells the RPC runtime to listen for remote procedure calls */

    status = RpcServerListen(cMinCalls, cMaxCalls, fDontWait);

    if(status)
        exit(status);

    if(fDontWait)
        {
        status = RpcMgmtWaitServerListen(); /* wait operation */

        if(status)
            exit(status);
        }
    }
```

Listing 9.2 — (continued)

```
/* Displays command line options */

void Usage(void)
    {
    printf("\nContext Handle prime number example.\n\n");
    printf("Usage: PRIMES4\n");
    printf(" -p protocol_sequence\n");
    printf(" -e endpoint\n");
    printf(" -m maxcalls\n");
    printf(" -n mincalls\n");
    printf(" -f flag_wait_op\n");
    printf(" -s security_descriptor\n");
    exit(EXIT_SUCCESS);
    }


/* MIDL allocate and free */

void *MIDL_user_allocate(size_t len)
    {
    return(malloc(len));
    }


void MIDL_user_free(void *ptr)
    {
    free(ptr);
    }


void InitializeApplication(void)
    {
    set_vid_mem();

    clearscreen(BACKGROUND_CYAN);

    box(0, 0, 79, 24, DOUBLE);
    mxyputs(37, 0, " PRIMES4 ", WHITE_ON_CYAN);

    mxyputs(TESTING_X1, 2, "Testing...", WHITE_ON_CYAN);

    box(TESTING_X1, TESTING_Y1, TESTING_X2, TESTING_Y2,SINGLE);

    mxyputs(PRIME_X1, 2, "Prime!", WHITE_ON_CYAN);
    box(PRIME_X1, PRIME_Y1, PRIME_X2, PRIME_Y2, SINGLE);

    mxyputs(32, 23, "Press Esc to exit", WHITE_ON_CYAN);

/* Create thread with low priority to display server activity */

    hthread_server = CreateThread(NULL, 0, (LPTHREAD_START_ROUTINE)thread_server, NULL,
                                  CREATE_SUSPENDED, &lpIDThread);

    SetThreadPriority(hthread_server, THREAD_PRIORITY_LOWEST);
    ResumeThread(hthread_server);
    }
```

Listing 9.2 — (continued)

```
/* Displays information about prime number production */

void thread_server()
   {
   while(1)
      {
      char Buffer[STRING_LENGTH], Buffert[STRING_LENGTH];
      unsigned char i;

      if(VK_ESCAPE == get_character_no_wait())
         {
         EnterCriticalSection(&GlobalCriticalSection);
         Sleep(WAIT);
         clearscreen(0);
         exit(EXIT_SUCCESS);
         LeaveCriticalSection(&GlobalCriticalSection);
         DeleteCriticalSection(&GlobalCriticalSection);
         }

      if(handles)
         {
         mxyputs(58, 2, "Number of Primes", WHITE_ON_CYAN);
         EnterCriticalSection(&GlobalCriticalSection);
         for(i = 0; i < handles; i++)
            {
            strncpy(Buffert, GlobalComputerNameBuffer[i], COMP_NAME_LENGTH);
            Buffert[COMP_NAME_LENGTH] = 0;
            sprintf(Buffer, " %7s:%5d ", Buffert, NoPrimes[i]);
            mxyputs(59, (unsigned char)(4+i), Buffer, WHITE_ON_CYAN);
            }
         box(58, 3, 74, (unsigned char)(4+handles), SINGLE);
         mxyputc(58, (unsigned char)(5+i), (char)32, 17, CYAN_ON_CYAN);
         LeaveCriticalSection(&GlobalCriticalSection);
         }
      else
         for(i = 0; i < 13; i++)
            mxyputc(58, (unsigned char)(2+i), (char)32, 17, CYAN_ON_CYAN);

      if(!handles)
         {
         mxyputs(23, 21, "Listening for prime number requests.",
            RED_ON_CYAN);
         Sleep(WAIT_DISPLAY);
         }
      mxyputc(23, 21, (char)32, 36, CYAN_ON_CYAN);
      }
   }

/* End of File */
```

Listing 9.3 — PRIMEP4.C

```c
/**********************************************************************\
*                                                                    *
* PRIMEP4.C - Distributed prime number example                       *
*            (c) Guy Eddon, 1993                                     *
*                                                                    *
* To build:   NMAKE PRIME4.MAK                                       *
*                                                                    *
* Usage:      PRIMES4                                                *
*                                                                    *
* Comments:   These are the remote procedures called by the clients. *
*                                                                    *
\**********************************************************************/

#include <STDIO.H>
#include <STRING.H>
#include <STDLIB.H>
#include <STDARG.H>
#include <LIMITS.H>
#include <CTYPE.H>
#include <WINDOWS.H>
#include <RPC.H>        /* RPC data structures and APIs          */
#include "prime4.h"     /* header file generated by MIDL compiler */
#include "directio.h"

/* If we found a prime then return PRIME, otherwise return NOT_PRIME */

#define PRIME        1
#define NOT_PRIME    0

/* Maximum Number of Clients to respond to */

#define MAX_CALLS    10

/* Coordinates for displaying numbers to be tested */

#define TESTING_X1    3
#define TESTING_Y1    3
#define TESTING_X2    23
#define TESTING_Y2    18

/* Coordinates for displaying prime numbers */

#define PRIME_X1     30
#define PRIME_Y1      3
#define PRIME_X2     50
#define PRIME_Y2     18

#define ERROR_EXIT    2
#define SUCCESS_EXIT  0
#define STRING_LENGTH 256
```

Listing 9.3 — (continued)

```
/* Time delay in microseconds */

#define WAIT         350
#define WAIT_DISPLAY 2000

/* Colors used in this application */

#define WHITE_ON_BLUE FOREGROUND_WHITE|FOREGROUND_INTENSITY|BACKGROUND_BLUE
#define WHITE_ON_CYAN FOREGROUND_WHITE|FOREGROUND_INTENSITY|BACKGROUND_CYAN
#define RED_ON_BLUE   FOREGROUND_RED|FOREGROUND_INTENSITY|BACKGROUND_BLUE
#define RED_ON_CYAN   FOREGROUND_RED|FOREGROUND_INTENSITY|BACKGROUND_CYAN
#define CYAN_ON_CYAN  FOREGROUND_CYAN|BACKGROUND_CYAN

/* Number of characters in computer name to display on the screen */

#define COMP_NAME_LENGTH 7

/* Critical Section for choosing next available number for testing */

extern CRITICAL_SECTION GlobalCriticalSection;

/* Number of clients that we are connected to */

unsigned long handles = 0,handlesp=0;

/* Names of clients that we are connected to */

char GlobalComputerNameBuffer[MAX_CALLS][MAX_COMPUTERNAME_LENGTH];

/* Number of primes for each client */

unsigned long NoPrimes[MAX_CALLS];

/* Unique identifier that we return to each client */

unsigned long GlobalComputerHandleBuffer[MAX_CALLS];

/* Global variable to help us to produce a unique number */

unsigned long handle_mod = 1;

/*
   This function is called by the client, we return a unique number,
   so in the future we can keep track who called us
*/

unsigned long InitializePrimeServer(PPCONTEXT_HANDLE_TYPE pphContext, unsigned char *ComputerName)
   {
   char Buffer[STRING_LENGTH];
   unsigned long unique_handle;

   EnterCriticalSection(&GlobalCriticalSection);
   unique_handle = handles + 10 * handle_mod++;
```

Listing 9.3 — (continued)

```
    strcpy(GlobalComputerNameBuffer[handles], ComputerName);

    mxyputc(2, 21, (char)32, 75, CYAN_ON_CYAN);
    sprintf(Buffer, "Computer %s logged in.", ComputerName);
    mxyputs(27, 21, Buffer, RED_ON_CYAN);
    sprintf(Buffer,  "(%ld)",unique_handle);
    mxyputs(54, 21, Buffer, RED_ON_CYAN);
    Sleep(2*WAIT_DISPLAY);
    mxyputc(2, 21, (char)32, 75, CYAN_ON_CYAN);

    GlobalComputerHandleBuffer[handles] = unique_handle;

    *pphContext = (PCONTEXT_HANDLE_TYPE)unique_handle;

    NoPrimes[handles] = 0;

    handles++;
    handlesp = handles;
    LeaveCriticalSection(&GlobalCriticalSection);

    return unique_handle;
    }

/*
    This function was called by the client. The client supplied his identifier
    and the number to test if it is a prime
*/

unsigned char RemoteIsPrime(unsigned long PrimeServerHandle,
    unsigned long TestNumber)
    {
    unsigned long count;
    unsigned long HalfNumber = TestNumber / 2 + 1;
    char Buffer[STRING_LENGTH];
    char LocalComputerName[MAX_COMPUTERNAME_LENGTH];
    int loop;

    SMALL_RECT psrctScrollRectTesting, psrctScrollRectPrime;
    COORD coordDestOriginTesting, coordDestOriginPrime;
    CHAR_INFO pchiFill;
    WORD Local[COMP_NAME_LENGTH];

    COORD ComputTestCoord;
    COORD ComputPrimeCoord;
    DWORD dummy;
```

Listing 9.3 — (continued)

```
/* Lets find out the name of client computer */

    EnterCriticalSection(&GlobalCriticalSection);
    for(loop = 0; loop < (int)handles; loop++)
        if(GlobalComputerHandleBuffer[loop] == PrimeServerHandle)
            {
            strcpy(LocalComputerName, GlobalComputerNameBuffer[loop]);
            PrimeServerHandle = loop;
            break;
            }
    LeaveCriticalSection(&GlobalCriticalSection);

    psrctScrollRectTesting.Left   = TESTING_X1+1;
    psrctScrollRectTesting.Top    = TESTING_Y1+2;
    psrctScrollRectTesting.Right  = TESTING_X2-1;
    psrctScrollRectTesting.Bottom = TESTING_Y2-1;

    coordDestOriginTesting.X = TESTING_X1+1;
    coordDestOriginTesting.Y = TESTING_Y1+1;

    psrctScrollRectPrime.Left   = PRIME_X1+1;
    psrctScrollRectPrime.Top    = PRIME_Y1+2;
    psrctScrollRectPrime.Right  = PRIME_X2-1;
    psrctScrollRectPrime.Bottom = PRIME_Y2-1;

    coordDestOriginPrime.X = PRIME_X1+1;
    coordDestOriginPrime.Y = PRIME_Y1+1;

    pchiFill.Char.AsciiChar = (char)32;
    pchiFill.Attributes = WHITE_ON_BLUE;

    ComputTestCoord.X  = TESTING_X2-7;
    ComputTestCoord.Y  = TESTING_Y2-1;
    ComputPrimeCoord.X = PRIME_X2-7;
    ComputPrimeCoord.Y = PRIME_Y2-1;

    for(loop = 0; loop < COMP_NAME_LENGTH; loop++)
        Local[loop] = WHITE_ON_BLUE;

    /* If the user pressed ESC then exit */

    if(VK_ESCAPE == get_character_no_wait())
        {
        EnterCriticalSection(&GlobalCriticalSection);
            Sleep(WAIT);
        clearscreen(0);
        exit(SUCCESS_EXIT);
        LeaveCriticalSection(&GlobalCriticalSection);
        DeleteCriticalSection(&GlobalCriticalSection);
        }
```

Listing 9.3 — (continued)

```
    sprintf(Buffer, "%d", TestNumber);

    EnterCriticalSection(&GlobalCriticalSection);
    ScrollConsoleScreenBuffer(hStdOut, &psrctScrollRectTesting, NULL, coordDestOriginTesting, &pchiFill);
    sprintf(Buffer, "%d", TestNumber);
    mxyputs((unsigned char)TESTING_X1+2, (unsigned char)(TESTING_Y2-1), Buffer, WHITE_ON_BLUE);
    WriteConsoleOutputAttribute(hStdOut, Local, COMP_NAME_LENGTH, ComputTestCoord, &dummy);
    LocalComputerName[COMP_NAME_LENGTH] = 0;
    mxyputs((unsigned char)(TESTING_X2-7), (unsigned char)TESTING_Y2-1, LocalComputerName, WHITE_ON_BLUE);
    LeaveCriticalSection(&GlobalCriticalSection);

    for(count = 2; count < HalfNumber; count++)
        if(TestNumber % count == 0)
            return NOT_PRIME;

    sprintf(Buffer, "%d", TestNumber);

    EnterCriticalSection(&GlobalCriticalSection);
    ScrollConsoleScreenBuffer(hStdOut, &psrctScrollRectPrime, NULL, coordDestOriginPrime, &pchiFill);
    sprintf(Buffer, "%d", TestNumber);
    mxyputs((unsigned char)(PRIME_X1+2), (unsigned char)PRIME_Y2-1, Buffer, WHITE_ON_BLUE);
    WriteConsoleOutputAttribute(hStdOut, Local, COMP_NAME_LENGTH, ComputPrimeCoord, &dummy);
    mxyputs((unsigned char)(PRIME_X2-7), (unsigned char)PRIME_Y2-1, LocalComputerName, WHITE_ON_BLUE);
    NoPrimes[PrimeServerHandle]++;
    LeaveCriticalSection(&GlobalCriticalSection);

    return PRIME;
    }

/* Notification from a client that he is done */

void TerminatePrimeServer(unsigned long PrimeServerHandle)
    {
    char Buffer[256+MAX_COMPUTERNAME_LENGTH];
    unsigned char loop, loopshift;

    EnterCriticalSection(&GlobalCriticalSection);

    for(loop = 0; loop < (unsigned char)handles; loop++)
        {
        if(GlobalComputerHandleBuffer[loop] == PrimeServerHandle)
            {
```

Listing 9.3 — (continued)

```
/* Let's put terminating message on the screen */

        mxyputc(2, 21, (char)32, 75, CYAN_ON_CYAN);
        sprintf(Buffer, "Computer %s Exited!", GlobalComputerNameBuffer[loop]);
        mxyputs(27, 21, Buffer, RED_ON_CYAN);
        mxyputc(59, (unsigned char)(4+loop), (char)32, 15, CYAN_ON_CYAN);
        Sleep(WAIT_DISPLAY);
        mxyputc(2, 21, (char)32, 75, CYAN_ON_CYAN);
        break;
        }
    }

  if(loop < handles-1)
    {
    loopshift = loop;

/* Let's remove his name from our table */

    for(loop = loopshift; loop < (unsigned char)(handles-1); loop++)
        {
        strcpy(GlobalComputerNameBuffer[loop], GlobalComputerNameBuffer[loop+1]);
        GlobalComputerHandleBuffer[loop] = GlobalComputerHandleBuffer[loop+1];
        NoPrimes[loop] = NoPrimes[loop+1];
        }
    }

/* We have one client less */

  handles--;
  LeaveCriticalSection(&GlobalCriticalSection);
  }

void PCONTEXT_HANDLE_TYPE_rundown(PCONTEXT_HANDLE_TYPE phContext)
  {
  if(handlesp==handles)
    {
    mxyputs(27, 2, "rundown Executed", RED_ON_CYAN);
    TerminatePrimeServer((unsigned long) phContext);
    Sleep(2000);
    mxyputs(27, 2, "                ", CYAN_ON_CYAN);
    }
  handlesp = handles;
  }

/* End of File */
```

Listing 9.4 — PRIME4.MAK

```
################################################################
#                                                              #
# PRIME4.MAK - Make file                                       #
#                                                              #
################################################################

!include <ntwin32.mak>

!if "$(CPU)" == "i386"
cvtomf =
cflags = $(cflags:G3=Gz)
!endif
!if "$(CPU)" == "MIPS"
cvtomf = mip2coff $@
!endif

.c.obj:
   $(cc) $(cflags) $(cvarsmt) $<
   $(cvtomf)

all : primec4 primes4

primec4 : primec4.exe
primec4.exe : primec4.obj prime4_c.obj prime4_x.obj directio.obj
    $(link) $(conflags) -out:primec4.exe primec4.obj prime4_c.obj prime4_x.obj directio.obj \
      rpcrt4.lib rpcndr.lib $(conlibsmt)

primec4.obj : primec4.c prime4.h

directio.obj : directio.c directio.h
   $(cc) $(cflags) $(cvarsmt) directio.c
   $(cvtomf)

prime4_c.obj : prime4_c.c prime4.h
   $(cc) $(cflags) $(cvarsmt) prime4_c.c
   $(cvtomf)

prime4_x.obj : prime4_x.c prime4.h
   $(cc) $(cflags) $(cvarsmt) prime4_x.c
   $(cvtomf)

primes4 : primes4.exe
primes4.exe : primes4.obj primep4.obj prime4_s.obj prime4_y.obj directio.obj
    $(link) $(conflags) -out:primes4.exe primes4.obj prime4_s.obj primep4.obj prime4_y.obj directio.obj \
      rpcrt4.lib rpcndr.lib $(conlibsmt)

primes4.obj : primes4.c prime4.h

primep4.obj : primep4.c prime4.h

prime4_s.obj : prime4_s.c prime4.h
   $(cc) $(cflags) $(cvarsmt) prime4_s.c
   $(cvtomf)
```

Listing 9.4 — (continued)

```
prime4_y.obj : prime4_y.c prime4.h
    $(cc) $(cflags) $(cvarsmt) prime4_y.c
    $(cvtomf)

prime4.h prime4_c.c prime4_x.c prime4_s.c prime4_y.c : prime4.idl prime4.acf
    midl -cpp_cmd $(cc) -cpp_opt "-E"  prime4.idl

# End of File #
```

Listing 9.5 — PRIME4.IDL

```
/**********************************************************************\
*                                                                    *
* PRIME4.IDL -  PRIME4 Interface Definition                          *
*              (c) Guy Eddon, 1993                                   *
*                                                                    *
\**********************************************************************/

[ uuid (72ABDE70-235B-5A4D-B352-026AB13562DA),
  version(1.0),
  pointer_default(unique)]
interface prime4
{
typedef [context_handle] void *PCONTEXT_HANDLE_TYPE;
typedef [ref] PCONTEXT_HANDLE_TYPE *PPCONTEXT_HANDLE_TYPE;

char RemoteIsPrime([in] unsigned long PrimeServerHandle,
   [in] unsigned long TestNumber);

unsigned long InitializePrimeServer([out] PPCONTEXT_HANDLE_TYPE pphcontext,
   [in, string] unsigned char *ComputerName);

void TerminatePrimeServer([in] unsigned long PrimeServerHandle);
}

/* End of File */
```

Listing 9.6 — *PRIME4.ACF*

```
/*********************************************************************\
* PRIME4.ACF -  PRIME4 Attribute Configuration File                 *
*               (c) Guy Eddon, 1993                                 *
\*********************************************************************/

[implicit_handle(handle_t prime_IfHandle)]
interface prime4
{

}

/* End of File */
```

Listing 9.7 — *DIRECTIO.C*

```
/*********************************************************************\
* DIRECTIO.C Direct screen access functions for MS-DOS              *
*               (c) Guy Eddon, 1993                                 *
\*********************************************************************/

#include <DOS.H>
#include <BIOS.H>
#include <GRAPH.H>
#include "directio.h"

#define MK_FP(seg,ofs) ((void far *) (((unsigned long)(seg) << 16) | (unsigned)(ofs)))

static char far *vid_mem_one, far *vid_mem_two;

void set_vid_mem(void)
   {
   union REGS r;
   int vmode;

   r.h.ah = 15;
   vmode = int86(0x10, &r, &r) & 255;

   if(vmode == 7)
      {
      vid_mem_one = (char*)MK_FP(0xB000,0000);
      vid_mem_two = (char*)MK_FP(0xB800,0000);
      }
   else
      {
      vid_mem_two = (char*)MK_FP(0xB000,0000);
      vid_mem_one = (char*)MK_FP(0xB800,0000);
      }
   }
```

Listing 9.7 — (continued)

```c
void mxyputs(unsigned char x, unsigned char y, char far *str, unsigned char attr)
   {
   while(*str)
      moutchar(x++, y, *str++, attr);
   }

void far mxyputc(unsigned char x, unsigned char y, char ch, unsigned char num, unsigned char attr)
   {
   unsigned char i;
   for(i = 0; i < num; i++)
      moutchar(x++, y, ch, attr);
   }

void far moutchar(unsigned char x, unsigned char y, char ch, unsigned char attr)
   {
   char far *v = vid_mem_one;
   v += y * 160 + x * 2;
   *v++ = ch, *v = attr;
   }

void far box(unsigned char x1, unsigned char y1, unsigned char x2, unsigned char y2, char S_D)
   {
   register int i;
   char far *v, far *t;
   char chr;

   t = v = vid_mem_one;
   chr = S_D ? 186 : 179;
   for(i = y1 + 1; i < y2; i++)
      {
      v += i * 160 + x1 * 2;
      *v++ = chr;
      *v = WHITE_ON_CYAN;
      v = t;
      v += i * 160 + x2 * 2;
      *v++ = chr;
      *v = WHITE_ON_CYAN;
      v = t;
      }
   chr = S_D ? 205 : 196;
   for(i = x1 + 1; i < x2; i++)
      {
      v += y1 * 160 + i * 2;
      *v++ = chr;
      *v = WHITE_ON_CYAN;
      v = t;
      v += y2 * 160 + i * 2;
      *v++ = chr;
      *v = WHITE_ON_CYAN;
      v = t;
      }
```

Listing 9.7 — (continued)

```
    chr = S_D ? 201 : 218;
    moutchar(x1, y1, chr, WHITE_ON_CYAN);
    chr = S_D ? 200 : 192;
    moutchar(x1, y2, chr, WHITE_ON_CYAN);
    chr = S_D ? 187 : 191;
    moutchar(x2, y1, chr, WHITE_ON_CYAN);
    chr = S_D ? 188 : 217;
    moutchar(x2, y2, chr, WHITE_ON_CYAN);
    }

void unsg_to_str(unsigned i, char far f[], unsigned char l)
    {
    int k = l - 1, h;
    for(h = 0; h < l; h++)
        {
        f[k--] = i % 10 + 0x30;
        i /= 10;
        }
    f[l] = 0;
    }

void read_field(unsigned char x1, unsigned char x2, unsigned char y, char *buffer)
    {
    unsigned char col = x1, row, count;
    gotoxy(x1, y);
    for(count = x1; count <= x2; count++)
        moutchar(count, y, (char)32, VID_REVERSE);
    for(count = x1; ; count++)
        {
        buffer[count - x1] = toupper(keyboard());
        if(buffer[count - x1] == '\r')
            break;
        if(buffer[count - x1] == '\b')
            {
            count--;
            if(col != x1)
                {
                moutchar(--col, y, (char)32, VID_REVERSE);
                count--;
                }
            }
        else
            moutchar(col++, y, buffer[count - x1], VID_REVERSE);
        if(col < x1)
            col = x1;
        else
            if(col > x2 + 1)
                {
                count--;
                col = x2 + 1;
                moutchar(col, y, (char)32, VID_NORMAL);
                }
        gotoxy(col, y);
        }
```

Listing 9.7 — (continued)

```c
    buffer[count - x1] = 0;
    }

void clear(unsigned char x1, unsigned char y1, unsigned char x2, unsigned char y2, unsigned char attr)
    {
    register unsigned char col, row;

    for(row = y1; row < y2; row++)
       for(col = x1; col < x2; col++)
          moutchar(col, row, (char)32, attr);
    }

void clearscreen(char attr)
    {
    clear(0, 0, 80, 25, attr);
    if(!attr)
       _setvideomode(_DEFAULTMODE);
    }

void gotoxy(unsigned char x, unsigned char y)
    {
    union REGS i;
    i.h.dh = y;
    i.h.dl = x;
    i.h.ah = 2;
    i.h.bh = 0;
    (void)int86(16, &i, &i);
    }

space getxy(void)
    {
    space cursor;
    union REGS i, o;
    i.h.bh = 0;
    i.h.ah = 3;
    (void)int86(16, &i, &o);
    cursor.x = o.h.dh;
    cursor.y = o.h.dl;
    return cursor;
    }

unsigned far keyboard(void)
    {
    unsigned ret_val = _bios_keybrd(_KEYBRD_READ);
    ret_val = (ret_val & 0x00ff) ? (ret_val & 0x00ff) :
       ((ret_val & 0xff00) / 0xff);

    return(ret_val);
    }

/* End of File */
```

Listing 9.8 — DIRECTIO.H

```
/*********************************************************************\
*                                                                   *
* DIRECTIO.H -  Definition for DIRECTIO.C for MS-DOS                *
*               (c) Guy Eddon, 1993                                 *
*                                                                   *
\*********************************************************************/

#define VID_NORMAL      0x07
#define VID_NORMAL_INT  0x0F
#define VID_REVERSE     0x70
#define VID_REVERSE_INT 0x78
#define VID_BLINK       0x87
#define VID_BLINK_INT   0x8F
#define VID_INVISIBLE   0x00
#define VID_BLUE        0x01
#define VID_CYAN        0x03
#define VID_WHITE       0x07
#define ESC             27
#define LWHITE          15
#define LRED            12

typedef struct
    {
    unsigned char x;
    unsigned char y;
    } space;

#define FOREGROUND_YELLOW    0x0006
#define FOREGROUND_CYAN      0x0003
#define FOREGROUND_WHITE     0x0007
#define FOREGROUND_BLUE      0x0001
#define FOREGROUND_GREEN     0x0002
#define FOREGROUND_RED       0x0004
#define FOREGROUND_INTENSITY 0x0008
#define BACKGROUND_CYAN      0x0030
#define BACKGROUND_BLUE      0x0010
#define BACKGROUND_GREEN     0x0020
#define BACKGROUND_RED       0x0040
#define BACKGROUND_INTENSITY 0x0080

#define SINGLE   0
#define DOUBLE   1
#define MAX_STR 100
```

Listing 9.8 — (continued)

```
extern void clearscreen(char screen);
extern void clear(unsigned char x1, unsigned char y1, unsigned char x2, unsigned char y2,
                  unsigned char attribute);
extern void gotoxy(unsigned char x, unsigned char y);
extern void read_field(unsigned char x1, unsigned char x2, unsigned char y, char *buffer);
extern void unsg_to_str(unsigned number, char far *buffer, unsigned char length);
extern void mxyputs(unsigned char x, unsigned char y, char far *buffer, unsigned char attribute);
extern void set_vid_mem(void);
extern void far mxyputc(unsigned char x, unsigned char y, char ch, unsigned char num, unsigned char attr);
extern void far moutchar(unsigned char x, unsigned char y, char character, unsigned char attribute);
extern void far box(unsigned char x1, unsigned char y1, unsigned char x2, unsigned char y2,char);
extern unsigned far keyboard(void);
extern space getxy(void);

#define WHITE_ON_CYAN FOREGROUND_WHITE|FOREGROUND_INTENSITY|BACKGROUND_CYAN

/* End of File */
```

Listing 9.9 — PRIME4.C

```
/**********************************************************************\
*                                                                    *
* PRIME4.C - Prime number example,  This example is for DOS          *
*           (c) Guy Eddon, 1993                                      *
*                                                                    *
* To build:  NMAKE PRIME4.DOS                                        *
*                                                                    *
* Usage:     PRIME4                                                  *
*                                                                    *
* Comments:  This example computes prime numbers.                    *
*                                                                    *
\**********************************************************************/

#include <STDIO.H>
#include <STRING.H>
#include <STDLIB.H>
#include <STDARG.H>
#include <LIMITS.H>
#include <WINDOWS.H>
#include <GRAPH.H>
#include <RPC.H>
#include <TIME.H>
#include "directio.h"
#include "prime4.h"

/* If we found a prime then return PRIME, otherwise return NOT_PRIME */

#define PRIME        1
#define NOT_PRIME    0

/* Coordinates for displaying numbers to be tested */

#define TESTING_X1   10
#define TESTING_Y1    3
#define TESTING_X2   30
#define TESTING_Y2   18

/* Coordinates for displaying prime numbers */

#define PRIME_X1     50
#define PRIME_Y1      3
#define PRIME_X2     70
#define PRIME_Y2     18

#define ERROR_EXIT    2
#define SUCCESS_EXIT  0
#define STRING_LENGTH 256

/* Colors used in this application */

#define WHITE_ON_BLUE FOREGROUND_WHITE|FOREGROUND_INTENSITY|BACKGROUND_BLUE
#define WHITE_ON_CYAN FOREGROUND_WHITE|FOREGROUND_INTENSITY|BACKGROUND_CYAN
#define RED_ON_BLUE   FOREGROUND_RED|FOREGROUND_INTENSITY|BACKGROUND_BLUE
```

Listing 9.9 — (continued)

```
/* Prototypes of functions used in this application */

extern void LocalComputer(void);
extern void RemoteComputer(void);
unsigned char IsPrime(unsigned long TestNumber);
unsigned long PrimeServerHandle;
void InitializeApplication(void);
void Usage(void);
extern void statistics(void);
extern void NotifyServer(void);
extern char ServerStatus(void);

/*
NextNumber      - Next available number to test
StartTime       - Time that we start to compute primes
CurrTime        - Current Computer time
NoPrimeLocal    - Number of primes computed locally
NoPrimeRemote   - Number of primes computed on the remote computer
StartNumber     - The starting number for testing primes
*/

unsigned long NextNumber = 1, NoPrimeLocal, NoPrimeRemote, StartNumber = 1;
clock_t StartTime, CurrTime, sleepTime;

char computer_name_buffer[255] = "MSDOS";
char Buffer[STRING_LENGTH];
unsigned  choice;
char rpc_on=FALSE;
char remote_only = FALSE;
PCONTEXT_HANDLE_TYPE phContext = NULL;

void main(int argc, char **argv)
    {
    RPC_STATUS status;
    DWORD Max_ComputerName_Length = 255;

    unsigned char * pszUuid             = NULL;
    unsigned char * pszProtocolSequence = "ncacn_np";
    unsigned char * pszNetworkAddress   = NULL;
    unsigned char * pszEndpoint         = "\\pipe\\prime";
    unsigned char * pszOptions          = NULL;
    unsigned char * pszStringBinding    = NULL;

    int count;
```

Listing 9.9 — (continued)

```
/* Allow the user to override settings with command line switches */
/* Default name MSDOS  ovrrride with C option*/

for(count = 1; count < argc; count++)
   {
   if((*argv[count] == '-') || (*argv[count] == '/'))
      {
      switch(tolower(*(argv[count]+1)))
         {
         case 'p': // protocol sequence
            pszProtocolSequence = argv[++count];
            break;

         case 'n': // network address
            pszNetworkAddress = argv[++count];
            break;

         case 'e':
            pszEndpoint = argv[++count];
            break;

         case 'o':
            pszOptions = argv[++count];
            break;

         case 'u':
            pszUuid = argv[++count];
            break;

         /* Default name MSDOS ovrrride with C option*/

         case 'c':
            strcpy(computer_name_buffer, argv[++count]);
            break;

         case 'f': /* first number */
            NextNumber = StartNumber = atol(argv[++count]);
            break;

         case 'r': /* remote_only */
            remote_only = atoi(argv[++count]);
            break;

         case 'h':
         case '?':
         default:
            Usage();
         }
      }
   else
      Usage();
   }
```

Listing 9.9 — (continued)

```
/* Use a convenience function to concatenate the elements of the string binding into the proper sequence */

status = RpcStringBindingCompose(pszUuid,
pszProtocolSequence,
pszNetworkAddress,
pszEndpoint,
pszOptions,
&pszStringBinding);

if(status)
    exit(ERROR_EXIT);

/* Set the binding handle that will be used to bind to the server */

status = RpcBindingFromStringBinding(pszStringBinding, &prime_IfHandle);

if(status)
    {
    printf("RpcBindingFromStringBinding  exit");
    printf(" %d",status);
    if(status == 6)
        printf("\n\n\t\tPlease load RPC runtime support!!");
    printf("\n\n\tPress any key");
    keyboard();
    exit(ERROR_EXIT);
    }

InitializeApplication();
ServerStatus();

while(1)
    {
    if(!(rpc_on==1 && remote_only ==1))
        {
        ++NextNumber;
        if((NextNumber-1)/2*2 == NextNumber - 1)
            ++NextNumber;
    LocalComputer();
    }

#define VID_BLINK 0x87
```

Listing 9.9 — (continued)

```
if(rpc_on)
   {
   ++NextNumber;
   if((NextNumber - 1) / 2 * 2 == NextNumber - 1)
      ++NextNumber;
   RemoteComputer();
   mxyputc((unsigned char)10, (unsigned char)21, (char)32, 65,
           FOREGROUND_CYAN|FOREGROUND_INTENSITY|BACKGROUND_CYAN);
   mxyputs((unsigned char)15, (unsigned char)21, "Prime number server is ",WHITE_ON_CYAN);
   mxyputs((unsigned char)35, (unsigned char)21, &pszNetworkAddress[2],WHITE_ON_CYAN);
   sprintf( Buffer, "(%ld)", PrimeServerHandle);
   mxyputs((unsigned char)(46),  21, Buffer, WHITE_ON_CYAN);
   }
else
   if(++choice > 100)
      {
      choice = 0;
      ServerStatus();
      if(rpc_on)
         {
         ++NextNumber;
         if((NextNumber - 1) / 2 * 2 == NextNumber - 1)
            ++NextNumber;
         RemoteComputer();
         mxyputc((unsigned char)10, (unsigned char)21, (char)32, 65,
                 FOREGROUND_CYAN|FOREGROUND_INTENSITY|BACKGROUND_CYAN);
         mxyputs((unsigned char)15, (unsigned char)21, "Prime number server is .", WHITE_ON_CYAN);
         mxyputs((unsigned char)15, (unsigned char)46, &pszNetworkAddress[2],WHITE_ON_CYAN);
         sprintf(Buffer, "(%ld)", PrimeServerHandle);
         mxyputs((unsigned char)(46),  21, Buffer, WHITE_ON_CYAN);
         }
      }
   else
      {
      if(strlen(pszNetworkAddress) < 3)
         mxyputs((unsigned char)15, (unsigned char)21,
            "Prime number server is off-line.  Please restart it.", WHITE_ON_CYAN|VID_BLINK);
      else
         {
         mxyputs((unsigned char)10, (unsigned char)21,
            "Prime number server ",WHITE_ON_CYAN|VID_BLINK);
         strcpy(Buffer,&pszNetworkAddress[2]);
         Buffer[10] = 0;
         mxyputs((unsigned char)30, (unsigned char)21, strupr(Buffer),WHITE_ON_CYAN|VID_BLINK);
         mxyputs((unsigned char)(30+strlen(Buffer)), (unsigned char)21,
            " is off-line.  Please restart it.", WHITE_ON_CYAN|VID_BLINK);
         }
      }
```

Listing 9.9 — (continued)

```c
         if(kbhit())
             if(ESC == keyboard())
                 {
                 NotifyServer();
                 clearscreen(0);
                 exit(0);
                 }
        }
   }

void LocalComputer(void)
   {
   while(NextNumber <= ULONG_MAX)
      {
      if(kbhit())
          if(ESC == keyboard())
              {
              NotifyServer();
              clearscreen(0);
              exit(0);
              }

      _settextwindow(5, 5, 18, 23);

      _settextcolor(1);
      _settextposition(14, 19);
      _outtext(" ");

      _settextcolor(LWHITE);

      sprintf(Buffer, "%ld", NextNumber - 1);
      _settextposition(14, 2);
      _setbkcolor(1);
      _outtext(Buffer);
      _settextposition(14, 13);
      _settextcolor(LWHITE);

      _outtext("LOCAL");

      if(IsPrime(NextNumber - 1) != 0)
         {
         _settextposition(14, 18);
         _settextcolor(LRED);
         _outtext("*");

         _settextwindow(5, 32, 18, 50);

         _settextcolor(1);
         _settextposition(14, 19);
         _outtext(" ");

         _setbkcolor(1);
```

Listing 9.9 — (continued)

```
            sprintf(Buffer, "%ld", NextNumber - 1);
            _settextcolor(LWHITE);
            _settextposition(14, 2);
            _outtext(Buffer);
            _settextposition(14, 13);
            _outtext("LOCAL ");

            NoPrimeLocal++;
            }
        statistics();
        return;
        }

    clearscreen(0);
    }

/* Test for prime numbers on the local computer */

unsigned char IsPrime(unsigned long TestNumber)
    {
    unsigned long count;
    unsigned long HalfNumber = TestNumber / 2 + 1;

    for(count = 2; count < HalfNumber; count++)
        if(TestNumber % count == 0)
            return NOT_PRIME;

    return PRIME;
    }

/* Allow the user to override settings with command line switches */

void Usage(void)
    {
    printf("\nSimple prime number example.\n\n");
    printf("Usage: PRIME4\n");
    printf(" -p protocol_sequence\n");
    printf(" -n network_address\n");
    printf(" -e endpoint\n");
    printf(" -o options\n");
    printf(" -u uuid\n");
    printf(" -f first number\n");
    printf(" -c Local Computer Name (Default: MSDOS)\n");
    printf(" -r 1 don't compute locally when the server is on\n");
    exit(SUCCESS_EXIT);
    }

void InitializeApplication(void)
    {
    set_vid_mem();
```

Listing 9.9 — (continued)

```
_clearscreen(_GCLEARSCREEN);
_settextwindow(1, 1, 25, 80);
_setbkcolor(3);
_clearscreen(_GWINDOW);
_settextwindow(5, 5, 18, 23);

_setbkcolor(1);

_clearscreen(_GWINDOW);

_settextwindow(5, 32, 18, 50);
_setbkcolor(1);

_clearscreen(_GWINDOW);

StartTime = clock();
box(0, 0, 79, 24, DOUBLE);
mxyputs(37, 0, " PRIME4 ", WHITE_ON_CYAN);

mxyputs(3, 2, "Testing...", WHITE_ON_CYAN);
box(3, 3, 23, 18, SINGLE);

mxyputs(30, 2, "Prime!", WHITE_ON_CYAN);
box(30, 3, 50, 18, SINGLE);

box(59, 3, 72, 6, SINGLE);

sprintf(Buffer,"First= %lu",StartNumber);
mxyputs(59, 9, Buffer, WHITE_ON_CYAN);
sprintf(Buffer,": (%s)",computer_name_buffer);
mxyputs(45, 0, Buffer, WHITE_ON_CYAN);

mxyputs(32, 23, "Press Esc to exit", WHITE_ON_CYAN);
}

void RemoteComputer(void)
{
char Buffer[STRING_LENGTH];
int loop;

while(1)
    {
    if(kbhit())
       if(ESC == keyboard())
          {
          NotifyServer();
          clearscreen(0);
          exit(0);
          }
    if(NextNumber >= ULONG_MAX)
       break;
    sprintf(Buffer, "%ld", NextNumber - 1);
    _settextwindow(5, 5, 18, 23);
```

Listing 9.9 — (continued)

```
      _settextcolor(1);
      _settextposition(14, 19);
      _outtext(" ");

      _settextcolor(LWHITE);
      _settextposition(14, 2);
      _outtext(Buffer);
      _settextposition(14, 13);
      _settextcolor(LRED);
      _outtext("REMOTE");

   RpcTryExcept
      {
      if(RemoteIsPrime(PrimeServerHandle, NextNumber - 1) != 0)
         {
         _settextwindow(5, 32, 18, 50);

         _settextcolor(1);
         _settextposition(14, 19);
         _outtext(" ");

         sprintf(Buffer, "%ld", NextNumber - 1);

         _settextcolor(LWHITE);

         _settextposition(14, 2);
         _outtext(Buffer);
         _settextposition(14, 13);

         _settextcolor(LRED);
         _outtext("REMOTE");

         NoPrimeRemote++;
         }

      statistics();
      }
   RpcExcept(1)
      {
      /* if exceptions occur */

      rpc_on = FALSE;
      return;


      }
   RpcEndExcept
   return;
   }
 }

void statistics(void)
   {
   char Buffer[STRING_LENGTH];
```

Listing 9.9 — (continued)

```
    CurrTime = (clock() - StartTime) / CLK_TCK;
    sprintf(Buffer, "Primes = %d", NoPrimeLocal + NoPrimeRemote);
    mxyputs(59, (unsigned char)(7), Buffer, WHITE_ON_CYAN);
    sprintf(Buffer, "Time = %ld.%02d min.", CurrTime/60, CurrTime%60);

    mxyputs(59, (unsigned char)(8), Buffer, WHITE_ON_CYAN);
    sprintf(Buffer, "%s:%5d", "LOCAL ", NoPrimeLocal);
    mxyputs((unsigned char)(60), (unsigned char)(4), Buffer, WHITE_ON_BLUE);
    sprintf(Buffer, "%s:%5d", "REMOTE", NoPrimeRemote);
    mxyputs((unsigned char)(60), (unsigned char)(5), Buffer, RED_ON_BLUE);
    }

/* Let the Server know that we are about to exit */

void NotifyServer(void)
    {
    RpcTryExcept
        {
        TerminatePrimeServer(PrimeServerHandle);
        }
    RpcExcept(1)
        {
        return;
        }
    RpcEndExcept
    }

/* Check the Server status if it is off line, then try to connect to it, returns Server status */

char ServerStatus(void)
    {
    char value = FALSE;

    RpcTryExcept
        {
        PrimeServerHandle = InitializePrimeServer(&phContext, computer_name_buffer);
        }
    RpcExcept(1)
        {
        value = TRUE;
        }
    RpcEndExcept
    rpc_on = !value;
    return value;
    }

void __RPC_FAR *__RPC_API MIDL_user_allocate(size_t len)
    {
    return(malloc(len));
    }
```

Listing 9.9 — (continued)

```
void __RPC_API MIDL_user_free(void __RPC_FAR *ptr)
    {
    free(ptr);
    }

/* End of File */
```

Listing 9.10 — PRIME4.DOS

```
################################################################
#                                                              #
# PRIME4.DOS - Make file for MS-DOS                            #
#                                                              #
################################################################

OSINCLUDE=C:\C700\INCLUDE\DOS

all : primec4

cc= cl
cflags= -c -AL -Gsw -Oas -Zpe -I$(OSINCLUDE)
linker= link
lflags= /NOD

# Make the client side application primec4
primec4 : primec4.exe

primec4.exe : primec4.obj prime4_c.obj prime4_x.obj directio.obj
    $(linker) $(lflags) primec4 prime4_c prime4_x directio,,NUL, oldnames llibce graphics rpc rpcndr;

# Update the object files if necessary

directio.obj: directio.c directio.h
    $(cc) $(cflags) $(cvars) directio.c

primec4.obj: primec4.c prime4.h
    $(cc) $(cflags) $(cvars) primec4.c

prime4_c.obj : prime4_c.c prime4.h
    $(cc) $(cflags) $(cvars) prime4_c.c

prime4_x.obj : prime4_x.c prime4.h
    $(cc) $(cflags) $(cvars) prime4_x.c

prime4.h prime4_c.c prime4_x.c : prime4.idl prime4.acf
    midl prime4.idl -cpp_cmd $(cc) -cpp_opt "-E"

# End of File #
```

Listing 9.11 — PRIME4.IDL

```
/*********************************************************************\
*                                                                   *
* PRIME4.IDL PRIME4 Interface Definition                            *
*           (c) Guy Eddon, 1993                                     *
*                                                                   *
\*********************************************************************/

[ uuid (72ABDE70-235B-5A4D-B352-026AB13562DA),
  version(1.0),
  pointer_default(unique)]
interface prime4
{
typedef [context_handle] void *PCONTEXT_HANDLE_TYPE;
typedef [ref] PCONTEXT_HANDLE_TYPE *PPCONTEXT_HANDLE_TYPE;

char RemoteIsPrime([in] unsigned long PrimeServerHandle, [in] unsigned long TestNumber);
unsigned long InitializePrimeServer([out] PPCONTEXT_HANDLE_TYPE pphcontext,
                                    [in, string] unsigned char *ComputerName);

void TerminatePrimeServer([in] unsigned long PrimeServerHandle);
}

/* End of File */
```

Listing 9.12 — PRIME4.ACF

```
/*********************************************************************\
*                                                                   *
* PRIME4.ACF PRIME4 Attribute Configuration File                    *
*           (c) Guy Eddon, 1993                                     *
*                                                                   *
\*********************************************************************/

[implicit_handle(handle_t prime_IfHandle)]
interface prime4
{

}

/* End of File */
```

Listing 9.13 — PRIMEC4.C (WFW)

```c
/**********************************************************************\
*                                                                    *
* PRIMEC4.C  -  PRIMEC4 client for Windows 3.1                       *
*              (c) Guy Eddon, 1993                                   *
*                                                                    *
\**********************************************************************/

#include <WINDOWS.H>
#include <STDIO.H>
#include <STRING.H>
#include <RPC.H>
#include <RPCNDR.H>
#include <STDLIB.H>
#include <MATH.H>
#include <LIMITS.H>
#include <TIME.H>

#define ERROR_EXIT     2
#define SUCCESS_EXIT   0
#define STRING_LENGTH 256
#define PRIME          1
#define NOT_PRIME      0

static cxChar, cyChar;

#include "prime4.h"              /* the RPC interface definitions     */
#include "primec4.h"             /* client-specific header file       */

HANDLE hInst;                    /* current instance                  */
HCURSOR hHourGlass, hOld;        /* during calls to RPC API functions */
char pszFail[MSGLEN];            /* RPC API failure message           */

RPC_STATUS status;               /* returned by RPC API function      */

unsigned char *pszUuid                      = NULL;
unsigned char *pszProtocolSequence          = "ncacn_np";
unsigned char  szNetworkAddress[UNCLEN+1]   = "\\\\servername";
unsigned char  szEndpoint[PATHLEN+1]        = "\\pipe\\prime";
unsigned char *pszOptions                   = NULL;
unsigned char *pszStringBinding             = NULL;

/* Prototypes of functions used in this application */

void  next_prime(void);
extern void LocalComputer(void);
extern void RemoteComputer(void);
unsigned char IsPrime(unsigned long TestNumber);
unsigned long PrimeServerHandle;
void InitializeApplication(void);
extern void statistics(void);
extern void NotifyServer(void);
extern char ServerStatus(void);
```

Listing 9.13 — (continued)

```c
/*
NextNumber     - Next available number to test
StartTime      - Time that we start to compute primes
CurrTime       - Current Computer time
NoPrimeLocal   - Number of primes computed locally
NoPrimeRemote  - Number of primes computed on the remote computer
StartNumber    - The starting number for testing primes
*/

unsigned long NextNumber = 1, NoPrimeLocal, NoPrimeRemote, StartNumber = 1;
clock_t StartTime, CurrTime, sleepTime;
char computer_name_buffer[255] = "WIN31";
unsigned choice;
char rpc_on = FALSE;
char remote_only = FALSE;
PCONTEXT_HANDLE_TYPE phContext = NULL;
char szString[MSGLEN + 1];

TEXTMETRIC tm;
HWND hWnd, hWndTest, hWndPrime, hWndStat;    /* Main window handle.    */

int APIENTRY WinMain(hInstance, hPrevInstance, lpCmdLine, nCmdShow)
    HANDLE hInstance;                           /* current instance    */
    HANDLE hPrevInstance;                       /* previous instance   */
    LPSTR  lpCmdLine;                           /* command line        */
    int nCmdShow;                               /* show-window type    */
    {
    MSG msg;
    UNREFERENCED_PARAMETER(lpCmdLine);

    if(!hPrevInstance)
       if(!InitApplication(hInstance))
          return(FALSE);

    if(!InitInstance(hInstance, nCmdShow))
       return(FALSE);

    StartTime = clock();

    while(TRUE)
       {
       if(PeekMessage(&msg, NULL, 0, 0, PM_REMOVE))
          {
          if(msg.message == WM_QUIT)
             break;
          TranslateMessage(&msg);
          DispatchMessage(&msg);
          }
       else
          {
          next_prime();
          }
       }
```

Listing 9.13 — (continued)

```
    NotifyServer();
    DestroyWindow(hWnd);

    return(msg.wParam);
    }

BOOL InitApplication(hInstance)
HANDLE hInstance;
    {
    WNDCLASS  wc;

    /* Fill in window class structure with parameters that describe the main window. */

    wc.style = NULL;
    wc.lpfnWndProc = (WNDPROC)MainWndProc;
    wc.cbClsExtra = 0;
    wc.cbWndExtra = 0;
    wc.hInstance = hInstance;
    wc.hIcon = LoadIcon(hInstance, "PrimeIcon");
    wc.hCursor = LoadCursor(NULL, IDC_ARROW);
    wc.hbrBackground = GetStockObject(WHITE_BRUSH);
    wc.lpszMenuName = "PrimeMenu";
    wc.lpszClassName = "PrimeWClass";

    /* Register the window class and return success/failure code. */

    return (RegisterClass(&wc));
    }

HDC hDC;

BOOL InitInstance(hInstance, nCmdShow)
HANDLE         hInstance;
int            nCmdShow;
    {
    hInst = hInstance;

    hDC = GetDC(hWnd);
    GetTextMetrics(hDC,&tm);
    cxChar = tm.tmAveCharWidth;
    cyChar = tm.tmHeight + tm.tmExternalLeading;
    ReleaseDC(hWnd,hDC);

    hHourGlass = LoadCursor(NULL, IDC_WAIT);
```

Listing 9.13 — (continued)

```
/* Create a main window for this application instance.  */

hWnd = CreateWindow("PrimeWClass",  "PRIMEC4 Windows Client",
                    WS_MINIMIZEBOX|WS_SYSMENU|WS_CLIPCHILDREN|WS_BORDER,
                    cxChar*5, cyChar*5, cxChar*66, cyChar*25,
                    NULL, NULL, hInstance, NULL );

/* If window could not be created, return "failure" */

if(!hWnd)
   return (FALSE);
ShowWindow(hWnd, nCmdShow);

hWndTest = CreateWindow("PrimeWClass", "Testing...", WS_CHILD|WS_VISIBLE|WS_BORDER,
                    cxChar*2, cyChar*2, cxChar*20, cyChar*18, hWnd,
                    NULL, hInstance, NULL );

/* If window could not be created, return "failure" */

if(!hWndTest)
   return (FALSE);
ShowWindow(hWndTest, SW_SHOW);

hWndPrime = CreateWindow("PrimeWClass", "PRIME...", WS_CHILD|WS_VISIBLE|WS_BORDER,
                    cxChar*(60-2-2-30), cyChar*2, cxChar*20, cyChar*18, hWnd,
                    NULL, hInstance, NULL);

/* If window could not be created, return "failure" */

if(!hWndPrime)
   return (FALSE);
ShowWindow(hWndPrime, SW_SHOW);

hWndStat = CreateWindow("PrimeWClass", "STATS...", WS_CHILD|WS_VISIBLE|WS_BORDER,
                    cxChar*(48), cyChar*2, cxChar*17, cyChar*7, hWnd,
                    NULL, hInstance, NULL);

/* If window could not be created, return "failure" */

if(!hWndPrime)
   return(FALSE);

ShowWindow(hWndPrime, SW_SHOW);
UpdateWindow(hWndPrime);

UpdateWindow(hWnd);
UpdateWindow(hWndTest);
UpdateWindow(hWndPrime);

rpc_on = FALSE;
```

Listing 9.13 — (continued)

```
        {
        FARPROC lpProc;
        lpProc = MakeProcInstance((FARPROC)Server, hInst);
        DialogBox(hInst, "ServerBox", hWnd, lpProc);
        FreeProcInstance(lpProc);
        }

/* Make the window visible; update its client area; and return "success" */

    return(TRUE);                   /* Returns the value from PostQuitMessage */
    }

long FAR PASCAL MainWndProc(hWnd, message, wParam, lParam)
HWND hWnd;
UINT message;
WPARAM wParam;
LPARAM lParam;
    {
    char Buffer[STRING_LENGTH];
    FARPROC lpProc;                 /* pointer to the dialog box function */
    PAINTSTRUCT ps;
    RECT rc;
    HBRUSH hBrush;

    switch(message)
        {
        case WM_PAINT:
            hDC = BeginPaint(hWnd, &ps);
            GetClientRect(hWnd, &rc);
            hBrush = CreateSolidBrush(RGB(255, 255, 255));
            FillRect(hDC, &rc, hBrush);
            DeleteObject(hBrush);
            EndPaint(hWnd, &ps);
            InitializeApplication();
            ValidateRect(hWnd, NULL);
            break;

        case WM_COMMAND:   /* message: command from application menu */
            switch (wParam)
                {
                case IDM_ABOUT:
                    lpProc = MakeProcInstance((FARPROC)About, hInst);
                    DialogBox(hInst,     /* current instance        */
                        "AboutBox",      /* resource to use         */
                        hWnd,            /* parent handle           */
                        lpProc);         /* About() instance address */
                    FreeProcInstance(lpProc);
                    break;
```

Listing 9.13 — (continued)

```
case IDM_SERVER:
  lpProc = MakeProcInstance((FARPROC)Server, hInst);
  DialogBox(hInst,     /* current instance      */
     "ServerBox",      /* resource to use       */
     hWnd,             /* parent handle         */
     lpProc);          /* Server  instance address */
  FreeProcInstance(lpProc);
  InvalidateRect(hWndStat,0,FALSE);
  break;

case IDM_ENDPOINT:
  lpProc = MakeProcInstance((FARPROC)Endpoint, hInst);
  DialogBox(hInst,     /* current instance      */
     "EndpointBox",    /* resource to use       */
     hWnd,             /* parent handle         */
     lpProc);          /* Server  instance address */
  FreeProcInstance(lpProc);
  break;

case IDM_FIRST:
  _ltoa(StartNumber, szString, 10);
  lpProc = MakeProcInstance((FARPROC)First, hInst);
  DialogBox(hInst,     /* current instance      */
     "FirstBox",       /* resource to use       */
     hWnd,             /* parent handle         */
     lpProc);          /* Server  instance address */
  FreeProcInstance(lpProc);
  NextNumber = StartNumber = strtoul(szString, NULL, 10);
  InvalidateRect(hWndTest, 0, FALSE);
  InvalidateRect(hWndPrime, 0, FALSE);
  InvalidateRect(hWndStat, 0, FALSE);
  break;

case IDM_REMOTE:
  {
  HMENU hmenu;
  BOOL fOwnerDraw;

  hmenu = GetMenu(hWnd);
  fOwnerDraw = GetMenuState(hmenu, IDM_REMOTE, MF_BYCOMMAND)
     & MF_CHECKED;
  if(fOwnerDraw)
     remote_only = FALSE;
  else
     remote_only = TRUE;
  CheckMenuItem(hmenu, IDM_REMOTE, MF_BYCOMMAND (fOwnerDraw ? MF_UNCHECKED : MF_CHECKED));
  }
  break;
```

Listing 9.13 — (continued)

```
        case IDM_LOCAL:
            strcpy(szString,computer_name_buffer);
            lpProc = MakeProcInstance((FARPROC)Local, hInst);
            DialogBox(hInst,     /* current instance        */
                "LocalBox",      /* resource to use         */
                hWnd,            /* parent handle           */
                lpProc);         /* Server  instance address */
            FreeProcInstance(lpProc);
            strcpy(computer_name_buffer, szString);
            InvalidateRect(hWndStat, 0, FALSE);
            break;

        case IDM_EXIT:
            NotifyServer();
            DestroyWindow(hWnd);
            break;

        default:               /* Lets Windows process it    */
            return(DefWindowProc(hWnd, message, wParam, lParam));
        }
        break;

    case WM_DESTROY:           /* message: window being destroyed */
        PostQuitMessage(0);
        break;

    default:                   /* Passes it on if unprocessed    */
        return (DefWindowProc(hWnd, message, wParam, lParam));
    }
    return (NULL);
    }

BOOL APIENTRY Server(
    HWND hDlg,                     /* window handle of the dialog box */
    UINT message,                  /* type of message              */
    UINT wParam,                   /* message-specific information   */
    LONG lParam)
    {
    UNREFERENCED_PARAMETER(lParam);

    switch(message)
        {
        case WM_INITDIALOG:             /* message: initialize dialog box */
            SetDlgItemText(hDlg, IDD_SERVERNAME, szNetworkAddress);
            return (TRUE);
```

Listing 9.13 — (continued)

```
    case WM_COMMAND:                    /* message: received a command */
        switch(wParam)
            {
            case IDCANCEL:              /* System menu close command? */
                EndDialog(hDlg, FALSE);
                return(TRUE);
            case IDOK:                  /* "OK" box selected?         */
                GetDlgItemText(hDlg, IDD_SERVERNAME, szNetworkAddress, UNCLEN);
                hOld = SetCursor(hHourGlass);
                if (Bind(hDlg) != 0)
                    {
                    EndDialog(hDlg, FALSE);
                    return(FALSE);
                    }
                SetCursor(hOld);
                EndDialog(hDlg, TRUE);
                return(TRUE);
            }
        }
    return (FALSE);                 /* Didn't process a message    */
    }


BOOL APIENTRY About(
    HWND hDlg,                      /* window handle of the dialog box */
    UINT message,                   /* type of message                 */
    UINT wParam,                    /* message-specific information     */
    LONG lParam)
    {
    UNREFERENCED_PARAMETER(lParam);

    switch(message)
        {
        case WM_INITDIALOG:         /* message: initialize dialog box */
            return (TRUE);

        case WM_COMMAND:            /* message: received a command     */
            if(wParam == IDOK       /* "OK" box selected?              */
            || wParam == IDCANCEL)
                {       /* System menu close command? */
                EndDialog(hDlg, TRUE);  /* Exits the dialog box        */
                return (TRUE);
                }
            break;
        }
    return (FALSE);                 /* Didn't process a message    */
    }


BOOL APIENTRY Endpoint(
    HWND hDlg,                      /* window handle of the dialog box */
    UINT message,                   /* type of message                 */
    UINT wParam,                    /* message-specific information     */
    LONG lParam)
    {
    UNREFERENCED_PARAMETER(lParam);
```

Listing 9.13 — (continued)

```
    switch(message)
        {
        case WM_INITDIALOG:            /* message: initialize dialog box */
            SetDlgItemText(hDlg, IDD_ENDPOINTNAME, szEndpoint);
            return (TRUE);

        case WM_COMMAND:               /* message: received a command    */
            switch(wParam)
                {
                case IDCANCEL:         /* System menu close command?     */
                    EndDialog(hDlg, FALSE);
                    return(TRUE);

                case IDOK:             /* "OK" box selected?             */
                    GetDlgItemText(hDlg, IDD_ENDPOINTNAME, szEndpoint, PATHLEN);
                    hOld = SetCursor(hHourGlass);
                    if(Bind(hDlg) != 0)      .
                        {
                        EndDialog(hDlg, FALSE);
                        return(FALSE);
                        }
                    SetCursor(hOld);
                    EndDialog(hDlg, TRUE);
                    return(TRUE);
                }
            }
    return (FALSE);                     /* Didn't process a message      */
    }

BOOL APIENTRY First(
    HWND hDlg,                         /* window handle of the dialog box */
    UINT message,                      /* type of message                */
    UINT wParam,                       /* message-specific information    */
    LONG lParam)
    {
    UNREFERENCED_PARAMETER(lParam);

    switch(message)
        {
        case WM_INITDIALOG:            /* message: initialize dialog box */
            SetDlgItemText(hDlg, IDD_MESSAGE, szString);
            return (TRUE);

        case WM_COMMAND:               /* message: received a command    */
            switch(wParam)
                {
                case IDCANCEL:         /* System menu close command?     */
                    EndDialog(hDlg, FALSE);
                    return(TRUE);
```

Listing 9.13 — (continued)

```
            case IDOK:                /* "OK" box selected?         */
                GetDlgItemText(hDlg, IDD_MESSAGE, szString, MSGLEN);
                RpcTryExcept
                    {
                    }
                RpcExcept(1)
                    {
                    MessageBox(hDlg, EXCEPT_MSG, "Remote Procedure Call", MB_ICONINFORMATION);
                    }
                RpcEndExcept
                EndDialog(hDlg, TRUE);
                return(TRUE);
            }                          /* end switch wParam          */
        }                              /* end switch message         */
    return(FALSE);                     /* Didn't process a message   */
    }

BOOL APIENTRY Local(
    HWND hDlg,                    /* window handle of the dialog box */
    UINT message,                /* type of message                 */
    UINT wParam,                 /* message-specific information    */
    LONG lParam)
    {
    UNREFERENCED_PARAMETER(lParam);
    switch(message)
        {
        case WM_INITDIALOG:          /* message: initialize dialog box */
            SetDlgItemText(hDlg, IDD_MESSAGE, szString);
            return(TRUE);

        case WM_COMMAND:             /* message: received a command    */
            switch(wParam)
                {
                case IDCANCEL:            /* System &menu close command?  */
                    EndDialog(hDlg, FALSE);
                    return(TRUE);

                case IDOK:                /* "OK" box selected?           */
                    GetDlgItemText(hDlg, IDD_MESSAGE, szString, MSGLEN);

                RpcTryExcept
                    {
                    }
                RpcExcept(1)
                    {
                    MessageBox(hDlg, EXCEPT_MSG, "Remote Procedure Call", MB_ICONINFORMATION);
                    }
                RpcEndExcept
                EndDialog(hDlg, TRUE);
                return(TRUE);
                }                          /* end switch wParam          */
            }                              /* end switch message         */
    return (FALSE);                        /* Didn't process a message   */
    }
```

Listing 9.13 — (continued)

```
RPC_STATUS Bind(HWND hWnd)
   {
   RPC_STATUS status;

   if(rpc_on == TRUE)
      {                              /* unbind only if bound       */
      NotifyServer();
      status = RpcBindingFree(&prime_IfHandle);
      if(status)
         {
         MessageBox(hWnd, "RpcBindingFree failed", "RPC Error", MB_ICONSTOP);
         return(status);
         }
      else
         rpc_on = FALSE;    /* unbind successful; reset flag */
      }

   status = RpcStringBindingCompose(pszUuid, pszProtocolSequence, szNetworkAddress,
                                    szEndpoint, pszOptions, &pszStringBinding);

   if(status)
      {
      wsprintf(pszFail, "RpcStringBindingCompose failed: (0x%x)\nNetwork Address = %s\n",
               status, szNetworkAddress);
      MessageBox(hWnd, pszFail, "RPC Runtime Error", MB_ICONEXCLAMATION);
      return(status);
      }
   status = RpcBindingFromStringBinding(pszStringBinding, &prime_IfHandle);

   if(status)
      {
      wsprintf(pszFail, "RpcBindingFromStringBinding failed:(0x%x)\nString = %s\n",
               status, pszStringBinding);
      MessageBox(hWnd, pszFail, "RPC Runtime Error", MB_ICONEXCLAMATION);
      if(status == 6)
         {
         wsprintf(pszFail,"Please load RPC runtime support!!");
         MessageBox(hWnd, pszFail, "RPC Runtime Error", MB_ICONEXCLAMATION);
         }
      return(status);
      }

   rpc_on = TRUE;                       /* bind successful; reset flag */
   ServerStatus();
   return(status);
   }
```

Listing 9.13 — (continued)

```c
void next_prime(void)
   {
   HDC hDC;
   char Buffer[STRING_LENGTH];

   memset(Buffer, ' ', STRING_LENGTH);
   hDC = GetDC(hWnd);
   if(!(rpc_on == 1 && remote_only == 1))
      {
      ++NextNumber;
      if((NextNumber - 1) / 2 * 2 == NextNumber - 1)
         ++NextNumber;
      LocalComputer();
      }

   if(rpc_on)
      {
      ++NextNumber;
      if((NextNumber - 1) / 2 * 2 == NextNumber - 1)
         ++NextNumber;
      RemoteComputer();

      TextOut(hDC,6 * cxChar, 21 * cyChar, Buffer, 16),
         TextOut(hDC, 15 * cxChar, 21 * cyChar, "Prime number server is ", 23);
      TextOut(hDC, 35 * cxChar, 21 * cyChar, &szNetworkAddress[2], strlen(&szNetworkAddress[2]));
      wsprintf(Buffer, " (%lu)", PrimeServerHandle);
      TextOut(hDC, 45 * cxChar, 21 * cyChar, Buffer, strlen(Buffer));
         {
         unsigned char len = strlen(Buffer);
         memset(Buffer, ' ', STRING_LENGTH);
         TextOut(hDC, (44 + len) * cxChar, 21 * cyChar, Buffer, 33);
         }
      }
   else
      if(++choice > 100)
         {
         choice =0;
         ServerStatus();
         if(rpc_on)
            {
            ++NextNumber;
            if((NextNumber - 1) / 2 * 2 == NextNumber - 1)
               ++NextNumber;
            RemoteComputer();
            TextOut(hDC, 6 * cxChar, 21 * cyChar, Buffer, 16),
               TextOut(hDC, 15 * cxChar, 21 * cyChar, "Prime number server is ", 23);
            TextOut(hDC, 35 * cxChar, 21 * cyChar, &szNetworkAddress[2], strlen(&szNetworkAddress[2]));
            wsprintf(Buffer, " (%lu)", PrimeServerHandle);
            TextOut(hDC, 45 * cxChar, 21 * cyChar, Buffer, strlen(Buffer));
               {
               unsigned char len = strlen(Buffer);
               memset(Buffer, ' ', STRING_LENGTH);
               TextOut(hDC, (44 + len) * cxChar, 21 * cyChar, Buffer, 33);
               }
```

Listing 9.13 — (continued)

```
            }
         }
      else
         {
         TextOut(hDC, 6 * cxChar, 21 * cyChar, "Prime number server ", 20);
         strcpy(Buffer, szNetworkAddress);
         Buffer[12] = 0;
         TextOut(hDC, 26 * cxChar, 21 * cyChar, Buffer, strlen(Buffer));
         TextOut(hDC, (27 + strlen(Buffer)) * cxChar, 21 * cyChar, " is off-line.  Please restart it.", 33);
         }
   ReleaseDC(hWnd,hDC);
   }

char nlineP = -1, nlineT = -1;

void LocalComputer(void)
   {
   RECT rUpdate;
   char Buffer[STRING_LENGTH];
   HDC hDCT,hDCP;

   if(NextNumber <= ULONG_MAX)
      {
      if(nlineT == 18)
         {
         ScrollWindow(hWndTest, 0, -cyChar, 0, 0);
         }
      else
         nlineT++;

      hDCT = GetDC(hWndTest);
      SetTextColor(hDCT, RGB(0, 0, 255));
      wsprintf(Buffer, "%lu", NextNumber - 1);
      TextOut(hDCT, cxChar, (nlineT - 1) * cyChar, Buffer, strlen(Buffer));
      TextOut(hDCT, 11 * cxChar, (nlineT - 1) * cyChar, "LOCAL    ", 9);
      GetUpdateRect(hWndTest, &rUpdate, FALSE);
      ValidateRect(hWndTest, &rUpdate);

      ReleaseDC(hWndTest, hDCT);

      if(IsPrime(NextNumber - 1) != 0)
         {
         if(nlineP == 18)
            {
            ScrollWindow(hWndPrime, 0, -cyChar, 0, 0);
            }
         else
            nlineP++;

         hDCP = GetDC(hWndPrime);
         SetTextColor(hDCP, RGB(0, 0, 255));
         wsprintf(Buffer, "%lu", NextNumber - 1);
         TextOut(hDCP, cxChar, (nlineP - 1) * cyChar, Buffer, strlen(Buffer));
         TextOut(hDCP, 11 * cxChar, (nlineP - 1) * cyChar, "LOCAL    ", 9);
```

Listing 9.13 — (continued)

```
        GetUpdateRect(hWndPrime, &rUpdate, FALSE);
        ValidateRect(hWndPrime, &rUpdate);
        ReleaseDC(hWndPrime, hDCP);

        NoPrimeLocal++;
        }
    statistics();

    return;
    }
}

unsigned char IsPrime(unsigned long TestNumber)
    {
    unsigned long count;
    unsigned long HalfNumber = TestNumber / 2 + 1;

    for(count = 2; count < HalfNumber; count++)
        if(TestNumber % count == 0)
            return NOT_PRIME;

    return PRIME;
    }

void InitializeApplication(void)
    {
    HDC hDC,hDCS;
    char Buffer[STRING_LENGTH];

    wsprintf(Buffer, "First= %lu", StartNumber);
    hDCS = GetDC(hWndStat);
    SetTextColor(hDCS, RGB(0, 0, 255));
    TextOut(hDCS, cxChar, 5 * cyChar, Buffer, strlen(Buffer));
    wsprintf(Buffer, "%s", computer_name_buffer);
    TextOut(hDCS, cxChar, 6 * cyChar, Buffer, strlen(Buffer));
    ReleaseDC(hWndStat, hDCS);

    hDC = GetDC(hWnd);
    TextOut(hDC, 2 * cxChar, 1 * cyChar, "Prime...", 8);
    TextOut(hDC, 26 * cxChar, 1 * cyChar, "Testing...", 10);
    ReleaseDC(hWnd, hDC);
    }

void RemoteComputer(void)
    {
    RECT rUpdate;
    HDC hDCT,hDCP;
    char Buffer[STRING_LENGTH];
```

Listing 9.13 — (continued)

```
if(NextNumber <= ULONG_MAX)
   {
   if(nlineT == 18)
      {
      ScrollWindow(hWndTest, 0, -cyChar, 0, 0);
      }
   else
      nlineT++;

   wsprintf(Buffer, "%lu", NextNumber - 1);
   hDCT = GetDC(hWndTest);
   SetTextColor(hDCT, RGB(255, 0, 0));
   TextOut(hDCT, cxChar, (nlineT - 1) * cyChar, Buffer, strlen(Buffer));
   TextOut(hDCT, 11 * cxChar, (nlineT - 1) * cyChar, "REMOTE", 6);
   GetUpdateRect(hWndTest, &rUpdate,FALSE);
   ValidateRect(hWndTest, &rUpdate);
   ReleaseDC(hWndTest, hDCT);
   RpcTryExcept
      {
      if(RemoteIsPrime(PrimeServerHandle, NextNumber - 1) != 0)
         {
         if(nlineP == 18)
            {
            ScrollWindow(hWndPrime, 0, -cyChar, 0, 0);
            }
         else
            nlineP++;

         hDCP = GetDC(hWndPrime);
         SetTextColor(hDCP, RGB(255, 0, 0));
         wsprintf(Buffer, "%lu", NextNumber - 1);
         TextOut(hDCP, cxChar, (nlineP - 1) * cyChar, Buffer, strlen(Buffer));
         TextOut(hDCP, 11 * cxChar, (nlineP - 1) * cyChar, "REMOTE", 6);
         GetUpdateRect(hWndPrime, &rUpdate, FALSE);
         ValidateRect(hWndPrime, &rUpdate);

         ReleaseDC(hWndPrime,hDCP);
         NoPrimeRemote++;
         }
      statistics();
      }
   RpcExcept(1)
      {
      rpc_on = FALSE;
      return;
      }
   RpcEndExcept

   return;
   }
}
```

Listing 9.13 — (continued)

```
void NotifyServer(void)
    {
    RpcTryExcept
        {
        TerminatePrimeServer(PrimeServerHandle);
        }
    RpcExcept(1)
        {
        return;
        }
    RpcEndExcept
    }

char ServerStatus(void)
    {
    char value = FALSE;

    RpcTryExcept
        {
        PrimeServerHandle = InitializePrimeServer(&phContext, computer_name_buffer);
        }
    RpcExcept(1)
        {
        value = TRUE;
        }
    RpcEndExcept
    rpc_on = !value;
    return value;
    }

void statistics(void)
    {
    HDC hDCS;
    char Buffer[STRING_LENGTH];

    CurrTime = (clock() - StartTime) / CLK_TCK;
    wsprintf(Buffer, "Primes = %lu", NoPrimeLocal + NoPrimeRemote);
    hDCS = GetDC(hWndStat);
    SetTextColor(hDCS, RGB(0, 0, 255));
    TextOut(hDCS, cxChar, 3 * cyChar, Buffer, strlen(Buffer));
    wsprintf(Buffer, "Time = %ld.%02d min.", CurrTime/60, CurrTime%60);

    TextOut(hDCS, cxChar, 4 * cyChar, Buffer, strlen(Buffer));

    wsprintf(Buffer, "%s:%5lu", "LOCAL    ", NoPrimeLocal);
    TextOut(hDCS, cxChar, 0, Buffer, strlen(Buffer));
    wsprintf(Buffer, "%s:%5lu", "REMOTE", NoPrimeRemote);
    SetTextColor(hDCS, RGB(255, 0, 0));
    TextOut(hDCS, cxChar, cyChar, Buffer, strlen(Buffer));

    ReleaseDC(hWndStat, hDCS);
    }
```

Listing 9.13 — (continued)

```
void __RPC_FAR *__RPC_API MIDL_user_allocate(size_t len)
    {
    return(malloc(len));
    }

void __RPC_API MIDL_user_free(void __RPC_FAR *ptr)
    {
    free(ptr);
    }
```

Listing 9.14 — PRIMEC4.H

```
/*********************************************************************\
*                                                                   *
* PRIMEC4.H  -  PRIMEC4 client header for Windows 3.1               *
*              (c) Guy Eddon, 1993                                  *
*                                                                   *
\*********************************************************************/

#ifdef WIN
#define APIENTRY PASCAL
#define UNREFERENCED_PARAMETER
#endif

#define IDM_ABOUT    100
#define IDM_SERVER   200
#define IDM_EXIT     300
#define IDM_ENDPOINT 400
#define IDM_FIRST    500
#define IDM_REMOTE   600
#define IDM_LOCAL    700

#define IDD_SERVERNAME   201
#define IDD_ENDPOINTNAME 401
#define IDD_MESSAGE      501

#define CNLEN   15      /* computer name length              */
#define UNCLEN  CNLEN+2 /* \\computername                    */
#define PATHLEN 260     /* Path                              */
#define MSGLEN  300     /* arbitrary large number for message size */

#define DEFAULT_SERVER NULL
#define DEFAULT_ENDPOINT    "\\pipe\\whello"
#define DEFAULT_MESSAGE     "hello, world"

#define EXCEPT_MSG "The remote procedure call failed. \
Please make sure the server application is running and \
that the server name and endpoint name are correct."

int APIENTRY WinMain(HANDLE, HANDLE, LPSTR, int);
BOOL InitApplication(HANDLE);
BOOL InitInstance(HANDLE, int);

LONG FAR APIENTRY MainWndProc(HWND, UINT, UINT, LONG);
BOOL APIENTRY About(HWND, UINT, UINT, LONG);
BOOL APIENTRY Server(HWND, UINT, UINT, LONG);
BOOL APIENTRY Endpoint(HWND, UINT, UINT, LONG);
BOOL APIENTRY First(HWND, UINT, UINT, LONG);
BOOL APIENTRY Remote(HWND, UINT, UINT, LONG);
BOOL APIENTRY Local(HWND, UINT, UINT, LONG);
RPC_STATUS Bind(HWND);

/* End of File */
```

Listing 9.15 — PRIME4.WIN

```
###################################################################
#                                                                 #
# PRIME4.WIN - Make file for Windows 3.1                          #
#                                                                 #
###################################################################

OSINCLUDE=C:\C700\INCLUDE\WIN

all: primec4.exe

cc= cl
cflags= -c -AL -Gsw -Oas -Zpe -I$(OSINCLUDE)
linker= link
lflags= /NOD

# Update the resource if necessary

prime4.res: prime4.rc primec4.h
    rc -r prime4.rc

# Update the executable file if necessary, and if so, add the resource back in.

primec4.exe: primec4.obj prime4.def prime4_c.obj prime4_x.obj prime4.res
    $(linker) $(lflags) primec4 prime4_c prime4_x,,NUL,\
    libw llibcew rpcw rpcndrw, prime4.def
    rc prime4.res primec4.exe

# Update the object files if necessary

primec4.obj: primec4.c primec4.h prime4.h
   $(cc) $(cflags) $(cvars) -DWIN primec4.c

prime4_c.obj : prime4_c.c primec4.h
   $(cc) $(cflags) $(cvars) prime4_c.c

prime4_x.obj : prime4_x.c primec4.h
   $(cc) $(cflags) $(cvars) prime4_x.c

prime4.h prime4_c.c prime4_s.c prime4_y.c prime4_x.c : prime4.idl prime4.acf
   midl prime4.idl -no_cpp

# End of File #
```

Listing 9.16 — PRIME4.IDL

```
/*********************************************************************\
*                                                                     *
* PRIMEC4.IDL - PRIMEC4 Interface Definition                          *
*              (c) Guy Eddon, 1993                                    *
*                                                                     *
\*********************************************************************/

[ uuid (72ABDE70-235B-5A4D-B352-026AB13562DA),
  version(1.0),
  pointer_default(unique)]
interface prime4
{
typedef [context_handle] void *PCONTEXT_HANDLE_TYPE;
typedef [ref] PCONTEXT_HANDLE_TYPE *PPCONTEXT_HANDLE_TYPE;

char RemoteIsPrime([in] unsigned long PrimeServerHandle, [in] unsigned long TestNumber);

unsigned long InitializePrimeServer([out] PPCONTEXT_HANDLE_TYPE pphcontext,
                                    [in, string] unsigned char *ComputerName);

void TerminatePrimeServer([in] unsigned long PrimeServerHandle);
}

/* End of File */
```

Listing 9.17 — PRIME4.ACF

```
/*********************************************************************\
*                                                                     *
* PRIMEC4.ACF - PRIMEC4 Attribute Configuration File                  *
*              (c) Guy Eddon, 1993                                    *
*                                                                     *
\*********************************************************************/

[implicit_handle(handle_t prime_IfHandle)]
interface prime4
{

}

/* End of File */
```

Listing 9.18 — PRIME4.DEF

```
;;;;;;;;;;;;;;;;;;;;;;;;;;;;;;;;;;;;;;;;;;;;;;;;;;;;;;;;;;;;;;;;
;                                                              ;
; PRIME4.DEF - Module Definition File                          ;
;              (c) Guy Eddon, 1993                             ;
;                                                              ;
;                                                              ;
;;;;;;;;;;;;;;;;;;;;;;;;;;;;;;;;;;;;;;;;;;;;;;;;;;;;;;;;;;;;;;;;

NAME        Client
DESCRIPTION 'PRIMEC4'
EXETYPE     WINDOWS
STUB        'WINSTUB.EXE'
CODE PRELOAD MOVEABLE DISCARDABLE
DATA PRELOAD MOVEABLE MULTIPLE
HEAPSIZE    1024
STACKSIZE   5120

EXPORTS
    MainWndProc   @1
    About         @2
    Server        @3
    Endpoint      @4
    First         @5
    Local         @7

; End of File ;
```

Listing 9.19 — PRIME4.RC

```
/*********************************************************************\
*                                                                   *
* PRIME4.RC  -  PRIMEC4 resource file                               *
*              (c) Guy Eddon, 1993                                  *
*                                                                   *
\*********************************************************************/

#include <WINDOWS.H>
#include "primec4.h"

PrimeMenu MENU
BEGIN
    POPUP               "&Remote Call"
        BEGIN
            MENUITEM            "&Server name",         IDM_SERVER
            MENUITEM            "&Endpoint name",       IDM_ENDPOINT
            MENUITEM            "&First Number",        IDM_FIRST
            MENUITEM            "&Remote Only",         IDM_REMOTE
            MENUITEM            "&Local Name",          IDM_LOCAL
            MENUITEM SEPARATOR
            MENUITEM            "E&xit",                IDM_EXIT
        END
    POPUP               "&Help"
        BEGIN
            MENUITEM            "&About RPC Prime...", IDM_ABOUT
        END
END

#include "prime4.dlg"

/* End of File */
```

Listing 9.20 — PRIME4.DLE

```
/*********************************************************************\
*                                                                   *
* PRIME4.DLG -  PRIMEC4 dialog boxes                                 *
*              (c) Guy Eddon, 1993                                   *
*                                                                   *
\*********************************************************************/


PrimeIcon ICON  prime4.ico

SERVERBOX DIALOG LOADONCALL MOVEABLE DISCARDABLE 67, 39, 102, 49
CAPTION "Server Name"
STYLE WS_BORDER | WS_CAPTION | WS_DLGFRAME | WS_SYSMENU | DS_MODALFRAME
BEGIN
    CONTROL "", IDD_SERVERNAME, "edit",
      ES_LEFT | ES_AUTOHSCROLL | WS_BORDER | WS_TABSTOP | WS_CHILD,
      4, 7, 95, 12
    CONTROL "OK", 1, "button", BS_DEFPUSHBUTTON | WS_TABSTOP | WS_CHILD,
      13, 26, 30, 14
    CONTROL "Cancel", 2, "button", BS_PUSHBUTTON | WS_TABSTOP | WS_CHILD,
      60, 26, 30, 14
END


ENDPOINTBOX DIALOG LOADONCALL MOVEABLE DISCARDABLE 67, 39, 102, 49
CAPTION "Endpoint Name"
STYLE WS_BORDER | WS_CAPTION | WS_DLGFRAME | WS_SYSMENU | DS_MODALFRAME
BEGIN
    CONTROL "", IDD_ENDPOINTNAME, "edit",
      ES_LEFT | ES_AUTOHSCROLL | WS_BORDER | WS_TABSTOP | WS_CHILD,
      4, 7, 95, 12
    CONTROL "OK", 1, "button", BS_DEFPUSHBUTTON | WS_TABSTOP | WS_CHILD,
      13, 26, 30, 14
    CONTROL "Cancel", 2, "button", BS_PUSHBUTTON | WS_TABSTOP | WS_CHILD,
      60, 26, 30, 14
END


FIRSTBOX DIALOG LOADONCALL MOVEABLE DISCARDABLE 67, 39, 102, 49
CAPTION "First Number"
STYLE WS_BORDER | WS_CAPTION | WS_DLGFRAME | WS_SYSMENU | DS_MODALFRAME
BEGIN
    CONTROL "", IDD_MESSAGE, "edit",
      ES_LEFT | ES_AUTOHSCROLL | WS_BORDER | WS_TABSTOP | WS_CHILD,
      4, 7, 95, 12
    CONTROL "OK", 1, "button", BS_DEFPUSHBUTTON | WS_TABSTOP | WS_CHILD,
      13, 26, 30, 14
    CONTROL "Cancel", 2, "button", BS_PUSHBUTTON | WS_TABSTOP | WS_CHILD,
      60, 26, 30, 14
END
```

Listing 9.20 — (continued)

```
LOCALBOX DIALOG LOADONCALL MOVEABLE DISCARDABLE 67, 39, 102, 49
CAPTION "Local Name"
STYLE WS_BORDER | WS_CAPTION | WS_DLGFRAME | WS_SYSMENU | DS_MODALFRAME
BEGIN
   CONTROL "", IDD_MESSAGE, "edit",
      ES_LEFT | ES_AUTOHSCROLL | WS_BORDER | WS_TABSTOP | WS_CHILD,
      4, 7, 95, 12
   CONTROL "OK", 1, "button", BS_DEFPUSHBUTTON | WS_TABSTOP | WS_CHILD,
      13, 26, 30, 14
   CONTROL "Cancel", 2, "button", BS_PUSHBUTTON | WS_TABSTOP | WS_CHILD,
      60, 26, 30, 14
END

ABOUTBOX DIALOG LOADONCALL MOVEABLE DISCARDABLE 25, 19, 144, 75
CAPTION "About RPC Prime"
STYLE WS_BORDER | WS_CAPTION | WS_DLGFRAME | WS_SYSMENU | DS_MODALFRAME |
   WS_POPUP
BEGIN
   CONTROL "Prime Number RPC", -1, "static",
      SS_CENTER | WS_GROUP | WS_CHILD, 0, 5, 144, 8
   CONTROL "Version 1.0", -1, "static", SS_CENTER | WS_GROUP | WS_CHILD,
      0, 14, 144, 8
   CONTROL "Microsoft Windows client example", -1, "static",
      SS_CENTER | WS_GROUP | WS_CHILD, 0, 23, 144, 8
   CONTROL "OK", 1, "button",
      BS_DEFPUSHBUTTON | WS_GROUP | WS_TABSTOP | WS_CHILD, 53, 59, 32, 14
   CONTROL "PrimeIcon", 104, "static", SS_ICON | WS_CHILD, 18, 43, 16, 21
END

/* End of File */
```

## Chapter 10

PRIME5 — *RPC Name Service*

Both the *PRIME3* and *PRIME4* clients require you to specify the name of a *PRIME* server. Unfortunately, users may not always be in the position to know the name of a compatible server and thus would be unable to use the application's distributed capacity. To solve this problem, the *PRIME5* client uses a special RPC mechanism, the Name Service, which allows it to bind to a server without knowing the server's name in advance.

The RPC Name Service, part of the OSF DCE specification, is a mechanism by which clients and servers locate each other. You can think of the Name Service as a piece of global memory spanning all the machines on the network. RPC applications manage the Name Service by calling special RPC runtime routines.

Applications that employ automatic binding incorporate the RPC Name Service automatically, since the function stubs generated by the MIDL compiler include the Name Service functions. In applications which are manual binding, however, the stubs do not contain the Name Service routines. Thus, with manual binding, the user must supply the computer's name when starting the client.

To expose the details of the Name Service mechanism, *PRIME5* uses the Name Service, but does not use the automatic binding stubs. Instead, it uses the manual binding stubs, meaning that the necessary Name Service code must be written as part of the application.

When you first load the server, it exports to the Name Service all the interfaces it wishes to make available. Each client process may then import all compatible server interfaces from the Name Service and choose those to which it wishes to bind. Once started, the client automatically finds the server and begins sending work to it.

The PRIME5 *Client*

The *PRIME5* client's user interface remain unchanged from *PRIME4*. In fact, the only notable addition to the *PRIME5* client code consists of the Name Service functions. The *PRIME5* client calls the *RpcNsBindingImportBegin()* function to begin importing the server interface.

The *RpcNsBindingImportBegin* function creates an import context for an interface and an object. The first parameter indicates the syntax of the second. The default value is *RPC_C_NS_SYNTX_DEFAULT*. The second parameter points to an entry name at which the search for compatible binding handles begins. The next parameter specifies the stub-generated interface handle. The fourth parameter is an optional UUID used for servers exporting multiple interfaces. In the *PRIME4* example, the default value *NULL* is used. The last parameter is a handle returned from this function that is used for later calls to the *RpcNsBindingImportNext* and *RpcNsBindingImportDone* functions.

```
status = RpcNsBindingImportBegin(RPC_C_NS_SYNTAX_DEFAULT,
                    "/.:/PRIME5",
                    PRIME5_ClientIfHandle, NULL,
                    &ImportContext);
```

As in the HELLO *program, starting the* PRIME5 *server the first time may take some time. The initial delay is caused by Windows NT starting the RPC Locator. Again, to avoid this initial lag, launch the RPC Services Control Panel and start the RPC services yourself.*

Before running PRIME5 *on two or more computers, you must modify each client computer's registry information. On the client computer, run the* C:\WINNT\SYSTEM32\REGEDT32.EXE *program. Select the* HKEY_LOCAL_MACHINE *window and choose* SOFTWARE — Microsoft — Rpc — NameService. *Then double-click on* ServerNetworkAddress *and enter* \\servercomputername, *where* servercomputername *is the name of the computer on which the* PRIME5 *server program will be running.*

It then calls *RpcNsBindingImportNext()* to cycle through the available interfaces.:

```
status = RpcNsBindingImportNext(ImportContext, &PRIME_IfHandle);
```

Finally, the client calls the *RpcNsImportDone()* function to end the import process:

```
status = RpcNsBindingImportDone(&ImportContext);
```

At this point, the client should have a valid server interface to which it can bind and make remote procedure calls.

Because the *PRIME5* client uses the Name Service, it does not need to supply the server's computer name as a command-line parameter. If, however, you want to use a specific *PRIME5* server, *PRIME5* lets you specify a computer name with a command-line switch.

The PRIME5 *Server*

The *PRIME5* server includes calls to the Name Service export functions used to export the server's interface:

```
status = RpcNsBindingExport(RPC_C_NS_SYNTAX_DEFAULT,
                    "/.:/PRIME5",
                    PRIME5_ServerIfHandle,
                    pBindingVector, NULL);
status = RpcNsBindingUnexport(RPC_C_NS_SYNTAX_DEFAULT,
                    "/.:/PRIME5",
                    PRIME5_ServerIfHandle, NULL);
```

Summary

While the Name Service functions are sometimes useful, they are often limited by a lack of flexibility. The *PRIME5* example uses the Name Service functions successfully. This provides the client program with the ability to automatically locate the *PRIME5* server. While Name Services are used productively in the *PRIME5* example, they might prove inadequate in other applications.

PRIME5   (CLIENT)   PRIME5

Command Syntax (Client)

```
PRIMEC5 [options]
```

Options

All options may be given in UNIX style (a leading hyphen) or DOS style (a leading slash).

```
-f n  Start search at n instead of one (one is the default).
-p    protocol_sequence
-n    network_address
-e    endpoint
-o    options
```

The *-p -n -e* and *-o* options correspond to the elements that determine the binding between the client and server. If you with to run *PRIME5* with a local server (on the same computer), do not specify a computer name (the -n option) on the command line.

```
-?
-h    Print usage summary and stop.
```

Termination

NextNumber reaches 4,294,967,296.

The user presses the *ESC* key.

Files

Makefile (builds both server and client)

```
PRIME5.MAK
```

File	Listing	Description
DIRECTIO.C	5.3	The *DIRECTIO* source code
DIRECTIO.H	5.4	The *DIRECTIO* header file
PRIMEC5.C	10.1	The *PRIME5* client C code
PRIMEP5.C	10.3	The *PRIME5* remote procedures C code
PRIME5.MAK	10.4	The *PRIME5* makefile
PRIME5.IDL	10.5	The *PRIME5* interface definition language file
PRIMEC5.ACF	10.6	The *PRIME5* attribute configuration file

Table 10.1   *Source files for* Prime5 *client.*

PRIME5   (SERVER)   PRIME5

Command Syntax (Server)

```
PRIMES5 [options]
```

Options

All options may be given in UNIX style (a leading hyphen) or DOS style (a leading slash).

```
-p   protocol_sequence
-e   endpoint
```

The -p and -e correspond to the elements that determine the binding between the client and server.

```
-m   maxcalls
-n   mincalls
-f   flag_wait_op
-s   security_descriptor
-?
-h   Print usage summary and stop.
```

Termination

NextNumber reaches 4,294,967,296.
The user presses the ESC key.

Files

Makefile (builds both server and client)

```
PRIME5.MAK
```

File	Listing	Description
DIRECTIO.C	4.1	The *DIRECTIO* source code
DIRECTIO.H	4.2	The *DIRECTIO* header file
PRIMES5.C	10.2	The *PRIME5* server C code
PRIMEP5.C	10.3	The *PRIME5* remote procedures C code
PRIME5.MAK	10.4	The *PRIME5* makefile
PRIME5.IDL	10.5	The *PRIME5* interface definition language file
PRIMEC5.ACF	10.6	The *PRIME5* attribute configuration file

Table 10.2   *Source files for the* PRIME5 *server.*

Listing 10.1 — PRIMEC5.C

```
/********************************************************************\
*                                                                   *
* PRIMEC5.C - Distributed prime number example                      *
*            (c) Guy Eddon, 1993                                    *
*                                                                   *
* To build:   NMAKE PRIME5.MAK                                      *
*                                                                   *
* Usage:      PRIMEC5                                               *
*                                                                   *
* Comments:   This is the client side prime number program.        *
*                                                                   *
\********************************************************************/

#include <STDIO.H>
#include <STRING.H>
#include <STDLIB.H>
#include <STDARG.H>
#include <LIMITS.H>
#include <CTYPE.H>
#include <WINDOWS.H>
#include <RPC.H>
#include "directio.h"
#include "prime5.h"

/* If we found a prime then return PRIME, otherwise return NOT_PRIME */

#define PRIME        1
#define NOT_PRIME    0

/* Max number of threads for this application */

#define MAX_THREADS    10

/* Coordinates for displaying numbers to be tested */

#define TESTING_X1    3
#define TESTING_Y1    3
#define TESTING_X2    23
#define TESTING_Y2    18

/* Coordinates for displaying prime numbers */

#define PRIME_X1    30
#define PRIME_Y1     3
#define PRIME_X2    50
#define PRIME_Y2    18
```

Listing 10.1 — (continued)

```
#define ERROR_EXIT     2
#define SUCCESS_EXIT    0
#define STRING_LENGTH 256
#define WAIT          350


/* Colors used in this application */

#define WHITE_ON_BLUE FOREGROUND_WHITE|FOREGROUND_INTENSITY|BACKGROUND_BLUE
#define WHITE_ON_CYAN FOREGROUND_WHITE|FOREGROUND_INTENSITY|BACKGROUND_CYAN
#define RED_ON_BLUE   FOREGROUND_RED|FOREGROUND_INTENSITY|BACKGROUND_BLUE
#define RED_ON_CYAN   FOREGROUND_RED|FOREGROUND_INTENSITY|BACKGROUND_CYAN


#define REMOTE_TRY       100
#define COMP_NAME_LENGTH   7


char on_line = 0;

/* Prototypes of functions used in this application */

unsigned char IsPrime(unsigned long TestNumber);
extern char ServerStatus(void);
extern void thread_local(void);
extern void thread_remote(void);
extern void Usage(void);
extern void InitializeApplication(void);
extern void statistics(void);
extern void NotifyServer(void);
extern void find_server(char);

/* Critical Section for choosing next available number for testing */

CRITICAL_SECTION GlobalCriticalSection;

/* Storage for local Computer Name */

char computer_name_buffer[MAX_COMPUTERNAME_LENGTH];

/* Storage for server Computer Name */

char ComputerNameServer[MAX_COMPUTERNAME_LENGTH];

/* Unique number returned by the server */

unsigned long PrimeServerHandle;
```

Listing 10.1 — (continued)

```
/*
NextNumber      - Next available number to test
StartTime       - Time that we start to compute primes
CurrTime        - Current Computer time
NoPrimeLocal    - Number of primes computed locally
NoPrimeRemote   - Number of primes computed on the remote computer
StartNumber     - The starting number for testing primes
*/

unsigned long NextNumber = 1, StartTime, CurrTime, NoPrimeLocal,
   NoPrimeRemote, StartNumber = 1;

/*
Context Handle - Contains binding information and information about
the state of the processing task on the server. State information is not
available to the client, it can be only accesses by the server
*/

PCONTEXT_HANDLE_TYPE phContext = NULL;

RPC_NS_HANDLE ImportContext;

void _CRTAPI1 main(int argc, char **argv)
   {
   RPC_STATUS status; /* returned by RPC API function */

   unsigned char *pszUuid            = NULL;
   unsigned char *pszProtocolSequence = "ncacn_np";
   unsigned char *pszNetworkAddress  = NULL;
   unsigned char *pszEndpoint        = "\\pipe\\prime";
   unsigned char *pszOptions         = NULL;
   unsigned char *pszStringBinding   = NULL;

   DWORD  Max_ComputerName_Length = MAX_COMPUTERNAME_LENGTH;
   DWORD  lpIDThread;
   HANDLE hthread_remote;

   int count;
```

Listing 10.1 — (continued)

```c
/* Allow the user to override settings with command line switches */

for(count = 1; count < argc; count++)
    {
    if((*argv[count] == '-') || (*argv[count] == '/'))
        {
        switch(tolower(*(argv[count] + 1)))
            {
            case 'p': /* protocol sequence */
                pszProtocolSequence = argv[++count];
                break;

            case 'n': /* network address   */
                pszNetworkAddress = argv[++count];
                break;

            case 'e':
                pszEndpoint = argv[++count];
                break;

            case 'o':
                pszOptions = argv[++count];
                break;

            case 'f': /* first number */
                NextNumber = StartNumber = atol(argv[++count]);
                break;

            case 'h':
            case '?':
            default:
                Usage();
            }
        }
    else
        Usage();
    }

if(pszNetworkAddress)
    {
    /*
    Use a convenience function to concatenate the elements of
    the string binding into the proper sequence
    */

    status = RpcStringBindingCompose(pszUuid, pszProtocolSequence, pszNetworkAddress,
                              pszEndpoint, pszOptions, &pszStringBinding);
```

Listing 10.1 — (continued)

```
    if(status)
       exit(ERROR_EXIT);

    /* Set the binding handle that will be used to bind to the server*/

    status = RpcBindingFromStringBinding(pszStringBinding, &prime_IfHandle);

    if(status)
       exit(ERROR_EXIT);
    }
else
    find_server(0);

GetComputerName(computer_name_buffer, &Max_ComputerName_Length);
ServerStatus();
InitializeApplication();

InitializeCriticalSection(&GlobalCriticalSection);

hthread_remote = CreateThread(NULL, 0, (LPTHREAD_START_ROUTINE)thread_remote,
                        NULL, 0, &lpIDThread);

thread_local();

DeleteCriticalSection(&GlobalCriticalSection);

/* The calls to the remote procedures are complete. Free the string and the binding handle */

/* remote calls done - unbind */

if(pszNetworkAddress)
   {
   status = RpcStringFree(&pszStringBinding);

   if(status)
      exit(ERROR_EXIT);
   }
else
   {
   /* remote calls done - unbind */

   status = RpcBindingFree(&prime5_ClientIfHandle);
```

Listing 10.1 — (continued)

```
    if(status)
        {
        printf("Unbinding from the prime number server. %d\n", status);
        exit(ERROR_EXIT);
        }
    }
  exit(SUCCESS_EXIT);
  }

void thread_local(void)
  {
  unsigned long temp;
  char Buffer[STRING_LENGTH];
  int loop;

  SMALL_RECT psrctScrollRectTesting, psrctScrollRectPrime;
  COORD coordDestOriginTesting, coordDestOriginPrime;
  CHAR_INFO pchiFill;
  WORD Color[TESTING_X2-TESTING_X1-3], Normal[TESTING_X2-TESTING_X1-3];

  COORD ComputTestCoord;
  COORD ComputPrimeCoord;

  DWORD dummy;
  COORD PrimeCoord;

  psrctScrollRectTesting.Left   = TESTING_X1+1;
  psrctScrollRectTesting.Top    = TESTING_Y1+2;
  psrctScrollRectTesting.Right  = TESTING_X2-1;
  psrctScrollRectTesting.Bottom = TESTING_Y2-1;

  coordDestOriginTesting.X = TESTING_X1+1;
  coordDestOriginTesting.Y = TESTING_Y1+1;

  psrctScrollRectPrime.Left   = PRIME_X1+1;
  psrctScrollRectPrime.Top    = PRIME_Y1+2;
  psrctScrollRectPrime.Right  = PRIME_X2-1;
  psrctScrollRectPrime.Bottom = PRIME_Y2-1;

  coordDestOriginPrime.X = PRIME_X1+1;
  coordDestOriginPrime.Y = PRIME_Y1+1;

  pchiFill.Char.AsciiChar = (char)32;
  pchiFill.Attributes = WHITE_ON_BLUE;
```

Listing 10.1 — (continued)

```
ComputTestCoord.X  = TESTING_X2-7;
ComputTestCoord.Y  = TESTING_Y2-1;
ComputPrimeCoord.X = PRIME_X2-7;
ComputPrimeCoord.Y = PRIME_Y2-1;

for(loop = 0; loop < TESTING_X2-TESTING_X1-3; loop++)
    {
    Color[loop]  = RED_ON_BLUE;
    Normal[loop] = WHITE_ON_BLUE;
    }

while(1)
    {
    if(VK_ESCAPE == get_character_no_wait())
        {

        /* If the user pressed ESC then notify the server and the exit*/

        EnterCriticalSection(&GlobalCriticalSection);
        Sleep(WAIT);
        NotifyServer();
        clearscreen(0);
        exit(0);
        LeaveCriticalSection(&GlobalCriticalSection);
        }

    /* To make sure that we won't test the same number twice */

    EnterCriticalSection(&GlobalCriticalSection);
    if((temp = ++NextNumber) >= ULONG_MAX)
        break;
    LeaveCriticalSection(&GlobalCriticalSection);

    EnterCriticalSection(&GlobalCriticalSection);
    ScrollConsoleScreenBuffer(hStdOut, &psrctScrollRectTesting, NULL,
                          coordDestOriginTesting, &pchiFill);
    sprintf(Buffer, "%d", temp - 1);
    mxyputs((unsigned char)TESTING_X1+2, (unsigned char)(TESTING_Y2-1),
            Buffer, WHITE_ON_BLUE);
    WriteConsoleOutputAttribute(hStdOut, Normal, 7, ComputTestCoord, &dummy);
    mxyputs((unsigned char)(TESTING_X2-7), (unsigned char)TESTING_Y2-1,
            "LOCAL ", WHITE_ON_BLUE);
    LeaveCriticalSection(&GlobalCriticalSection);

    if(IsPrime(temp - 1) != 0)
        {
        PrimeCoord.X = PRIME_X1 + 2;
        PrimeCoord.Y = PRIME_Y2 - 1;
```

Listing 10.1 — (continued)

```
        EnterCriticalSection(&GlobalCriticalSection);
        ScrollConsoleScreenBuffer(hStdOut, &psrctScrollRectPrime, NULL,
                            coordDestOriginPrime, &pchiFill);
        sprintf(Buffer, "%-17d", temp - 1);
        mxyputs((unsigned char)(PRIME_X1+2), (unsigned char)PRIME_Y2-1,
                Buffer, WHITE_ON_BLUE);
        WriteConsoleOutputAttribute(hStdOut, Normal, 7, ComputPrimeCoord,&dummy);
        mxyputs((unsigned char)(PRIME_X2-7), (unsigned char)PRIME_Y2-1,
                "LOCAL ", WHITE_ON_BLUE);
        LeaveCriticalSection(&GlobalCriticalSection);
        NoPrimeLocal++;
        }

    statistics();
      }
   }

void thread_remote(void)
   {
   unsigned long temp;
   char Buffer[STRING_LENGTH];
   int loop;

   SMALL_RECT psrctScrollRectTesting, psrctScrollRectPrime;
   COORD coordDestOriginTesting, coordDestOriginPrime;
   CHAR_INFO pchiFill;
   WORD Color[TESTING_X2-TESTING_X1-3], Normal[TESTING_X2-TESTING_X1-3];

   COORD ComputTestCoord;
   COORD ComputPrimeCoord;

   DWORD dummy;
   COORD PrimeCoord;

   psrctScrollRectTesting.Left   = TESTING_X1+1;
   psrctScrollRectTesting.Top    = TESTING_Y1+2;
   psrctScrollRectTesting.Right  = TESTING_X2-1;
   psrctScrollRectTesting.Bottom = TESTING_Y2-1;

   coordDestOriginTesting.X = TESTING_X1+1;
   coordDestOriginTesting.Y = TESTING_Y1+1;

   psrctScrollRectPrime.Left   = PRIME_X1+1;
   psrctScrollRectPrime.Top    = PRIME_Y1+2;
   psrctScrollRectPrime.Right  = PRIME_X2-1;
   psrctScrollRectPrime.Bottom = PRIME_Y2-1;
```

Listing 10.1 — *(continued)*

```
coordDestOriginPrime.X = PRIME_X1+1;
coordDestOriginPrime.Y = PRIME_Y1+1;

pchiFill.Char.AsciiChar = (char)32;
pchiFill.Attributes = WHITE_ON_BLUE;

ComputTestCoord.X  = TESTING_X2-7;
ComputTestCoord.Y  = TESTING_Y2-1;
ComputPrimeCoord.X = PRIME_X2-7;
ComputPrimeCoord.Y = PRIME_Y2-1;

for(loop = 0; loop < TESTING_X2-TESTING_X1-3; loop++)
   {
   Color[loop]  = RED_ON_BLUE;
   Normal[loop] = WHITE_ON_BLUE;
   }

while(1)
   {
   static unsigned char Notry=0;

   if(VK_ESCAPE == get_character_no_wait())
      {
      /* If the user pressed ESC then notify the server and the exit*/

      EnterCriticalSection(&GlobalCriticalSection);
      Sleep(WAIT);
      NotifyServer();
      clearscreen(0);
      exit(0);
      LeaveCriticalSection(&GlobalCriticalSection);
      }

   if(!on_line)
      {
      if(Notry++ > REMOTE_TRY)
         {
         Notry = 0;
         mxyputs((unsigned char)15, (unsigned char)21,
                 "        Attempting to connect to Prime Server        ", WHITE_ON_CYAN);
         find_server(1);
         ServerStatus();
         }
      else
          continue;
      }
```

Listing 10.1 — (continued)

```
        if(!on_line)
            continue;

        /* To make sure that we won't test the same number twice */

        EnterCriticalSection(&GlobalCriticalSection);
        if((temp = ++NextNumber) >= ULONG_MAX)
            break;
        LeaveCriticalSection(&GlobalCriticalSection);

        EnterCriticalSection(&GlobalCriticalSection);
        ScrollConsoleScreenBuffer(hStdOut, &psrctScrollRectTesting, NULL,
                                coordDestOriginTesting, &pchiFill);
        sprintf(Buffer, " %-17d", temp - 1);
        mxyputs((unsigned char)TESTING_X1+1, (unsigned char)(TESTING_Y2-1),
                Buffer, RED_ON_BLUE);
        WriteConsoleOutputAttribute(hStdOut, Color, 7, ComputTestCoord, &dummy);
        mxyputs((unsigned char)(TESTING_X2-7), (unsigned char)TESTING_Y2-1,
                strupr(ComputerNameServer), RED_ON_BLUE);
        LeaveCriticalSection(&GlobalCriticalSection);

        RpcTryExcept
            {
            if(RemoteIsPrime(PrimeServerHandle, temp - 1) != 0)
                {
                EnterCriticalSection(&GlobalCriticalSection);
                PrimeCoord.X = TESTING_X1 + 2;
                LeaveCriticalSection(&GlobalCriticalSection);

                PrimeCoord.X = PRIME_X1 + 2;
                PrimeCoord.Y = PRIME_Y2 - 1;

                EnterCriticalSection(&GlobalCriticalSection);
                ScrollConsoleScreenBuffer(hStdOut, &psrctScrollRectPrime, NULL,
                                        coordDestOriginPrime, &pchiFill);
                sprintf(Buffer, " %-17d", temp - 1);
                mxyputs((unsigned char)(PRIME_X1+1), (unsigned char)PRIME_Y2-1,
                        Buffer, RED_ON_BLUE);
                WriteConsoleOutputAttribute(hStdOut, Color, 7, ComputPrimeCoord,& dummy);
                mxyputs((unsigned char)(PRIME_X2-7), (unsigned char)PRIME_Y2-1,
                        strupr(ComputerNameServer), RED_ON_BLUE);
                LeaveCriticalSection(&GlobalCriticalSection);

                NoPrimeRemote++;
                }

            statistics();
            }
```

Listing 10.1 — (continued)

```
        RpcExcept(1)
            {
            /* if exceptions occur */

            find_server(1);

            ServerStatus();
            mxyputs((unsigned char)15, (unsigned char)21,
                    "Prime number server is off-line.  Please restart it.", WHITE_ON_CYAN);
            Sleep(WAIT);
            mxyputc((unsigned char)15, (unsigned char)21, (char)32, 52,
                    FOREGROUND_CYAN|FOREGROUND_INTENSITY|BACKGROUND_CYAN);
            Sleep(WAIT);
            }
        RpcEndExcept
        }
    }

/* Tests for prime number on the local computer */

unsigned char IsPrime(unsigned long TestNumber)
{
    unsigned long count;
    unsigned long HalfNumber = TestNumber / 2 + 1;

    for(count = 2; count < HalfNumber; count++)
        if(TestNumber % count == 0)
            return NOT_PRIME;

    return PRIME;
}

/* Displays command line options */

void Usage(void)
    {
    printf("\nDistributed client/server prime number example.\n\n");
    printf("Usage: PRIME5\n");
    printf(" -p protocol_sequence\n");
    printf(" -n network_address\n");
    printf(" -e endpoint\n");
    printf(" -o options\n");
    printf(" -f first number\n");
    printf("no parameters  auto find server\n");
    exit(1);
    }
```

Listing 10.1 — (continued)

```
/* Screen Initialization and colors and title lines */

void InitializeApplication(void)
    {
    char Buffer[STRING_LENGTH];
    set_vid_mem();

    clearscreen(BACKGROUND_CYAN);
    StartTime = GetTickCount();

    box(0, 0, 79, 24,DOUBLE);
    mxyputs(37, 0, " PRIMEC5 ", WHITE_ON_CYAN);

    mxyputs(TESTING_X1, 2, "Testing...", WHITE_ON_CYAN);
    box(TESTING_X1, TESTING_Y1, TESTING_X2, TESTING_Y2, SINGLE);

    mxyputs(PRIME_X1, 2, "Prime!",WHITE_ON_CYAN);
    box(PRIME_X1, PRIME_Y1, PRIME_X2, PRIME_Y2, SINGLE);

    mxyputs(58, 2, "Number of Primes", WHITE_ON_CYAN);
    box(58, 3, 73, (unsigned char)(1+5), SINGLE);

    sprintf(Buffer,"First = %d", StartNumber);
    mxyputs(58,(unsigned char)(1+5+3), Buffer, WHITE_ON_CYAN);

    mxyputs(32, 23, "Press Esc to exit", WHITE_ON_CYAN);
    }

/* Check the Server status if it is of line, then try to connect, return server status */

char ServerStatus(void)
    {
    char value = FALSE;

    RpcTryExcept
        {
        PrimeServerHandle = InitializePrimeServer(&phContext,
                                        computer_name_buffer, ComputerNameServer);
        ComputerNameServer[COMP_NAME_LENGTH] = 0;
        on_line = TRUE;
        mxyputc((unsigned char)15, (unsigned char)21, (char)32, 52,
                FOREGROUND_CYAN|FOREGROUND_INTENSITY|BACKGROUND_CYAN);
        }
    RpcExcept(1)
        {
        on_line = FALSE;
        value = TRUE;
        mxyputs((unsigned char)(60), (unsigned char)(5), "REMOTE", RED_ON_BLUE);
```

Listing 10.1 — (continued)

```
        mxyputs((unsigned char)15, (unsigned char)21,
                "Prime number server is off-line.  Please restart it.", WHITE_ON_CYAN);
        }
    RpcEndExcept

    return value;
    }

/* Dislay information about the progress of computing prime numbers */

void statistics(void)
    {
    char Buffer[STRING_LENGTH];

    CurrTime = (GetTickCount() - StartTime) / 1000;
    sprintf(Buffer, "Primes = %d", NoPrimeLocal+NoPrimeRemote);
    mxyputs(58, (unsigned char)(7), Buffer, WHITE_ON_CYAN);
    sprintf(Buffer, "Time = %d.%02d min.", CurrTime/60, CurrTime%60);
    mxyputs(58, (unsigned char)(8), Buffer, WHITE_ON_CYAN);
    sprintf(Buffer, "%s:%5d", "LOCAL ", NoPrimeLocal);
    mxyputs((unsigned char)(60), (unsigned char)(4), Buffer, WHITE_ON_BLUE);

    strcpy(Buffer,strupr(ComputerNameServer));
    Buffer[COMP_NAME_LENGTH-1] = 0;

    sprintf(Buffer, "%s:%5d", on_line?Buffer:"REMOTE", NoPrimeRemote);
    mxyputs((unsigned char)(60), (unsigned char)(5), Buffer, RED_ON_BLUE);
    }

/* Let the Server know that we are about to exit */

void NotifyServer(void)
    {
    RpcTryExcept
        {
        TerminatePrimeServer(PrimeServerHandle);
        }
    RpcExcept(1)
        {
        return;
        }
    RpcEndExcept
    }
```

Listing 10.1 — (continued)

```
/* Obtain binding information from a global name-service database */

void find_server(FromException)
   {
   RPC_STATUS status; /* returned by RPC API function */

   /* Create an import context for an interface and an object */

   status = RpcNsBindingImportBegin(RPC_C_NS_SYNTAX_DEFAULT, "/.:/Prime5"
                                 prime5_ClientIfHandle,NULL, &ImportContext);

   if(status == RPC_S_ENTRY_NOT_FOUND)
      {
      mxyputs((unsigned char)15, (unsigned char)21,
            "Prime number server is off-line.  Please restart it.", WHITE_ON_CYAN);
      Sleep(WAIT);
      mxyputc((unsigned char)15, (unsigned char)21, (char)32, 52,
            FOREGROUND_CYAN|FOREGROUND_INTENSITY|BACKGROUND_CYAN);
      Sleep(WAIT);
      }
   else
      if(status == RPC_S_NAME_SERVICE_UNAVAILABLE)
         {
         printf("\n\tNAME SERVICE UNAVAILABLE\n");
         exit(ERROR_EXIT);
         }

   else
      if(status)
         {
         printf("RpcNsBindingImportBegin  %d\n",status);
         exit(ERROR_EXIT);
         }

   /* Looks up an interface  from a name-service database */

   status = RpcNsBindingImportNext(ImportContext, &prime_IfHandle);

   if(status == RPC_S_NO_CONTEXT_AVAILABLE)
      {
      mxyputs((unsigned char)15, (unsigned char)21,
            "      No Rights to access Prime Server   !!!!!       ", RED_ON_BLUE);
      Sleep(WAIT);
      }
```

Listing 10.1 — (continued)

```
else
    if(status && status != RPC_S_NAME_SERVICE_UNAVAILABLE)
    {
    printf("RpcNsBindingImportNext  %d %d\n", status, prime5_ClientIfHandle);
    exit(ERROR_EXIT);
    }

status = RpcEpResolveBinding(prime_IfHandle, prime5_ClientIfHandle);
if(status)
    {
    printf("RpcEpResolveBinding  %d %d %d\n", status, prime_IfHandle, prime5_ClientIfHandle);
    exit(ERROR_EXIT);
    }

/* We are done looking for a compatible server */

status = RpcNsBindingImportDone(&ImportContext);

if(status && status != RPC_S_NAME_SERVICE_UNAVAILABLE)
    {
    printf("RpcNsBindingImportDone  %d  %d\n", status, ImportContext);
    exit(ERROR_EXIT);
    }
}

/* End of File */
```

Listing 10.2 — *PRIMES5.C*

```c
/********************************************************************\
*                                                                  *
* PRIMES5.C - Distributed prime number example                     *
*             (c) Guy Eddon, 1993                                  *
*                                                                  *
* To build:   NMAKE PRIME5.MAK                                     *
*                                                                  *
* Usage:      PRIMES5                                              *
*                                                                  *
* Comments:   This is the server side prime number example.        *
*                                                                  *
\********************************************************************/

#include <STDIO.H>
#include <STRING.H>
#include <STDLIB.H>
#include <STDARG.H>
#include <LIMITS.H>
#include <CTYPE.H>
#include <WINDOWS.H>
#include <RPC.H>
#include "prime5.h"
#include "directio.h"

/* If we found a prime then return PRIME, otherwise return NOT_PRIME */

#define PRIME          1
#define NOT_PRIME      0

/* Maximum Number of Clients to respond to */

#define MAX_CALLS      10

/* Coordinates for displaying numbers to be tested */

#define TESTING_X1     3
#define TESTING_Y1     3
#define TESTING_X2     23
#define TESTING_Y2     18

/* Coordinates for displaying prime numbers */

#define PRIME_X1       30
#define PRIME_Y1       3
#define PRIME_X2       50
#define PRIME_Y2       18
```

Listing 10.2 — (continued)

```
#define ERROR_EXIT      2
#define SUCCESS_EXIT    0
#define STRING_LENGTH 256

/* Delay time in microseconds */

#define WAIT           350
#define WAIT_DISPLAY 2000

/* Colors used in this application */

#define WHITE_ON_BLUE FOREGROUND_WHITE|FOREGROUND_INTENSITY|BACKGROUND_BLUE
#define WHITE_ON_CYAN FOREGROUND_WHITE|FOREGROUND_INTENSITY|BACKGROUND_CYAN
#define RED_ON_BLUE   FOREGROUND_RED|FOREGROUND_INTENSITY|BACKGROUND_BLUE
#define RED_ON_CYAN   FOREGROUND_RED|FOREGROUND_INTENSITY|BACKGROUND_CYAN
#define CYAN_ON_CYAN  FOREGROUND_CYAN|BACKGROUND_CYAN

/* Number of characters in computer name to display on the screen */

#define COMP_NAME_LENGTH 7

extern char IsPrime(unsigned long TestNumber);
extern void Usage(void);
extern void InitializeApplication(void);
extern unsigned long NoPrimes[MAX_CALLS];
extern unsigned long handles;
extern void thread_server(void);

extern char GlobalComputerNameBuffer[MAX_CALLS][MAX_COMPUTERNAME_LENGTH];

DWORD  lpIDThread;
HANDLE hthread_server;
CRITICAL_SECTION GlobalCriticalSection;

RPC_BINDING_VECTOR * pBindingVector;

void _CRTAPI1 main(int argc, char *argv[])
   {
   RPC_STATUS status;

   unsigned char *pszProtocolSequence = "ncacn_np";
   unsigned char *pszSecurity       = NULL;
   unsigned char *pszEndpoint        = "\\pipe\\prime";
   unsigned int cMinCalls          = 1;
   unsigned int cMaxCalls          = MAX_CALLS;
   unsigned int fDontWait          = FALSE;

   int i;
```

Listing 10.2 — (continued)

```c
/* allow the user to override settings with command line switches */

for(i = 1; i < argc; i++)
   {
   if((*argv[i] == '-') || (*argv[i] == '/'))
      {
      switch(tolower(*(argv[i]+1)))
         {
         case 'p': /* protocol sequence */
            pszProtocolSequence = argv[++i];
            break;

         case 'e':
            pszEndpoint = argv[++i];
            break;

         case 'm':
            cMaxCalls = (unsigned int) atoi(argv[++i]);
            break;

         case 'f':
            fDontWait = (unsigned int) atoi(argv[++i]);
            break;

         case 'h':
         case '?':
         default:
            Usage();
         }
      }
   else
      Usage();
   }

/* Tells the RPC runtime to use the specified protocol sequence combined
with the specified endpoint for receiving remote procedure calls */

status = RpcServerUseProtseqEp(pszProtocolSequence,
   cMaxCalls,      /* max concurrent calls */
   pszEndpoint,
   pszSecurity);  /* Security descriptor  */

if(status)
   {
   printf("RpcServerUseProtseqEp  %d\n", status);
   exit(status);
   }
```

Listing 10.2 — (continued)

```
/* Registers an interface with RPC runtime */

status = RpcServerRegisterIf(
    prime5_ServerIfHandle, /* interface to register    */
    NULL,                  /* MgrTypeUuid              */
    NULL);                 /* MgrEpv; null means use default */

if(status)
    {
    printf("RpcServerRegisterIf  %d\n", status);
    exit(status);
    }

status = RpcServerInqBindings(&pBindingVector);

if(status)
    {
    printf("RpcServerInqBindings  %d", status);
    exit(status);
    }

status = RpcNsBindingExport(
    RPC_C_NS_SYNTAX_DEFAULT,     // entry name syntax
    "/.:/Prime5",                // entry name
    prime5_ServerIfHandle,
    pBindingVector,
    NULL);

if(status==RPC_S_NAME_SERVICE_UNAVAILABLE)
    {
    printf("\n\tNAME SERVICE UNAVAILABLE\n");
    exit(ERROR_EXIT);
    }
else
    if(status)
        {
        printf("RpcNsBindingExport %d\n", status);
        exit(status);
        }

InitializeCriticalSection(&GlobalCriticalSection);

InitializeApplication();

mxyputs(23, 21, "Listening for prime number requests.", RED_ON_CYAN);

status = RpcServerListen(cMinCalls, cMaxCalls, fDontWait);
```

Listing 10.2 — (continued)

```
    if(status)
       exit(status);

    if(fDontWait)
       {
       status = RpcMgmtWaitServerListen(); /* wait operation */

       if(status)
          exit(status);
       }
    }

/* Displays command line options */

void Usage(void)
   {
   printf("\nDistributed client/server prime number example.\n\n");
   printf("Usage: PRIME5\n");
   printf(" -p protocol_sequence\n");
   printf(" -e endpoint\n");
   printf(" -m maxcalls\n");
   exit(EXIT_SUCCESS);
   }

/* MIDL allocate and free */
void *MIDL_user_allocate(size_t len)
   {
   return(malloc(len));
   }

void MIDL_user_free(void * ptr)
   {
   free(ptr);
   }

void InitializeApplication(void)
   {
   set_vid_mem();

   clearscreen(BACKGROUND_CYAN);

   box(0, 0, 79, 24, DOUBLE);
   mxyputs(37, 0, " PRIMES5 ", WHITE_ON_CYAN);

   mxyputs(TESTING_X1, 2, "Testing...", WHITE_ON_CYAN);

   box(TESTING_X1, TESTING_Y1, TESTING_X2, TESTING_Y2,SINGLE);
```

Listing 10.2 — (continued)

```
    mxyputs(PRIME_X1, 2, "Prime!", WHITE_ON_CYAN);
    box(PRIME_X1, PRIME_Y1, PRIME_X2, PRIME_Y2, SINGLE);

    mxyputs(32, 23, "Press Esc to exit", WHITE_ON_CYAN);

    hthread_server = CreateThread(NULL, 0, (LPTHREAD_START_ROUTINE)thread_server, NULL,
                        CREATE_SUSPENDED, &lpIDThread);

    SetThreadPriority(hthread_server, THREAD_PRIORITY_LOWEST);
    ResumeThread(hthread_server);
    }

/* Displays information about prime number production */

void thread_server()
    {
    RPC_STATUS status;

    while(1)
        {
        char Buffer[STRING_LENGTH], Buffert[STRING_LENGTH];
        unsigned char i;

        if(VK_ESCAPE == get_character_no_wait())
            {
            EnterCriticalSection(&GlobalCriticalSection);
            Sleep(WAIT);
            clearscreen(0);

            status = RpcNsBindingUnexport(
                RPC_C_NS_SYNTAX_DEFAULT,    // entry name syntax
                "/.:/Prime5", prime5_ServerIfHandle, NULL);

            if(status)
                {
                printf("RpcNsBindingUnExport %d\n",status);
                exit(status);
                }
            status = RpcEpUnregister(prime5_ServerIfHandle, pBindingVector, NULL);

            if(status)
                {
                printf("RpcEpUnregister %d\n", status);
                exit(status);
                }
```

Listing 10.2 — (continued)

```
        exit(EXIT_SUCCESS);
        LeaveCriticalSection(&GlobalCriticalSection);
        DeleteCriticalSection(&GlobalCriticalSection);
        }

    if(handles)
        {
        mxyputs(58, 2, "Number of Primes", WHITE_ON_CYAN);
        EnterCriticalSection(&GlobalCriticalSection);
        for(i = 0; i < handles; i++)
            {
            strncpy(Buffert, GlobalComputerNameBuffer[i], COMP_NAME_LENGTH);
            Buffert[COMP_NAME_LENGTH] = 0;
            sprintf(Buffer, " %7s:%5d ", Buffert, NoPrimes[i]);
            mxyputs(59, (unsigned char)(4+i), Buffer, WHITE_ON_CYAN);
            }
        box(58, 3, 74, (unsigned char)(4+handles), SINGLE);
        mxyputc(58, (unsigned char)(5+i), (char)32, 17, CYAN_ON_CYAN);
        LeaveCriticalSection(&GlobalCriticalSection);
        }
    else
        for(i = 0; i < 13; i++)
            mxyputc(58, (unsigned char)(2+i), (char)32, 17, CYAN_ON_CYAN);

    if(!handles)
        {
        mxyputs(23, 21, "Listening for prime number requests.", RED_ON_CYAN);
        Sleep(WAIT_DISPLAY);
        }
    mxyputc(23, 21, (char)32, 36, CYAN_ON_CYAN);
    }
  }

/* End of File */
```

Listing 10.3 — PRIMEP5.C

```
/********************************************************************\
*                                                                  *
* PRIMEP5.C - Distributed prime number example                     *
*            (c) Guy Eddon, 1993                                    *
*                                                                  *
* To build:   NMAKE PRIME5.MAK                                      *
*                                                                  *
* Usage:      PRIMES5                                               *
*                                                                  *
* Comments:   These are the remote procedures called by the clients. *
*                                                                  *
\********************************************************************/

#include <STDIO.H>
#include <STRING.H>
#include <STDLIB.H>
#include <STDARG.H>
#include <LIMITS.H>
#include <CTYPE.H>
#include <WINDOWS.H>
#include <RPC.H>
#include "prime5.h"
#include "directio.h"

/* If we found a prime then return PRIME, otherwise return NOT_PRIME */

#define PRIME        1
#define NOT_PRIME    0

/* Maximum Number of Clients to respond to */

#define MAX_CALLS    10

/* Coordinates for displaying numbers to be tested */

#define TESTING_X1   3
#define TESTING_Y1   3
#define TESTING_X2   23
#define TESTING_Y2   18

/* Coordinates for displaying prime numbers */

#define PRIME_X1     30
#define PRIME_Y1     3
#define PRIME_X2     50
#define PRIME_Y2     18

#define ERROR_EXIT   2
```

Listing 10.3 — (continued)

```
#define SUCCESS_EXIT    0
#define STRING_LENGTH 256

/* Time delay in microseconds */

#define WAIT          350
#define WAIT_DISPLAY 2000

/* Colors used in this application */

#define WHITE_ON_BLUE FOREGROUND_WHITE|FOREGROUND_INTENSITY|BACKGROUND_BLUE
#define WHITE_ON_CYAN FOREGROUND_WHITE|FOREGROUND_INTENSITY|BACKGROUND_CYAN
#define RED_ON_BLUE   FOREGROUND_RED|FOREGROUND_INTENSITY|BACKGROUND_BLUE
#define RED_ON_CYAN   FOREGROUND_RED|FOREGROUND_INTENSITY|BACKGROUND_CYAN
#define CYAN_ON_CYAN  FOREGROUND_CYAN|BACKGROUND_CYAN

/* Number of characters in computer name to display on the screen */

#define COMP_NAME_LENGTH 7

/* Critical Section for choosing next available number for testing */

extern CRITICAL_SECTION GlobalCriticalSection;

/* Number of clients that we are connected to */

unsigned long handles = 0,handlesp=0;

/* Name of server that we are connected to */

char ComputerNameServer[MAX_COMPUTERNAME_LENGTH];

char GlobalComputerNameBuffer[MAX_CALLS][MAX_COMPUTERNAME_LENGTH];

/* Number of primes for each client */

unsigned long NoPrimes[MAX_CALLS];

/* Unique identifier that we return to each client */

unsigned long GlobalComputerHandleBuffer[MAX_CALLS];

/* Global variable to help us to produce a unique number */

unsigned long handle_mod = 1;
```

Listing 10.3 — (continued)

```c
/* This function is called by the client, we return a unique number,
so in the future we can keep track who called us */

unsigned long InitializePrimeServer(PPCONTEXT_HANDLE_TYPE pphContext,
                                unsigned char *ComputerName, char *ComputerNameServer)
  {
  DWORD  Max_ComputerName_Length = MAX_COMPUTERNAME_LENGTH;
  char Buffer[STRING_LENGTH];
  unsigned long unique_handle;

  EnterCriticalSection(&GlobalCriticalSection);
  unique_handle = handles + 10 * handle_mod++;

  GetComputerName(ComputerNameServer, &Max_ComputerName_Length);

  strcpy(GlobalComputerNameBuffer[handles], ComputerName);

  mxyputc(2, 21, (char)32, 75, CYAN_ON_CYAN);
  sprintf(Buffer, "Computer %s logged in.", ComputerName);
  mxyputs(27, 21, Buffer, RED_ON_CYAN);
  sprintf(Buffer, "(%ld)", unique_handle);
  mxyputs(54, 21, Buffer, RED_ON_CYAN);
  Sleep(2 * WAIT_DISPLAY);
  mxyputc(2, 21, (char)32, 75, CYAN_ON_CYAN);

  GlobalComputerHandleBuffer[handles] = unique_handle;

  *pphContext = (PCONTEXT_HANDLE_TYPE)unique_handle;

  NoPrimes[handles] = 0;

  handles++;
  handlesp = handles;
  LeaveCriticalSection(&GlobalCriticalSection);

  return unique_handle;
  }
```

Listing 10.3 — (continued)

```c
/*  This function was called by the client. The client supplied his
    identifier and the number to test if it is a prime          */

unsigned char RemoteIsPrime(unsigned long PrimeServerHandle, unsigned long TestNumber)
    {
    unsigned long count;
    unsigned long HalfNumber = TestNumber / 2 + 1;
    char Buffer[STRING_LENGTH];
    char LocalComputerName[MAX_COMPUTERNAME_LENGTH];
    int loop;

    SMALL_RECT psrctScrollRectTesting, psrctScrollRectPrime;
    COORD coordDestOriginTesting, coordDestOriginPrime;
    CHAR_INFO pchiFill;
    WORD Local[COMP_NAME_LENGTH];

    COORD ComputTestCoord;
    COORD ComputPrimeCoord;
    DWORD dummy;

    EnterCriticalSection(&GlobalCriticalSection);

    /* Lets find out the name of client computer */

    for(loop = 0; loop < (int)handles; loop++)
       if(GlobalComputerHandleBuffer[loop] == PrimeServerHandle)
          {
          strcpy(LocalComputerName, GlobalComputerNameBuffer[loop]);
          PrimeServerHandle = loop;
          break;
          }

    LeaveCriticalSection(&GlobalCriticalSection);

    psrctScrollRectTesting.Left   = TESTING_X1+1;
    psrctScrollRectTesting.Top    = TESTING_Y1+2;
    psrctScrollRectTesting.Right  = TESTING_X2-1;
    psrctScrollRectTesting.Bottom = TESTING_Y2-1;

    coordDestOriginTesting.X = TESTING_X1+1;
    coordDestOriginTesting.Y = TESTING_Y1+1;

    psrctScrollRectPrime.Left   = PRIME_X1+1;
    psrctScrollRectPrime.Top    = PRIME_Y1+2;
    psrctScrollRectPrime.Right  = PRIME_X2-1;
    psrctScrollRectPrime.Bottom = PRIME_Y2-1;
```

Listing 10.3 — (continued)

```
coordDestOriginPrime.X = PRIME_X1+1;
coordDestOriginPrime.Y = PRIME_Y1+1;

pchiFill.Char.AsciiChar = (char)32;
pchiFill.Attributes = WHITE_ON_BLUE;

ComputTestCoord.X  = TESTING_X2-7;
ComputTestCoord.Y  = TESTING_Y2-1;
ComputPrimeCoord.X = PRIME_X2-7;
ComputPrimeCoord.Y = PRIME_Y2-1;

for(loop = 0; loop < COMP_NAME_LENGTH; loop++)
   Local[loop] = WHITE_ON_BLUE;

sprintf(Buffer, "%d", TestNumber);

EnterCriticalSection(&GlobalCriticalSection);
ScrollConsoleScreenBuffer(hStdOut, &psrctScrollRectTesting, NULL,
                          coordDestOriginTesting, &pchiFill);
sprintf(Buffer, "%d", TestNumber);
mxyputs((unsigned char)TESTING_X1+2, (unsigned char)(TESTING_Y2-1),
        Buffer, WHITE_ON_BLUE);
WriteConsoleOutputAttribute(hStdOut, Local, COMP_NAME_LENGTH, ComputTestCoord, &dummy);
LocalComputerName[COMP_NAME_LENGTH] = 0;
mxyputs((unsigned char)(TESTING_X2-7), (unsigned char)TESTING_Y2-1,
       LocalComputerName, WHITE_ON_BLUE);
LeaveCriticalSection(&GlobalCriticalSection);

for(count = 2; count < HalfNumber; count++)
   if(TestNumber % count == 0)
     return NOT_PRIME;

sprintf(Buffer, "%d", TestNumber);

EnterCriticalSection(&GlobalCriticalSection);
ScrollConsoleScreenBuffer(hStdOut, &psrctScrollRectPrime, NULL,
                          coordDestOriginPrime, &pchiFill);
sprintf(Buffer, "%d", TestNumber);
mxyputs((unsigned char)(PRIME_X1+2),
   (unsigned char)PRIME_Y2-1, Buffer, WHITE_ON_BLUE);
WriteConsoleOutputAttribute(hStdOut, Local, COMP_NAME_LENGTH, ComputPrimeCoord, &dummy);
mxyputs((unsigned char)(PRIME_X2-7), (unsigned char)PRIME_Y2-1,
        LocalComputerName, WHITE_ON_BLUE);
NoPrimes[PrimeServerHandle]++;
LeaveCriticalSection(&GlobalCriticalSection);

return PRIME;
}
```

Listing 10.3 — (continued)

```c
/* If the user pressed ESC then exit */

void TerminatePrimeServer(unsigned long PrimeServerHandle)
    {
    char Buffer[256+MAX_COMPUTERNAME_LENGTH];
    unsigned char loop, loopshift;

    EnterCriticalSection(&GlobalCriticalSection);

    for(loop = 0; loop < (unsigned char)handles; loop++)
        {
        if(GlobalComputerHandleBuffer[loop] == PrimeServerHandle)
            {
             /* Let's put terminating message on the screen */

            mxyputc(2, 21, (char)32, 75, CYAN_ON_CYAN);
            sprintf(Buffer, "Computer %s Exited!", GlobalComputerNameBuffer[loop]);
            mxyputs(27, 21, Buffer, RED_ON_CYAN);
            mxyputc(59, (unsigned char)(4+loop), (char)32, 15, CYAN_ON_CYAN);
            Sleep(WAIT_DISPLAY);
            mxyputc(2, 21, (char)32, 75, CYAN_ON_CYAN);
            break;
            }
        }

    /* Let's remove his name from our table */

    if(loop < handles-1)
        {
        loopshift = loop;
        for(loop = loopshift; loop < (unsigned char)(handles-1); loop++)
            {
            strcpy(GlobalComputerNameBuffer[loop], GlobalComputerNameBuffer[loop+1]);
            GlobalComputerHandleBuffer[loop] = GlobalComputerHandleBuffer[loop+1];
            NoPrimes[loop] = NoPrimes[loop+1];
            }
        }

    /* We have one client less */

    handles--;
    LeaveCriticalSection(&GlobalCriticalSection);
    }
```

Listing 10.3 — (continued)

```
void PCONTEXT_HANDLE_TYPE_rundown(PCONTEXT_HANDLE_TYPE phContext)
   {
   if(handlesp == handles)
     {
     mxyputs(27, 2, "rundown Executed", RED_ON_CYAN);
     TerminatePrimeServer((unsigned long) phContext);
     Sleep(2000);
     mxyputs(27, 2, "                ", CYAN_ON_CYAN);
     }
   handlesp = handles;
   }

/* End of File */
```

Listing 10.4 — PRIME5.MAK

```
##################################################################
#                                                                #
# PRIME5.MAK - Makefile                                          #
#                                                                #
##################################################################

!include <ntwin32.mak>

!if "$(CPU)" == "i386"
cvtomf =
cflags = $(cflags:G3=Gz)
!endif
!if "$(CPU)" == "MIPS"
cvtomf = mip2coff $@
!endif

.c.obj:
    $(cc) $(cflags) $(cvarsmt) $<
    $(cvtomf)

all : primec5 primes5

primec5 : primec5.exe
primec5.exe : primec5.obj prime5_c.obj prime5_x.obj directio.obj
    $(link) $(conflags) -out:primec5.exe \
      primec5.obj prime5_c.obj prime5_x.obj directio.obj \
      rpcrt4.lib rpcndr.lib rpcns4.lib $(conlibsmt)

primec5.obj : primec5.c prime5.h

directio.obj : directio.c directio.h
    $(cc) $(cflags) $(cvarsmt) directio.c
    $(cvtomf)

prime5_c.obj : prime5_c.c prime5.h
    $(cc) $(cflags) $(cvarsmt) prime5_c.c
    $(cvtomf)

prime5_x.obj : prime5_x.c prime5.h
    $(cc) $(cflags) $(cvarsmt) prime5_x.c
    $(cvtomf)
```

Listing 10.4 — (continued)

```
primes5 : primes5.exe
primes5.exe : primes5.obj primep5.obj prime5_s.obj
  prime5_y.obj directio.obj
    $(link) $(conflags) -out:primes5.exe \
      primes5.obj prime5_s.obj primep5.obj prime5_y.obj directio.obj \
      rpcrt4.lib rpcndr.lib rpcns4.lib $(conlibsmt)

primes5.obj : primes5.c prime5.h

primep5.obj : primep5.c prime5.h

prime5_s.obj : prime5_s.c prime5.h
  $(cc) $(cflags) $(cvarsmt) prime5_s.c
  $(cvtomf)

prime5_y.obj : prime5_y.c prime5.h
  $(cc) $(cflags) $(cvarsmt) prime5_y.c
  $(cvtomf)

prime5.h prime5_c.c prime5_x.c prime5_s.c
  prime5_y.c : prime5.idl prime5.acf
    midl -cpp_cmd $(cc) -cpp_opt "-E"  prime5.idl

# End of File #
```

Listing 10.5 — PRIMEC5.IDL

```
/******************************************************************\
*                                                                  *
* PRIMEC5.IDL PRIME5 Interace Definition File                      *
*          (c) Guy Eddon, 1993                                     *
*                                                                  *
\******************************************************************/

[ uuid (26521ABE-C35B-10A5-B027-01BE7351D2DA),
  version(1.0),
  pointer_default(unique)]
interface prime5
{
typedef [context_handle] void *PCONTEXT_HANDLE_TYPE;
typedef [ref] PCONTEXT_HANDLE_TYPE *PPCONTEXT_HANDLE_TYPE;

char RemoteIsPrime([in] unsigned long PrimeServerHandle, [in] unsigned long TestNumber);

unsigned long InitializePrimeServer([out] PPCONTEXT_HANDLE_TYPE pphcontext,
                                    [in, string] unsigned char *ComputerName,
                                    [in, out, string] unsigned char *ComputerNameServer);

void TerminatePrimeServer([in] unsigned long PrimeServerHandle);
}

/* End of File */
```

Listing 10.6 — PRIMEC5.ACF

```
/******************************************************************\
*                                                                  *
* PRIMEC5.ACF PRIME5 Attribute Configuration File                  *
*          (c) Guy Eddon, 1993                                     *
*                                                                  *
\******************************************************************/

[implicit_handle(handle_t prime_IfHandle)]
interface prime5
{

}

/* End of File */
```

## Chapter 11

PRIME6 - *Overview*

The *PRIME6* application builds upon the foundation laid in *PRIME4*. *PRIME6* does not expand on the Name Service developed in *PRIME5*. Instead, it offers an important new feature: a client that can maintain concurrent connections to multiple servers.

Multiple Clients, Multiple Servers

In previous *PRIME* examples, the server could support multiple clients. The client, however, was unable to issue remote procedure calls to more than one server at a time. This limitation was due to the clients' use of implicit binding handles generated by the MIDL compiler. Since the RPC runtime automatically packages the implicit binding handle as the first parameter to every RPC, a client that relies upon implicit binding handles can bind to only one server at a time.

PRIME6, on the other hand, uses explicit binding handles. Explicit binding handles provide the developer with the control necessary to bind to multiple servers concurrently. This crucial feature achieves the goal I outlined early in the book: A program on a heavily-taxed machine should be able to tap the resources of all available computers spread across a network.

If you test *PRIME6* on at least three computers, you should see quite a show. Though *PRIME6* will run satisfactorily on one computer, it will not be nearly as interesting as on several machines. To see this show, launch the client on one or two computers and launch at least two servers, each on a different computer. Then bind each client to both servers. Each client's display will list the servers with which it is connected, and each server will display those clients it is currently servicing. When you terminate a client, normally or abnormally, the server removes that client from its list of current clients via the context rundown routine introduced in *PRIME4*. If a server terminates, all the clients that were connected to that server notify the user that the server is off-line. This drama can be quite exciting if you position the computers close enough to see the actions taken on one machine reflected in the others.

The PRIME6 *Client*

When you load the *PRIME6* client, it creates a binding for each server you specify on the command line. The client will run whether a *PRIME6* server is available or not since, like earlier *PRIME* clients, it creates a local thread that computes prime numbers. These bindings are created with calls of the form:

```
status = RpcStringBindingCompose(pszUuid,
    pszProtocolSequence, pszNetworkAddress[i],
    pszEndpoint[i], pszOptions, &pszStringBinding[i]);
status = RpcBindingFromStringBinding(pszStringBinding[i],
    &BindingHandle[i]);
```

The client then calls the *CreateThread()* function to create a thread to manage each server:

```
hthread_remote[count - 1] = CreateThread(NULL, 0,
    (LPTHREAD_START_ROUTINE)thread_remote, count, 0,
    &lpIDThread[count - 1]);
```

It then passes each thread a number (*iserver*) to designate the server to which it will bind. If a thread fails to bind to its server, it waits a predetermined period of time before trying to rebind. Once the client has obtained a valid binding to each server, it attempts to initialize the servers on a logical level via the *InitializePrimeServer()* RPC.

```
RpcTryExcept
    {
    PrimeServerHandle[iserver] = InitializePrimeServer(
        BindingHandle[iserver],
        &phContext[iserver], computer_name_buffer);
    IsActiveServer[iserver] = TRUE;
    }
RpcExcept(1)
    {
    value = TRUE;
    IsActiveServer[iserver] = FALSE;
    }
RpcEndExcept
```

The *PRIME6* client parts company with its predecessors by utilizing explicit binding handles. As you may recall from Chapter 6, explicit binding handles require the programmer to include the binding handle as the first parameter in each remote procedure call. The *PRIME6* client manages the binding handles by maintaining them in an array:

```
handle_t BindingHandle[MAX_THREADS];
```

The variable *iserver* serves as an index into the array. Each thread then calls the remote procedures on its designated server by using the server's binding handle.

After the client threads complete their initialization, each begins computing prime numbers by calling *RemoteIsPrime()* on its assigned server. In addition, the local thread computes prime numbers on the client machine. If an exception occurs, indicating that a server is off-line, the client thread waits some fraction of time before attempting to rebind.

The *PRIME6* server code remains nearly unchanged from the *PRIME4* server. The only difference is the use of explicit binding handles, so that each remote procedure now receives one extra parameter, the binding handle, explicitly.

The PRIME6 *Interface*

The *PRIME6* Interface Definition file specifies the interface between the client and server. The file contains the UUID, version number, and pointer type used for the interface header:

```
[ uuid (906B0CE0-C70B-1067-B317-00DD010662DA),
  version(1.0),
  pointer_default(unique) ]
interface prime6
    {
    /* Function Definitions */
    }
```

Other than the use of explicit binding handles in the remote procedures, the *PRIME6* interface remains unchanged from that of *PRIME5*.

Debugging PRIME6

As mentioned in earlier chapters, the issue of the network makes debugging distributed RPC applications different from debugging "conventional" applications. For this reason, it is best to separate the server initialization code from the remote procedures themselves. I divided the *PRIME6* server code into the *PRIMES6.C* and *PRIMEP6.C* source files. Ultimately, I will link both files to produce the server, but separating them for the debugging stage can prove invaluable.

By dividing the server into two parts, you permit yourself the option of linking the remote procedures with the client to produce a non-distributed application that you can test without worrying about the network. Once you verify that your program works properly as a standard program, you can divide it into its client and server parts and test it as a distributed application.

Summary

After all the effort we have invested in building an application to compute prime numbers, it's a shame there is not more demand for them. Yet, what advantage exists in computing prime numbers in a distributed manner, rather than on a single computer? *PRIME6* provides some simple timing routines that let you monitor the time the computations take.

Table 11.1 shows that distributing the computation of relatively small prime numbers (1-1000) actually worsens overall performance. While RPC makes programming a distributed application much easier, its overhead weighs heavily. When an application begins testing very large numbers (10,000,000 and up), the RPC overhead becomes negligible, and the extra CPU power available to the distributed application significantly enhances performance. When I clocked times for these large numbers, the improvement with the distributed prime computations on four computers approached an order of 3.5 times faster than computing on only one machine. A smart application might therefore make remote procedure calls only when the potential gain outweighs its overhead.

Range	1 computer (sec.)	4 computers (sec.)	Ratio
1 - 1,000	35	40	0.88
100,000 - 101,000	40	42	0.95
1,000,000 - 1,001,000	100	61	1.64
10,000,000 - 10,001,000	581	170	3.42

Table 11.1   *Timing of Prime Number Computations in* PRIME6.

PRIME6　　　　　　　　(CLIENT)　　　　　　　PRIME6

Command Syntax (Client)

```
PRIMEC6 [options]
```

Options

All options may be given in UNIX style (a leading hyphen) or DOS style (a leading slash).

-f n Start search at n instead of one (one is the default).
-p   protocol_sequence
-n   network_address
-e   endpoint
-o   options

The -p -n -e and -o options correspond to the elements that determine the binding between the client and server. If you with to run *PRIME6* with a local server (on the same computer), do not specify a computer name (the -n option) on the command line. To connect the *PRIME6* client to several *PRIME6* servers use the form:

```
PRIMEC6 -n \\ServerMachineName1;\\ServerMachineName2;...
```

-?
-h   Print usage summary and stop.

Example

```
PRIMEC6 -n \\ServerMachineName1;\\ServerMachineName2; -f 1000
```

begins computing prime numbers at 1000, using the servers resident on machines named *ServerMachineName1* and *ServerMachineName2*.

Termination

NextNumber reaches 4,294,967,296.
The user presses the *ESC* key.

Files

Makefile (builds both server and client)

File	Listing	Description
DIRECTIO.C	5.3	The *DIRECTIO* source code
DIRECTIO.H	5.4	The *DIRECTIO* header file
PRIMEC6.C	11.1	The *PRIME6* client C code
PRIMEP6.C	11.3	The *PRIME6* remote procedures C code
PRIME6.MAK	11.4	The *PRIME6* makefile

Table 11.2　　*Source files for the* PRIME6 *client.*

PRIME6   (SERVER)   PRIME6

Command Syntax (Server)

```
PRIMES6 [options]
```

Options

All options may be given in UNIX style (a leading hyphen) or DOS style (a leading slash).

```
-p   protocol_sequence
-e   endpoint
```

The -p and -e correspond to the elements that determine the binding between the client and server.

```
-m   maxcalls
-n   mincalls
-f   flag_wait_op
-s   security_descriptor
-?
-h   Print usage summary and stop.
```

Termination

NextNumber reaches 4,294,967,296.
The user presses the *ESC* key.

Files

Makefile (builds both server and client)

```
PRIME6.MAK
```

File	Listing	Description
DIRECTIO.C	5.3	The *DIRECTIO* source code
DIRECTIO.H	5.4	The *DIRECTIO* header file
PRIMES6.C	11.2	The *PRIME6* server C code
PRIMEP6.C	11.3	The *PRIME6* remote procedures C code
PRIME6.MAK	11.4	The *PRIME6* makefile

Table 11.3   *Source files for the* PRIME6 *server.*

Listing 11.1 — PRIMEC6.C

```
/*********************************************************************\
*                                                                    *
* PRIMEC6.C - Distributed prime number example                      *
*             (c) Guy Eddon, 1993                                   *
*                                                                    *
* To build:   NMAKE PRIME6.MAK                                      *
*                                                                    *
* Usage:      PRIMEC6                                               *
*                                                                    *
* Comments:   This is the client side prime number program.        *
*                                                                    *
\*********************************************************************/

#include <STDIO.H>
#include <STRING.H>
#include <STDLIB.H>
#include <STDARG.H>
#include <LIMITS.H>
#include <CTYPE.H>
#include <WINDOWS.H>
#include <RPC.H>
#include "directio.h"
#include "prime6.h"

/* If we found a prime then return PRIME, otherwise return NOT_PRIME */

#define PRIME          1
#define NOT_PRIME      0

/* Coordinates for displaying numbers to be tested */

#define TESTING_X1     3
#define TESTING_Y1     3
#define TESTING_X2     23
#define TESTING_Y2     18

/* Coordinates for displaying prime numbers */

#define PRIME_X1       30
#define PRIME_Y1       3
#define PRIME_X2       50
#define PRIME_Y2       18

#define ERROR_EXIT     2
#define SUCCESS_EXIT   0
#define STRING_LENGTH 256
```

Listing 11.1 — (continued)

```
/* Delay time in microseconds */

#define WAIT          350
#define WAIT_DISPLAY 2000

/* Colors used in this application */

#define WHITE_ON_BLUE FOREGROUND_WHITE|FOREGROUND_INTENSITY|BACKGROUND_BLUE
#define WHITE_ON_CYAN FOREGROUND_WHITE|FOREGROUND_INTENSITY|BACKGROUND_CYAN
#define RED_ON_BLUE   FOREGROUND_RED|FOREGROUND_INTENSITY|BACKGROUND_BLUE
#define RED_ON_CYAN   FOREGROUND_RED|FOREGROUND_INTENSITY|BACKGROUND_CYAN
#define CYAN_ON_CYAN  FOREGROUND_CYAN|BACKGROUND_CYAN
#define BLUE_ON_CYAN  FOREGROUND_BLUE|FOREGROUND_INTENSITY|BACKGROUND_CYAN

/* Max number of threads for this application */

#define MAX_THREADS      9
#define COMP_NAME_LENGTH 7

int NumThreads;

/* Prototypes of functions used in this application */

unsigned char IsPrime(unsigned long TestNumber);
extern char ServerStatus(char);
extern void thread_local(void);
extern void thread_remote(int count);
extern void Usage(void);
extern void InitializeApplication(void);
extern void NotifyServer(char);
extern void thread_client(void);
char IsActiveServer[MAX_THREADS];

DWORD  lpIDThreadClient;
HANDLE hthread_client;

/* Critical Section for choosing next available number for testing */

CRITICAL_SECTION GlobalCriticalSection;

/* Storage for Computer Name */

char computer_name_buffer[MAX_COMPUTERNAME_LENGTH];

/* Unique number returned by the server */

unsigned long PrimeServerHandle[MAX_THREADS];
```

Listing 11.1 — (continued)

```
/*
NextNumber    - Next available number to test
StartTime     - Time that we start to compute primes
CurrTime      - Current Computer time
NoPrimeLocal  - Number of primes computed locally
NoPrimeRemote - Number of primes computed on the remote computer
StartNumber   - The starting number for testing primes
*/

unsigned long NextNumber = 1, StartTime, CurrTime, NoPrimeLocal,
    NoPrimeRemoteT, StartNumber = 1;

handle_t BindingHandle[MAX_THREADS];
unsigned long NoPrimeRemote[MAX_THREADS];

PCONTEXT_HANDLE_TYPE phContext[MAX_THREADS];

int ipszNetAdd = 0;

RPC_NS_HANDLE ImportContext;

unsigned char pszRemoteName[MAX_THREADS][MAX_COMPUTERNAME_LENGTH];

#define REMOTE_TRY 100

unsigned char Notry[MAX_THREADS];

void _CRTAPI1 main(int argc, char **argv)
    {
    RPC_STATUS status; /* returned by RPC API function */

    unsigned char *pszUuid                 = NULL;
    unsigned char *pszProtocolSequence     = "ncacn_np";
    unsigned char *pszNetworkAddress[MAX_THREADS]  = { NULL };
    unsigned char *pszEndpoint[MAX_THREADS]        =
        {
        "\\pipe\\prime", "\\pipe\\prime", "\\pipe\\prime", "\\pipe\\prime",
        "\\pipe\\prime", "\\pipe\\prime", "\\pipe\\prime", "\\pipe\\prime",
        "\\pipe\\prime"
        };
    unsigned char *pszOptions              = NULL;
    unsigned char *pszStringBinding[MAX_THREADS]  = { NULL };

    DWORD  Max_ComputerName_Length = MAX_COMPUTERNAME_LENGTH;
    DWORD  lpIDThread[MAX_THREADS];
    HANDLE hthread_remote[MAX_THREADS];

    int count;
```

Listing 11.1 — (continued)

```c
/* Allow the user to override settings with command line switches */

for(count = 1; count < argc; count++)
    {
    if((*argv[count] == '-') || (*argv[count] == '/'))
        {
        switch(tolower(*(argv[count]+1)))
            {
            case 'p': /* protocol sequence */
                pszProtocolSequence = argv[++count];
                break;

            case 'n': /* network address */
                {
                char tokensep[] = " \t,;", *token;
                token = strtok(argv[++count], tokensep);

                while(token != NULL)
                    {
                    pszNetworkAddress[ipszNetAdd] = token;
                    token = strtok(NULL, tokensep);
                    strcpy(pszRemoteName[ipszNetAdd],
                            strupr(&pszNetworkAddress[ipszNetAdd][2]));
                    pszRemoteName[ipszNetAdd][COMP_NAME_LENGTH] = 0;
                    ipszNetAdd++;
                    }
                }
                break;

            case 'e':
                {
                char tokensep[] = " \t,;", *token;
                token =strtok(argv[++count], tokensep);

                while(token != NULL)
                    {
                    pszEndpoint[ipszNetAdd] = token;
                    token = strtok(NULL, tokensep);
                    ipszNetAdd++;
                    }
                }
                break;

            case 'o':
                pszOptions = argv[++count];
                break;
```

Listing 11.1 — (continued)

```
        case 'f': /* first number */
            NextNumber = StartNumber = atol(argv[++count]);
            break;

        case 't': /* number of threads */
            NumThreads = atoi(argv[++count]);
            if(NumThreads > MAX_THREADS)
                NumThreads = MAX_THREADS;
            break;

        case 'h':
        case '?':
        default:
            Usage();
        }
    }
    else
        Usage();
    }

if(pszNetworkAddress)
    {
    int i;

    /*
    Use a convenience function to concatenate the elements of
    the string binding into the proper sequence
    */

    for(i = 0; i < ipszNetAdd; i++)
        {
        status = RpcStringBindingCompose(pszUuid, pszProtocolSequence, pszNetworkAddress[i],
                                pszEndpoint[i], pszOptions, &pszStringBinding[i]);

        if(status)
            exit(ERROR_EXIT);
        }

    /* Set the binding handle that will be used to bind to the server*/

    for(i = 0; i < ipszNetAdd; i++)
        {
        status = RpcBindingFromStringBinding(pszStringBinding[i], &BindingHandle[i]);

        if(status)
            exit(ERROR_EXIT);
        }
    }
```

Listing 11.1 — (continued)

```
GetComputerName(computer_name_buffer, &Max_ComputerName_Length);

InitializeCriticalSection(&GlobalCriticalSection);

   {
   char i;

   for(i = 0; i < ipszNetAdd; i++)
      ServerStatus(i);
   }

for(count = 1; count <= ipszNetAdd ; count++)
   hthread_remote[count-1] = CreateThread(NULL, 0, (LPTHREAD_START_ROUTINE)thread_remote,
                                  count, 0, &lpIDThread[count-1]);

InitializeApplication();

hthread_client = CreateThread(NULL, 0, (LPTHREAD_START_ROUTINE)thread_client, NULL,
                        CREATE_SUSPENDED, &lpIDThreadClient);

SetThreadPriority(hthread_client, THREAD_PRIORITY_NORMAL);
ResumeThread(hthread_client);
thread_local();
DeleteCriticalSection(&GlobalCriticalSection);

/* The calls to the remote procedures are complete. Free the string and the binding handle */

/* remote calls done - unbind */

if(pszNetworkAddress)
   {
   int i;

   for(i = 0; i < ipszNetAdd; i++)
      {
      status = RpcStringFree(&pszStringBinding[i]);

      if(status)
         exit(ERROR_EXIT);
      }
   }

exit(SUCCESS_EXIT);
}
```

Listing 11.1 — (continued)

```c
void thread_local(void)
   {
   unsigned long temp;
   char Buffer[STRING_LENGTH];
   int loop;

   SMALL_RECT psrctScrollRectTesting, psrctScrollRectPrime;
   COORD coordDestOriginTesting, coordDestOriginPrime;
   CHAR_INFO pchiFill;
   WORD Color[TESTING_X2-TESTING_X1-3], Normal[TESTING_X2-TESTING_X1-3];

   COORD ComputTestCoord;
   COORD ComputPrimeCoord;

   DWORD dummy;
   COORD PrimeCoord;

   psrctScrollRectTesting.Left   = TESTING_X1+1;
   psrctScrollRectTesting.Top    = TESTING_Y1+2;
   psrctScrollRectTesting.Right  = TESTING_X2-1;
   psrctScrollRectTesting.Bottom = TESTING_Y2-1;

   coordDestOriginTesting.X = TESTING_X1+1;
   coordDestOriginTesting.Y = TESTING_Y1+1;

   psrctScrollRectPrime.Left   = PRIME_X1+1;
   psrctScrollRectPrime.Top    = PRIME_Y1+2;
   psrctScrollRectPrime.Right  = PRIME_X2-1;
   psrctScrollRectPrime.Bottom = PRIME_Y2-1;

   coordDestOriginPrime.X = PRIME_X1+1;
   coordDestOriginPrime.Y = PRIME_Y1+1;

   pchiFill.Char.AsciiChar = (char)32;
   pchiFill.Attributes = WHITE_ON_BLUE;

   ComputTestCoord.X  = TESTING_X2-7;
   ComputTestCoord.Y  = TESTING_Y2-1;
   ComputPrimeCoord.X = PRIME_X2-7;
   ComputPrimeCoord.Y = PRIME_Y2-1;

   for(loop = 0; loop < TESTING_X2-TESTING_X1-3; loop++)
      {
      Color[loop]  = RED_ON_BLUE;
      Normal[loop] = WHITE_ON_BLUE;
      }
```

Listing 11.1 — (continued)

```
    while(1)
        {
        EnterCriticalSection(&GlobalCriticalSection);
        if((temp = ++NextNumber) >= ULONG_MAX)
            break;
        LeaveCriticalSection(&GlobalCriticalSection);

        EnterCriticalSection(&GlobalCriticalSection);
        ScrollConsoleScreenBuffer(hStdOut, &psrctScrollRectTesting, NULL,
                            coordDestOriginTesting, &pchiFill);
        sprintf(Buffer, "%d", temp - 1);
        mxyputs((unsigned char)TESTING_X1+2, (unsigned char)(TESTING_Y2-1),
                Buffer, WHITE_ON_BLUE);
        WriteConsoleOutputAttribute(hStdOut, Normal, 7, ComputTestCoord, &dummy);
        mxyputs((unsigned char)(TESTING_X2-7), (unsigned char)TESTING_Y2-1,
                "LOCAL ", WHITE_ON_BLUE);
        LeaveCriticalSection(&GlobalCriticalSection);

        if(IsPrime(temp - 1) != 0)
            {
            PrimeCoord.X = PRIME_X1 + 2;
            PrimeCoord.Y = PRIME_Y2 - 1;

            EnterCriticalSection(&GlobalCriticalSection);
            ScrollConsoleScreenBuffer(hStdOut, &psrctScrollRectPrime, NULL,
                                coordDestOriginPrime, &pchiFill);
            sprintf(Buffer, "%-17d", temp - 1);
            mxyputs((unsigned char)(PRIME_X1+2), (unsigned char)PRIME_Y2-1,
                    Buffer, WHITE_ON_BLUE);
            WriteConsoleOutputAttribute(hStdOut, Normal, 7, ComputPrimeCoord &dummy);
            mxyputs((unsigned char)(PRIME_X2-7), (unsigned char)PRIME_Y2-1,
                    "LOCAL ", WHITE_ON_BLUE);
            LeaveCriticalSection(&GlobalCriticalSection);
            NoPrimeLocal++;
            }
        }
    }

void thread_remote(int count)
    {
    unsigned long temp;
    char Buffer[STRING_LENGTH];
    int loop;
```

Listing 11.1 — (continued)

```
SMALL_RECT psrctScrollRectTesting, psrctScrollRectPrime;
COORD coordDestOriginTesting, coordDestOriginPrime;
CHAR_INFO pchiFill;
WORD Color[TESTING_X2-TESTING_X1-3], Normal[TESTING_X2-TESTING_X1-3];

COORD ComputTestCoord;
COORD ComputPrimeCoord;

DWORD dummy;
COORD PrimeCoord;

psrctScrollRectTesting.Left   = TESTING_X1+1;
psrctScrollRectTesting.Top    = TESTING_Y1+2;
psrctScrollRectTesting.Right  = TESTING_X2-1;
psrctScrollRectTesting.Bottom = TESTING_Y2-1;

coordDestOriginTesting.X = TESTING_X1+1;
coordDestOriginTesting.Y = TESTING_Y1+1;

psrctScrollRectPrime.Left   = PRIME_X1+1;
psrctScrollRectPrime.Top    = PRIME_Y1+2;
psrctScrollRectPrime.Right  = PRIME_X2-1;
psrctScrollRectPrime.Bottom = PRIME_Y2-1;

coordDestOriginPrime.X = PRIME_X1+1;
coordDestOriginPrime.Y = PRIME_Y1+1;

pchiFill.Char.AsciiChar = (char)32;
pchiFill.Attributes = WHITE_ON_BLUE;

ComputTestCoord.X  = TESTING_X2-7;
ComputTestCoord.Y  = TESTING_Y2-1;
ComputPrimeCoord.X = PRIME_X2-7;
ComputPrimeCoord.Y = PRIME_Y2-1;

for(loop = 0; loop < TESTING_X2-TESTING_X1-3; loop++)
   {
   Color[loop]  = RED_ON_BLUE;
   Normal[loop] = WHITE_ON_BLUE;
   }
```

Listing 11.1 — (continued)

```
while(1)
    {
    if(!IsActiveServer[count-1])
        {
        if(Notry[count-1]++ > REMOTE_TRY)
            {
            Notry[count - 1] = 0;
            EnterCriticalSection(&GlobalCriticalSection);
             ServerStatus((char)(count - 1));
            LeaveCriticalSection(&GlobalCriticalSection);
            }
        else
            continue;
        }
    if(!IsActiveServer[count-1])
        continue;

/* To make sure that we won't test the same number twice */

    EnterCriticalSection(&GlobalCriticalSection);
    if((temp = ++NextNumber) >= ULONG_MAX)
        break;
    LeaveCriticalSection(&GlobalCriticalSection);

    EnterCriticalSection(&GlobalCriticalSection);
    ScrollConsoleScreenBuffer(hStdOut, &psrctScrollRectTesting, NULL,
                            coordDestOriginTesting, &pchiFill);
    sprintf(Buffer, " %-17d", temp - 1);
    mxyputs((unsigned char)TESTING_X1+1, (unsigned char)(TESTING_Y2-1),
            Buffer, RED_ON_BLUE);
    WriteConsoleOutputAttribute(hStdOut, Color, 7, ComputTestCoord, &dummy);
    mxyputs((unsigned char)(TESTING_X2-7), (unsigned char)TESTING_Y2-1,
            pszRemoteName[count-1], RED_ON_BLUE);
    LeaveCriticalSection(&GlobalCriticalSection);

    RpcTryExcept
        {
        if(RemoteIsPrime(BindingHandle[count-1], PrimeServerHandle[count-1], temp - 1) != 0)
            {
            EnterCriticalSection(&GlobalCriticalSection);
            PrimeCoord.X = TESTING_X1 + 2;
            LeaveCriticalSection(&GlobalCriticalSection);

            PrimeCoord.X = PRIME_X1 + 2;
            PrimeCoord.Y = PRIME_Y2 - 1;
```

Listing 11.1 — (continued)

```
            EnterCriticalSection(&GlobalCriticalSection);
            ScrollConsoleScreenBuffer(hStdOut, &psrctScrollRectPrime, NULL,
                            coordDestOriginPrime, &pchiFill);
            sprintf(Buffer, " %-17d", temp - 1);
            mxyputs((unsigned char)(PRIME_X1+1), (unsigned char)PRIME_Y2-1,
                    Buffer, RED_ON_BLUE);
            WriteConsoleOutputAttribute(hStdOut, Color, 7, ComputPrimeCoord,&dummy);
            mxyputs((unsigned char)(PRIME_X2-7), (unsigned char)PRIME_Y2-1,
                    pszRemoteName[count-1], RED_ON_BLUE);
            LeaveCriticalSection(&GlobalCriticalSection);
                NoPrimeRemote[count-1]++;
            NoPrimeRemoteT++;
            }
        }
    RpcExcept(1)
        {
        /* if exceptions occurs */

        EnterCriticalSection(&GlobalCriticalSection);
        ServerStatus((char)(count - 1));
        LeaveCriticalSection(&GlobalCriticalSection);
        }
    RpcEndExcept
    }
}

/* Tests for prime number on the local computer */

unsigned char IsPrime(unsigned long TestNumber)
    {
    unsigned long count;
    unsigned long HalfNumber = TestNumber / 2 + 1;

    for(count = 2; count < HalfNumber; count++)
        if(TestNumber % count == 0)
            return NOT_PRIME;

    return PRIME;
    }
```

Listing 11.1 — (continued)

```c
/* Displays command line options */

void Usage(void)
   {
   printf("\nDistributed client/server prime number example.\n\n");
   printf("Usage: PRIME6\n");
   printf(" -p protocol_sequence\n");
   printf(" -n network_address\n");
   printf(" -e endpoint\n");
   printf(" -o options\n");
   printf(" -f first number\n");
   exit(1);
   }

/* Screen Initialization and colors and title lines */

void InitializeApplication(void)
   {
   set_vid_mem();

   clearscreen(BACKGROUND_CYAN);
   StartTime = GetTickCount();

   box(0, 0, 79, 24, DOUBLE);
   mxyputs(37, 0, " PRIMEC6 ", WHITE_ON_CYAN);

   mxyputs(TESTING_X1, 2, "Testing...", WHITE_ON_CYAN);
   box(TESTING_X1, TESTING_Y1, TESTING_X2, TESTING_Y2, SINGLE);

   mxyputs(PRIME_X1, 2, "Prime!",WHITE_ON_CYAN);
   box(PRIME_X1, PRIME_Y1, PRIME_X2, PRIME_Y2, SINGLE);
   mxyputs(32, 23, "Press Esc to exit", WHITE_ON_CYAN);
   }

/* Check the Server status if it is of line, then try to connect, return server status */

char ServerStatus(char iserver)
   {
   char value = FALSE;

   RpcTryExcept
      {
      PrimeServerHandle[iserver] = InitializePrimeServer(BindingHandle[iserver],
                                                         &phContext[iserver],
                                                         computer_name_buffer);

      IsActiveServer[iserver] = TRUE;
      }
```

Listing 11.1 — (continued)

```
   RpcExcept(1)
      {
      value = TRUE;
      IsActiveServer[iserver] = FALSE;
      }
   RpcEndExcept

   return value;
   }

/* Let the Server know that we are about to exit */

void NotifyServer(char iserver)
   {
   RpcTryExcept
      {
      TerminatePrimeServer(BindingHandle[iserver], PrimeServerHandle[iserver]);
      }
   RpcExcept(1)
      {
      return;
      }
   RpcEndExcept
   }

void thread_client()
   {
   unsigned char no_active =0;

   while(1)
      {
      char Buffer[STRING_LENGTH];
      int  i;

      if(VK_ESCAPE == get_character_no_wait())
         {
         EnterCriticalSection(&GlobalCriticalSection);
         Sleep(WAIT);
         for(i = 0;i < ipszNetAdd; i++)
            NotifyServer((char)i);
         clearscreen(0);
         exit(0);
         LeaveCriticalSection(&GlobalCriticalSection);
         }
```

Listing 11.1 — (continued)

```c
    mxyputs(58, 2, "Number of Primes", WHITE_ON_CYAN);
    sprintf(Buffer, "%s:%5d", "LOCAL  ", NoPrimeLocal);
    mxyputs((unsigned char)(60), (unsigned char)(4), Buffer, WHITE_ON_CYAN);
        {
        no_active = 0;
        EnterCriticalSection(&GlobalCriticalSection);
        for(i = 0; i < ipszNetAdd; i++)
            if(IsActiveServer[i])
                {
                sprintf(Buffer, " %7s:%5d ", pszRemoteName[i], NoPrimeRemote[i]);
                mxyputs(59, (unsigned char)(4+1+no_active), Buffer, RED_ON_CYAN);
                no_active++;
                }
        box(58, 3, 74, (unsigned char)(5 + no_active), SINGLE);
        mxyputc(58, (unsigned char)(6 + no_active), (char)32, 17, CYAN_ON_CYAN);
        }

    no_active = 0;
    for(i = 0; i < ipszNetAdd; i++)
        if(!IsActiveServer[i])
            {
            sprintf(Buffer, " %7s:%5d ", pszRemoteName[i], NoPrimeRemote[i]);
            mxyputs(59, (unsigned char)(4+15+no_active), Buffer, RED_ON_CYAN);
            no_active ++;
            }

    if(no_active)
        {
        mxyputs(58, (unsigned char)(17), "Inactive Servers", WHITE_ON_CYAN);
        box(58, (unsigned char)(18), 74, (unsigned char)(19 + no_active), SINGLE);
        mxyputc(58, (unsigned char)(20 + no_active), (char)32, 17, CYAN_ON_CYAN);
        }
    else
        for(i = 0; i < 5; i++)
            mxyputc(58, (unsigned char)(17 + no_active + i), (char)32, 17, CYAN_ON_CYAN);

    LeaveCriticalSection(&GlobalCriticalSection);
    CurrTime = (GetTickCount() - StartTime) / 1000;
    sprintf(Buffer, "Primes = %d", NoPrimeLocal + NoPrimeRemoteT);
    mxyputs(58, (unsigned char)(7 + ipszNetAdd), Buffer, WHITE_ON_CYAN);
    sprintf(Buffer, "Time = %d.%02d min.", CurrTime/60, CurrTime%60);
    mxyputs(58, (unsigned char)(8 + ipszNetAdd), Buffer, WHITE_ON_CYAN);

    sprintf(Buffer,"First = %d", StartNumber);
    mxyputs(58,(unsigned char)(1+5+3+ipszNetAdd), Buffer, WHITE_ON_CYAN);
    }
 }
/* End of File */
```

Listing 11.2 — PRIMES6.C

```
/*********************************************************************\
*                                                                    *
* PRIMES6.C - Distributed prime number example                       *
*            (c) Guy Eddon, 1993                                      *
*                                                                    *
* To build:   NMAKE PRIME6.MAK                                        *
*                                                                    *
* Usage:      PRIMES6                                                 *
*                                                                    *
* Comments:   This is the server side prime number example.          *
*                                                                    *
\*********************************************************************/

#include <STDIO.H>
#include <STRING.H>
#include <STDLIB.H>
#include <STDARG.H>
#include <LIMITS.H>
#include <CTYPE.H>
#include <WINDOWS.H>
#include <RPC.H>
#include "prime6.h"
#include "directio.h"

/* If we found a prime then return PRIME, otherwise return NOT_PRIME */

#define PRIME        1
#define NOT_PRIME    0

/* Maximum Number of Clients to respond to */

#define MAX_CALLS    10

/* Coordinates for displaying numbers to be tested */

#define TESTING_X1   3
#define TESTING_Y1   3
#define TESTING_X2   23
#define TESTING_Y2   18
```

Listing 11.2 — (continued)

```
/* Coordinates for displaying prime numbers */

#define PRIME_X1        30
#define PRIME_Y1         3
#define PRIME_X2        50
#define PRIME_Y2        18

#define ERROR_EXIT       2
#define SUCCESS_EXIT     0
#define STRING_LENGTH 256

/* Delay time in microseconds */

#define WAIT           350
#define WAIT_DISPLAY 2000

/* Colors used in this application */

#define WHITE_ON_BLUE FOREGROUND_WHITE|FOREGROUND_INTENSITY|BACKGROUND_BLUE
#define WHITE_ON_CYAN FOREGROUND_WHITE|FOREGROUND_INTENSITY|BACKGROUND_CYAN
#define RED_ON_BLUE   FOREGROUND_RED|FOREGROUND_INTENSITY|BACKGROUND_BLUE
#define RED_ON_CYAN   FOREGROUND_RED|FOREGROUND_INTENSITY|BACKGROUND_CYAN
#define CYAN_ON_CYAN  FOREGROUND_CYAN|BACKGROUND_CYAN

/* Number of characters in computer name to display on the screen */

#define COMP_NAME_LENGTH 7

extern char IsPrime(unsigned long TestNumber);
extern void Usage(void);
extern void InitializeApplication(void);
extern unsigned long NoPrimes[MAX_CALLS];
extern unsigned long handles;
extern void thread_server(void);
extern char GlobalComputerNameBuffer[MAX_CALLS][MAX_COMPUTERNAME_LENGTH];

DWORD  lpIDThread;
HANDLE hthread_server;
CRITICAL_SECTION GlobalCriticalSection;

RPC_BINDING_VECTOR * pBindingVector;
```

Listing 11.2 — (continued)

```c
void _CRTAPI1 main(int argc, char **argv)
    {
    RPC_STATUS status;

    unsigned char *pszProtocolSequence = "ncacn_np";
    unsigned char *pszSecurity         = NULL;
    unsigned char *pszEndpoint         = "\\pipe\\prime";
    unsigned int cMinCalls             = 1;
    unsigned int cMaxCalls             = MAX_CALLS;
    unsigned int fDontWait             = FALSE;

    int i;

    /* allow the user to override settings with command line switches */

    for(i = 1; i < argc; i++)
        {
        if((*argv[i] == '-') || (*argv[i] == '/'))
            {
            switch(tolower(*(argv[i]+1)))
                {
                case 'p': /* protocol sequence */
                    pszProtocolSequence = argv[++i];
                    break;

                case 'e':
                    pszEndpoint = argv[++i];
                    break;

                case 'm':
                    cMaxCalls = (unsigned int) atoi(argv[++i]);
                    break;

                case 'n':
                    cMinCalls = (unsigned int) atoi(argv[++i]);
                    break;

                case 'f':
                    fDontWait = (unsigned int) atoi(argv[++i]);
                    break;

                case 's':
                    pszSecurity = argv[++i];
                    break;
```

Listing 11.2 — (continued)

```
        case 'h':
        case '?':
        default:
            Usage();
        }
    }
    else
      Usage();
    }

status = RpcServerUseProtseqEp(
    pszProtocolSequence,
    cMaxCalls,     /* max concurrent calls */
    pszEndpoint,
    pszSecurity); /* Security descriptor */

if(status)
    {
    printf("RpcServerUseProtseqEp  %d\n", status);
    exit(status);
    }

status = RpcServerRegisterIf(
    prime6_ServerIfHandle, /* interface to register      */
    NULL,                  /* MgrTypeUuid                */
    NULL);                 /* MgrEpv; null means use default */

if(status)
    {
    printf("RpcServerRegisterIf  %d\n", status);
    exit(status);
    }

InitializeCriticalSection(&GlobalCriticalSection);

InitializeApplication();

mxyputs(23, 21, "Listening for prime number requests.", RED_ON_CYAN);

status = RpcServerListen(cMinCalls, cMaxCalls, fDontWait);

if(status)
    exit(status);

if(fDontWait)
    {
    status = RpcMgmtWaitServerListen(); /* wait operation */
```

Listing 11.2 — (continued)

```
        if(status)
            exit(status);
        }
    }

void Usage(void)
    {
    printf("\nDistributed client/server prime number example.\n\n");
    printf("Usage: PRIME6\n");
    printf(" -p protocol_sequence\n");
    printf(" -e endpoint\n");
    printf(" -m maxcalls\n");
    printf(" -n mincalls\n");
    printf(" -f flag_wait_op\n");
    printf(" -s security_descriptor\n");
    exit(EXIT_SUCCESS);
    }

/* MIDL allocate and free */

void *MIDL_user_allocate(size_t len)
    {
    return(malloc(len));
    }

void MIDL_user_free(void *ptr)
    {
    free(ptr);
    }

void InitializeApplication(void)
    {
    set_vid_mem();

    clearscreen(BACKGROUND_CYAN);

    box(0, 0, 79, 24, DOUBLE);
    mxyputs(37, 0, " PRIMES6 ", WHITE_ON_CYAN);

    mxyputs(TESTING_X1, 2, "Testing...", WHITE_ON_CYAN);

    box(TESTING_X1, TESTING_Y1, TESTING_X2, TESTING_Y2,SINGLE);

    mxyputs(PRIME_X1, 2, "Prime!", WHITE_ON_CYAN);
    box(PRIME_X1, PRIME_Y1, PRIME_X2, PRIME_Y2, SINGLE);

    mxyputs(32, 23, "Press Esc to exit", WHITE_ON_CYAN);
```

Listing 11.2 — (continued)

```
    hthread_server = CreateThread(NULL, 0, (LPTHREAD_START_ROUTINE)thread_server, NULL,
                       CREATE_SUSPENDED, &lpIDThread);

    SetThreadPriority(hthread_server, THREAD_PRIORITY_LOWEST);
    ResumeThread(hthread_server);
    }

void thread_server()
    {
    while(1)
       {
       char Buffer[STRING_LENGTH], Buffert[STRING_LENGTH];
       unsigned char i;

       if(VK_ESCAPE == get_character_no_wait())
           {
           EnterCriticalSection(&GlobalCriticalSection);
           Sleep(WAIT);
           clearscreen(0);
           exit(EXIT_SUCCESS);
           LeaveCriticalSection(&GlobalCriticalSection);
           DeleteCriticalSection(&GlobalCriticalSection);
           }

       if(handles)
           {
           mxyputs(58, 2, "Number of Primes", WHITE_ON_CYAN);
           EnterCriticalSection(&GlobalCriticalSection);
           for(i = 0; i < handles; i++)
               {
               strncpy(Buffert, strupr(GlobalComputerNameBuffer[i]), COMP_NAME_LENGTH);
               Buffert[COMP_NAME_LENGTH] = 0;
               sprintf(Buffer, " %7s:%5d ", Buffert, NoPrimes[i]);
               mxyputs(59, (unsigned char)(4+i), Buffer, WHITE_ON_CYAN);
               }

           box(58, 3, 74, (unsigned char)(4+handles), SINGLE);
           mxyputc(58, (unsigned char)(5+i), (char)32, 17, CYAN_ON_CYAN);
           LeaveCriticalSection(&GlobalCriticalSection);
           }
       else
           for(i = 0; i < 13; i++)
               mxyputc(58, (unsigned char)(2+i),
               (char)32, 17, CYAN_ON_CYAN);
```

Listing 11.2 — (continued)

```
    if(!handles)
       {
       mxyputs(23, 21, "Listening for prime number requests.", RED_ON_CYAN);
       Sleep(WAIT_DISPLAY);
       }

    mxyputc(23, 21, (char)32, 36, CYAN_ON_CYAN);
       }
   }

/* End of File */
```

Listing 11.3 — PRIMEP6.C

```
/*********************************************************************\
*                                                                   *
* PRIMEP6.C - Distributed prime number example                      *
*            (c) Guy Eddon, 1993                                     *
*                                                                   *
* To build:   NMAKE PRIME6.MAK                                       *
*                                                                   *
* Usage:      PRIMES6                                                *
*                                                                   *
* Comments:   These are the remote procedures called by the clients. *
*                                                                   *
\*********************************************************************/

#include <STDIO.H>
#include <STRING.H>
#include <STDLIB.H>
#include <STDARG.H>
#include <LIMITS.H>
#include <CTYPE.H>
#include <WINDOWS.H>
#include <RPC.H>
#include "prime6.h"
#include "directio.h"

/* If we found a prime then return PRIME, otherwise return NOT_PRIME */

#define PRIME         1
#define NOT_PRIME     0

/* Maximum Number of Clients to respond to */

#define MAX_CALLS     10

/* Coordinates for displaying numbers to be tested */

#define TESTING_X1    3
#define TESTING_Y1    3
#define TESTING_X2    23
#define TESTING_Y2    18
```

Listing 11.3 — (continued)

```
/* Coordinates for displaying prime numbers */

#define PRIME_X1      30
#define PRIME_Y1       3
#define PRIME_X2      50
#define PRIME_Y2      18

#define ERROR_EXIT     2
#define SUCCESS_EXIT   0
#define STRING_LENGTH 256

/* Time delay in microseconds */

#define WAIT          350
#define WAIT_DISPLAY 2000

/* Colors used in this application */

#define WHITE_ON_BLUE FOREGROUND_WHITE|FOREGROUND_INTENSITY|BACKGROUND_BLUE
#define WHITE_ON_CYAN FOREGROUND_WHITE|FOREGROUND_INTENSITY|BACKGROUND_CYAN
#define RED_ON_BLUE   FOREGROUND_RED|FOREGROUND_INTENSITY|BACKGROUND_BLUE
#define RED_ON_CYAN   FOREGROUND_RED|FOREGROUND_INTENSITY|BACKGROUND_CYAN
#define CYAN_ON_CYAN  FOREGROUND_CYAN|BACKGROUND_CYAN

/* Number of characters in computer name to display on the screen */

#define COMP_NAME_LENGTH 7

extern CRITICAL_SECTION GlobalCriticalSection;
unsigned long handles = 0, handlesp = 0;

/* Critical Section for choosing next available number for testing */

char GlobalComputerNameBuffer[MAX_CALLS][MAX_COMPUTERNAME_LENGTH];

/* Number of primes for each client */

unsigned long NoPrimes[MAX_CALLS];
unsigned long GlobalComputerHandleBuffer[MAX_CALLS];
unsigned long handle_mod = 1;
```

Listing 11.3 — (continued)

```
/*
   This function is called by the client, we return a unique number,
   so in the future we can keep track who called us
*/

unsigned long InitializePrimeServer(handle_t h1, PPCONTEXT_HANDLE_TYPE pphContext,
                                     unsigned char *ComputerName)
   {
   char Buffer[STRING_LENGTH];
   unsigned long unique_handle;

   EnterCriticalSection(&GlobalCriticalSection);
   unique_handle = handles + 10 * handle_mod++;

   strcpy(GlobalComputerNameBuffer[handles], ComputerName);

   mxyputc(2, 21, (char)32, 75, CYAN_ON_CYAN);
   sprintf(Buffer, "Computer %s logged in.", ComputerName);
   mxyputs(27, 21, Buffer, RED_ON_CYAN);
   sprintf(Buffer,  "(%ld)",unique_handle);
   mxyputs(54, 21, Buffer, RED_ON_CYAN);
   Sleep(2*WAIT_DISPLAY);
   mxyputc(2, 21, (char)32, 75, CYAN_ON_CYAN);

   GlobalComputerHandleBuffer[handles] = unique_handle;

   *pphContext = (PCONTEXT_HANDLE_TYPE)unique_handle;

   NoPrimes[handles] = 0;

   handles++;
   handlesp = handles;
   LeaveCriticalSection(&GlobalCriticalSection);

   return unique_handle;
   }
```

Listing 11.3 — (continued)

```
/*
    This function was called by the client. The client supplied his identifier
    and the number to test if it is a prime
*/

unsigned char RemoteIsPrime(handle_t h1, unsigned long PrimeServerHandle,
                            unsigned long TestNumber)
    {
    unsigned long count;
    unsigned long HalfNumber = TestNumber / 2 + 1;
    char Buffer[STRING_LENGTH];
    char LocalComputerName[MAX_COMPUTERNAME_LENGTH];
    int loop;

    SMALL_RECT psrctScrollRectTesting, psrctScrollRectPrime;
    COORD coordDestOriginTesting, coordDestOriginPrime;
    CHAR_INFO pchiFill;
    WORD Local[COMP_NAME_LENGTH];

    COORD ComputTestCoord;
    COORD ComputPrimeCoord;
    DWORD dummy;

/* Lets find out the name of client computer */

    EnterCriticalSection(&GlobalCriticalSection);
    for(loop = 0; loop < (int)handles; loop++)
        if(GlobalComputerHandleBuffer[loop] == PrimeServerHandle)
            {
            strcpy(LocalComputerName, GlobalComputerNameBuffer[loop]);
            PrimeServerHandle = loop;
            break;
            }

    LeaveCriticalSection(&GlobalCriticalSection);

    psrctScrollRectTesting.Left   = TESTING_X1+1;
    psrctScrollRectTesting.Top    = TESTING_Y1+2;
    psrctScrollRectTesting.Right  = TESTING_X2-1;
    psrctScrollRectTesting.Bottom = TESTING_Y2-1;

    coordDestOriginTesting.X = TESTING_X1+1;
    coordDestOriginTesting.Y = TESTING_Y1+1;

    psrctScrollRectPrime.Left   = PRIME_X1+1;
    psrctScrollRectPrime.Top    = PRIME_Y1+2;
    psrctScrollRectPrime.Right  = PRIME_X2-1;
    psrctScrollRectPrime.Bottom = PRIME_Y2-1;
```

Listing 11.3 — (continued)

```c
    coordDestOriginPrime.X = PRIME_X1+1;
    coordDestOriginPrime.Y = PRIME_Y1+1;

    pchiFill.Char.AsciiChar = (char)32;
    pchiFill.Attributes = WHITE_ON_BLUE;

    ComputTestCoord.X  = TESTING_X2-7;
    ComputTestCoord.Y  = TESTING_Y2-1;
    ComputPrimeCoord.X = PRIME_X2-7;
    ComputPrimeCoord.Y = PRIME_Y2-1;

    for(loop = 0; loop < COMP_NAME_LENGTH; loop++)
        Local[loop] = WHITE_ON_BLUE;

    if(VK_ESCAPE == get_character_no_wait())
        {

/* If the user pressed ESC then exit */

        EnterCriticalSection(&GlobalCriticalSection);
        Sleep(WAIT);
        clearscreen(0);
        exit(SUCCESS_EXIT);
        LeaveCriticalSection(&GlobalCriticalSection);
        DeleteCriticalSection(&GlobalCriticalSection);
        }

    sprintf(Buffer, "%d", TestNumber);

    EnterCriticalSection(&GlobalCriticalSection);
    ScrollConsoleScreenBuffer(hStdOut, &psrctScrollRectTesting, NULL,
                        coordDestOriginTesting, &pchiFill);
    sprintf(Buffer, "%d", TestNumber);
    mxyputs((unsigned char)TESTING_X1+2, (unsigned char)(TESTING_Y2-1),
            Buffer, WHITE_ON_BLUE);
    WriteConsoleOutputAttribute(hStdOut, Local, COMP_NAME_LENGTH, ComputTestCoord, &dummy);
    LocalComputerName[COMP_NAME_LENGTH] = 0;
    mxyputs((unsigned char)(TESTING_X2-7), (unsigned char)TESTING_Y2-1,
            LocalComputerName, WHITE_ON_BLUE);
    LeaveCriticalSection(&GlobalCriticalSection);
```

Listing 11.3 — (continued)

```
    for(count = 2; count < HalfNumber; count++)
        if(TestNumber % count == 0)
            return NOT_PRIME;

    sprintf(Buffer, "%d", TestNumber);

    EnterCriticalSection(&GlobalCriticalSection);
    ScrollConsoleScreenBuffer(hStdOut, &psrctScrollRectPrime, NULL,
                              coordDestOriginPrime, &pchiFill);
    sprintf(Buffer, "%d", TestNumber);
    mxyputs((unsigned char)(PRIME_X1+2), (unsigned char)PRIME_Y2-1, Buffer, WHITE_ON_BLUE);
    WriteConsoleOutputAttribute(hStdOut, Local, COMP_NAME_LENGTH, ComputPrimeCoord, &dummy);
    mxyputs((unsigned char)(PRIME_X2-7), (unsigned char)PRIME_Y2-1,
            LocalComputerName, WHITE_ON_BLUE);
    NoPrimes[PrimeServerHandle]++;
    LeaveCriticalSection(&GlobalCriticalSection);

    return PRIME;
    }

/* Notification from a client that he is done */

void TerminatePrimeServer(handle_t h1, unsigned long PrimeServerHandle)
    {
    char Buffer[256+MAX_COMPUTERNAME_LENGTH];
    unsigned char loop, loopshift;

    EnterCriticalSection(&GlobalCriticalSection);

    for(loop = 0; loop < (unsigned char)handles; loop++)
        {
        if(GlobalComputerHandleBuffer[loop] == PrimeServerHandle)
            {
            mxyputc(2, 21, (char)32, 75, CYAN_ON_CYAN);
```

Listing 11.3 — (continued)

```
/* Let's put terminating message on the screen */

        sprintf(Buffer, "Computer %s Exited!", GlobalComputerNameBuffer[loop]);
        mxyputs(27, 21, Buffer, RED_ON_CYAN);
        mxyputc(59, (unsigned char)(4+loop), (char)32, 15, CYAN_ON_CYAN);
        Sleep(WAIT_DISPLAY);
        mxyputc(2, 21, (char)32, 75, CYAN_ON_CYAN);
        break;
        }
    }

    if(loop < handles-1)
        {
        loopshift = loop;
        for(loop = loopshift; loop < (unsigned char)(handles - 1); loop++)
            {
            strcpy(GlobalComputerNameBuffer[loop], GlobalComputerNameBuffer[loop+1]);
            GlobalComputerHandleBuffer[loop] = GlobalComputerHandleBuffer[loop+1];
            NoPrimes[loop] = NoPrimes[loop+1];
            }
        }

/* Let's remove his name from our table */

    handles--;
    LeaveCriticalSection(&GlobalCriticalSection);
    }

void PCONTEXT_HANDLE_TYPE_rundown(PCONTEXT_HANDLE_TYPE phContext)
    {
    handle_t dummmy;

    if(handlesp == handles)
        {
        mxyputs(27, 2, "rundown Executed", RED_ON_CYAN);
        TerminatePrimeServer(dummmy, (unsigned long)phContext);
        Sleep(2000);
        mxyputs(27, 2, "                ", CYAN_ON_CYAN);
        }
    handlesp = handles;
    }

/* End of File */
```

Listing 11.4 — PRIME6.MAK

```
################################################################
#                                                              #
# PRIME6.MAK - Makefile                                        #
#                                                              #
################################################################

!include <ntwin32.mak>

!if "$(CPU)" == "i386"
cvtomf =
cflags = $(cflags:G3=Gz)
!endif
!if "$(CPU)" == "MIPS"
cvtomf = mip2coff $@
!endif

.c.obj:
   $(cc) $(cflags) $(cvarsmt) $<
   $(cvtomf)

all : primec6 primes6

primec6 : primec6.exe
primec6.exe : primec6.obj prime6_c.obj prime6_x.obj directio.obj
   $(link) $(conflags) -out:primec6.exe \
     primec6.obj prime6_c.obj prime6_x.obj directio.obj \
     rpcrt4.lib rpcndr.lib rpcns4.lib $(conlibsmt)

primec6.obj : primec6.c prime6.h

directio.obj : directio.c directio.h
   $(cc) $(cflags) $(cvarsmt) directio.c
   $(cvtomf)

prime6_c.obj : prime6_c.c prime6.h
   $(cc) $(cflags) $(cvarsmt) prime6_c.c
   $(cvtomf)

prime6_x.obj : prime6_x.c prime6.h
   $(cc) $(cflags) $(cvarsmt) prime6_x.c
   $(cvtomf)
```

Listing 11.4 — (continued)

```
primes6 : primes6.exe
primes6.exe : primes6.obj primep6.obj prime6_s.obj
  prime6_y.obj directio.obj
    $(link) $(conflags) -out:primes6.exe \
      primes6.obj prime6_s.obj primep6.obj prime6_y.obj directio.obj \
      rpcrt4.lib rpcndr.lib rpcns4.lib $(conlibsmt)

primes6.obj : primes6.c prime6.h

primep6.obj : primep6.c prime6.h

prime6_s.obj : prime6_s.c prime6.h
  $(cc) $(cflags) $(cvarsmt) prime6_s.c
  $(cvtomf)

prime6_y.obj : prime6_y.c prime6.h
  $(cc) $(cflags) $(cvarsmt) prime6_y.c
  $(cvtomf)

#prime6.h prime6_c.c prime6_x.c prime6_s.c
  prime6_y.c : prime6.idl prime6.acf
prime6.h prime6_c.c prime6_x.c prime6_s.c prime6_y.c : prime6.idl
    midl -cpp_cmd $(cc) -cpp_opt "-E"  prime6.idl

# End of File #
```

Listing 11.5 — PRIME6.IDL

```
/*********************************************************************\
*                                                                   *
* PRIME6.IDL -  PRIME6 Interface Definition                         *
*              (c) Guy Eddon, 1993                                  *
*                                                                   *
\*********************************************************************/

[ uuid (24D37AB0-460B-2567-B357-08DBA524257A),
  version(1.0),
  pointer_default(unique)]
interface prime6
{
typedef [context_handle] void *PCONTEXT_HANDLE_TYPE;
typedef [ref] PCONTEXT_HANDLE_TYPE *PPCONTEXT_HANDLE_TYPE;

char RemoteIsPrime([in] handle_t h1, [in] unsigned long PrimeServerHandle,
                   [in] unsigned long TestNumber);

unsigned long InitializePrimeServer([in] handle_t h1,
                                    [out] PPCONTEXT_HANDLE_TYPE pphcontext,
                                    [in, string] unsigned char *ComputerName);

void TerminatePrimeServer([in] handle_t h1, [in] unsigned long PrimeServerHandle);
}

/* End of File */
```

Chapter 12

A Distributed Mandelbrot Application

The *PRIME* programs introduced the basic components of RPC and showed how to implement them. My goal in this chapter is to develop a distributed application that applies RPC to a problem with commercial applications. As Figures 12.1 and 12.2 show, this application computes and displays the *Mandelbrot* set.(The full-color displays that will appear on your screen are shown on the back cover.) While many existing programs can generate this image, nearly all do so on only one processor and may take as long as an hour to complete. The *Mandelbrot* application in this chapter uses RPC to exploit multiple CPUs, thus speeding the lengthy computations normally required to produce the graphic. By adding more computers (especially those that use such processors as the DEC Alpha or MIPS R4000) you can compute the entire *Mandelbrot* set in less time than was possible on even the fastest workstations. While this power may sound thrilling, you might ask how applying RPC to computing a *Mandelbrot* set is commercially valuable.

Lossless vs. Lossy Compression

Despite the advances made in data storage technology, the capacity to store and catalog information continues to lag behind ever-increasing quantities of data. This point is reinforced by the many successful commercial products that provide compression and decompression as a means of managing growing volumes of data.

Certain data compression techniques are static, while others are dynamic. PKZIP's compression is considered static because it requires user intervention to compress the data. Dynamic, or on-the-fly, compression

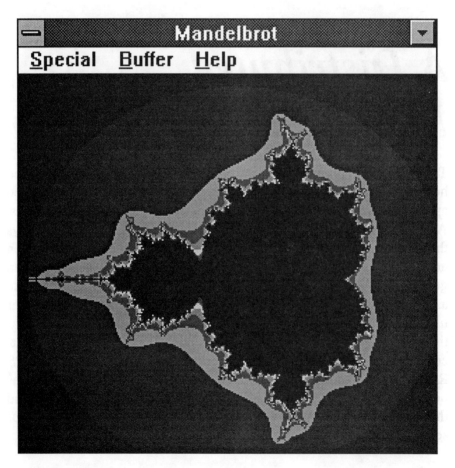

Figure 12.1   *Mandelbrot display.*

and decompression programs such as Stacker and DoubleDisk perform their jobs automatically when data is stored or retrieved.

All these products are examples of lossless compression technology. Lossless compression is usually reserved for data that must be reproduced precisely and cannot be subjected to approximation. Examples of such data might be bank records or executable programs. Unfortunately, lossless compression quickly reaches a ceiling, roughly a 2-to-1 compression ratio, beyond which it is impossible to reconstruct the data precisely, at least with today's technology.

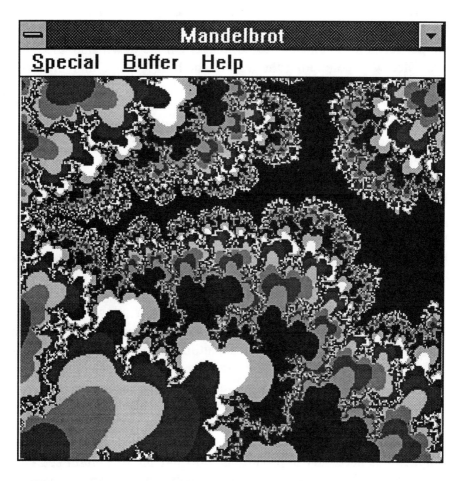

Figure 12.2 *Mandelbrot display.*

Lossy compression technology, on the other hand, is often used for sound and video data. Graphic images contain an enormous amount of information, amounting to more visual detail than the human eye can detect. Thus lossy compression techniques like JPEG can produce pleasing images even though they can't precisely replicate the original data. Similarly, one cannot differentiate sound produced from a file compressed to one-fourth its original size from that of the original, uncompressed file. Since precise reconstruction is not absolutely necessary, this kind of data can be subjected to lossy compression methods.

One interesting new technology in lossy compression is that of fractal compression. Tools that incorporate this technology compress and decompress images into fractals with astounding rates of compression. These fractals can then be transmitted in a fraction of the time it would take to transmit the uncompressed image. On the down side, the costs associated with computing the fractals, both in the time and advanced hardware, are quite high.

Visionaries see many practical uses for graphic compression, including live motion video where animated, true-color sequences of images run at rates comparable to film quality (30 frames per second). The problem, however, is to quickly decompress these fractals into viewable images. Conventional techniques require hours to recreate the images from these fractal compressions. The ability to decompress fractal images quickly might enable a whole new technology to emerge. For instance, people could carry medical records, including X-rays and other graphic images, stored in a key ring on their person. Such technology has enormous potential if harnessed correctly.

Using the distributed *Mandelbrot* application developed in this chapter, you can harness the processing power of multiple Windows NT computers to decompress fractals quickly, reducing decompression time to minutes or perhaps even seconds. By utilizing the *Mandelbrot* application's distributed processing, you can set a number of computers to the task of quickly building the fractal image.

I based the *Mandelbrot* application on an example supplied with the Microsoft RPC SDK. Microsoft's example is a simple program that makes remote procedure calls to a server, which then performs the computations necessary to produce and display the *Mandelbrot* set. One can barely call the Microsoft example a distributed application, since one server performs all the computations and simply returns the result to the client for display.

In contrast, the Mandelbrot application presented here offers the following features:

- □ One client can distribute work to many servers.
- □ Each server can support multiple clients.
- □ Rebinding to lost connections is handled automatically.
- □ A client dialog box displays which servers are currently active.
- □ The server displays current computations.

The Mandelbrot Set

According to Benoit Mandelbrot's classic definition, "A fractal is a curve whose Hausdorff-Besicovitch dimension is larger than its Euclidean dimension." Mandelbrot discovered this fractal while investigating the behavior of the iterated function

$$z_n = z^2_{(n-1)} + c$$

Where z and c are complex numbers.

To better understand this function, consider the hypothetical situation where z_0 is a real number and c is zero. If z_0 is 1, then the value of z always remains one, regardless of the number of iterations performed:

$$z_n = 1, 1, 1, 1, 1... \lim z_n = 1 \text{ as n approaches infinity}$$

If $z_0 = 1/2$ and $c = 0$, the sequence will be:

$$z_n = 1/2, 1/4, 1/8, 1/16, 1/32... \lim z_n = 0 \text{ as n approaches infinity}$$

z_n will approach zero faster if the starting number z_0 is smaller:

$$z_n = 1/5, 1/25, 1/125, 1/625, 1/3125... \lim z_n = 0 \text{ as n approaches infinity}$$

However, starting with z_0 greater than one, the sequence then becomes:

$$z_n = 2, 4, 8, 16, 32... \lim z_n = \text{infinity as n approaches infinity}$$

If the starting number z_0 is bigger still, the above sequence will approach infinity still faster, for example, 5, 25, 125, 625, 3125...

While this example is fairly simple, the results are much more complex when z_0 is a complex number, such as $x + iy$, or c is a complex number instead of zero. While mathematicians have known about these problems for years, it is only with modern computing power that we have been able to explore the chaotic behavior that yields fractal curves.

Design Issues

Unlike the PRIME programs, the Mandelbrot client does not perform computations locally. (However, the user can still take advantage of the client's CPU by launching a server locally. See the "Using Local Servers" section.) I chose this division of labor because it makes for a smaller, simpler, and more modular client. I can modify the server application, either increasing efficiency or adding functionality, without changing the client, and vice versa. For example, instead of producing a Mandelbrot fractal, a server could compute a Newton fractal. Alternatively, a user might want to use both a Mandelbrot and a Newton server simultaneously.

The Mandelbrot client's job is to quickly display the Mandelbrot fractal. In a non-distributed fractal application, the color of each pixel is computed and then displayed in a sequential manner until the entire picture is completed. The RPC-based Mandelbrot application cannot follow this model, since the RPC overhead does not permit the luxury of making a remote procedure call for every pixel. Instead, the client sends an entire buffer of memory as a parameter to each remote procedure call. Most of the buffer is empty, except for the first four bytes which contain pixel coordinates denoting the location at which the returned image will be displayed. The server then computes the color for each pixel in the desired range and stores it in the buffer. When finished, it returns the buffer, which now contains a fragment of the fractal.

The size of the buffer is determined by the user from a pull-down menu. Valid choices are 1, 2, 4, 8, or 16 columns per remote procedure call. Since a column is fixed at 300 pixels, the server computes 300, 600, 1200, 2400, or 4800 pixels per remote procedure call, respectively. When the client receives the buffer back, it displays the pixels in the correct location based upon the original coordinates sent in the first four bytes.

You could improve the *Mandelbrot* application's performance by using variant arrays, which I discussed in Chapter 8. Using a variant array would allow the client to transmit only the first four bytes (the location coordinates) of the buffer to the server, thus minimizing the amount of network traffic. (The rest of the buffer is just garbage until the server fills it with a portion of the fractal image.) Only after the server has finished computing the pixel values, would the application need to transmit the complete buffer.

Using a Local Server

The *Mandelbrot* client can also connect to a local server instead of, or in addition to, connecting to a remote server. If you don't have multiple computers at your disposal, you can still demonstrate the application by launching multiple servers and clients on a single computer. Even with multiple computers, you might launch a local server so that the power of the local CPU can also be used to compute pixel information.

You must launch each local server with a different endpoint. The default endpoint is *\pipe\mandel*. You may load the first server with the default, but you must start the second with a different endpoint, such as

```
server -e \pipe\testing
```

After starting the servers on different endpoints, you must inform the client of the server's endpoint by using the second edit control of the *Connections* dialog box.

Using NT's local RPC (*ncalrpc*) protocol sequence to communicate with the local server can improve the *Mandelbrot* application's performance. The local RPC protocol sequence is a special protocol for making remote procedure calls to servers on the same computer as the client. Since this protocol informs the RPC runtime that the two applications reside on the same server, the runtime can enhance performance by employing a more efficient message-passing mechanism.

Running Mandelbrot

When you start the *Mandelbrot* client, its main window appears, along with a modal dialog box that requests the computer name of the *Mandelbrot* server. If you are running a local *Mandelbrot* server, simply press the *Enter* key.

The *Mandelbrot* client then attempts to bind to the requested server. If successful, the server will begin computing the *Mandelbrot* set. Otherwise, the client will wait for the server to come on-line. If more than one server is available, you may choose *Connections* from the *Special* menu and enter another server name. You must repeat this process for each available server.

Once the *Mandelbrot* application begins computing, you may sit back and enjoy. Each time the client completes a frame of the *Mandelbrot* set, it automatically chooses a portion of that frame to enlarge. This process will continue indefinitely. To stop the continuous enlargement of the fractal image, uncheck *Continuous* in the *Special* menu. If you wish to manually enlarge a portion of the window, select it with the mouse.

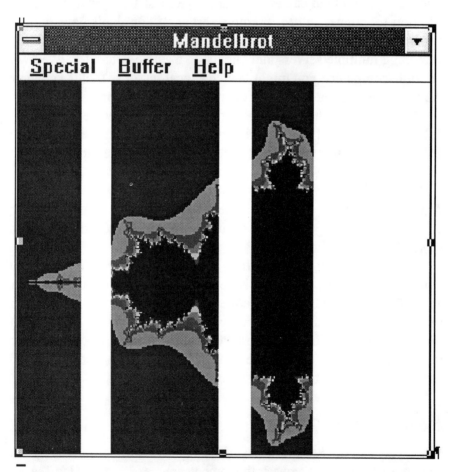

Figure 12.3   Mandelbrot *client waiting for servers to return their portions of the fractal.*

Since the time required to compute a portion of the fracal may vary
from server to server, the client may not display the columns in sequential
order. For this reason, the user may see sections of the fractal appear in
seemingly random order. Figure 12.3 shows a *Mandelbrot* client waiting
for several servers to return their portions of the fractal.

The *Statistics* dialog box, chosen from the client's *Special* menu,
lists the active servers and the columns of the fractal they are computing
(see Figure 12.4). The box displays an asterisk next to all inactive servers.
If a server goes off-line in the middle of a computation, the client will
attempt to re-route that server's work to another server so that the fractal
image is not damaged by a missing block. The *Mandelbrot* program even
lets you connect to servers that are off-line, as indicated by the asterisk.
When the server comes on-line, the *Mandelbrot* client recognizes this
event and begins to send work to it.

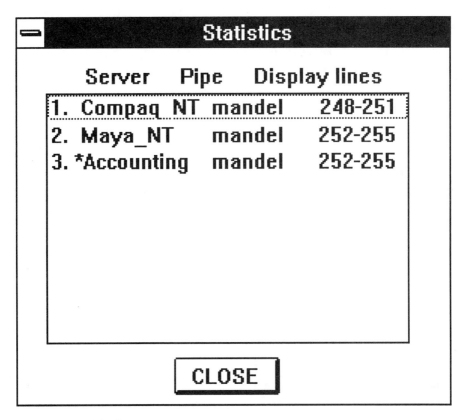

Figure 12.4   *The* Statistics *dialog box lists active servers and the
columns of the fractal they are computing.*

The *Buffer* menu lets you select the number of columns computed in each remote procedure call. This setting translates into the granularity of columns displayed on the client. The menu choices are 1, 2, 4, 8, or 16 columns. For better user response, choose a low granularity. For more efficient fractal computations, choose a higher granularity.

The Mandelbrot Server

The *Mandelbrot* server waits for client remote procedure calls. When the server receives a *MandelCalc()* remote procedure call from a client, it begins to compute the requested fractal portion. Among the parameters passed to *MandelCalc()* is the empty buffer that the server fills with pixel color values:

```
typedef struct _calcbuf
  {
  LONGRECT  rclDraw;
  double    dblPrecision;
  DWORD     dwThreshold;
  CPOINT    cptLL;
  } CALCBUF;

extern handle_t BindingHandle[];
static CPOINT cptLL;
CALCBUF cb;
static double dPrecision;  /* precision of draw      */
static DWORD dwThreshold;  /* threshold for iterations */
PDWORD  pbBuf;
```

X	Y	Precision	Threshold
0	3	0.010000	25
4	7	0.010000	25
8	11	0.010000	25
12	15	0.010000	25
16	19	0.010000	25
20	23	0.010000	25
24	27	0.010000	25

Table 12.1　　*Format of* Mandelbrot *server screen display.*

```
MandelCalc(BindingHandle[iServer], &cptLL, &(cb.rclDraw),
           dPrecision, dwThreshold, (PLINEBUF)pbBuf);
```

The server displays information about the portion of the fractal it is currently computing. The information on a *Mandelbrot* server screen takes the form of Table 12.1, in which the X and Y coordinates denote the portion of the fractal image currently being processed. These numbers correspond to the entries in the client's *Statistics* dialog box. Since the server solves the *Mandelbrot* function by approximation, the precision value determines how close it must be to the solution. The threshold specifies the maximum number of iterations computed before the function decides to give up. The threshold starts with the value 25 and doubles every 100 frames.

To run the *Mandelbrot* server, type the command *SERVER*. You may specify several command-line parameters, which you should recognize from the *PRIME* program examples:

```
-p protocol_sequence
-e endpoint
-m maxcalls
-n mincalls
-f flag_wait_op
-s security_descriptor
```

The *MANDEL.MAK* file will build the *Mandelbrot* application from the source files in Table 12.2.

File	Listing	Description
MANDEL.C	12.1	*Mandelbrot* client source
SERVER.C	12.2	*Mandelbrot* server source
REMOTE.C	12.3	*Mandelbrot* Remote procedures
CALC.C	12.4	*Mandelbrot* Fractal computation functions
MANDEL.H	12.5	*Mandelbrot* header file
MDLRPC.IDL	12.6	*Mandelbrot* interface definition
MDLRPC.ACF	12.7	*Mandelbrot* Attribute configuration file
MANDEL.RC	12.8	*Mandelbrot* Resource file
MANDEL.DEF	12.9	*Mandelbrot* Module definition file
MANDEL.MAK	12.10	*Mandelbrot* Makefile

Table 12.2   *Source files for* Mandelbrot *application.*

Summary

Unlike the *Prime* examples, the `Mandelbrot` application fully exploits the graphic capabilities of the Windows environment. Thus, the `Mandelbrot` client is a full Windows program — and has the structure of a Windows program — complete with message loop. Despite this radical change in programming style, the programmer need not learn any new techniques to create a distributed version. The simple elegance of the RPC model, because it so effectively emulates the ever-present function call, is just as effective for Windows programs as for more traditional programs.

Listing 12.1 — MANDEL.C

```
/*************************************************************************\
*                                                                       *
* MANDEL.C - Mandelbrot example                                         *
*           (c) Guy Eddon, 1993                                         *
*                                                                       *
* To build:  NMAKE MANDEL.MAK                                           *
*                                                                       *
* Comments:  Main code for the Windows Mandelbrot Set distributed drawing *
*            program.                                                   *
*                                                                       *
\*************************************************************************/

#define NCOLORS 11

#include <SYS\TYPES.H>
#include <SYS\STAT.H>
#include <DIRECT.H>
#include <DOS.H>
#include <STRING.H>
#include <CTYPE.H>
#include <MALLOC.H>
#include <STDIO.H>
#include <STDLIB.H>
#include <TIME.H>
#include <WINDOWS.H>
#include <WINDOWSX.H>
#include <RPC.H>

#include "mdlrpc.h"
#include "mandel.h"

#define MAX_THREADS 9

/* An array of binding handles */

handle_t BindingHandle[MAX_THREADS];

/* Previous cordinates from specific server. (To monitor server progress) */

extern UINT prev_coord[];

HWND hWnd;
HWND hWndSecondary;

/* Critical Section for choosing next available number for testing */

CRITICAL_SECTION GlobalCriticalSection;
```

Listing 12.1 — (continued)

```c
/* Storage for Computer Name */

char computername[MAX_COMPUTERNAME_LENGTH];
int computerlength = 9;
char szTitle[] = "Mandelbrot";
char szBitmap[] = "Mandel";

CPOINT  cptUL = { (double) -2.05, (double) 1.4 };
double  dPrec = (double) .01;
extern  int ipszNetAdd;
char    iServerUnBound = 0;

/* Display the buffer of colors received from server */

void PaintLine( HWND, svr_table *, HDC, int, long);

/* Map iterations receved from server to colors */

COLORREF MapColor(DWORD, DWORD);

/*  This function draws (or undraws) the zoom rectangle */

void DrawRect(HWND, PRECT, BOOL, HDC);

HANDLE hInst;
HANDLE GlobalhDlg;

/* Number of active servers */

int ipszNetAdd = 0;

DWORD  lpIDThread[MAX_THREADS];
HANDLE hthread_remote[MAX_THREADS];

/* number of vertical lines (each line is 300 pixel) to send to server */

int iLines = LINES;

/* info about servers */

svr_table SvrTable[20];
int SvrTableSz = 0;
int fContinueZoom = TRUE;
int fZoomIn = TRUE;

/* split current picture into 16 regions */

int Histogram[4][4][NCOLORS+1] = { 0 };
```

Listing 12.1 — (continued)

```
/* zoom on most complex region; region with most colors represented */

int ColorCount[4][4] = { 0 };
int Max[4][4] = { 0 };
int iHistMaxI = 2;
int iHistMaxJ = 3;
RECT rcZoom;
BOOL fRectDefined = FALSE;

/* flag indicates whether bound to svr */

int fBound[MAX_THREADS] = { FALSE };

/* returned by RPC API function */

RPC_STATUS status;

unsigned char * pszUuid            = NULL;
unsigned char * pszProtocolSequence = "ncacn_np";
unsigned char   pszEndpoint[MAX_THREADS][UNCLEN+1] = { "\\pipe\\mandel",
  "\\pipe\\mandel", "\\pipe\\mandel", "\\pipe\\mandel", "\\pipe\\mandel",
  "\\pipe\\mandel", "\\pipe\\mandel", "\\pipe\\mandel", "\\pipe\\mandel" };
unsigned char * pszOptions          = NULL;
unsigned char * pszStringBinding[MAX_THREADS] = { NULL };
unsigned char   szNetworkAddress[MAX_THREADS][UNCLEN+1] = { '\0' };

/* pointer to the dialog box function */

DLGPROC lpProcSecondary;

int APIENTRY WinMain(HANDLE hInstance, HANDLE hPrevInstance, LPSTR lpCmdLine, int nCmdShow)
   {
   MSG msg;
   unsigned long ulRpcException;

   RpcTryExcept
      {
      UNREFERENCED_PARAMETER(lpCmdLine);

      if(!hPrevInstance)
         if(!InitApplication(hInstance))
            return(FALSE);
```

Listing 12.1 — (continued)

```
/* Perform initializations that apply to a specific instance */

        if(!InitInstance(hInstance, nCmdShow))
            return (FALSE);

/* Acquire and dispatch messages until a WM_QUIT message is received. */

        while(GetMessage(&msg, (HWND)NULL, 0, 0))
            {
            if(hWndSecondary == 0 || !IsDialogMessage(hWndSecondary,&msg))
                {
                TranslateMessage(&msg);
                DispatchMessage(&msg);
                }
            }
        }
    RpcExcept(1)
        {
        ulRpcException = RpcExceptionCode();
        sprintf(pszFail, "Runtime exception 0x%lx = %ld\n", ulRpcException, ulRpcException);
        MessageBox(msg.hwnd, pszFail, "RPC Sample Application", MB_ICONINFORMATION | MB_SYSTEMMODAL);
        }
    RpcEndExcept

    return(msg.wParam);
    }

BOOL InitApplication(HANDLE hInstance)
    {
    WNDCLASS wc;

    wc.style = 0;
    wc.lpfnWndProc = (WNDPROC)MainWndProc;
    wc.cbClsExtra = 0;
    wc.cbWndExtra = 0;
    wc.hInstance = hInstance;
    wc.hIcon = LoadIcon(hInstance, "RPC_ICON");
    wc.hbrBackground = GetStockObject(WHITE_BRUSH);
    wc.lpszMenuName =  MENUNAME;
    wc.lpszClassName = CLASSNAME;

    return (RegisterClass(&wc));
    }
```

Listing 12.1 — (continued)

```
BOOL InitInstance(HANDLE hInstance, int nCmdShow)
   {
   RECT  rc;
   HMENU hMenu;

/* Save the instance handle in static variable, which will be used in
   many subsequence calls from this application to Windows.          */

   hInst = hInstance;

/* Create a main window for this application instance.  */

   hWnd = CreateWindow(CLASSNAME, szTitle,
                       WS_OVERLAPPED | WS_CAPTION | WS_SYSMENU | WS_BORDER | WS_MINIMIZEBOX,
                       25, 40, WIDTH, HEIGHT, (HWND)NULL, (HMENU)NULL, hInstance,
                       (void FAR *)NULL);

   if(!hWnd)
      return(FALSE);

   ShowWindow(hWnd, nCmdShow);
   UpdateWindow(hWnd);

   hWndSecondary = CreateDialog(hInst,"Secondary",hWnd, lpProcSecondary =
                               MakeProcInstance(Secondary, hInst));

   ShowWindow(hWndSecondary,SW_HIDE);

   rc.top = rc.left = 0;
   rc.bottom = HEIGHT - 1;
   rc.right = WIDTH - 1;

   SetNewCalc(cptUL, dPrec, rc);
   hMenu = GetMenu(hWnd);

   return (TRUE);
   }

LONG APIENTRY MainWndProc(HWND hWnd, UINT message, UINT wParam, LONG lParam)
/* additional information      */
   {
/* pointer to the dialog box function */

   DLGPROC lpProc;
```

Listing 12.1 — (continued)

```
PAINTSTRUCT  ps;
HDC hdc;
static HDC    hdcMem;
static HBITMAP hbmMem;
static int    width;
static int    height;
RECT          rc;
static BOOL   fButtonDown = FALSE;
static POINT  pSelected;
POINT         pMove;
int           iWidthNew;
int           iHeightNew;
static int    miOldLines;
double        scaling;

switch(message)
    {
    case WM_CREATE:

        /* bind to server */

        PostMessage(hWnd, WM_COMMAND, IDM_SERVER, 0L);
        InitializeCriticalSection(&GlobalCriticalSection);

        InitHistogram();

        hdc = GetDC(hWnd);
        hdcMem = CreateCompatibleDC(hdc);
        GetWindowRect(hWnd, &rc);
        width = rc.right - rc.left;
        height = rc.bottom - rc.top;
        hbmMem = CreateCompatibleBitmap(hdc, width, height);
        SelectObject(hdcMem, hbmMem);

        ReleaseDC(hWnd,hdc);

        rc.left = rc.top = 0;
        rc.right = width + 1;
        rc.bottom = height + 1;
        FillRect(hdcMem, &rc, GetStockObject(WHITE_BRUSH));

        CheckMenuItem(GetMenu(hWnd), IDM_4LINES, MF_CHECKED);
        CheckMenuItem(GetMenu(hWnd), IDM_CONTINUOUS, MF_CHECKED);

         /* save to uncheck  */

        miOldLines = IDM_4LINES;
```

Listing 12.1 — (continued)

```
        break;

    case WM_PAINT:

        hdc = BeginPaint(hWnd, &ps);

        BitBlt(hdc, ps.rcPaint.left, ps.rcPaint.top, ps.rcPaint.right - ps.rcPaint.left,
                ps.rcPaint.bottom - ps.rcPaint.top, hdcMem, ps.rcPaint.left,
                ps.rcPaint.top, SRCCOPY);
        EndPaint(hWnd, &ps);
        break;

    case WM_COMMAND:
        switch(wParam)
          {
          case IDM_BIND:
            if(Bind(hWnd,TRUE))
                PostMessage(hWnd, WM_DESTROY, 0, 0L);
            break;

          case IDM_ABOUT:
            lpProc = MakeProcInstance(About, hInst);
            DialogBox(hInst, ABOUTBOX, hWnd, lpProc);
            FreeProcInstance(lpProc);
            break;

          case IDM_SECONDARY:
            ShowWindow(hWndSecondary, SW_RESTORE);
            break;

          case IDM_ZOOMOUT:

            /* don't allow the zoom out */

            if(dPrec > (double)MAXPREC)
               break;

            /* center square */

            rcZoom.left = WIDTH/4 + (WIDTH/8);
            rcZoom.top   = HEIGHT/4 + (HEIGHT/8);
            rcZoom.right = rcZoom.left + (WIDTH/4);
            rcZoom.bottom = rcZoom.top + (HEIGHT/4);

             /* inverse of zoom in */
```

Listing 12.1 — (continued)

```
                cptUL.real -= (rcZoom.left * dPrec);
                cptUL.imag += (rcZoom.top * dPrec);
                iWidthNew = (rcZoom.right - rcZoom.left + 1);
                iHeightNew = (rcZoom.bottom - rcZoom.top + 1);
                scaling = ((double)((iWidthNew > iHeightNew) ? iWidthNew : iHeightNew)
                        / (double)width);
                dPrec /= scaling;

                rc.left = rc.top = 0;
                rc.bottom = height - 1;
                rc.right = width - 1;

                SetNewCalc(cptUL, dPrec, rc);
                fRectDefined = FALSE;
                break;

                /* zoom in on selected rectangle */

            case IDM_ZOOMIN:

                /* if no rectangle, don't zoom in  */

                if(!fRectDefined)
                    break;
                if(dPrec < (double)MINPREC)  // don't allow zoom in
                    break;

                DrawRect(hWnd, &rcZoom, TRUE, hdcMem);  // draw new rect

                // calculate new upper-left
                cptUL.real += (rcZoom.left * dPrec);
                cptUL.imag -= (rcZoom.top * dPrec);

                iWidthNew = (rcZoom.right - rcZoom.left + 1);
                iHeightNew = (rcZoom.bottom - rcZoom.top + 1);
                scaling = ((double)((iWidthNew > iHeightNew) ? iWidthNew : iHeightNew)
                    / (double)width);

                dPrec *= scaling;

                rc.left = rc.top = 0;
                rc.bottom = height - 1;
                rc.right = width - 1;

                SetNewCalc(cptUL, dPrec, rc);
                IncPictureID();
```

Listing 12.1 — (continued)

```
            fRectDefined = FALSE;
            break;

            /*  continuous zoom in  */

        case IDM_CONTINUOUS:
            if(fContinueZoom == TRUE)
               {
               CheckMenuItem(GetMenu(hWnd), IDM_CONTINUOUS, MF_UNCHECKED);
               fContinueZoom = FALSE;
               }
            else
               {
               CheckMenuItem(GetMenu(hWnd), IDM_CONTINUOUS, MF_CHECKED);
               fContinueZoom = TRUE;
               }
            break;

        case IDM_REDRAW:
            if(fContinueZoom == TRUE)
               InitHistogram();
            rc.left = rc.top = 0;
            rc.right = width+1;
            rc.bottom = height + 1;
            FillRect(hdcMem, &rc, GetStockObject(WHITE_BRUSH));
            InvalidateRect(hWnd, NULL, TRUE);

            rc.left = rc.top = 0;
            rc.bottom = height - 1;
            rc.right = width - 1;
            SetNewCalc( cptUL, dPrec, rc);

            fRectDefined = FALSE;
            break;

        case IDM_EXIT:
            DestroyWindow(hWnd);
            break;

        case IDM_TOP:
            cptUL.real = (double) -2.05;
            cptUL.imag = (double) 1.4;
            dPrec = .01;
```

Listing 12.1 — (continued)

```
            rc.left = rc.top = 0;
            rc.bottom = height - 1;
            rc.right = width - 1;
            SetNewCalc( cptUL, dPrec, rc);
            cPictureID = 0;

            fRectDefined = FALSE;
            break;

    case IDM_1LINE:
    case IDM_2LINES:
    case IDM_4LINES:
    case IDM_8LINES:
    case IDM_16LINES:

        CheckMenuItem(GetMenu(hWnd), miOldLines, MF_UNCHECKED);
        miOldLines = wParam;
        switch(wParam)
            {
            case IDM_1LINE:
                iLines = 1;
                break;
            case IDM_2LINES:
                iLines = 2;
                break;
            case IDM_4LINES:
                iLines = 4;
                break;
            case IDM_8LINES:
                iLines = 8;
                break;
            case IDM_16LINES:
                iLines = 16;
                break;
            }

        CheckMenuItem(GetMenu(hWnd), miOldLines, MF_CHECKED);
        break;

    case IDM_SERVER:
        lpProc = MakeProcInstance(Server, hInst);
        DialogBox(hInst, "ServerBox", hWnd, lpProc);
        FreeProcInstance(lpProc);
        break;

        /* Lets Windows process it */
```

Listing 12.1 — (continued)

```
        default:
            return (DefWindowProc(hWnd, message, wParam, lParam));
        }
        break;

    case WM_DESTROY:
        PostQuitMessage(0);
        DeleteDC(hdcMem);
        DeleteObject(hbmMem);
        DestroyWindow(GlobalhDlg);
        hWndSecondary = 0;

        {
        RPC_STATUS status;
        int i;

        for(i = 0; i < ipszNetAdd; i++)
            {
            /* remote calls done; unbind */

            status = RpcBindingFree(&BindingHandle[i]);

            sprintf(pszFail, "RpcBindingFree returned 0x%x", status);
            MessageBox(hWnd, pszFail, "RPC Sample Application", MB_ICONINFORMATION);
            }
        }
        break;

    case WM_PAINTLINE:

        /* The shared buffer contains a line of data; draw it */

        PaintLine(hWnd, (svr_table *)&SvrTable[(signed int)wParam], hdcMem, height, lParam);
        break;

    case WM_LBUTTONDOWN:

        /* left button down; start to define a zoom rectangle; undraw old rectangle */

        if(fRectDefined)
            DrawRect(hWnd, &rcZoom, FALSE, hdcMem);

        /* initialize rectangle */

        rcZoom.left = rcZoom.right = pSelected.x = LOWORD(lParam);
        rcZoom.top = rcZoom.bottom = pSelected.y = HIWORD(lParam);
```

Listing 12.1 — (continued)

```
        /* draw the new rectangle */

        DrawRect(hWnd, &rcZoom, TRUE, hdcMem);

        fRectDefined = TRUE;
        fButtonDown = TRUE;
        SetCapture(hWnd);          // capture all mouse events
        break;

    case WM_MOUSEMOVE:

        /* mouse move -- if the button is down, change the rect */

        if(!fButtonDown)
            break;

        /* undraw old rect */

        DrawRect(hWnd, &rcZoom, FALSE, hdcMem);

        pMove.x = LOWORD(lParam);
        pMove.y = HIWORD(lParam);

        /* update the selection rectangle */

        if(pMove.x <= pSelected.x)
            rcZoom.left = pMove.x;
        if(pMove.x >= pSelected.x)
            rcZoom.right = pMove.x;
        if(pMove.y <= pSelected.y)
            rcZoom.top = pMove.y;
        if(pMove.y >= pSelected.y)
            rcZoom.bottom = pMove.y;

        /* draw new rect */

        DrawRect(hWnd, &rcZoom, TRUE, hdcMem);
        break;

    case WM_LBUTTONUP:

        /* button up; end selection */

        fButtonDown = FALSE;
        ReleaseCapture();
        break;
```

Listing 12.1 — (continued)

```
            /* Passes it on if unproccessed    */

        default:
            return (DefWindowProc(hWnd, message, wParam, lParam));
        }

    return (0L);
    }

BOOL APIENTRY About(HWND hDlg, UINT message, UINT wParam, LONG lParam)
    {
    UNREFERENCED_PARAMETER(lParam);

    switch(message)
        {

        /* message: initialize dialog box */

        case WM_INITDIALOG:
            return (TRUE);

        /* message: received a command */

        case WM_COMMAND:

            /* "OK" box selected?  or  System menu close command? */

            if(wParam == IDOK || wParam == IDCANCEL)
                {

                /* Exits the dialog box      */

                EndDialog(hDlg, TRUE);
                return (TRUE);
                }
                break;
        }

    /* Didn't process a message    */

    return (FALSE);
    }
```

Listing 12.1 — (continued)

```
/* DrawRect -- This function draws (or undraws) the zoom rectangle. */

void DrawRect(HWND hwnd, PRECT prc, BOOL fDrawIt, HDC hdcBM)
   {
   HDC   hdc;
   DWORD dwRop;

   hdc = GetDC(hwnd);

   if(fDrawIt)
      dwRop = NOTSRCCOPY;
   else
      dwRop = SRCCOPY;

   /* top side */

   BitBlt(hdc, prc->left, prc->top, (prc->right - prc->left) + 1,
         1, hdcBM, prc->left, prc->top, dwRop);

   /* bottom side */

   BitBlt(hdc, prc->left, prc->bottom, (prc->right - prc->left) + 1,
         1, hdcBM, prc->left, prc->bottom, dwRop);

   /* left side */

   BitBlt(hdc,prc->left, prc->top, 1, (prc->bottom - prc->top) + 1, hdcBM, prc->left, prc->top, dwRop);

   /* right side */

   BitBlt(hdc,prc->right, prc->top, 1, (prc->bottom - prc->top) + 1,
         hdcBM, prc->right, prc->top, dwRop);

   ReleaseDC(hwnd, hdc);
   }

/* PaintLine -- This function paints a buffer of data into the bitmap. */

void PaintLine(HWND hwnd, svr_table * pst, HDC hdcBM, int cHeight, long iServer)
   {
   PWORD   pwDrawData;
   int     y;
   int     x;
   DWORD   dwThreshold;
   RECT    rc;
   WORD    lines;
   WORD    calc_left;
   WORD    calc_right;
```

Listing 12.1 — (continued)

```
/* picture ID had better match, or else we skip it */

if(CheckDrawingID(pst->cPicture))
   {

   /* figure out our threshold */

   dwThreshold = QueryThreshold();

   /* get a pointer to the draw buffer */

   pwDrawData = (PWORD)GetDrawBuffer(iServer);
   calc_left = *pwDrawData;
   pwDrawData+=2;
   calc_right = *pwDrawData;
   pwDrawData+=2;
   lines = calc_right-calc_left + 1;
   if(pwDrawData == NULL)
      {
      ReturnDrawBuffer(iServer);
      return;
      }

if(fBound[iServer] == FALSE)
   {
   ReturnDrawBuffer(iServer);
   return;
   }

/* starting x coordinate */

x = (int)calc_left + 1;

/* now loop through the rectangle */

while(lines-- > 0)
   {

   /* bottom to top, since that's the order of the data in the buffer */
   y = (int) cHeight-1;

   while(y >= 0)
      {
      /* draw a pixel */
      SetPixel(hdcBM, x,y, MapColor((DWORD)*pwDrawData, dwThreshold));
      if(fContinueZoom == TRUE)
         CalcHistogram(x, y, (DWORD)*pwDrawData, dwThreshold);
```

Listing 12.1 — (continued)

```
        /* now increment buffer pointer and y coord */

        y--;
        pwDrawData++;
        }

    /* increment X coordinate */

    x++;
    }

    /* figure out the rectangle to invalidate */

    rc.top = 0;
    rc.bottom = cHeight;
    rc.left = (int)calc_left;
    rc.right = (int)calc_right+2;

    FreeDrawBuffer(iServer);

    /* and invalidate it on the screen so we redraw it  */

    InvalidateRect(hwnd, &rc, FALSE);
    }

/* free this for someone else to use */

ReturnDrawBuffer(iServer);

/* and change the pipe state, if necessary */

if(pst->iStatus == SS_PAINTING)
    pst->iStatus = SS_IDLE;
}

#define CLR_BLACK        RGB(0,0,0)
#define CLR_DARKBLUE     RGB(0,0,127)
#define CLR_BLUE         RGB(0,0,255)
#define CLR_CYAN         RGB(0,255,255)
#define CLR_DARKGREEN    RGB(0,127,0)
#define CLR_GREEN        RGB(0,255,0)
#define CLR_YELLOW       RGB(255,255,0)
#define CLR_RED          RGB(255,0,0)
#define CLR_DARKRED      RGB(127,0,0)
#define CLR_WHITE        RGB(255,255,255)
#define CLR_PALEGRAY     RGB(194,194,194)
#define CLR_DARKGRAY     RGB(127,127,127)
```

Listing 12.1 — (continued)

```
static COLORREF ColorMapTable[] =
    {
    CLR_DARKBLUE,
    CLR_BLUE,
    CLR_CYAN,
    CLR_DARKGREEN,
    CLR_GREEN,
    CLR_YELLOW,
    CLR_RED,
    CLR_DARKRED,
    CLR_WHITE,
    CLR_PALEGRAY,
    CLR_DARKGRAY
    };

/* MapColor -- This function maps an iteration count into a corresponding RGB color. */

COLORREF MapColor(DWORD  dwIter, DWORD  dwThreshold)
    {
    /* if it's beyond the threshold, call it black */

    if(dwIter >= dwThreshold)
        {
        return CLR_BLACK;
        }

    /* get a modulus based on the number of colors */

    dwIter = (dwIter / 3) % NCOLORS;

    /* and return the appropriate color */
    return ColorMapTable[dwIter];
    }

/* CalcHistogram -- This function is used to select the region that
 is the most complex and will be used to zoom in for the next picture;
 it contains the most colors. The number of colors are counted. */

void CalcHistogram(int x, int y, DWORD  dwIter, DWORD  dwThreshold)
    {
    /* if it's beyond the threshold, call it black */

    if (dwIter >= dwThreshold)
        {
        Histogram[x/(WIDTH/4)][y/(HEIGHT/4)][NCOLORS]++;
        return;
        }
```

Listing 12.1 — (continued)

```
    /* get a modulus based on the number of colors */

    dwIter = (dwIter / 3) % NCOLORS;

    /* and bump the count for the appropriate color */

    Histogram[x/(WIDTH/4)][y/(HEIGHT/4)][dwIter]++;

    return;
    }

/* InitHistogram - This function initializes the histogram data structures. */

void InitHistogram(void)
    {
    int i, j, k;

    for(i = 0; i < 4; i++)
       for(j = 0; j < 4; j++)
          for(k = 0; k <= NCOLORS; k++)

             /* count of colors */

             Histogram[i][j][k] = 0;
    }

/* CountHistogram
    This function determines the number of colors represented within a region. The region with
    the most colors is selected using the maxi and maxj values. X and Y coordinates corresponding
    to these regions are stored in the HistRegion table and are used for the next picture. */

void CountHistogram(void)
    {
    int i, j, k;

    /* count the number of colors in each region  find the color that dominates each region */

    for(i = 0; i < 4; i++)
       {
       for (j = 0; j < 4; j++)
          {
          ColorCount[i][j] = 0;
          Max[i][j] = 0;
          for(k = 0; k <= NCOLORS; k++)
             {
             if(Histogram[i][j][k] > Max[i][j])
                Max[i][j] = Histogram[i][j][k];
```

Listing 12.1 — (continued)

```
            /* count of colors */

            if(Histogram[i][j][k] != 0)
                ColorCount[i][j]++;
            }
        }
    }

iHistMaxI = 0;
iHistMaxJ = 0;

/* if several regions have the same number of colors,
   select the region with the most variety:  the smallest max */

for(i = 0; i < 4; i++)
    {
    for(j = 0; j < 4; j++)
        {
        if((ColorCount[i][j] >= ColorCount[iHistMaxI][iHistMaxJ])
            && (Max[i][j] < Max[iHistMaxI][iHistMaxJ]))
            {
            iHistMaxI = i;
            iHistMaxJ = j;
            }
        }
    }

/* initialize for next time */

InitHistogram();
}

/* need this function to link properly; ndrlib needs it */

void *MIDL_user_allocate(size_t len)
    {
    UNREFERENCED_PARAMETER(len);
    return(NULL);
    }

BOOL APIENTRY Server(HWND hDlg, UINT message, UINT wParam, LONG lParam)
    {
    UNREFERENCED_PARAMETER(lParam);

    switch(message)
        {
```

Listing 12.1 — (continued)

```
    /* message: initialize dialog box */

    case WM_INITDIALOG:
        SetDlgItemText(hDlg, IDD_SERVERNAME, szNetworkAddress[ipszNetAdd]);
        SetDlgItemText(hDlg, IDD_ENDPOINT, pszEndpoint[ipszNetAdd]);
        return (TRUE);

    /* message: received a command */

    case WM_COMMAND:
        switch(wParam)
            {

            /* System menu close command? */

            case IDCANCEL:
                EndDialog(hDlg, FALSE);
                return(TRUE);

                /* "OK" box selected?    */

            case IDOK:
                GetDlgItemText(hDlg, IDD_SERVERNAME, szNetworkAddress[ipszNetAdd], UNCLEN);
                GetDlgItemText(hDlg, IDD_ENDPOINT, pszEndpoint[ipszNetAdd], UNCLEN);

                if(szNetworkAddress[ipszNetAdd][0] != '\\')
                    {
                    computername[0] = computername[1] = '\\';
                    GetComputerName(&computername[2], &computerlength);
                    GetComputerName(&computername[2], &computerlength);
                    strcpy(szNetworkAddress[ipszNetAdd],computername);
                    }

                if(Bind(hDlg,TRUE) != RPC_S_OK)
                    {
                    EndDialog(hDlg, FALSE);
                    return(FALSE);
                    }
                EndDialog(hDlg, TRUE);
                return(TRUE);
            }
        }

/* Didn't process a message    */

return (FALSE);
}
```

Listing 12.1 — (continued)

```
UINT prev_coord[MAX_THREADS];

/*
FUNCTION: Bind(HWND)

PURPOSE:  Make RPC API calls to bind to the server application

COMMENTS:
   The binding calls are made from InitInstance() and whenever
   the user changes the server name or endpoint. If the bind
   operation is successful, the global flag fBound is set to TRUE.

   The global flag fBound is used to determine whether to call
   the RPC API function RpcBindingFree.
*/

RPC_STATUS Bind(HWND hWnd,char flag)
   {
   RPC_STATUS status[MAX_THREADS];
   if(!flag)
      {
      if(fBound[iServerUnBound] == TRUE)
         {
         fBound[iServerUnBound] = FALSE;
         iServerUnBound = 0;
         return(status[iServerUnBound]);
         }
      return 0;
      }

   if(!InitRemote(hWnd,ipszNetAdd))
      return FALSE;

   status[ipszNetAdd] = RpcStringBindingCompose(pszUuid, pszProtocolSequence,
                                  szNetworkAddress[ipszNetAdd],
                                  pszEndpoint[ipszNetAdd], pszOptions,
                                  &pszStringBinding[ipszNetAdd]);

   if(!status[ipszNetAdd])
      {
      status[ipszNetAdd] = RpcBindingFromStringBinding(pszStringBinding[ipszNetAdd],
                                       &BindingHandle[ipszNetAdd]);
      }

   if(!status[ipszNetAdd])
      {
      /* bind successful; reset flag */
```

Listing 12.1 — (continued)

```
            fBound[ipszNetAdd] = TRUE;
            hthread_remote[ipszNetAdd] = CreateThread(NULL, 0,
                                        (LPTHREAD_START_ROUTINE)CheckDrawStatus,
                                        ipszNetAdd, CREATE_SUSPENDED,
                                        &lpIDThread[ipszNetAdd]);
        SetThreadPriority(hthread_remote[ipszNetAdd], THREAD_PRIORITY_LOWEST);
        ResumeThread(hthread_remote[ipszNetAdd]);
        if(hWndSecondary)
            {
            char Buffer[MAX_COMPUTERNAME_LENGTH];

            memset(Buffer, '\0', MAX_COMPUTERNAME_LENGTH);
            GetComputerName(Buffer, &computerlength);

            if(strlen(szNetworkAddress[ipszNetAdd]) <= 3)
                {
                memset(Buffer, '\0', MAX_COMPUTERNAME_LENGTH);
                GetComputerName(Buffer, &computerlength);
                }
            else
                {
                memset(Buffer, '\0', MAX_COMPUTERNAME_LENGTH);
                lstrcpy(Buffer, &szNetworkAddress[ipszNetAdd][2]);
                Buffer[computerlength] = 0;
                lstrcat(Buffer, " ");
                lstrcat(Buffer, &pszEndpoint[ipszNetAdd][6]);
                lstrcat(Buffer, " bound.");
                }

            SendMessage(GetDlgItem(GlobalhDlg, SERVER_LB), LB_ADDSTRING, 0,
                                (LPARAM)(LPCSTR)Buffer);
            }
        ipszNetAdd++;
        }
    else
        {
        fBound[ipszNetAdd] = FALSE;
        }
    return(0);
    }

BOOL APIENTRY Secondary(HWND hDlg, UINT message, UINT wParam, LONG lParam)
/* additional information      */
    {
    char Buffer[300];
```

Listing 12.1 — (continued)

```
switch(message)
    {
    case WM_INITDIALOG:
        GlobalhDlg = hDlg;
        return TRUE;

    case WM_PAINTDLG:
        memset(Buffer, '\0', 300);
        strcpy(Buffer, &szNetworkAddress[lParam][2]);
        sprintf(Buffer, "%d.  %-10s %-10s  %d-%d ", lParam + 1,&szNetworkAddress[lParam][2],
                &pszEndpoint[lParam][6], wParam, wParam + iLines - 1);

        if(prev_coord[lParam] == wParam)
            Buffer[2] = '*';
        else
            prev_coord[lParam] = wParam;

        SendMessage(GetDlgItem(hDlg, SERVER_LB), WM_SETREDRAW,FALSE,0L);
        SendMessage(GetDlgItem(hDlg, SERVER_LB), LB_DELETESTRING, lParam, 0L);
        SendMessage(GetDlgItem(hDlg, SERVER_LB), LB_INSERTSTRING,
                    lParam, (LPARAM)(LPCSTR)Buffer);
        SendMessage(GetDlgItem(hDlg, SERVER_LB), WM_SETREDRAW,TRUE,0L);

        return FALSE;

    case WM_COMMAND:
        switch(wParam)
            {
            case WM_DESTROY:
            case 3:
                ShowWindow(hWndSecondary, SW_HIDE);
                return TRUE;
            }
        return FALSE;
    }
    return FALSE;
    }

/* End of File */
```

Listing 12.2 — SERVER.C

```
/***************************************************************************\
* SERVER.C - Mandelbrot example                                           *
*            (c) Guy Eddon, 1993                                          *
*                                                                         *
* To build:  NMAKE                                                        *
\***************************************************************************/

#include <STDLIB.H>
#include <WINDOWS.H>
#include <STDIO.H>
#include <CTYPE.H>
#include <RPC.H>

#include "mdlrpc.h"
#include "mandel.h"

HANDLE hSharedBuf = NULL;

/* Displays command line options */

void Usage(char * pszProgramName)
    {
    fprintf(stderr, "Usage:  %s\n", pszProgramName);
    fprintf(stderr, " -p protocol_sequence\n");
    fprintf(stderr, " -e endpoint\n");
    fprintf(stderr, " -m maxcalls\n");
    fprintf(stderr, " -n mincalls\n");
    fprintf(stderr, " -f flag_wait_op\n");
    fprintf(stderr, " -s security_descriptor\n");
    exit(1);
    }

void _CRTAPI1 main(int argc, char *argv[])
    {
    RPC_STATUS status;
    unsigned char * pszProtocolSequence = "ncacn_np";
    unsigned char * pszSecurity    = NULL;
    unsigned char * pszEndpoint     = "\\pipe\\mandel";
    unsigned int    cMinCalls       = 1;
    unsigned int    cMaxCalls       = 20;
    unsigned int    fDontWait       = FALSE;
    int i;
```

Listing 12.2 — (continued)

```
/* allow the user to override settings with command line switches */

for(i = 1; i < argc; i++)
   {
   if((*argv[i] == '-') || (*argv[i] == '/'))
      {
      switch(tolower(*(argv[i]+1)))
         {
         case 'p':
             pszProtocolSequence = argv[++i];
             break;
         case 'e':
             pszEndpoint = argv[++i];
             break;
         case 'm':
             cMaxCalls = (unsigned int)atoi(argv[++i]);
             break;
         case 'n':
             cMinCalls = (unsigned int)atoi(argv[++i]);
             break;
         case 'f':
             fDontWait = (unsigned int)atoi(argv[++i]);
             break;
         case 's':
             pszSecurity = argv[++i];
             break;
         case 'h':
         case '?':
         default:
             Usage(argv[0]);
         }
      }
   else
      Usage(argv[0]);
   }

hSharedBuf = GlobalAlloc(GMEM_FIXED, MAX_BUFSIZE);

/* Tells the RPC runtime to use the specified protocol sequence combined
   with the specified endpoint for receiving remote procedure calls */

status = RpcServerUseProtseqEp(pszProtocolSequence, cMaxCalls, pszEndpoint, pszSecurity);
printf("RpcServerUseProtseqEp returned 0x%x\n", status);
if(status)
   {
   exit(status);
   }
```

Listing 12.2 — (continued)

```
    /* Registers an interface with RPC runtime */

    status = RpcServerRegisterIf(mdlrpc_ServerIfHandle, NULL, NULL);
    printf("RpcServerRegisterIf returned 0x%x\n", status);
    if(status)
        {
        exit(status);
        }

    printf("Calling RpcServerListen\n");

    /* Tells the RPC runtime to listen for remote procedure calls */

    status = RpcServerListen(cMinCalls, cMaxCalls, fDontWait);
    printf("RpcServerListen returned: 0x%x\n", status);
    if(status)
        {
        exit(status);
        }

    if(fDontWait)
        {
        printf("Calling RpcMgmtWaitServerListen\n");
        status = RpcMgmtWaitServerListen();  // wait operation
        printf("RpcMgmtWaitServerListen returned: 0x%x\n", status);
        if(status)
            {
            exit(status);
            }
        }
    }

/* Memory allocation and deallocation  for RPC runtime */

static HANDLE hMidlUserFunc;

void *MIDL_user_allocate(size_t len)
    {
    hMidlUserFunc = GlobalAlloc(GMEM_FIXED, len);
    return(PDWORD)(GlobalLock(hMidlUserFunc));
    }

void MIDL_user_free(void *ptr)
    {
    GlobalUnlock(hMidlUserFunc);
    GlobalFree(hMidlUserFunc);
    }
/* End of File */
```

Listing 12.3 — REMOTE.C

```
/*************************************************************************\
* REMOTE.C - Mandelbrot example                                          *
*           (c) Guy Eddon, 1993                                          *
*                                                                        *
* To build:  NMAKE                                                       *
*                                                                        *
* Comments:                                                              *
*   Code to do the remote calculations for the Windows Mandelbrot Set    *
*   distributed drawing program.                                         *
*                                                                        *
*   Information coming into this module (via API calls) is based on      *
*   upper-left being (0,0) (the Windows standard). We translate that     *
*   to lower-left is (0,0) before we ship it out onto                    *
*   the net, and we do reverse translations accordingly.                 *
*                                                                        *
*   The iteration data is passed back to the main window procedure       *
*   (by means of a WM_PAINTLINE message) which draws the picture.        *
*           program.                                                     *
\*************************************************************************/

#include <STRING.H>
#include <STDIO.H>
#include <FCNTL.H>
#include <SYS\TYPES.H>
#include <SYS\STAT.H>
#include <SHARE.H>
#include <IO.H>
#include <MALLOC.H>
#include <WINDOWS.H>
#include <RPC.H>

#include "mdlrpc.h"
#include "mandel.h"

#define SVR_TABLE_SZ 20

/* errno from c runtime */

extern int errno;

/* Main window handle.  */

extern HWND hWnd;
```

Listing 12.3 — (continued)

```
/* Dialog Box window handle.  */

extern HWND hWndSecondary;

extern char      iServerUnBound;
extern handle_t BindingHandle[];
extern int       ipszNetAdd;

/* Data structures */

extern svr_table    SvrTable[];
extern int          SvrTableSz;
char pszFail[255];

BOOL fRemoteWork = FALSE;

/* picture id, in case we reset in the middle */

int cPictureID = 0;

/* upper-left */

static CPOINT cptLL;

/* precision of draw */

static double dPrecision;

/* rectangle defining client window */

static LONGRECT rclPicture;

/* next line to be drawn */

static DWORD dwCurrentLine;

/* threshold for iterations */

static DWORD dwThreshold;

extern CRITICAL_SECTION GlobalCriticalSection;

static char szLocal[] = "Local machine";

/* returned by RPC API function */

RPC_STATUS status;
```

Listing 12.3 — (continued)

```
/* function prototypes for local procs */

DWORD CalcThreshold(double);

extern UINT prev_coord[];

/* InitRemote --
   This function initializes everything for our remote connections.
   It gets the local wksta name (making sure the wksta is started)
   and it creates the mailslot with which to collect replies to our poll.
   RETURNS
       TRUE        - initialization succeeded
       FALSE       - initialization failed, can't go on */

BOOL InitRemote( HWND hWnd,int iServer )
   {
   UNREFERENCED_PARAMETER(hWnd);

   SvrTableSz++;
   strcpy(SvrTable[iServer].name, szLocal);
   SvrTable[iServer].iStatus = SS_LOCAL;

   /* value out of range */

   prev_coord[iServer]= 30000;

   /* good, we succeeded */

   return TRUE;
   }
/* CheckDrawStatus --
   This function does a check of all buffers being drawn.
   If it finds an idle pipe, and there is work to be done, it assigns
       a line, and writes out the request.
   If it finds a read-pending pipe, it checks if the read has completed.
       If it has, it is read and a message is sent so the read data can
       be processed.
   RETURNS
       TRUE        - we did a piece of work
       FALSE       - we could not find any work to do.*/

static int  iThreadWork = 0;
void CheckDrawStatus(int iServer)
   {
   int      iWork = iServer;
   int      iLast;
   CALCBUF  cb;
   PDWORD   pbBuf;
```

Listing 12.3 — (continued)

```
char flag = 0;
DWORD dwCurtLine;
dwCurtLine = dwCurrentLine;

while(1)
    {
    WORD wIteration = 0;

    iLast = iWork;

    while(TRUE)
        {
        /* Check the status */

        switch(SvrTable[iWork].iStatus)
            {
            case SS_PAINTING:
                break;

            case SS_IDLE:
                if((long)dwCurtLine > rclPicture.xRight)
                    break;

                if(!fRemoteWork)
                    break;
                if(!flag)
                    {
                    EnterCriticalSection(&GlobalCriticalSection);
                    dwCurtLine = dwCurrentLine;
                    dwCurrentLine += iLines;
                    LeaveCriticalSection(&GlobalCriticalSection);
                    flag = 1;
                    }

                /* cb is of type CALCBUF -- rectangle, precision, threshold and complex point */

                cb.rclDraw.xLeft = dwCurtLine;
                cb.rclDraw.xRight = dwCurtLine + iLines - 1;
                cb.rclDraw.yTop = rclPicture.yTop;
                cb.rclDraw.yBottom = rclPicture.yBottom;
                cb.dblPrecision = dPrecision;
                cb.dwThreshold = dwThreshold;
                cb.cptLL = cptLL;
                SvrTable[iWork].dwLine = dwCurtLine;
                SvrTable[iWork].iStatus = SS_READPENDING;
                SvrTable[iWork].cPicture = cPictureID;
                SvrTable[iWork].cLines = iLines;
                break;
```

Listing 12.3 — (continued)

```
case SS_LOCAL:
    if(!flag)
        {
        EnterCriticalSection(&GlobalCriticalSection);
        dwCurtLine = dwCurrentLine;
        dwCurrentLine += iLines;
        LeaveCriticalSection(&GlobalCriticalSection);
        flag = 1;
        }

    if(fBound[iServer] == FALSE)
        {
        Sleep(400);
        fBound[iServer] = TRUE;
        }

    if((long)dwCurtLine > rclPicture.xRight)
        {
        if(fContinueZoom == TRUE)
            {
            if((fZoomIn == TRUE) && (dPrec < (double)MINPREC))
                fZoomIn = FALSE;
            if((fZoomIn == FALSE) && (dPrec > (double)MAXPREC))
                fZoomIn = TRUE;
            if(fZoomIn)
                {
                CountHistogram();
                rcZoom.top    = iHistMaxJ * (WIDTH/4);
                rcZoom.bottom = rcZoom.top + (WIDTH/4) - 1;
                rcZoom.left   = iHistMaxI * (HEIGHT/4);
                rcZoom.right  = rcZoom.left + (HEIGHT/4) - 1;
                fRectDefined  = TRUE;
                PostMessage(hWnd, WM_COMMAND, IDM_ZOOMIN, 0L);
                }
            else
                PostMessage(hWnd, WM_COMMAND, IDM_ZOOMOUT, 0L);
            }
        dwCurtLine = 0;
        break;
        }
```

Listing 12.3 — (continued)

```
if(!TakeDrawBuffer(iServer))
   break;

if(!flag)
   {
   EnterCriticalSection(&GlobalCriticalSection);
   dwCurtLine = dwCurrentLine;
   dwCurrentLine += iLines;
   LeaveCriticalSection(&GlobalCriticalSection);
   flag = 1;
   }

pbBuf = GetDrawBuffer(iServer);

cb.rclDraw.xLeft  = dwCurtLine;
cb.rclDraw.xRight = dwCurtLine+ iLines-1;
cb.rclDraw.yTop = rclPicture.yTop;
cb.rclDraw.yBottom = rclPicture.yBottom;
*pbBuf++ = dwCurtLine;
*pbBuf++ = dwCurtLine +iLines - 1;

RpcTryExcept
   {
   MandelCalc(BindingHandle[iServer], &cptLL, &(cb.rclDraw),
            dPrecision, dwThreshold, (PLINEBUF)pbBuf);
   flag = 0;
   }
RpcExcept(1)
   {
   iServerUnBound = iServer;
   fBound[iServer] = FALSE;
   Bind(hWnd,FALSE);
   }
RpcEndExcept
```

Listing 12.3 — (continued)

```
            if(hWndSecondary)
                PostMessage(hWndSecondary, WM_PAINTDLG, (UINT)(cb.rclDraw.xLeft), iServer);

            FreeDrawBuffer(iServer);

            SvrTable[iWork].cPicture = cPictureID;
            SvrTable[iWork].dwLine = dwCurtLine;
            SvrTable[iWork].cLines = iLines;

            PostMessage(hWnd, WM_PAINTLINE, (UINT)iWork, iServer);
            }
        }
    }
}

/* SetNewCalc --
    This sets up new information for a drawing and updates the drawing
    ID so any calculations in progress will not be mixed in. */

void SetNewCalc(CPOINT cptUL, double dPrec, RECT rc)
    {
    /* First, the base point. We need to translate from upper left to lower left */

    cptLL.real = cptUL.real;
    cptLL.imag = cptUL.imag - (dPrec * (rc.bottom - rc.top));

    dPrecision = dPrec;

    rclPicture.xLeft = (long)rc.left;
    rclPicture.xRight = (long)rc.right;
    rclPicture.yBottom = (long)rc.top;
    rclPicture.yTop = (long)rc.bottom;

    dwCurrentLine = rclPicture.xLeft;

    dwThreshold = CalcThreshold(dPrecision);
    }

void IncPictureID(void)
    {
    cPictureID++;
    }
```

Listing 12.3 — (continued)

```
/* CheckDrawing --
   Just a sanity check here -- a function to check to make sure that we're
   on the right drawing */

BOOL CheckDrawingID(int id)
   {
   return (id == cPictureID) ? TRUE : FALSE;
   }

/* TakeDrawBuffer / GetDrawBuffer / FreeDrawBuffer / ReturnDrawBuffer
   These functions hide a handle to a buffer of memory.
    TakeDrawBuffer ensures only one pipe read at a time.
   GetDrawBuffer locks the handle and returns a pointer.
   FreeDrawBuffer unlocks the handle.
   ReturnDrawBuffer unlocks the handle and lets another pipe read go. */

#define MAX_THREADS 9

static BOOL fBufferTaken[MAX_THREADS] = { FALSE };
static HANDLE hSharedBuf[MAX_THREADS] = { (HANDLE)NULL };

BOOL TakeDrawBuffer(int pipe)
   {
   if(fBufferTaken[pipe])
      {
      return FALSE;
      }

   if(hSharedBuf[pipe] == NULL)
      {
      hSharedBuf[pipe] = GlobalAlloc(GMEM_MOVEABLE, MAX_BUFSIZE);
      if(hSharedBuf[pipe] == NULL)
         return FALSE;
      }
   fBufferTaken[pipe] = TRUE;
   return TRUE;
   }

PDWORD GetDrawBuffer(int pipe)
   {
   if(hSharedBuf[pipe] == NULL)
      return NULL;

   return (PDWORD)GlobalLock(hSharedBuf[pipe]);
   }
```

Listing 12.3 — (continued)

```c
void FreeDrawBuffer(int pipe)
   {
   GlobalUnlock(hSharedBuf[pipe]);
   }

void ReturnDrawBuffer(int pipe)
   {
   fBufferTaken[pipe] = FALSE;
   }

/* CalcThreshold --
   We need an iteration threshold beyond which we give up. We want it to
   increase the farther we zoom in. This code generates a threshold value
   based on the precision of drawing.
   RETURNS
       threshold calculated based on precision */

DWORD CalcThreshold(double precision)
   {
   DWORD  thres = 25;
   double multiplier = (double)100.0;

   /* for every 100, multiply by 2 */

   while((precision *= multiplier) < (double)1.0)
      thres *= 2;

   return thres;
   }

/* QueryThreshold --
   Callback for finding out what the current drawing's threshold is. */

DWORD QueryThreshold(void)
   {
   return dwThreshold;
   }

/* GetServerCount -- Returns the number of servers in the table. */

int GetServerCount(void)
   {
   return (int)SvrTableSz - 1;
   }

/* End of File */
```

Listing 12.4 — CALC.C

```
/***************************************************************************\
* CALC.C   - Mandelbrot example                                           *
*           (c) Guy Eddon, 1993                                           *
*                                                                         *
* To build:  NMAKE MANDEL.MAK                                             *
*                                                                         *
* Comments:  Code to do the calculations for the Windows Mandelbrot Set   *
*            distributed drawing program.                                 *
\***************************************************************************/

#include <WINDOWS.H>
#include <MALLOC.H>
#include <STRING.H>
#include <STDIO.H>
#include <RPC.H>

#include "mdlrpc.h"
#include "mandel.h"

/*
   h1      - explicit binding handle
   pcptLL  - pointer to complex number
   prcDraw - drawing rectangle
   pbBuf   - number of iterations are stuff here
*/

void MandelCalc(handle_t h1, PCPOINT pcptLL, PLONGRECT  prcDraw,
                double precision, DWORD  ulThreshold, PLINEBUF pbBuf)
   {
   char Buffer[300];

   DWORD  h, height;
   DWORD  width;
   PWORD  pbPtr;
   double dreal, dimag, dimag2;
   short  maxit = 0;

/* Show what the server is computing */

   sprintf(Buffer,"%3ld  %3ld  %f  %ld \n", prcDraw->xLeft,
      prcDraw->xRight, precision, ulThreshold);
   printf(Buffer);

/* PLINEBUF points to the struct LINEBUF, LINEBUF is an array of WORDS */

   pbPtr = (PWORD)pbBuf;
```

Listing 12.4 — (continued)

```c
    dreal = pcptLL->real + ((double)prcDraw->xLeft * precision);
    dimag = pcptLL->imag + ((double)prcDraw->yBottom * precision);

    maxit = (short)ulThreshold;

    height = (prcDraw->yTop - prcDraw->yBottom) + 1;
    width = (prcDraw->xRight - prcDraw->xLeft) + 1;

    for(; width > 0; --width, dreal += precision)
        {
        for(dimag2 = dimag, h = height; h > 0; --h, dimag2 += precision)
            {
            if((dreal > 4.0) || (dreal < -4.0) || (dimag2 > 4.0) || (dimag2 < -4.0))
                *(pbPtr++) = 0L;
            else
                *(pbPtr++) = (WORD)(calcmand(dreal, dimag2, maxit));
            }
        }

    return;
    }

/* The actual calculations are done here */

short calcmand(double dreal, double dimag, short maxit)
    {
    double x, y, xsq, ysq;
    short k;

    k = (short)maxit;
    x = dreal;
    y = dimag;

    while(1)
        {
        xsq = x * x;
        ysq = y * y;
        y = 2.0 * x * y + dimag;
        x = (xsq - ysq) + dreal;
        if(--k == 0)
            return((short)(maxit - k));
        if((xsq + ysq) > 4.0)
            return((short)(maxit - k));
        }
    }

/* End of File */
```

Listing 12.5 — MANDEL.H

```
/*************************************************************************\
* MANDEL.H - Mandelbrot example                                         *
*            (c) Guy Eddon, 1993                                        *
*                                                                       *
* To build:  NMAKE MANDEL.MAK                                           *
\*************************************************************************/

#define SERVER_LB 1

#define IDM_ABOUT       100
#define IDM_SECONDARY   1990
#define IDM_ZOOMIN      101
#define IDM_ZOOMOUT     105
#define IDM_TOP         106
#define IDM_REDRAW      107
#define IDM_EXIT        108
#define IDM_CONTINUOUS  109
#define IDM_SERVER      110
#define IDD_SERVERNAME  111
#define IDD_ENDPOINT    113
#define IDM_BIND        112
#define IDM_1LINE       200
#define IDM_2LINES      201
#define IDM_4LINES      202
#define IDM_8LINES      203
#define IDM_16LINES     204
#define ID_REMOVE       1000
#define ID_CLOSE        3

#define IDD_LB_SERVER   205

#define ID_OK           304

#define WM_DOSOMEWORK   (WM_USER+0)
#define WM_PAINTLINE    (WM_USER+1)
#define WM_PAINTDLG     (WM_USER+2)

#define LBID_SERVERS    102

#define WIDTH           300
#define HEIGHT          300

#define MAXLINES        16

#define MAXID           64      // saved zoomin operations

#define MAX_BUFSIZE     (HEIGHT * sizeof(long) * MAXLINES)
```

Listing 12.5 — (continued)

```c
#define MENUNAME        "MandelMenu"
#define CLASSNAME       "MandelClass"
#define ABOUTBOX        "AboutBox"
#define SERVERBOX       "ServerBox"
#define SECONDBOX       "SecondBox"


#define POLL_TIME       100
#define LINES           4


#define CNLEN           15   /* computer name length */
#define UNCLEN          CNLEN+2 /* \\computername */
#ifndef MAXPATHLEN
#define MAXPATHLEN      260
#endif
#ifndef APIENTRY
#define APIENTRY FAR PASCAL
#endif
#ifndef UNREFERENCED_PARAMETER
#define UNREFERENCED_PARAMETER(P)       \
    { \
        (P) = (P); \
    }
#endif

extern int iLines;

// A table of servers we know about
typedef struct _svr_table
    {
    char    name[16+1];                 // name of remote server
    int     hfPipe;                     // RPC handle
    int     iStatus;                    // status of connection
    int     cPicture;                   // picture id for this line
    DWORD   dwLine;                     // line we're drawing
    int     cLines;                     // lines in this chunk
    } svr_table;

// if RPC, this data is defined within the IDL file
// For LOCAL COMPUTATIONS
typedef struct _clpoint
    {
    double    real;
    double    imag;
    } CLPOINT;
```

Listing 12.5 — (continued)

```c
typedef CLPOINT *PCLPOINT;

typedef struct _LLONGRECT
    {      /* rcl */
    long    xLeft;
    long    yBottom;
    long    xRight;
    long    yTop;
    } LLONGRECT;

typedef LLONGRECT *PLLONGRECT;

typedef struct _LLINEBUF
    {
    WORD adw[MAX_BUFSIZE];
    } LLINEBUF;

typedef LLINEBUF * PLLINEBUF;

extern svr_table    SvrTable[];         // the table
extern int          SvrTableSz;         // # of objects in it
extern int          cPictureID;         // current picture; index to table
extern RECT         rcHistory[];

int APIENTRY WinMain(HANDLE, HANDLE, LPSTR, int);
BOOL InitApplication(HANDLE);
BOOL InitInstance(HANDLE, int);
LONG APIENTRY MainWndProc(HWND, UINT, UINT, LONG);
BOOL APIENTRY About(HWND, UINT, UINT, LONG);
BOOL APIENTRY Secondary(HWND, UINT, UINT, LONG);
BOOL APIENTRY Server(HWND, UINT, UINT, LONG);
BOOL APIENTRY SaveAsDlgProc(HWND, UINT, UINT, LONG);

RPC_STATUS Bind(HWND,char);
extern int fBound[];

void DoSomeWork(HWND, BOOL);
void IncPictureID(void);

void InitHistogram(void);
void CountHistogram(void);
void CalcHistogram(int  x, int y, DWORD  dwIter, DWORD  dwThreshold);
```

Listing 12.5 — (continued)

```
#define NCOLORS 11

extern int fContinueZoom;
extern int fZoomIn;
extern int iHistMaxI;
extern int iHistMaxJ;
extern int Histogram[4][4][NCOLORS+1];
extern int ColorCount[4][4];
extern BOOL fRectDefined;

extern char pszFail[];

BOOL InitRemote(HWND, int);
void PollForServers(void);
void CheckPoll(void);

void CheckDrawStatus(int);

void RetryConnections(void);
void SetNewCalc(CPOINT cptUL, double dPrecision, RECT rcl);
BOOL CheckDrawingID(int);

extern BOOL fRemoteWork;

// Status of connection to server

#define SS_IDLE          1
#define SS_READPENDING   2
#define SS_PAINTING      3
#define SS_LOCAL         4

// Buffer routines

BOOL TakeDrawBuffer(int);
PDWORD GetDrawBuffer(int);
void FreeDrawBuffer(int);
void ReturnDrawBuffer(int);
DWORD QueryThreshold(void);

int GetServerCount(void);
void GetServerName(int, char *);

extern RECT rcZoom;
extern double dPrec;
```

Listing 12.5 — (continued)

```
#define MINPREC 5.0E-9
#define MAXPREC 5.0E-3

typedef struct _calcbuf
    {
    LONGRECT  rclDraw;
    double    dblPrecision;
    DWORD     dwThreshold;
    CPOINT    cptLL;
    } CALCBUF;

short calcmand(double dreal, double dimag, short maxit);

typedef struct _mults
    {
    double  rs;      /* real squared    */
    double  is;      /* imag squared    */
    double  ri;      /* real * imaginary */
    } mults;

/* End of File */
```

Listing 12.6 — MDLRPC.IDL

```
/***********************************************************************\
* MDLRPC.IDL -  Interface Definition for Mandelbrot                    *
*              (c) Guy Eddon, 1993                                     *
\***********************************************************************/

[ uuid (3523EF40-CA38-114B-BD42-2033552BDE2A),
  version (1.0),
  pointer_default(unique)
]
interface mdlrpc
{
#define HEIGHT        300
#define MAXLINES      4
#define LONGSIZE      8
#define MAX_BUFSIZE   9600

typedef struct _cpoint
   {
   double real;
   double imag;
   } CPOINT;

typedef CPOINT *PCPOINT;

typedef struct _LONGRECT
   {
   long xLeft;
   long yBottom;
   long xRight;
   long yTop;
   } LONGRECT;

typedef LONGRECT *PLONGRECT;

typedef struct _LINEBUF
   {
   unsigned short adw[MAX_BUFSIZE];
   } LINEBUF;
```

Listing 12.6 — (continued)

```
typedef [ref] LINEBUF *PLINEBUF;

void MandelCalc( [in]  handle_t        h1,
                 [in]  PCPOINT         pcptLL,
                 [in]  PLONGRECT       prcDraw,
                 [in]  double          precision,
                 [in]  unsigned long ulThreshold,
                 [out] LINEBUF *       pbBuf);
}

/* End of File */
```

Listing 12.7 — MDLRPC.ACF

```
/*************************************************************************\
*                                                                         *
* MDLRPC.ACF -  Attribute Configuration for Mandelbrot                    *
*              (c) Guy Eddon, 1993                                        *
*                                                                         *
\*************************************************************************/

[implicit_handle(handle_t hMandel)]
interface mdlrpc
{

}

/* End of File */
```

Listing 12.8 — MANDEL.RC

```
/************************************************************************\
*                                                                      *
* MANDEL.RC- Mandelbrot resource file                                  *
*          (c) Guy Eddon, 1993                                         *
*                                                                      *
* To build:  NMAKE MANDEL.MAK                                          *
*                                                                      *
* Comments:  Menus and dialog boxes                                    *
*                                                                      *
\************************************************************************/

#include <WINDOWS.H>
#include "mandel.h"

RPC_ICON ICON MANDEL.ICO

MandelMenu MENU
BEGIN
    POPUP            "&Special"
    BEGIN
    MENUITEM             "&Connections...",      IDM_SERVER
        MENUITEM         "S&tatistics",          IDM_SECONDARY
    MENUITEM SEPARATOR
        MENUITEM         "&Zoom in",             IDM_ZOOMIN
        MENUITEM         "Zoom &out",            IDM_ZOOMOUT
    MENUITEM             "&Top",                 IDM_TOP
        MENUITEM         "&Redraw",              IDM_REDRAW
        MENUITEM SEPARATOR
    MENUITEM             "&Continuous",          IDM_CONTINUOUS
        MENUITEM         "E&xit",                IDM_EXIT
    END
    POPUP            "&Buffer"
    BEGIN
        MENUITEM         "1 Line",               IDM_1LINE
        MENUITEM         "2 Lines",              IDM_2LINES
        MENUITEM         "4 Lines",              IDM_4LINES
        MENUITEM         "8 Lines",              IDM_8LINES
        MENUITEM         "16 Lines",             IDM_16LINES
    END
    POPUP            "&Help"
    BEGIN
        MENUITEM         "&About Mandelbrot...", IDM_ABOUT
    END
END
```

Listing 12.8 — (continued)

```
AboutBox DIALOG 22, 17, 144, 105
STYLE DS_MODALFRAME | WS_CAPTION | WS_SYSMENU | WS_VISIBLE
CAPTION "About Mandelbrot"
BEGIN
    CTEXT "Mandelbrot RPC Application" -1, 0,  5, 144, 8
    CTEXT "Copyright Guy Eddon, 1993" -1, 0, 14, 144, 8
    CTEXT "Based on a Microsoft sample program"  -1, 0, 23, 144, 8
    CONTROL "RPC_ICON", 104, "static", SS_ICON | WS_CHILD, 18, 43, 16, 21
    DEFPUSHBUTTON "OK" IDOK, 53, 89,  32, 14, WS_GROUP
END


ServerBox DIALOG LOADONCALL MOVEABLE DISCARDABLE 67, 39, 200, 40
CAPTION "Connections..."
STYLE WS_BORDER | WS_CAPTION | WS_DLGFRAME | WS_SYSMENU | DS_MODALFRAME
BEGIN
    LTEXT "Server" -1, 4, 6, 30, 8
    CONTROL "", IDD_SERVERNAME, "edit",
        ES_LEFT | ES_AUTOHSCROLL | WS_BORDER | WS_TABSTOP | WS_CHILD,
        35, 6, 95, 12
    LTEXT  "Endpoint" -1,4,20,30,8
    CONTROL "", IDD_ENDPOINT, "edit",
        ES_LEFT | ES_AUTOHSCROLL | WS_BORDER | WS_TABSTOP | WS_CHILD,
        35, 20, 95, 12
    CONTROL "OK", 1, "button",
        BS_DEFPUSHBUTTON | WS_TABSTOP | WS_CHILD, 160, 6, 35, 12
    CONTROL "Cancel", 2, "button",
        BS_PUSHBUTTON | WS_TABSTOP | WS_CHILD, 160, 20, 35, 12
END


Secondary DIALOG WIDTH, 17, 144, 115
STYLE WS_POPUP | WS_CAPTION | WS_SYSMENU
CAPTION "Statistics"
BEGIN
    CTEXT "Server     Pipe     Display lines" -1, 0, 5, 144, 8
    CONTROL "", SERVER_LB, "LISTBOX",
        LBS_HASSTRINGS | LBS_NOTIFY | WS_VSCROLL | WS_CHILD | WS_BORDER |
        WS_TABSTOP, 10, 15, 120, 85
    CONTROL "CLOSE", 3, "button", BS_PUSHBUTTON | WS_TABSTOP | WS_CHILD,
        52, 100, 35, 12
END

/* End of File */
```

Listing 12.9 — MANDEL.DEF

```
;;;;;;;;;;;;;;;;;;;;;;;;;;;;;;;;;;;;;;;;;;;;;;;;;;;;;;;;;;;;;;;;;;;;;;;;;;
;                                                                      ;
; MANDEL.DEF - Module Definition File                                  ;
;              (c) Guy Eddon, 1993                                     ;
;                                                                      ;
;;;;;;;;;;;;;;;;;;;;;;;;;;;;;;;;;;;;;;;;;;;;;;;;;;;;;;;;;;;;;;;;;;;;;;;;;;

NAME        MANDEL
DESCRIPTION 'Mandelbrot Drawing'
EXETYPE     WINDOWS
STUB        'WINSTUB.EXE'

CODE  PRELOAD MOVEABLE DISCARDABLE
DATA  PRELOAD MOVEABLE MULTIPLE
HEAPSIZE    10240
STACKSIZE   5120

EXPORTS
        MainWndProc   @1
        About         @2
        Server        @3
        Secondary     @4

; End of File ;
```

Listing 12.10 — MANDEL.MAK

```
#############################################################################
#                                                                          #
# MANDEL.MAK - Makefile                                                    #
#                                                                          #
#############################################################################

!include <ntwin32.mak>

RPCFLAG = -DRPC

cvtomf =
!if "$(CPU)" == "MIPS"
cvtomf = mip2coff $@
!endif

!if "$(CPU)" == "i386"
cflags = $(cflags:G3=Gz)
!endif

.c.obj:
    $(cc) $(cflags) $(cvars) $(RPCFLAG) $<
    $(cvtomf)

all: client.exe server.exe

client.exe: mandel.obj remote.obj mandel.def mandel.rbj \
            mdlrpc_c.obj mdlrpc_x.obj
    $(link) $(guiflags) -out:client.exe \
      mandel.obj remote.obj mdlrpc_c.obj mdlrpc_x.obj \
      mandel.rbj rpcrt4.lib rpcndr.lib $(guilibs)

server.exe: server.obj calc.obj mdlrpc_s.obj mdlrpc_y.obj
    $(link) $(conflags) -out:server.exe \
      server.obj calc.obj mdlrpc_s.obj mdlrpc_y.obj \
      rpcrt4.lib rpcndr.lib $(conlibs)

# Update the resource if necessary
mandel.rbj: mandel.rc mandel.h
    rc -r mandel.rc
    cvtres -$(CPU) mandel.res -o mandel.rbj
```

Listing 12.10 — (continued)

```
# Object file dependencies

# server only built for RPC version; always needs mdlrpc.h
server.obj: server.c mandel.h mdlrpc.h

mandel.obj: mandel.c mandel.h mdlrpc.h
remote.obj: remote.c mandel.h mdlrpc.h
calc.obj  : calc.c mandel.h mdlrpc.h

# client stub
mdlrpc_c.obj : mdlrpc_c.c mdlrpc.h
!if "$(CPU)"=="i386"
    $(cc) $(cflags) $(cvars) mdlrpc_c.c
!endif

# client auxiliary file
mdlrpc_x.obj : mdlrpc_x.c mdlrpc.h
!if "$(CPU)"=="i386"
    $(cc) $(cflags) $(cvars) mdlrpc_x.c
!endif

# server stub file
mdlrpc_s.obj : mdlrpc_s.c mdlrpc.h
!if "$(CPU)"=="i386"
    $(cc) $(cflags) $(cvars) mdlrpc_s.c
!endif

# server auxiliary file
mdlrpc_y.obj : mdlrpc_y.c mdlrpc.h
!if "$(CPU)"=="i386"
    $(cc) $(cflags) $(cvars) mdlrpc_y.c
!endif

# Stubs, auxiliary and header file from the IDL file
mdlrpc.h mdlrpc_c.c mdlrpc_x.c mdlrpc_s.c mdlrpc_y.c: mdlrpc.idl
    midl mdlrpc.idl

# End of File #
```

Evolution
of PC Operating Systems

When IBM began building their own personal computer, the mainframe giant contracted with Bill Gates and his small software company, Microsoft, to supply an operating system for the new machine. At that time, Microsoft's most popular products were BASIC interpreters for a variety of personal computers including Tandy, Commodore, and Apple.

Rather than write a new operating system from scratch, Microsoft bought 86-DOS from Seattle Computer Products, and ported it to the IBM PC. Tim Paterson had originally written 86-DOS for Seattle Computer Products in 1980. The new port, PC-DOS v1.0, was released for the IBM PC computer in 1982. This was the foundation of the IBM/Microsoft partnership.

IBM management regarded their own PC as a toy, an addendum to their real business, which was building powerful and expensive mainframes. This was a serious tactical error, as evidenced by the millions of PCs sold each year. Had IBM developed their own operating system or bought Microsoft's instead of licensing it, they might not find themselves in their current situation. However, this toy mentality permeated IBM management long after it became abundantly clear that the future will not belong to mainframes.

MS-DOS proved tremendously successful in the PC marketplace and quickly became the defacto standard for the IBM PC. MS-DOS, however, had (and still has) a very serious flaw: It internalizes the addressing limitations of the original 8086 CPU. The 8086 CPU could address only 1Mb of memory, using only 16-bit offsets. At the time, one megabyte of memory seemed more than a program would ever need. After all, the most successful micro operating system of the day, CP/M, could address only 64Kb. Thus, throughout its internals, MS-DOS assumes there will be no usable memory above 1Mb and that offsets will always be limited to 16 bits.

Now there are millions of 80286 and 80386 PCs with multiple megabytes of memory available, and many widely used applications that require more than single megabyte of program space. Therefore, both IBM and Microsoft collaborated in an effort to develop a protected mode version of DOS, to take advantage of the new features of the 80286 Intel chip, such as memory protection and the ability to access extended memory.

Compatibility

MS-DOS can trace its ancestry directly to an earlier micro operating system: CP/M. CP/M, from Digital Research, Inc., was the semi-standard operating system used with early microcomputers. Though 86-DOS was developed independently, the core services in the original release were designed to be compatible with the services offered by CP/M. Many of these functions remain in current releases of MS-DOS, though Microsoft strongly encourages developers to use alternate versions in new development. Thus, even in the "middle ages" of microcomputing (1981), compatibility was an important issue. Today, compatibility with previous versions of an application, or even with entirely different operating systems, is still a central issue facing all operating system developers.

OS/2 and the 286

This protected mode version of DOS was eventually named OS/2 v1.0 and was first released in 1987. OS/2 was seen as rightful successor to MS-DOS, and was widely regarded as the new standard for the IBM AT. OS/2, however, was a disappointment; it had performance, reliability, and compatibility problems. In retrospect, the early versions of OS/2 should be regarded as a learning experience for the industry. No one knew how to work with protected mode or with the other advanced features of the 80286 chip. In fact, the 80286 chip itself was an early attempt at innovation by Intel.

Intel planned many good features into the 80286 design but left several important things on the cutting room floor. The most important of these was the ability to switch the CPU from real mode into protected mode and back. The 80286 chip boots in real mode and from software can be switched to protected mode. Intel never considered the possibility of switching it back to real mode. This and other design flaws were later corrected in the 80386 chip.

Consequently, OS/2 was dealing with several handicaps, including a limited CPU, which hampered its performance and reliability. Microsoft and IBM realized that eventually a separate 32-bit version of OS/2 would

DOS Extenders

When DOS extenders first came out in 1989, they were extraordinary products. They allowed an application to take advantage of the larger memory space in newer computers but still run MS-DOS. A DOS extender lets an MS-DOS program allocate and execute code above the 1Mb boundary imposed by the real mode MS-DOS. DOS extenders work by switching the CPU into protected mode and then intercepting MS-DOS calls. When an MS-DOS call is made, the DOS extender either provides the service itself or switches back into real mode and passes the call along to MS-DOS. In this way a DOS extender temporarily becomes the protected mode operating system.

have to be written for 80386 chips. This became OS/2 v2.0. Times were changing, and Microsoft never collaborated with IBM on OS/2 v2.0.

The Surrogate OS/2

In 1985 Microsoft released Windows as one of the first desktop GUIs (Graphics User Interface) to run on the IBM PC. While it ran in real mode only, it was a graphical multitasking environment that sat on top of MS-DOS. Microsoft urged developers to start writing Windows applications until OS/2 v1.0 came out in 1987. According to Microsoft, Windows applications would easily port to OS/2 Presentation Manager (PM) when it became available. In effect, Windows was supposed to be a temporary surrogate for OS/2.

Although Windows applications were not difficult to port to OS/2 PM, little Windows-to-OS/2 porting ever took place because most developers waited until OS/2 was released in 1987. Most developers that is, except Microsoft. When it became clear that OS/2 was not all it was cracked up to be, Microsoft intensified its own development of Windows. They

Enhanced Mode in Three Flavors

Many programmers are not aware that enhanced mode Windows 3.1 operates in three different modes internally. These modes can be enumerated as follows:

1	V86 mode	When MS-DOS programs are executing, Windows is in V86 mode.
2	16-bit protected mode	When Windows programs are executing, Windows is in 286 protected mode.
3	32-bit protected mode	When virtual device drivers are executing, Windows is in 386 protected mode.

The best way to see how and when Windows 3.1 switches among these modes is to use the Soft-Ice/W debugger for Windows. This excellent debugger from Nu-Mega Technologies is one of the few that can show you how Windows 3.1 internals operate. I certainly hope that Nu-Mega Technologies will release a version of Soft-Ice/W for Windows NT.

applied knowledge gained during the development of OS/2 to creating a superior version of Windows. This new version was released amid an intense media blitz as Windows 3.0 in 1990. When Windows 3.0 began selling (as OS/2 should have done), Microsoft dropped IBM like a hot "potatoe" (to quote a great American).

Windows 3.0

While Windows 3.0 was far from perfect, it had several points in its favor. It was relatively fast, ran on top of MS-DOS so that users could always drop back to a familiar environment, and had excellent MS-DOS compatibility. In enhanced mode, it could run multiple MS-DOS applications simultaneously, and had significantly lower hardware requirements than OS/2. In addition, for the novice computer user, it provided an intuitive, easy to learn computing environment.

The marketplace responded. Where before, OS/2 had been seen as the rightful successor to MS- DOS, the marketplace became divided between supporters of two different operating systems, neither one completely compatible with the other. The success of Windows and the failure of OS/2 can be attributed largely to timing. When OS/2 was released in 1987, the marketplace was not prepared for its seemingly extreme hardware requirements (four megabytes of RAM and 80 megabytes of hard disk space). By the time Windows 3.0 was released in 1990 with similar hardware requirements, the necessary hardware was readily available.

The other difference between OS/2 and Windows was design philosophy. OS/2 took the ground-up approach of building an entirely new operating system, while Windows took the incremental approach of working on top of MS-DOS and adding more features slowly. Windows NT is a ground-up redesign, but retains compatibility with the windows feature set.

The Fallout

The success of Windows created many negative feelings toward Microsoft — and not just from IBM. Many software developers felt they had been misled by Microsoft into developing applications for OS/2 instead of Windows. Developers were saddled with their poorly selling

OS/2 applications, while Microsoft had several unopposed Windows applications that were doing quite well. Even today, Microsoft's domination over the word processing and spreadsheet applications for Windows is largely due to the lead of more than a year over competitors' Windows applications.

Windows acquired market-leader status, leaving OS/2 2.0 (though it may be a good operating system) in the unenviable position of "an also ran." Even so, Windows was not without problems of its own. For example, dreaded UAEs (Unrecoverable Application Errors) could cause users to lose all unsaved data. In response, Microsoft released a much improved version of Windows in 1992 as Windows 3.1.

Windows 3.1

Considering the amount of work that went into it, Windows 3.1 really should have been named "Windows 4.0." Microsoft dropped real mode support, and improved overall stability and performance. They also added support for TrueType fonts, multimedia, and OLE.

Windows 3.1 is often denied operating system status because it runs on top of MS-DOS. Microsoft appears to have settled on the term "environment" for Windows 3.1. While Windows 3.1 does run on top of MS-DOS it uses fewer MS-DOS services then any previous version of Windows. With the new FastDisk service, Windows 3.1 can now even access some hard drives without calling MS-DOS.

Windows 3.1 supports two modes of operation: Standard and Enhanced. Enhanced mode is the only practical alternative for new development. Most new Windows software will require enhanced mode operation. (For instance, Windows for Workgroups runs in enhanced mode only.)

Windows for Workgroups

Windows for Workgroups version 3.1 was released in November 1992. While not all Windows 3.1 users have switched yet, I believe they will soon, due in part to Windows NT. On a developmental scale Windows for Workgroups is a product positioned between Windows 3.1 and Windows NT. In fact, Windows for Workgroups is Windows 3.1 with added and enhanced Windows applets, extensions, and protected mode network drivers.

Windows for Workgroups supports peer-to-peer communication between MS-DOS, Windows 3.1, and Windows NT. In Windows for Workgroups you can share a local device with a computer running Windows NT. Windows for Workgroups is packaged with the network drivers necessary to make remote procedure calls from MS-DOS and Windows 3.1. It is important to note, however, that Windows for Workgroups runs in enhanced mode only and therefore requires at least an 80386 processor.

The Future of MS-DOS, Windows on DOS, and Windows NT

The release of Windows NT does not indicate the demise of MS-DOS, nor Windows on DOS. With an estimated 100 million MS-DOS users, and millions of Windows 3.1 users, it will be a long time before these systems disappear. In addition, Microsoft continues to plan and release new versions of these systems. The release of MS-DOS 6.0, with improved memory management, integrated disk compression, utilities, and configuration options, shows a strong commitment to the bread and butter of the operating system market.

Microsoft's future plans include MS-DOS 7.0, rumored to be a 32-bit multitasking environment, and Windows 4.0 (Chicago) which will be a scaled down version of Windows NT running on top of MS-DOS. Future enhancements of Windows NT include a major revision (Cairo), which will provide an object-oriented user interface. As these projects come to fruition, the phrase "Windows Everywhere" may become a reality.

The Future

The purpose of an operating system is to allow a standardized method of accessing application software. An operating system is a standard which allows multiple application programs to coexist peacefully. Today's operating systems aim at providing as many standard services as possible without compromising efficiency and hardware requirements.

Since 1981, MS-DOS has been that standard, in part because of its parsimonious approach to resources. MS-DOS allows an application to request only very simple services. Thus, most programs rely upon MS-DOS to provide only two services:

□ Load the program into memory and begin execution.
□ Perform file I/O functions at the program's request.

Other than that, a commercial MS-DOS application is practically on its own. MS-DOS allows one to go anywhere and do anything within the first megabyte of memory.

Unfortunately one megabyte is no longer adequate to sate the appetites of developers or users. Alone, MS-DOS is simply no longer an acceptable choice for most users. While add-on environments like Windows 3.1, DESQview, and DOS extenders overcome some of these limitations, and farther extend the life of MS-DOS, they do not offer acceptable long term solutions.

Even so, Windows 3.1 and its successors will probably be around for some time yet. This means that MS-DOS will stick around a while longer. This is not necessarily bad as long as the users of these systems are happy. When users outgrow these environments, which they eventually will, Windows NT will be there for them.

Will Windows NT be able to bring users of today's diverse operating systems and environments together to agree on a new standard? Not immediately, but in the long run, almost certainly. Its extensive compatibility with the applications of other operating systems will win over many potential users. As native Windows NT applications hit the stands (many of them are available now at a software store near you), the new features of Windows NT will shine through.

What is Win32?

Win32 is a 32-bit API (Application Programming Interface) which takes advantage of the 32-bit processing power of 80386 CPUs. As such, Win32 is *not* the Windows NT operating system. Win32 is a set of functions used to write applications that will work on any platform that supports the Win32 API. Of course, Windows NT is *currently* the only implementation of the Win32 API.

Since Win32 is only an API, developers can build on top of Windows NT without conforming to the Win32 specification. And, while Win32 has Microsoft's backing, conceivably some other API could emerge as the preferred developer's interface to NT. In fact several alternative APIs are already available.

Most notable are the Multiplatform Development Systems (MDS), such as XVT, which make one API available on several platforms. XVT, for instance, provides its API for MS-DOS, Windows 3.1, Windows NT, Macintosh, OS/2, Presentation Manager, and several flavors of UNIX. If you write to a portable API, then the difficulty of porting your application to another operating system is greatly reduced, especially if you write it in a widely implemented language such as C.

How Win32s Differs from Win32

Win32s is a subset of the Win32 API. (The 's' on the end of Win32s stands for "subset.") Win32s is a subset API that works on both Windows NT and Windows 3.1. The purpose of Win32s, is to allow a native Windows NT program written to the Win32s API, to run on Windows 3.1. This means that even if you write a 32-bit Windows NT application, your user can run it on Windows 3.1 without having the hardware Windows NT requires. Win32s will be a major force in the PC software market, as almost all applications written for Windows NT will try to claim Win32s compatibility. This is because Windows 3.1 has an enormous installed base of users, while Windows NT is just starting out.

The Win32s system consists of several 32-bit DLLs and one virtual device (VxD). These facilities provide the ability to load and execute 32-bit applications written for Windows NT. (See Figure A2.1, Win32s System Architecture. The dark gray boxes are the Win32s modules, while

Developing Win32s Applications

When writing a Win32s program, you draft the program as a regular Windows NT application, using Windows NT development tools to compile and link the application. Then, to confirm that the application uses only Win32s calls, you test the application in Windows 3.1. If you have two computers you can set up one with Windows for Workgroups to share the directory with the program in Windows NT. This assumes that network cards have been installed in both computers.

If you would prefer to develop on a single machine, you can of course reboot your computer to switch between Windows 3.1 and Windows NT. Or, if rebooting to switch between environments sounds too barbaric, you can use TNT DOS Extender 6.1 from PharLap Software.

TNT DOS Extender 6.1 is a special version of Phar Lap's 386 DOS extender that can load and execute programs in the Portable Executable (PE) format used by Windows NT. With TNT DOS Extender 6.1 you can run Microsoft's Windows NT C compiler, linker, and other Windows NT tools in MS-DOS, thus simplifying your development cycle. I highly recommend TNT DOS Extender 6.1 for Win32s development.

Interestingly, one could conceivably use Win32s to write a set of DLLs and a VxD device to support some other 32-bit operating system, for instance OS/2 2.0 PM. I wouldn't be surprised to see a third party vendor, or even Microsoft, attempt to market an OS/2 API subset for Windows 3.1. The likelihood of this occurring will be dependent upon the number of OS/2 2.0 applications actually brought to market.

the light gray boxes make up the Windows 3.1 code.) A Win32 application should call only Win32s modules. Most of the Win32s modules simply translate and then forward the Win32 calls to the 16-bit modules of Windows 3.1. In addition, the Win32s virtual device (VxD), is used to handle low-level system services such as exception handling, floating-point trap emulation, and memory management.

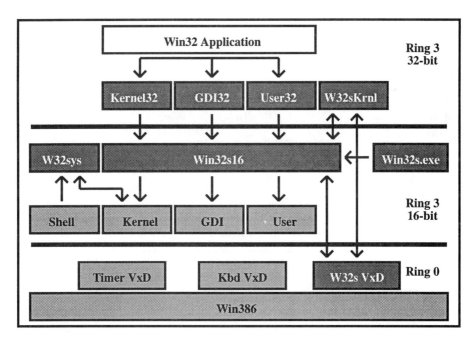

Figure A2.1 *Win32s system architecture.*

Windows 3.0 does not support Win32s. Windows 3.1 includes both the Win32s modules and a loader that can recognize apps that need to have the Win32s modules available. If Windows 3.1 cannot recognize an executable's format, then it attempts to locate the Win32s system. If available, it transfers control to the Win32s system. Otherwise it displays a message informing the user that the program the user attempted to start is in an unknown executable format. When the Win32s system receives control, it identifies the application as a Windows NT executable, and loads it accordingly.

API	Windows 3.0	Windows 3.1	Windows NT
Win16	X	X	X
Win32s		X	X
Win32			X

Table A2.1   *Compatibility of Windows versions with Win APIs.*

Features	Win16	Win32s	Win32
Bezier Curves			X
Console			X
File mapping			X
Multitasking	X	X	X
Multithreading			X
RPC clients	X		X
RPC servers			X
Security			X
SEH		X	X
Unicode		X	X
Virtual memory	X	X	X
32-bit code		X	X
32-bit flat model		X	X

Table A2.2   *Features available with the Windows APIs.*

OSF DCE

The goals of the OSF DCE standards are to allow interoperability and portability across heterogeneous platforms. Within OSF DCE, you can create a network of computers ranging from mainframes to minis to workstations to PCs and create distributed applications that will share the services and advantages of each.(See the Bibliography for a list of books on the OSF DCE standards.)

OSF DCE supports three main types of distributed computing models — client/server, remote procedure call, and data sharing:

> **The client/server model.** This model divides an application into two parts. Each part resides on one of the two computers participating in the distributed application. The client/server model is often implemented using RPC. Microsoft SQL Server is a good example of the client/server model.

> **The remote procedure call model.** This model usually implements the communication mechanism between the client and the server. The client makes what looks like a local procedure call, which the underlying RPC mechanism translates into network messages. The remote procedure executes on the server. RPC is used by most of the other DCE technology components for their network communications. The remote procedure call is a low-level

service for implementing client/server and data sharing applications. Microsoft RPC is an example of an RPC service.

The data sharing model. This model focuses on distributed data rather than distributed execution. Data sharing is implemented by distributing data throughout the system. Lotus Notes is an example of the data sharing model.

Traditionally, network software for personal computers has been built upon the model of a powerful computer designated as a server to share resources among workstations. In this model, however, the resources the server supplies are usually specialized, such as file, print, and communication services. RPC represents an evolutionary step in this model. You can now designate a server as a compute server, allowing clients to share its CPU power as a resource.

OSF cites the following reasons for endorsing the RPC model:

□ The three most important properties of a remote procedure call are simplicity, transparency, and performance.

□ The selected RPC model adheres to the local procedure model as closely as possible. This minimizes the amount of time developers spend learning the new environment.

□ The selected RPC model permits interoperability; its core protocol is well-defined and can't be modified by the user.

□ The selected RPC model allows applications to remain independent of the transport and protocol on which they run, while supporting a variety of transports and protocols.

□ The selected RPC model can easily be integrated with other components of the DCE.

Integration of the DCE Technology Components

One of the benefits of OSF's DCE is its coherence: although the components themselves are modular with well-defined interfaces, they are also well integrated. The various DCE components make use of the other components' services wherever possible. For example, the OSF RPC facility uses the Directory Service to advertise and look up RPC-based servers and their characteristics. OSF's RPC uses the Security Service to ensure message integrity and privacy. It also uses DCE Threads to handle concurrent execution of multiple RPCs.

DCE Threads

DCE Threads supports the creation, management, and synchronization of multiple threads of control within a single process. As threads are sometimes a part of the operating system, DCE can use the existing software of the host operating system if it supports threads. Threads support concurrent programming, allowing an application to perform many actions simultaneously. OSF DCE includes DCE Threads because many DCE components require threads, including Remote Procedure Calls, Security, Directory, Time services, and the Distributed File System. While some operating systems implement multithreading, some do not and for those, DCE Threads are required. Windows NT supports multithreading and therefore does not require DCE Threads.

DCE Remote Procedure Call (RPC)

The DCE Remote Procedure Call (RPC) facility consists of both a development tool and a runtime service. The development tool consists of a language (and its compiler) that supports the development of distributed applications within the client/server model. This language automatically generates code that transforms procedure calls into network messages. The runtime service utilizes the network protocols by which the client and the server sides of an application communicate. DCE RPC also includes software for generating unique identifiers, which indentify service interfaces and other resources. Microsoft RPC v1.0 implements the DCE RPC facility.

DCE Directory Service

In the distributed system, the DCE Directory Service is a central depot for information about resources. Typical resources include users, machines, and RPC-based services. The information contains the name of the resource as well as its associated attributes, such as a user's home directory or the location of an RPC-based server.

The DCE Directory Service is made up of several parts: the Cell Directory Service (CDS), the Global Directory Service (GDS), the Global Directory Agent (GDA), and a directory service programming interface. The Cell Directory Service manages a database of information about the resources in a group of machines called a DCE cell. The global

Directory Service implements an international standard directory service and creates a global namespace that connects the local DCE cells into one worldwide hierarchy. The Global Directory Agent (GDA) acts as a go-between for cell and global directory services. Both CDS and GDS are accessed using a single directory service application programming interface, the X/Open Directory Service (XDS) API.

DCE Time

The DCE Distributed Time Service (DTS) provides synchronized time on the computers participating in a Distributed Computing Environment. DTS synchronizes a DCE host's time with Coordinated Universal Time (UTC), an international time standard.

DCE Security

The DCE Security provides secure communications and controlled access to resources in the distributed system. There are three aspects to DCE security: authentication, secure communications, and authorization. These aspects are put to use by several services and facilities that together comprise the DCE Security Service, including the Registry Service, the Authentication Service, the Privilege Service, the Access Control List (ACL) Facility, and the Login Facility.

DCE Distributed File Service

The DCE Distributed File Service (DFS) allows users to access and share files stored on a File Server anywhere on the network, without the user having to know the physical location of the file. Files are part of a single, global namespace, so no matter where in the network a user might be, the file can be found using the same name. The Distributed File Service achieves high performance, particularly through caching of file system data, so that many users can access files that are located on a given File Server without prohibitive amounts of network traffic and accompanying delays.

DCE DFS includes a physical file system, the DCE Local File System (LFS), which supports special features that are useful in a distributed environment. They include the ability to replicate data; log file system data; enable quick recovery after a crash; simplify administration by dividing the file system into easily managed units called filesets; and associate ACLs with files and directories.

DCE also offers Diskless Support Service, which provides the tools to allow a diskless node to acquire an operating system over the network, obtain configuration information, connect to DFS to obtain the diskless node's root file system, and perform remote swapping.

Management

The Management block is actually not a single component, but a cross-section of the other components. Each DCE service contains an administrative component so that it can be managed over the network.

Cells

A group of DCE machines that work together and are administered as a unit is called a cell. For example, imagine an organization comprised of several departments, each in a different building and operating on its own budget. Each department in such an organization could have its own DCE cell.

Appendix 4

What's New in Windows NT?

Many people who look at Windows NT for the first time are pleasantly surprised to find the familiar looks of Windows 3.1. Windows NT is meant to look like Windows 3.1 so that users of Windows 3.1 will not be intimidated by the prospect of learning a whole new system (again!). Developers, however, should not be misled by the similarity in appearances. Windows NT is a powerful new operating system with many new features which will impact developers and users for many years to come. Most significant among these are improved compatibility and portability, a simpler memory model, better process management, and changes to the GDI.

Compatibility and Portability

The Windows NT designers made compatibility and portability explicit design goals. To support these goals, machine-dependent code is carefully isolated in a few assembly language modules, and applications interface with independent subsystems instead of directly with the (minimal) kernel. The resulting operating system (when running on an Intel processor) offers binary compatibility to existing OS/2, MS-DOS, and Windows 3.1 applications, and source-code compatibility to POSIX applications. Windows NT is already hosted on Intel and Alpha processors and is slated to be released for PowerPC.

Subsystems and Compatibility

This means that any application that works on these platforms will run under Windows NT. Any of these applications can be started seamlessly from a single command shell (the Windows NT command line). POSIX is a government standard that stands for Portable Operating System Interface to UNIX.

Windows NT was designed following in the steps of the popular Mach kernel created at MIT. The keystone of this design is a small low-level kernel which provides a slightly higher-level API that is hardware independent. The kernel, or Windows NT Executive, runs at a special privilege level (kernel mode). Subsystems (running in user mode) translate primitive kernel services into the services needed by applications. The subsystems are the only user-level processes which directly call the operating system services. In NT, such subsystems aren't an "add-on." Many crucial operating system services (such as security) are provided by "integral" subsystems.

These subsystems use the low-level APIs provided by the NT Executive to provide other high-level APIs to user-mode applications. Each subsystem provides a different API depending upon the environment being emulated. The Win32 subsystem, for instance, provides the Win32 API, and the Windows 3.1 subsystem provides compatibility for those applications. The same approach is taken for all other emulated environments: Each has a dedicated subsystem.

Since every application interacts with the kernel and other NT processes by making calls to a subsystem, the distinction between a "native" and a "hosted" application is somewhat arbitrary. However, since the Win32 subsystem always "owns" the attached display and I/O devices, Win32 applications running under the Win32 subsystem are considered "native."

Currently Windows NT ships with subsystems that provide compatibility with the following operating systems and environments:

- ☐ Win32
- ☐ MS-DOS
- ☐ Windows 3.1
- ☐ OS/2 1.3 Character Mode
- ☐ POSIX

The subsystem model allows third party vendors to create other subsystems. For instance, it is possible to implement a Macintosh subsystem that will enable Windows NT to load and execute applications written for the Macintosh. This is contrary to the design of OS/2 which built compatibility directly into the operating system. If OS/2 decided to support a new operating system such as NeXTStep/486, this support would have to be built directly into OS/2 from the ground up and could not be added as a subsystem by a third party vendor.

File Systems and Compatibility

While some PC operating systems support multiple file systems, each has a native file system that it prefers. MS-DOS supports the FAT file system only. OS/2 supports both FAT and the more advanced HPFS. Windows NT supports both FAT and HPFS and adds its own file system: NTFS. See Table A4.1 for details about each.

Portability

To promote portability, Windows NT was written in C, hardware dependent code was carefully encapsulated in separate modules, and processor-specific features were avoided. The designers chose C because it is widely available and is well-suited to systems coding. With the exception of processor-specific kernel operations (such as exception trapping), portions of various device drivers, some performance critical modules, and a layer that abstracts architecture specifics (called the HAL — hardware abstraction layer), the entire operating system is written in portable C.

To insure portability to other computer architectures, Windows NT does not make use of specific CPU features for which a compatible facility might not exist on other microprocessors.

Hardware Abstraction Layer

The concept of a Hardware Abstraction Layer (HAL) is integral to any portable operating system. At some point every operating system must perform low-level hardware manipulations. A traditional operating system will have this type of code sprinkled throughout. However, in a portable operating system, this code must be encapsulated in a black box.

Operating System	FAT	HPFS	NTFS
MS-DOS	X		
OS/2	X	X	
Windows NT	X	X	X
File Allocation Table	FAT is the standard MS-DOS file system. The File Allocation Table (FAT) gets its name from the structure that keeps information about each file stored on the disk. It supports file names of eight characters with an extension of three characters leading to the familiar 12345678.123 file. There are really no advantages to using this file system in Windows NT, unless you intend to use MS-DOS.		
High Performance File System	The High Performance File System was first implemented in OS/2. This file system was a big improvement over the MS-DOS file allocation table. It is considerably faster than the FAT system and allows case-sensitive file names up to 256 characters in length. It also has support for large drive volumes.		
New Technology File System	The Windows NT file system, NTFS, is the most advanced of the three. One of the advanced features of NTFS is its data striping capabilities. Data striping is a method of storing data on a hard disk. With the data striping mechanism, data can be saved and read from multiple hard disks concurrently, thus increasing throughput. To do this, each file is divided into as many pieces as there are disks, and each disk saves its part of the file, all at the same time. When reading, the file is read from all disks simultaneously and then reassembled. The NTFS supports case sensitive file names up to 256 characters in length and extremely large drive volumes.		

Table A4.1   *File systems supported by PC operating systems.*

This black box provides functions which other parts of the operating system call.

HAL provides a low-level API (called only by high-level parts of the operating system) to perform hardware-related services. Implemented as a DLL (*HAL.DLL*), this layer encapsulates all platform specific hardware knowledge. Processor specific services are abstracted in the kernel. All other hardware variances (e.g., caching mechanisms, inter-processor communications mechanisms, and interrupt controllers) are abstracted in the HAL.

If the hardware platform changes, the hardware abstraction layer must be rewritten (probably by the machine vendor) and then recompiled along with the rest of the operating system (that presumably did not need to be changed), under the new platform.

Segmented Memory Models

At the hardware level, an Intel segment-based architecture must split applications into 64Kb (one 16-bit segment) blocks. Whether this partitioning is visible to the application programmer working in a high-level language depends upon how the compiler-writer chooses to implement pointers and certain other features in the language. On Intel processors, the natural choices for pointer sizes are either 16 bits or 32 bits. Since data and code are referenced relative to separate segment registers, it can also make sense for code and data pointers to be differently sized. These variables have given rise to the following memory models available in segment-based PC operating systems:

Model	Data	Code	Description
Small	Single	Single	Both data and code addresses are 16-bit offsets.
Medium	Single	Multiple	Data addresses are 16-bit offsets, but code addresses use explicit segments and offsets.
Compact	Multiple	Single	Code addresses are offset only, but data addresses use segments and offsets.
Large	Multiple	Multiple	Both data and code addresses include explicit segments and offsets. A single data item cannot exceed a 64Kb segment.
Huge	Multiple	Multiple	Same as the large model, but address arithmetic is performed so that an array can cross segment boundaries.

Memory Model

Unlike other PC operating systems, Windows NT supports a flat 32-bit programming model, and gives each application a separate address space. MS-DOS, earlier incarnations of Windows (including Windows 3.1), and OS/2 v1.3, all have segment-based architectures. These segment-based operating systems also run all applications into a single, common address space.

The segment-based architecture of the 16-bit Intel CPUs has been the cause of much grief in the software industry. A lot of programming effort has been required to overcome these hardware limitations. Windows NT is no longer subject to these problems because the 80386 CPU provides hardware support for the flat 32-bit address space. In Windows NT one segment encompasses the entire four gigabyte address space. This means that programmers no longer have to worry about the different memory models, and the problems associated with near and far pointers. Everything is near.

Thunking

When applied to Win32s, "thunking" refers to the process by which 16-bit values are converted to 32-bit values, and back. These values can be messages, handles, or actual data. For instance, a 16-bit Windows application that enumerates the handles to all the other windows on the system will receive only 16-bit handles, even if some of those are 32-bit windows. Thunking can also occur in the opposite direction, when a 32-bit application sees all other windows as having 32-bit handles. This translation is performed by the thunking layer.

The same translation occurs when DDE conversations take place among 16- and 32-bit applications. Each application sees all other applications as being of its own type. Applications running in Win32s experience a deterioration in performance because of the thunking layer through which all messages pass. However, this is offset by a 10% to 50% improvement in application performance due to the 32-bit code generated by the compiler and the 32-bit system functions.

Separate Address Spaces

In Windows 3.1, all Windows applications run in the same address space. For this reason, an errant application can corrupt another. In Windows NT, each application runs in its own assigned virtual address space. Therefore, applications cannot corrupt each other.

Upon execution, Windows NT assigns each application a 4Gb virtual address space. The upper two gigabytes are kept for use by the operating system. The lower two are available to the application program.

Running each application in its own address space also facilitates debugging. Program bugs can no longer corrupt the operating system or the debugger, and references through an invalid pointer are easier to trap.

As a security feature, Windows NT also wipes clean each application address space upon termination. This insures that other (unscrupulous) applications won't be able to read "leftover" data.

Preemptive Multitasking

Preemptive multitasking gives Windows NT the ability to run several different applications simultaneously. While earlier versions of Windows could multitask, in those versions the multitasking mechanism worked only if the applications cooperated with the operating system. Because all applications (and the system) shared a common message queue, the system would work correctly only if each application periodically surrendered control and properly processed all its messages. If a Windows 3.1 application crashed, got stuck in an infinite loop, or simply ignored the rules, it and all other applications in the system would crash. To overcome this problem, in Windows NT the operating system periodically

Model	Segmented	Flat
MS-DOS	X	
Windows 3.1	X	
Windows NT		X
OS/2 1.3	X	
OS/2 2.0		X

Table A4.2   *Memory models implemented by PC operating systems.*

preempts each application, avoiding the possibility of a program locking the system. Thus, under Windows NT, if an application enters an infinite loop, only that application will be affected.

The shared system message queue of Windows 3.1 creates a related multitasking problem. If an application enters an infinite loop or has some other problem that prevents it from checking the system message queue, then the system message queue will fill up, preventing the messages pertaining to other applications from entering the queue. The result is that all applications will be inoperative. OS/2 v2.0 also suffers from the same problem.

Windows NT avoids this problem by eliminating the system message queue. When a window message is created, Windows NT determines the message owner (by identifying which window has the input focus), and enters the message directly into the correct application's message queue. Since each application will retrieve its messages from its private message

Windows 3.1 and the Virtual Machine

When comparing operating systems, it is often noted that OS/2 v2.0 supports preemptive multitasking while Windows 3.1 does not. This is not correct, as Windows 3.1 does in fact support a preemptive multitasking mechanism — at least among all virtual machines on the system.

Virtual Machines (VMs) are used by Windows 3.1 to emulate real mode for MS-DOS compatibility. VMs are supported in hardware by the 80386 CPU and are therefore a very efficient mechanism to emulate the real mode environment of MS-DOS. The Windows 3.1 Virtual Machine Manager (VMM), preemptively time-slices between all virtual machines on the system. This allows multiple MS-DOS and Windows applications to run concurrently in enhanced mode.

Unfortunately, all Windows 3.1 applications run in one virtual machine: the System VM. Thus, Windows applications are non-preemptively multitasked in the System VM, by a cooperative, message based mechanism. See Figure A4.1, Windows 3.1 System Architecture, for an illustration of a theoretical example of the Windows 3.1 operating system.

queue, a faulty application that stops checking its message queue will not affect the operation of any other application.

Multithreading

In addition to multitasking, Windows NT allows an application to run multiple threads of execution. These threads work simultaneously on one or more processors.

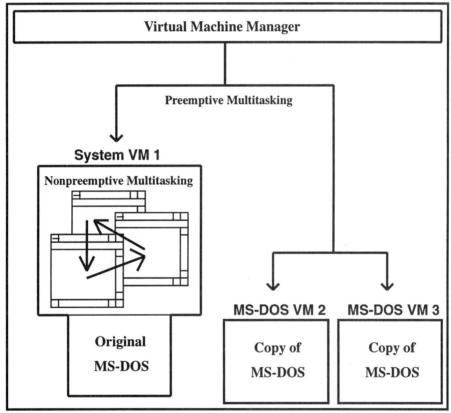

Figure A4.1   *Windows system architecture. In this diagram, the Virtual Machine Manager (VMM) is preemptively multitasking three virtual machines. Two of these VMs are running MS-DOS applications, while the other, the System VM, runs Windows applications. Thus, we can see that while the Windows interface appears to be the center of the operating system, in fact it is only one part of the puzzle.*

Multithreading allows an application to continue execution while a user is pulling down a menu or moving or resizing a window. Usually, a main application thread is created first, which in turn manages all other threads. The child threads are usually given specific tasks. For instance, one thread can wait for keyboard input while another can re-index a database. When the main thread terminates, all child threads are also terminated. See Figure A4.2 for a comparison of multitasking and multithreading mechanisms.

Threads

While threads are an integral part of the Windows NT operating system, they are usually unnecessary for application programs. This is evidenced by the fact that many great MS-DOS and Windows applications have been written without the availability of threads.

Multiple threads can, however, make the programmer's life easier. An application may create several threads which are dedicated to specific tasks. One thread can wait for keyboard and mouse input, while another searches for a database record, while still another handles video output.

In MS-DOS and Windows 3.1, where threads were not readily available, programmers had to be very clever if they wanted their users to think that more than one thing was happening at the same time. For instance an application could hook the timer interrupt (INT 8h) to perform some specific action on a regular basis. The application could also hook the keyboard interrupt (INT 16h) to be notified whenever a key was pressed. This required a lot of work on the part of the programmers but led to very responsive and impressive applications.

The multithreading facility in Windows NT cuts down on much of this work and moves it out of the programmer's control. Nevertheless, one should be aware that threads are not free. They come with the overhead of task switching and stack management. This means that you should not use a thread arbitrarily because it seems like an easy way to accomplish a specific task. Instead you should use a thread only when it is really important to the design and functionality of your application.

Symmetric Multiprocessing

A multiprocessing system can execute several tasks *on several separate processors* simultaneously. By comparison, multitasking executes multiple tasks on *a single* processor by time-slicing the processor. Whereas multitasking software merely *appears* to execute multiple threads simultaneously, multiprocessing software actually does so, by executing one or more threads on each processor. While several operating systems are able to support the multitasking mechanism, very few are able to support multiprocessing.

Depending upon how the operating system distributes kernel and user tasks, multiprocessing systems are classified as either asymmetric or symmetric. Asymmetric multiprocessing systems typically choose one processor as a dedicated operating system processor, while all the others execute the user's applications only. This model, being easy to implement, is often chosen to extend an existing single processor system.

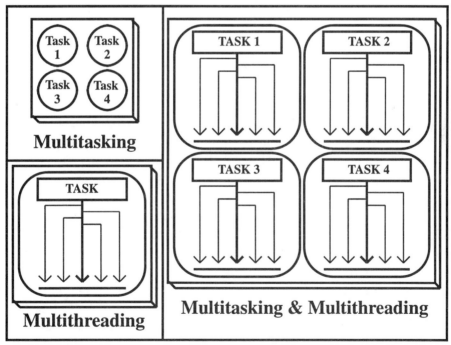

Figure A4.2 *A multitasking operating system (upper left block) can run several tasks concurrently. A threaded single task operating system (lower left block) can only run one task, but that task may create multiple concurrent threads. NT can run several tasks, each of which may create several threads (right block).*

Asymmetric systems tend to use custom-built hardware and require at least two processors.

Symmetric multiprocessing operating systems, on the other hand, are able to run system and user code on any available processor. See Figure A4.3, which compares multitasking and multiprocessing. As a result, symmetric systems tend to be more flexible and robust. Symmetric multiprocessing is built into the basic structure of Windows NT, creating a very efficient and powerful mechanism for exploiting the potential of (relatively) inexpensive microprocessors. As the prices of processors drop servers with four or more processors will become more and more common.

Improved Graphics Device Interface (GDI)

In Windows NT, the entire graphics device interface has been rewritten. Although the Win32 GDI interface appears the same, it is now a fully 32-bit graphics engine. Some of the new features of the GDI now include matrix transformations, Bezier splines, paths, and bitmap rotation. In addition, almost all the GDI functions that had 16-bit parameters and

GUIs

It appears to me as though we are suffering from a reversal of trends. At first PC software developers and corporations were very slow to accept the need of graphical interfaces, saying that their applications worked fine in character mode, and who needs a mouse anyway. Now we are going full swing in the opposite direction, everyone is porting all applications to a graphic interface, which is also more aesthetically pleasing to the eye. While GUIs certainly make it easier to use many applications, some applications should definitely stay in character mode versions. These types of applications include text editors and programs that involve large amounts of data entry. In some cases, even a well-written graphic application cannot match one in character mode. A Graphic User Interface (GUI), contributes to code complexity and frequently results in performance time deterioration. A conscious decision has to be made every time one opts for the visual seamlessness of a GUI at the expense of performance.

return values in Windows 3.1, have now been widened to 32 bits in Windows NT. This should not affect most existing programs, as the change to the 32-bit types is hidden by the Windows header file. For more information about new GDI features refer to Charles Petzold, "GDI Comes of Age: Exploring the 32-bit Graphics of WIndows NT," *Microsoft Systems Journal,* September, 1992.

Console

Windows NT also supplies a character mode display called the console API. Console applications look very similar to MS-DOS application running in windowed mode in Windows 3.1 enhanced mode. Console applications can be started from the Program Manager, File Manager, or from the Single Command Shell (the Windows NT command line).

The console API is quite similar to the memory mapped video input/output used by most commercial quality character mode MS-DOS

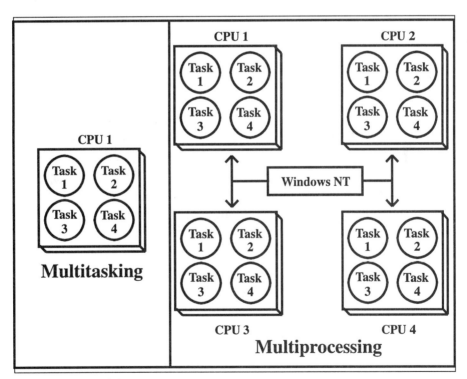

Figure A4.3   *Because NT supports multiprocessing, it can run tasks independently on each of the CPUs of a multi-processor machine.*

applications. It allows you to set characters and attributes in a memory buffer and have that buffer displayed properly, either in full screen mode, or in windowed mode (when the user presses *Alt-Enter*). Console applications, however, have much more flexibility and control than do MS-DOS applications running in Windows. A console application can get and set the window title and has access to all the features of Windows NT, except those that relate to the graphic user interface. This includes multithreading, file mapping, structured exception handling, and security.

The console API has the added advantage of allowing many software developers to release native Windows NT versions of their popular MS-DOS applications easily without moving to the native Windows interface.

Other Features

Several other Windows NT features deserve brief mention. For a complete overview of NT's capabilities and design, I recommend Helen Custer's book *Inside Windows NT*.

□ Windows NT is designed to qualify for a U.S. Department of Defense Class C2 security rating. This rating is supported by a separate logon process, password identification, resource access control, and accounting capabilities.

□ Support for Unicode — a character coding scheme that can encode up to 64,000 different characters — is built into Windows NT, much as support for TrueType was built into Windows 3.1. Instead of recompiling or reconfiguring for different language markets, Microsoft can market one version of Windows NT that is completely compatible with all applications written for it.

□ Windows 3.1 initialization (*.ini*) files have been replaced by individual "registries" assigned to each user on the system. Different users can store different values in their personal registry, so that if others use your computer, they can modify only their own settings.

□ In Windows NT, almost all system settings can be changed dynamically. (In MS-DOS, changing your system configuration usually means rebooting your PC.) This feature is very important for servers that cannot be restarted without affecting many users.

Glossary

A

ACF   See *Attribute Configuration File*.

Active context handle   A context handle that is not *NULL*. See also *Context handle*.

Aliasing   Aliasing occurs when two pointers passed to a remote procedure point at the same data object.

Allocation size   The quantity of memory necessary to represent a variable-length data object, such as an array specified by the MIDL attribute `size_is`.

Allocation value   The value which determines the allocation size of a data object. See also *Allocation size*.

Association   One or more connections between a client and server. The purpose of an association is to bind the client to the server.

Attribute   A keyword of the Interface Definition Language that appears within square brackets in the IDL file and that conveys information about an interface, type, field, parameter, or operation.

Attribute Configuration File   A file with the *.ACF* extension that contains statements written in the MIDL. The Attribute Configuration File and the Interface Definition Language file both specify the interface between the client and the server. The *.ACF* file contains attributes specific to Microsoft RPC. See also *Interface Definition File.*

Auto handle   An implicit primitive handle automatically generated for the client and managed entirely by the client stub and the runtime library.

Auxiliary file   A source file composed in the C programming language which contains support routines that marshall data and manage complex, user-defined data types. The server auxiliary file is named `file_y.c` by default and the client auxiliary file is named `file_x.c`, where `file` is the name of the interface. Auxiliary files are generated by the MIDL compiler and are determined by the interface definition contained in the IDL and ACF files. You can override the default names by using the MIDL compiler command line switches.

B

Base type   A standard data type defined within the Interface Definition Language that can be used to define all other types.

Big endian   A computer architecture in which the least significant byte of data is stored in the highest memory address associated with the data. See also *Little endian.*

Bind   The act of establishing a logical connection between a client and server to direct the remote procedure call to a specific server. See also *Binding.*

Binding   1. A logical connection between the client and the server involved in a remote procedure call. 2. The process by which the client establishes a logical connection to the server and obtains a handle to indicate that logical connection. See also *Handle.*

Binding handle   A primitive handle that the client uses to represent the logical connection to the server. The client uses the binding handle to direct the remote procedure call to the server.

C

Client   The application that initiates the remote procedure call to a server. Some applications act as both a client a server.

Client runtime library   The library that contains the RPC functions which manage network communications for the client relative to the remote procedure call. The client runtime import library is linked with the client application program.

Client-server architecture   A distributed computing model in which a computer process makes requests from another process or another computer. The party that requests help completing the task is called the client, and the party accepting the request is called the server.

Client stub   A stand-in procedure that is visible on the client computer and that makes the remote procedure call appear to the client program as a local call. The client stub is a C language source file generated by the MIDL compiler from an interface defined in the IDL file. The generated stub is linked with the client application and runtime import library. This source code contains all essential information which allows the client application to make remote procedure calls while preserving the appearance of a local procedure call.

Communications link   A network connection between a client and server that uses a valid transport and a network protocol that are available to both the client and server RPC runtimes.

Compile time   The time at which a program is compiled. Compile time occurs during development of the program and is distinguished from "runtime." Compile time errors are caused by syntax errors in the program, while runtime errors are usually caused by the state of the computer, such as network connections or stack size.

Conformant array   An array passed to the remote procedure call whose size is determined at runtime.

Conformant varying array   An open array; an array whose range of transmitted data and whose size are both determined at runtime; an open array.

Connection   A transport-level virtual circuit between the client and server. If there is no virtual circuit between the client and server, the Microsoft RPC runtime library establishes the connection when the client binds to the server interface instance. A client may have more than one connection to the server.

Context handle   A reference to that state maintained across remote procedure calls, by a server on behalf of the client. State information maintained by the context handle is not available to the client and can be accessed only by the server that is processing the remote procedure call. A context handle is defined with the *context_handle* attribute.

Context rundown   An optional cleanup routine executed when the connection to the processing task on the server is lost, such as when there are network communication errors. The name of the context rundown routine is determined by the name of the context handle type.

D

Daemon   An attendant spirit. A process that runs continuously in the background until some condition is met.

Data representation   The format of a data type; data representation usually refers to the binary standard used for data types transferred across the network during a remote procedure call.

DCE   See *Distributed Computing Environment*.

Declarator   A language statement that defines the type of an identifier, such as a function or a variable. A declarator is also defined as part of the interface definition language.

Directional attribute An attribute that specifies how parameters are passed between the client and server.

Discriminant A variable that determines the valid type, or member, of a discriminated union used in a remote procedure call. When the union is defined within a structure, the discriminant is provided as a field of that structure. See also *Encapsulated union* and *Non-encapsulated union*.

Discriminated union A union that is accompanied by a data item that specifies the valid type of the union. A discriminated union can either be classified as encapsulated or non-encapsulated.

Distributed application An application program that distributes its computational tasks between two or more networked computers. The remote procedure call facility permits a programmer to write a distributed application using a procedure model. The RPC facility directs network communication so the programmer does not have to write code for specific network types, conditions, and events.

Distributed Computing Environment A set of integrated services that enables users to share computer processing power; specifically, the services identified and recommended by the Open Software Foundation (OSF). These include remote procedure call, naming, threads, time, distributed file system, distributed security, operating system and transport, and integration services. The Microsoft Interface Definition Language and run-time libraries are based on the remote procedure call technology as recommended by the Open Software Foundation. This OSF DCE toolkit contains remote procedure calling and data representation libraries.

DLL See *Dynamic Link Library*.

Dynamic Link Library A library that can be loaded into memory once and then called by multiple applications, such that the operating system dynamically resolves the entry points, or the addresses of the called routines, at runtime.

E

Encapsulated union   A discriminated union passed to a remote procedure call as a structure that contains the discriminant as the first field of the structure and contains the union as the second and last field of the structure.

Endian   See *Little endian* and *Big endian*.

Endpoint   A network dependent address of a particular server instance on a host.

Entry point vector   A list of addresses for the entry points of a given set of remote procedures that implement the operation stated in an interface definition. These addresses are listed in the same corresponding order as the operation statements. These vectors are not implemented in MIDL version 1.0.

Enumerator   A named constant within the set of constants that determines the range of values for an enumerated type.

Explicit generic handle   A user-defined handle type that is passed as an argument to the remote procedure call. The explicit handle specifies the binding to the server that will process the remote procedure call. See also *Handle*.

Explicit handle   A primitive or generic handle transferred as an argument to the remote procedure call. The explicit determines the binding to the server which invokes the remote procedure call. See also *Handle*.

Explicit primitive handle   A primitive or generic handle that is passed as an argument during the remote procedure call. The primitive handle specifies a binding to the server which will execute the remote procedure call.

F

Field attribute   A MIDL language construct that appears in an array declaration. This is used to specify the size of the array or the range of valid entries within the array. The size is defined by a parameter that is associated with the array.

Full pointer   A pointer parameter to a remote procedure call that can be changed in value by the remote procedure that supports aliasing. Not supported by Microsoft RPC version 1.0.

Function prototype   A declaration of a function that includes its name, the number and types of its arguments, and its return type, but does not include the body of the function. The definition of the function must match the function prototype.

G

Generic handle   A user-defined handle that is associated with the user-defined bind and unbind routines. The generic handle may be either implicit or explicit. See also *Primitive handle*.

Globally Unique IDentifier   A unique identification string associated with the remote procedure call interface. The GUID is compatible with the Universally Unique IDentifier (UUID). These identifiers consist of eight hexadecimal digits followed by a hyphen, followed by three groups of four hexadecimal digits with each group followed by a hyphen, followed by twelve hexadecimal digits. For example, 12345678-1234-1234-1234-123456789ABC is a syntactically correct identifier. The identifiers on both the client and server must match for them to bind.

(GUID)   See *Globally Unique IDentifier*.

H

Handle   A reference to transparent information. An object available after a client binds to the server that directs that client's remote procedure calls to the server. The handle is created by the runtime library according to its specification in the attribute configuration file (*.ACF*) and interface definition language (*.IDL*) files.

I

Idempotent   An attribute of a remote procedure call indicating that an operation does not modify any state information; the operation produces the same results regardless of when or how often it is performed.

IDL   See *Interface Definition Language*.

Implicit binding   A binding that is established using an implicit handle.

Implicit generic handle   A user-defined handle accessed from a variable specified in the attribute configuration and interface definition language files and defined in the client stub.

Implicit handle   A handle used for a remote procedure call that is automatically retrieved by the client stub from a variable defined in the client stub. This hidden mechanism makes the handle usage invisible to the client-side programmer. An implicit handle may be either primitive or generic (user-defined). The global variable that contains the handle may be specified by the attribute. See also *Explicit handle*.

Import library   A special library that is associated with a dynamic link library (DLL); the import library is statically linked with application programs and provides information that enables the application to dynamically link with the DLL at runtime.

Import list   A list of files specified by the user containing data types that are made available to the interface by the MIDL compiler. The import operation is similar to the C language *#include* preprocessor directive, except that the import directive ignores function prototypes.

In parameter   A directional attribute of a remote procedure call argument referencing the parameter passed from the client to the server.

In, out parameter   A directional attribute of a remote procedure call argument indicating that the data is passed from client to server and server to client.

Interface   A collection of data types and function prototypes designating remote operations, together with the specification of the binding used by each operation. The interface definition is compiled from a specification in the IDL and ACF files.

Interface definition   1. The MIDL language production that defines an interface definition as an interface header (including the identifier, GUID, and attributes) and interface body (including data types and function prototypes). 2. The formal definition of the interface that appears in the ACF file, and that can be considered as the equivalent of a C header file. A description of the RPC interface written in the IDL file. See also *Interface*.

Interface Definition Language   A high-level language which provides the syntax for interface definitions. This language is used to specify the interface for remote procedure calls and was selected as a language standard by the Open Software Foundation (OSF) Distributed Computing Environment (DCE).

Interface Definition File   A file with extension *.IDL* that contains information written in the Microsoft Interface Definition Language. The Interface Definition File and the Attribute Configuration File (*.ACF* file) specify the remote procedure call interface between the client and the server. The *.IDL* file contains attributes that are compatible with OSF DCE RPC. See also *Attribute Configuration File*.

Interface header   A statement in the MIDL language that formally defines the interface definition. The interface header includes an attribute list describing the interface, the GUID, and the version attribute.

Interface instance   A combination of protocol stack version, protocol, and transport options selected from a set of options available on the server that are available to the client when it attempts to bind to the server.

Interface lookup   A process by which the client queries the server for the interface information and obtains a set of protocol stacks containing information about possible server interface instances.

L

Little endian   A computer architecture design in which the least significant byte of data is stored in the lowest memory address associated with the data. Intel processors use the little endian scheme. See also *Big endian*.

Location service   Any service that uses the locator functions in the runtime libraries to find a compatible interface between available clients and servers. A location service must be running if you are using auto handles. The locator maintains a database of servers that support remote procedure calls.

Locator scope   The extent over which server interface information is sent by the locator procedures either to the local machine alone or to additional computers. The scope is determined by a variable of the enumerated type *RPC_SCOPE*.

M

Major version number   A number that identifies the version of the interface, specified in the structure *RPC_VERSION*. In order to bind, the major version numbers must be compatible on both the client and the server.

Manager   A set of remote procedures that implement the operations of an RPC interface and can be dedicated to a given type of object.

Marshalling   The procedure by which a stub converts its local format into network data format and packages it for transmission. Marshalling procedures are provided in the client and server stub and auxiliary files.

MIDL   See *Microsoft Interface Definition Language*.

Microsoft Interface Definition Language   The Microsoft implementation of the Interface Definition Language (IDL), used to specify remote procedure prototypes. The Microsoft IDL language can be considered an extension to the C programming language. Programs written in the MIDL language are compiled by the Microsoft MIDL compiler to produce C language header files and client and server stub source files.

Minor version number   A number that identifies the version of the interface, specified in the structures *RPC_VERSION*. To be compatible, the client and server major version numbers must adhere, and the server minor version number must be greater than or equal to the client minor version number.

N

NDR   See Network Data Representation.

Network address   An address that identifies a specific server on a network.

Network Data Representation   A standard format for all data types during network transmission that is independent of the data type format on any particular computer architecture.

Network Interface Definition Language   The standard language used to specify the interface for remote procedure calls that was selected by the Open Software Foundation (OSF) Distributed Computing Environment (DCE). The NIDL language standard was specified by Hewlett-Packard, Apollo, and DEC. It is also known as IDL.

NIDL   See *Network Interface Definition Language*.

Non-encapsulated union   A discriminated union that neither requires the discriminant to be in the same structure as the union nor requires the discriminant to be the first field of the structure when the union is a structure. The discriminant may be another parameter if the union is a parameter or may be any other field of the structure if the union is part of a structure.

NULL **binding handle**   A binding handle containing the *NULL* value.

NULL **context handle**   1. A context handle that has the value *NULL* and does not signify any saved context. 2. Any context handle that is passed to a remote procedure call that has only the out attribute, regardless of the value of the context handle.

O

Open array   A conformant and varying array; an array parameter passed to the remote procedure call whose range of transmitted entries and whose size are determined at runtime by other parameters, structure fields, or constant expressions.

Open Software Foundation   A non-profit company composed of members from throughout the computing community that encourages computer interoperability through requests for technology, evaluation, and promulgation of standards. The OSF has published standards for technologies needed to provide a distributed computing environment (DCE), including the remote procedure call (RPC) standard.

Operation   The work performed by a given routine or procedure.

Orphan   An object which is semantically isolated when it is no longer referenced by another object. For example, a remote procedure on the server becomes an orphan when the network or client crashes after the client makes the remote procedure call. A data object is orphaned when a pointer to that data object is changed to *NULL* or to point to another value that does not reference the data object.

OSF   See *Open Software Foundation*.

Out parameter   A directional attribute of a remote procedure call parameter referencing the parameter passed from the server to the client.

P

Package   An interface. See *Interface*.

Parameter callback   A callback function that is defined using the *typedef* facility of MIDL and passed as a function pointer parameter to the remote procedure call. See also *Static callback*.

Password   A security mechanism consisting of a string of characters that the user must match before the user is allowed access to computer resources.

Pipe   1. A mechanism for transferring large amounts of data in a remote procedure call. 2. The data structure that represents this structure.

Presented type   The data type as it is visible and manipulated on the client and server computers. The presented type is distinguished from the transmitted type, which is the format of the data type as it is transmitted over the network. The data type that clients and servers manipulate.

Primitive binding handle   A binding handle of the predefined type *handle_t* that can only be used to direct a call to a specific RPC server and cannot contain user-defined information.

Priority   A value associated with the client that can be used by the server event handler to determine whether to accept or reject a new client's request for a binding.

Protocol   The version of the OSF connection-oriented RPC protocol that is supported by an interface; a structure within the protocol stack consisting of major and minor protocol numbers. A set of conventions used to exchange messages between entities over a medium. In this case it oversees communication across a network.

Protocol stack   A data structure defined within the runtime libraries that contains a complete description of all available server interface instances, including GUID, interface version, RPC protocol version, and security and transport information.

R

Reference pointer   A non-*NULL* pointer whose value is invariant during a remote procedure call and cannot point at aliased storage. See also *Unique pointer* and *Full pointer*.

Remote operation   See *Remote procedure*.

Remote procedure   An application procedure located in a separate address space from the calling code.

Remote Procedure Call   A procedure call invoked by an application procedure located in a separate address space from the calling code. Under the client-server model, a procedure on the client computer makes a call to the remote procedure on the server computer. The remote procedure is then executed on the server and any return data is transferred from the server to the client.

Runtime   The time the application program is executed, as opposed to the time the program is compiled. See *Compile time*.

Runtime library   Routines of the RPC runtime that support the RPC applications. Libraries containing remote procedure call application program interface (API) functions that are linked with applications.

S

Server   The program or computer that processes remote procedure calls from the client.

Server runtime library   The library that contains RPC API functions that manage network communications on behalf of the server side of the distributed application during the remote procedure call. The server runtime import library is linked with the server application program, the client stub, and auxiliary programs. The Microsoft server runtime import library is named *WINRPC.LIB*.

Server stub   C program source code generated by the MIDL compiler containing all the necessary functions to allow a server application to satisfy remote procedure requests using local procedure calls. The MIDL compiler's naming convention for server stubs is to name the generated file *file_X.C* where *file* is the name of the interface.

Service   A software component that is usually implemented as an independent program that runs on a server and handles requests from client computers. This set of RPC interfaces are offered together by a server to meet a specific goal.

Static callback   A callback procedure that is defined as part of the interface and appears in the stub. See also *Parameter callback.*

Static link library   A library that is combined with the application program to form a single executable program. All function calls to static link library functions are completely resolved at the time the application program is linked. See also *Dynamic link library.*

String   A one-dimensional array of characters.

Stub   A code module unique to an RPC interface that is generated by the DCE IDL compiler to support remote procedure calls for the interface. RPC stubs are linked with the client and server application and hide the complexity of the remote procedure calls from the application code. Client and server stubs are generated from the interface description files that contain statements written in the interface description language. The stubs manage packaging and unpackaging of data, transmission and reception, and communication over the network. See also *Client stub* and *Server stub.*

T

Transfer syntax   A formal definition of data formats to be used for transmission over the network. The network data representation format is a specific implementation of a transfer syntax. A set of rules used for transmitting data over a network.

Transmitted type The data type that is transmitted over the network, which may or may not be the same type as presented on the client and server computers. The transmitted type is specified by the `transmit as` attribute.

Transport layer 1. A particular layer of the OSI Reference Model between the network layer and the session layer. 2. A communications protocol between two different computers on a network. The client must use the same transport as the server in order to bind and make remote procedure calls. It provides end to end communication between two parties while hiding details of the network communication.

U

Unbind To remove a binding; to end the logical connection between the client and server that is necessary for remote procedure calls. See also *Bind*.

Unique pointer A pointer passed as a parameter to a remote procedure call that can be null, or non-null and that can change to null or non-null. A unique pointer does not cause aliasing. See also *Reference pointer* and *Full pointer*.

Universally Unique IDentifier A unique identification string associated with the remote procedure call interface. See *Globally Unique IDentifier*.

UUID See *Universally Unique IDentifier*.

V

Variant record A discriminated union.

Varying array An array passed to the remote procedure call whose range of transmitted entries is determined at runtime by another parameter, structure field, or constant expression. An array whose elements do not necessarily all get transmitted during a remote procedure call.

Annotated Bibliography

A.D. Birrell and B.J. Nelson, "Implementing Remote Procedure Calls, ACM Trans. on Computer Systems," vol. 2, pp. 39-59, Feb. 1984. First proposal for Remote Procedure Calls.

John Bloomer, *Power Programming with RPC*, Sebastopol CA: O'Reilly & Associates, Inc., 1992, 486 pp., ISBN 0-937175-77-3. Explanation of RPC relating to UNIX, X/Windows and ONC standards. Little mention of OSF DCE and none of Windows NT.

Ralph Brown and Jim Kyle, *PC Interrupts: A Programmer's Reference to BIOS, DOS, and Third-Party Calls*, Reading MA: Addison-Wesley, 1994, ISBN 0-201-62485-0. A must-have reference for Windows 3.1, and MS-DOS programmers. Not applicable to Windows NT.

Helen Custer, *Inside Windows NT*, Redmond WA: Microsoft Press, 1992, 385 pp., ISBN 1-55615-481-X. Lucid insiders overview of the Windows NT system. Not only for programmers.

Ralph Davis, *Windows Network Programming*, Reading MA: Addison-Wesley, 1993, 562 pp., ISBN 0-201-58133-7. How to integrate networking in your Windows applications. Many extensive examples.

Guy Eddon, "TNT DOS-Extender" v6. 1, *Windows/DOS Developer's Journal*, July 1994. All about Phar Lap Software's new Totally New Technology (TNT) DOS Extender.

Guy Eddon, "Fundamental Techniques for Sprite Animation in Windows-based Applications," *Microsoft Systems Journal*, December 1993. How to do flicker-free sprite animation in Windows and Windows NT.

Guy Eddon, "DDE to DOS," *Windows/DOS Developer's Journal*, August 1993. How to connect DOS applications to Windows via DDE.

Guy Eddon, "Monitoring Hardware Interrupts in Real Time," *Windows/DOS Developer's Journal*, March 1993. Example TSR shows hardware interrupts in real time. Full explanation of hardware interrupts.

Guy Eddon, "OS/2 Power Under DOS," *Windows/DOS Developer's Journal*, February 1992. Explanation of Phar Lap's 286\DOS extender, and its multithreading features.

Guy Eddon, "Remote Procedure Calls in Windows NT," *Windows/DOS Developer's Journal*, September 1993. Introduction to RPC. Covers all the major areas of RPC.

Guy Eddon, "WinBox," *Windows/DOS Developer's Journal*, December 1992, Tech Tips. Example shows how DOS programs can switch from windowed to full-screen mode in Windows.

Brian Kernighan and Dennis Ritchie, *The C Programming Language*, Englewood Cliffs, NJ: Prentice Hall, 1978, 228 pp., ISBN 0-13-110163-3. The definitive guide to the C programming language.

Microsoft, *Remote Procedure Call Programmer's Guide* and *Reference The Microsoft RPC* manual. Lacking in some areas, but still a must-have.

Robert Orfali and Don Harkey, *Client/Server Programming with OS/2 2.0*, New York, NY: Von Nostrand Reinhold, 1992, 1088 pp., ISBN 0-442-01219-5. Some useful explanations of client/server computing. Some OS/2 2.0 material is applicable to Windows NT.

OSF DCE, Application Development Reference, Englewood Cliffs NJ: Prentice Hall, 1993, ISBN 0-13-643834-2. The reference for all the

OSF DCE calls. Useful if you want to know where Microsoft RPC came from.

OSF DCE, Introduction to OSFDCE, Englewood Cliffs NJ: Prentice Hall, 1992, ISBN 0-13-490624-1. A full overview of OSF DCE. Not only for programmers.

Charles Petzold, "GDI Comes of Age: Exploring the 32-bit Graphics of Windows NT," *Microsoft Systems Journal*, September, 1992. An excellent article covering most new features of the GDI available in Windows NT.

Charles Petzold, *Programming Windows*, Redmond WA: Microsoft Press, 1992, 983 pp., ISBN 1-55615-395-3. The "classic" Windows programming book. Excellent for beginners, invaluable for experts. All the examples are well written.

Greg Pope, "Software Testophobia," *CASE Trends*, November 1992. Description of the software quality problem, and its solution in extensive testing.

Jeffrey Richter, *Advanced Windows NT*, Redmond WA: Microsoft Press, 1994, 700 pp., ISBN 1-55616-567-0. One of the best Windows NT programming books available.

Jeffrey Richter, *Windows 3.1: A Developer's Guide*, Redwood City CA: M&T Books, 1992, 715 pp., ISBN 1-55851-276-4. Explanation and examples of advanced Windows programming at its best. Examples are the key to understanding this book.

Ward Rosenberry, David Kenney, and Gerry Fisher, *Understanding DCE*, Sebastopol CA: O'Reilly & Associates, Inc., 1992, 233 pp., ISBN 1-56592- 005-8. Extensive overview of OSF DCE. Covers many facets with full explanations, including client/server, cells, RPC, security, and threads.

Andrew Schulman et al., *Undocumented DOS*, Reading MA: Addison-Wesley, 1990, 694 pp., ISBN 0-201-57064-5. An incredible compilation of undocumented DOS functions and data structures. Many useful explanations of these data structures and how they are used by DOS.

Andrew Schulman, David Maxey, and Matt Pietrek, *Undocumented Windows*, Reading MA: Addison-Wesley, 1992, 715 pp., ISBN 0-201-60834-0. A must for any serious Windows programmer; contains a "jumble of material on undocumented functions and internal data structures in KERNEL, USER, and GDI."

John Shirley, *Guide to Writing DCE Applications*, Sebastopol CA: O'Reilly & Associates, Inc., 1992, 251 pp., ISBN 1-56592-004-X. Explanation of DCE and how these issues relate to UNIX programmers. Many extensive examples utilizing RPC; no floppy disk available!

Roger T. Stevens, *Fractal Programming in C*, Redwood City CA: M&T Books, 1989, 583 pp., ISBN 1-55851-038-9. An excellent description of fractals, and how to program them in C.

Bjarne Stroustrup, *The C++ Programming Language*, Addison-Wesley, 1991, 669 pp., ISBN 0-201-53992-6. The official guide to the C++ programming language, from its creator.

Andrew Tanenbaum, *Modern Operating Systems*, Englewood Cliffs NJ: Prentice Hall, 1992, 728 pp., ISBN 0-13-588187-0. An excellent book about operating systems in general, and UNIX and MS-DOS in particular. Very applicable to Windows NT, even though NT is never explicitly mentioned.

Winn Rosch, *Hardware Bible*, New York NY: Brady Publishing, 1992, 1060 pp., ISBN 0-13-932260-4. Excellent for a full understanding of the IBM PC hardware architecture.

Index

A

abnormally terminated client *150*
ACF file *92, 95*
address
    internet *26*
    network *25–26*
address space differences *7*
aliasing *47–48*
allocation function *29*
Apollo computer *9*
Application Interface *6*
array *49*
    variable or variant *51*
array bounds *49*
attribute
    [auto_handle] *32, 94*
    handle *93*
    MIDL *49*
    min_is *49*
    security *126*

attribute (continued)
    string *51*
Attribute Configuration File
    HELLO.ACF *30*
Attribute Control File *30*
auxiliary files *18*

B

binding *7, 23–29, 32, 91–98, 101, 228–229*
    automatic *18, 92, 94, 227*
    components *25, 96*
    manual *91–92, 95, 227–228*
    string *96–98*
    terminating a *105*
    vector *28*
binding handles *32, 92–97, 148, 152*
    creating *92*
    explicit *96*
    implicit *95, 103*
    primitive *93*
    retreiving *28*

binding handles (continued)
  user-defined *93*
Birrell and Nelson *2, 413*
blocking, and threads *11*
box 56–58
building RPC applications *31, 33*

C

call-by-reference *46*
call-by-value *44, 46*
calling conventions *46*
  cdecl 46
  PASCAL 46
  stdcall 46
$(cflags) 60
character sets *3*
char_from_ndr 103
child thread *76*
clean-up tasks *150*
clear 56
clearscreen 56
client *3*
  abnormally terminated *149–150*
  hello 19
  maximum *127*
  PRIME3 91, 98, 107
  PRIME4 156, 159, 190, 202
  PRIME5 231
  PRIME6 266
  runtime *4*
  runtime library *33*
  termination *104*
client stub *4, 43–44, 92–93, 102, 104, 108*
client/server architecture *53*
client/server compatibility *30, 227*
client/server model *3*

code, start up *130*
communication server *3*
compatibility *9*
compatible server *101*
compiler
  IDL *5*
  MIDL *17, 31, 33–34*
compute server *3*
concurrency problems *77*
$(conflags) 59–60
$(conlibs) 59–60
conlibsmt 34
console application interface *54*
console functions *57*
console I/O library *56*
console libraries *34*
console management *53–54*
constant pointers *47*
context handle *95, 147–149, 152–153*
context rundown routines *147, 149–150, 153*
crash of client *149*
CreateProcess 76
CreateThread 10, 75–76, 85, 99, 126
creating binding handles *92*
critical sections *76–79, 125*
$(cvars) 60

D

data structures, passing large *44*
DCE *1, 377–381*
  services *9*
  standard *9*
DDE conversation *10*
deadlock *78*
deallocation function *29*

debugging *34*
DECNet *26*
DeleteCriticalSection 85
development cycle *33*
dialog boxes *224*
DIRECTIO library *56*
DIRECTIO.C 67, 184
DIRECTIO.H 73, 188
direction tag *30*
distributed computing *9*
Distributed Computing Environment; see DCE
distributed file services *9*
distributed prime number example *110*
distributed system *3*
distributing work *80*
DOS client *190*
dynamic linking *23–25*
Dynamic Link Library (DLL) *24*

E

efficiency, and pointer emulation *45, 48*
end point *25, 27, 96, 126*
endian schemes *3*
EnterCriticalSection 78, 86
error
    network *3*
    pointer *44–45*
event objects *77*
exception handling *14, 17, 20, 35, 100, 103*
    execution focus *11*
    macros *18*
    and portability *14*

exception handling (continued)
    structured *100, 103*
explicit binding handles *96*
exported functions *7*
exporting interface *28*
exporting multiple interfaces *228*
extern 51
external, unresolved *7*

F

fault tolerance *147–155*
file server *3*
file-naming conventions *33*
FillConsoleOutputAttribute 57
FillConsoleOutputCharacter 57
finding a server *228*
first_is 49–50
FlushConsoleInputBuffer 57
focus *11*
full pointers *48*
function
    allocation *29*
    box 56, 58
    char_from_ndr 103
    clear 56
    clearscreen 56
    conlibsmt 34
    console *57*
    CreateProcess 76
    CreateThread 10, 75–76, 85, 99, 126
    deallocation 29
    DeleteCriticalSection 85
    EnterCriticalSection 78, 86
    exported *7*
    extern 51
    FillConsoleOutputAttribute 57

function (continued)

FillConsoleOutputCharacter 57
FlushConsoleInputBuffer 57
get_character_no_wait 56
get_character_wait 56
GetComputerName 102, 113
GetConsoleMode 57
GetConsoleScreenBufferInfo 57
handle_t 92–93
HelloRPC 29
InitializeCriticalSection 77, 85
InitializePrimeServer 124
IsPrime 55, 57, 59, 64–65, 76–77, 79
LeaveCriticalSection 78, 87
long_from_ndr 127
moutchar 56
mxyputc 56
mxyputs 56
pBindingVector 28
PeekConsoleInput 57
read_field 56
RemoteIsPrime 99
RpcAbnormalTermination 18
RpcBindingFree 105, 114
RpcBindingFromStringBinding 91, 97
RpcBindingToStringBinding 97
RpcEndExcept 17–18
RpcEndFinally 18
RpcExcept 17–18, 100
RpcExceptionCode 18
RpcFinally 18
RPC.H 18
RpcRaiseException 103
RpcServerInqBindings 28

function (continued)

RpcNsBindingExport 28
RpcServerListen 28–29, 127
RpcServerRegisterIf 28, 126
RpcServerUseProtseqEp 27, 125
RpcStringBindingCompose 97, 102, 105, 113
RpcStringBindingParse 97
RpcStringFree 97, 105, 114
RpcTryExcept 17–18, 100
RpcTryFinally 18
screen access 184
ScrollConsoleScreenBuffer 59
ServerStatus 100, 113
SetConsoleCtrl Handler 57
SetConsoleMode 57
set_vid_mem 56
Thread 77–78, 85, 99
WriteConsoleOutputAttribute 57
WriteConsoleOutputCharacter 57
function parameters 43, 45
function prototypes 30

G

generating stubs 31
get_character_no_wait 56
get_character_wait 56
GetComputerName 102, 113
GetConsoleMode 57
GetConsoleScreenBufferInfo 57
global variable 7, 77
Globally Unique IDentifier 26
graceful shutdown 149
graphical user interface (GUI) 54

H

handle *32*
    attribute *93*
    binding *32, 92–97, 148, 152*
    context *95, 147–149, 152–153*
    implicit binding *18*
handler, exception *14, 17, 20, 35, 100, 103*
handle_t 92–93
Hello, world 15
    HELLO client *19*
    HELLO interface definition *30*
    HELLO procedure *29*
    HELLO project source files *35*
    HELLO remote procedure *39*
    HELLO server *23, 27, 37*
    HELLO.ACF 40
    HELLO.IDL 28, 30, 40
    HELLO.MAK 41
    HELLOP.C 29
    HelloRPC 29

I

Interface Definition Language (IDL) *5, 30*
    compiler *5*
    file *7, 30, 92, 105*
    HELLO.IDL 30
    .IDL extension *7*
    IDL types *6*
    parameters *30*
implicit binding handles *18, 95, 103*
import context *228*
import process *229*
importing interface *28*

IN parameter *30*
InitializeCriticalSection 77, 85
InitializePrimeServer 124
interface
    address *26*
    console application *54*
    exporting *28, 228*
    graphical user *54*
    handle *228*
    importing *28*
    name *30*
    name manipulations *126*
    registration *28, 126*
    PRIME4 183
interprocess communications *9*
I/O library *56*
IsPrime 55, 57, 59, 64–65, 76–77, 79

K

kerberos security *126*
Kernighan and Ritchie *15, 414*

L

last_is 49–50
LeaveCriticalSection 78, 87
length_is 49–50
$(link) 60
linker *15*
linking *7*
    dynamic *23–25*
    RPC applications *31*
    static *23, 25*
local procedure call *2*
long_from_ndr 127

M

macros, exception handling *18*

major version numbers *30*

makefile *31, 34*

manual binding *91–92, 95, 227–228*

manual page

    PRIME1 61

    PRIME2 82

    PRIME3 107, 129

    PRIME4 156, 158

    PRIME5 231–232

    PRIME6 270–271

marshalling routines *93*

maximum calls, server *125*

maximum clients *127*

max_is 49–50

memory

    allocator *29*

    user-defined allocation *29*

memory fault *44–45*

memory management *9*

Microsoft Interface Definition Language (MIDL) *5*

    attributes *49*

    base types *6*

    compilation *31*

    compiler *17, 33–34*

    name manipulations *127, 150*

Microsoft RPC *53*

min_is 49

moutchar 56

MS-DOS *9*

multiple servers *96*

multitasking *9*

multithreaded prime number example *83*

multithreading *10–11, 14, 53, 75–81*

multithreading, preemptive *75*

Mutex objects *77*

mutual exclusion *14, 77*

mxyputc 56

mxyputs 56

N

name manipulations

    interface *126*

    MIDL *127, 150*

    server stub *127*

Name Service *95, 227–231*

    automatic binding *227*

    export functions *229*

    manual binding *227*

named pipes *10, 26, 126*

    named pipes and security *27*

naming conventions, RPC *33*

ncacn_dnet_nsp 26

ncacn_ip_tcp 26

ncacn_nb 26

ncacn_np 26

ncacn_osi_dna 26

ncadg_dds 26

ncadg_ip_udp 26

ncalrpc 26

NetBIOS *26*

network address *25–26, 96*

Network Computing System (NCS) *9*

Network Data Representation (NDR) *4, 104*

network error *3*

network protocol *3, 26*
networking
    peer-to-peer *10*
    and Windows NT *10*
NMAKE 34
NMAKE HELLO.MAK 35
NTWIN32.MAK 34, 59
NULL 47–48

O

Object Oriented Programming
    (OOP) *11*
Open Software Foundation (OSF) *1, 8*
operating system
    PC, history of *365–372*
    theory *77*
Options 27, 96
OSF DCE *1, 9, 377–381*
OUT parameter *30*

P

parameters
    function *43, 45*
    IDL *30*
    IN 30
    Options 27
    OUT 30
PASCAL calling convention *46*
pBindingVector 28
peak performance *11*
PeekConsoleInput 57
peer-to-peer networking *10*
performance *44*
    and threads *11*
    peak *11*
pointer aliasing *48*

pointer emulation *44*
    and efficiency *45*
pointer error *44–45*
pointers *46*
    constant *47*
    and efficiency *48*
    full *48*
    reference *47*
    and RPC *44*
    types of *47*
    unique *48*
POP *2*
portability *9*
    and exception handling *14*
    of existing applications *48*
POSIX *9*
preemptive multithreading *75*
prime number algorithm *55*
PRIME1 55–73
    manual page *61*
    usage *58*
    PRIME1.C 62
    PRIME1.MAK 59, 66
PRIME2 75–89
    manual page *82*
    PRIME2.C 83
    PRIME2.MAK 89
PRIME3 91–145
    client *98, 107*
    manual pages *107, 129*
    server *123, 129*
    PRIMEC3.C 110
    PRIMEP3.C 137
    PRIMES3.C 130
    PRIME3.ACF 106, 145

PRIME3 (continued)
    PRIME3.IDL 105, 145
    PRIME3.MAK 143
PRIME4 147–225
    client *156, 159*
    DOS client *190*
    interface definition *183*
    manual pages *156–158*
    PRIMEC4.ACF 221
    PRIMEC4.C 159, 202
    PRIMEC4.H 219
    PRIMEC4.IDL 221
    PRIMEP4.C 176
    PRIMES4.C 170
    PRIME4.ACF 184, 201
    PRIME4.C 190
    PRIME4.DEF 222
    PRIME4.DLG 224
    PRIME4.DOS 200
    PRIME4.IDL 183, 201
    PRIME4.MAK 182
    PRIME4.RC 223
    PRIME4.WIN 220
    remote procedures *176*
    server *158, 170*
    Windows client *202*
PRIME5 227–229
    client *231*
    manual pages *231–232*
    PRIMEC5.C 233
    PRIMEP5.C 255
    PRIMES5.C 248
    PRIME5.ACF 264
    PRIME5.IDL 264
    PRIME5.MAK 262

PRIME5 (continued)
    server *229, 232*
PRIME6 265–301
    client *266*
    interface *268*
    manual pages *270–271*
    PRIMEC6.C 272
    PRIMES6.C 286
    PRIMEP6.C 293
    PRIME6.MAK 300
    PRIME6.IDL 302
primitive binding handles *93*
print server *3*
priority, thread's *126*
procedure call
    local *2*
    remote *16–17, 29, 39, 91, 137, 176*
Procedure Oriented Programming
    languages *2*
protocol, network *3, 26*
protocol sequence *25–26, 96, 125*
PVIEW 79

R

read_field 56
reentrancy *14*
reference pointers *44, 47*
REGEDT32.EXE 35, 229
registering the end point *126*
registering the interface *28, 126*
registering the protocol sequences *125*
registering the server interface *125*
registry information *35, 229*
remote procedure, see procedure
RemoteIsPrime 99
resources, shared *77*

routines
    context rundown *147, 149–150, 153*
    marshalling *93*
    rundown *149–153*
    unmarshalling *93*
RPC
    development cycle *32*
    development issues *53*
    file-naming conventions *33*
    Microsoft *8*
    and references *44*
    transparency *7*
    user-defined features *29*
    and Windows NT *8*
RPC application
    building *31, 33*
    linking *31*
RPC Locator *36, 228*
RPC Service *36*
RpcAbnormalTermination 18
RpcBindingFree 105, 114
RpcBindingFromStringBinding 91, 97
RpcBindingToStringBinding 97
RpcEndExcept 17–18
RpcEndFinally 18
RpcExcept 17–18, 100
RpcExceptionCode 18
RpcFinally 18
RPC.H 17–18, 20
RpcNsBindingExport 28, 229
RpcNsBindingImportBegin 228
RpcNsBindingImportDone 228
RpcNsBindingImportNext 228, 229
RpcNsBindingUnexport 229

RpcNsImportDone 229
RpcRaiseException 103
RpcServerInqBindings 28
RpcServerListen 28–29, 127
RpcServerRegisterIf 28, 126
RpcServerUseProtseqEp 27, 125
RpcStringBindingCompose 97, 102, 105, 113
RpcStringBindingParse 97
RpcStringFree 97, 105, 114
RpcTryExcept 17–18, 100
RpcTryFinally 18
rundown routines *149–150, 152–153*
runtime, client *4*
runtime library
    client *33*
    server *33*

S

screen access functions *184*
ScrollConsoleScreenBuffer 59
security *9*
    and named pipes *27*
    kerberos *126*
security attribute *126*
Semaphores *77*
sequence, protocol *25*
serialized access *77*
server *3*
    communication *3*
    compatibity with client *30, 101, 227*
    compute *3*
    file *3*
    finding a *228*
    HELLO 23, 27, 37

server (continued)
    interface *229*
    maximum calls *125*
    print *3*
    registering interface *125*
    remote procedures *137*
    runtime library *33*
    start up code *130*
    stateful *151*
    stateless *151*
    stub *4, 43, 45, 127*
    stub, name manipulations *127*
    terminating *128*
ServerStatus *100, 113*
SetConsoleCtrl Handler *57*
SetConsoleMode *57*
set_vid_mem *56*
shared data *10*
shared resources *14, 77*
shared volume *10*
shutdown, graceful *149*
size of an array *49*
size_is *49–50*
start up code, for server *130*
state information *148*
stateful server *151*
stateless server *151*
static linking *23, 25*
stdcall convention *46*
string attribute *51*
string binding *96–98*
strings *51*
strongly typed language *6*
Structured Exception Handling
    (SEH) *14, 100, 103*

stub
    client *4, 43–44, 92–93, 102, 104, 108*
    generating *31*
    role in binding *95*
    server *4, 43, 45, 127*
suspended threads *126*
synchronization *14, 77*
synchronization objects *77*
system makefile *34*

T

TCP/IP *10*
termination
    abnormal (of client) *150*
    binding *105*
    client *104*
    server *128*
    thread *79*
testing *123*
Thread *77–78, 85, 99*
threads *9, 76–77, 155*
    and blocking *11*
    child *76*
    monitoring *79*
    priority *126*
    and RPC performance *11*
    suspended *126*
    termination of *79*
    Thread *77–78, 85, 99*
timers *9*
transparency, in RPC *7*
transport layer *4*
transport services *9*
types, MIDL base *6*

U

unique pointers *48*

Universally Unique IDentifier (UUID) *7, 25–26, 30, 96*

unmarshalling routines *93*

unresolved external *7*

user heap *149*

user-defined binding handles *93*

user-defined features, in RPC *29*

user-defined memory allocation *29*

UUIDGEN 26

V

variable, global *7, 77*

variable or variant array *51*

version numbers, major *30*

VFS layer *9*

W

Win32 API *10, 373–376*

Win32 console functions *56*

Windows, client *202*

Windows for Workgroups *9, 147, 153–155, 157*

Windows NT *8–9*

   and networking *10*

   and RPC *8*

   what's new in *383–396*

WinExec *76*

work scheduling *79*

WriteConsoleOutputAttribute 57

WriteConsoleOutputCharacter 57